HARK FO

The Life of a Lakeland Huntsman

~

Anthony Chapman

Edited by Anne Bonney

HELM
PRESS

Dedicated to all fox hunters past and present

Published by Helm Press
10 Abbey Gardens, Natland, Kendal, Cumbria LA9 7SP

Tel: 015395 61321

E.mail: HelmPress@natland.freeserve.co.uk

Copyright – Anne Bonney

First published 2004

ISBN 0 9540497 9 9

Typeset and printed by
MTP Media Ltd, The Sidings, Beezon Fields, Kendal. Cumbria LA9 6BL

Contents

Foxhound

Introduction

THIS BOOK CONTAINS THE MEMOIRS of Anthony Chapman, born in 1914 and the fourth generation of his family to be Lakeland huntsman, who proudly hunted the fells with his hounds and terriers, as his forefathers has done and in particular the Coniston Foxhounds. Indeed hunting has been carried on in this area for centuries, partly out of necessity and partly from the love of the sport.

Farmers on the fells had to protect their livestock in particular new born lambs in the springtime. As farming involved people from all walks of life it was only natural that the hunt should reflect this social mix and it quickly became integrated into the fabric of local society. As such it became as much a social event where people from the widely spread out farms and villages could gather together at different meets.

The Lakeland packs: Windermere Harriers, Eskdale and Ennerdale, Blencathra, Ullswater and Melbreak and of course the Coniston, each had their own area they hunted, with their own masters, huntsmen, whipper-ins, hounds and terriers. They had sometimes a few meets (hunts) a week during the season, where many miles were covered across fells and wooded areas all in the pursuit of the fox. Sometimes the huntsman could be away from home for a week or so and would be put up at a farm and the hounds bedded down for the night in outbuildings. They walked many miles to hunts, sometimes travelling the day before so they were ready for the hunt early the very next morning. The different meets would be advertised in the local papers and farmers living in outlying areas if not joining in would sometimes welcome a crack (chat) and would meet them travelling through.

Each pack would have to cover their own expenses for their upkeep – wages though small for the huntsman, whipper-in (assistant), hounds to be fed, kennels maintained and any other expenses which were kept to a minimum. The kennels also gratefully received or collected dead livestock from local farms to supplement the foxhounds' meals. The

Coniston received money from farmers, landowners and other follow-ers through voluntary subscriptions. The various villages raised money through having Hunt Balls, Whist Drives and Raffles. Huntsmen were only paid during the hunting season – September to May and to fill in the rest of the year they took on other seasonal work such as farming.

Anthony knew the fells like the back of his hand. The huntsmen and their supporters then would never have conceived or dreamt in their very worst nightmare that hunting as they knew it could possibly be banned by the Government in the beginning of the twenty-first century and become a thing of the past.

Anthony in the last few years of his life in the early 1980s sat down and penned the seasons of his hunting life, with the help of his diary, various paper cuttings and with the generous help of Peter Martin and Mrs Margaret (Sid) Dixon's diaries. Intermingled amongst his beloved hounds, terriers, foxes, supporters, farmers, dalesmen, inn-keepers – his fells – where he knew more or less every square inch, the borrans, earths, benks, intakes, allotments, you name it – he knew where the hounds and foxes could or would go – and he kept up with them every step of the way. He encouraged the young to follow and take part – they were the next generation of followers. Many will read fondly of their fathers and grandparents who took part.

Intermixed in this is the way of life then, when there was only the odd car and motorbike, with no electricity or telephone. They hunted from late September – usually started the Monday after Eskdale Show – on until mid May. The hounds then went to their respective houses and farms where they were looked after; had a well-earned rest during the summer until the season began in the autumn. This was known as 'out at walk'. They were then gathered back in to Greenbank Kennels, Ambleside. During the summer months Anthony helped out on farms or shepherding. He enjoyed taking part in the local Lakeland Shows he attended and became one of the main persons who helped with Ambleside Sports and in particular laying trails for various hound trail-ing events from Grasmere Sports right through to the Westmorland Show at Kendal. There was also the popular Puppy Show usually held on Ambleside Sheep Fair Day on White Platts, now a park, and there were prizes for the various foxhound puppies; groups of foxhounds entered from different packs and many other classes. Anthony liked these shows as this kept up the enthusiasm and interest of the followers during the summer season.

As we read his memoirs we come across many dialect and hunting terms that are explained or given in the glossary at the back of the book. Also included are some of the verses of the many poems written about him and fellow huntsmen, and his great respect for the Logan family, who were Masters (head) of the Coniston Foxhounds and the important role they played. It was a way of life for Anthony – they were not well paid in his day, his wife Annie and three of a family, Edward, Mavis and Ann lived at Huntsman Cottage, Rydal. The family have their own memories of their dad and the life they were born into. We hear about the Shepherd's Meet, Hunt Balls and later the Hunt Suppers and of the sing songs they had at the end of a successful hunting day. Each had their own particular songs that they sang! Anthony's was 'It's a fine hunting day!'

They were not all good times but in reading this you will imagine yourself up on the fells among the heather and bracken with Anthony, his hounds, terriers and followers walking many miles after the fox who at times could lead them 'a merry dance!' Out in all weathers and a master of the hounds he knew so well, each one by name and sound. It was a way of life for many country folk and is now part of history.

We owe a debt of gratitude to Anthony for penning these pages and also to his family who have kept and handed over his carefully written work, in order that it may be published.

Every effort has been made to check, correct and alter any errors along the way but please forgive any that I may have inadvertently made. The photographs used are from Anthony's own family albums and any others have been credited accordingly. I have found useful the book by R. Clapham, *Fox Hunting on the Fells*, an author known by Anthony. I have also listened to the copy tapes by Ambleside Oral History Group when Dr Forrester interviewed Anthony a few years before he died – it was fascinating hearing him actually speaking of his times on the fells.

So please read on and enjoy this remarkable story of his life on the fells as only he could have told it, which will bring memories to some and will undoubtedly be new to others but will hopefully make you think when next time you are up on Anthony's beloved fells and conjure up the way of life as it was then.

Anne Bonney
October 2004

Anthony Chapman – grandfather

Miss Hilda Chapman – (aunt to
author) with pet fox 'Jacky'

I

Family History

I WAS BORN AT COTE HOW COTTAGE, Rydal, Ambleside, on 29 March 1914 and I was the second son of George and Hannah Chapman. My father was a local man and my mother came from Ashstead Farm, Whinfell near Kendal. My father was hunting born and bred, the son of Anthony Chapman, another well-known Lakeland huntsman, who was born at Noran Bank Farm, Patterdale.

Early in his life my grandfather went as a shepherd to Borrowdale and later to Pavement End Farm, Grasmere. He was taken on by Mr Fleming Green, a notable Grasmere sportsman, to hunt a pack of rough hounds after the mart (Pine Martin) and hare.

A few seasons later Anthony became huntsman to Colonel Ridehalgh of the Windermere Harriers, after his Uncle Tom retired. The late Mr Ullock was a hotel and property owner from Bowness, and had originally started the pack and later transferred them to the Colonel. The pack was kennelled at Fell Foot, Newby Bridge. Colonel Ridehalgh gave up the Harriers in 1892 and they were then taken over by Mr Bruce Logan of Windermere – a grand man!

My grandfather still being huntsman, moved then from Grasmere to Brow Head Farm, Ambleside and the Windermere Harriers were kennelled there also. He continued as huntsman until 1905 and then they were taken over by his eldest son, Tom, and kept going until the 'Great War' and were disbanded between 1914–18.

When my grandfather finished in 1905, he went into the hotel trade and had many changes of domicile. First the Travellers Rest, Kirkstone Pass, followed by the Dungeon Ghyll (Old), Langdale; the Mortal Man, Troutbeck; then the Kirkstone Foot, Brotherswater; leaving in 1922 to go to the Hare and Hounds at Bowland Bridge. After another eight years he retired and finished his days at Glen Side, Troutbeck. He was a fine hound man besides being a great hunter. He had a wonderful ringing voice, like his Uncle Tom. He hunted hounds almost entirely by his voice, seldom using horn, except to call them home or signal a kill. After hare

Huntsman, Jim Dalton and Ernie Parker whipper-in of the Blencathra

hunting had ceased fox was hunted, the Harriers having some help from some larger and faster hounds.

Hunting was in the Chapman blood and including myself who later became a huntsman there have been four generations that have hunted hounds. Starting with Anthony, his Uncle Tom and his cousin Harrison. Anthony's son Tom – huntsman to the Harriers, and his second son George recently retired from hunting the Coniston Foxhounds and now me, Anthony's grandson.

Sir Robert Farquhar, Grasmere's sporting and musical baronet, composed a tuneful hunting song of which Chapman was the hero:

> *'For the dalesmen love to hear*
> *The bonny hounds draw near*
> *And everyone knows Chapman's rousing cry*
> *As he sends the startled fox*
> *That shelters in the rocks*
> *A tally-ho which makes the distant hills reply'*

But Anthony had been the hero of many a hunting song in his name, along with Bowman, Porter, Crozier, Dalton and Tommy Dobson his name is repeatedly heard at a hunt sing song.

I have here details of an old Windermere Harriers Hunt – 28 October to 4 November 1890. They were kennelled at the Prince of Wales Hotel, Grasmere, for a week. Three meets for the week was put in, one in Little Langdale with good sport from two hares. Found another meet at the Nags Head, Wythburn, one hare was run and killed on Helvelyn. On the Saturday went across the valley to Allan Bank, no sign of game was found until the intakes behind Allan Bank Wood were reached. Here some good questing took place, some perseverance by Anthony and hounds before Pussy (hare) was roused and made out by the savins (gorse) to Megs Ghyll to Langdale, coming back through Silver How in by Score Crag intakes (area of low ground surrounded by wall) to Boothwaite, where they killed a fine mountain hare.

Another by the Harriers was when at the spring of year they used to change from hunting the hare onto the fox after March. This was during Mr Logan's time, they put a fox off about Wansfell Pike and away they did go by Wark How, Black Busk to cross the Stock Valley out of Petts Quarries, Snow Cove into Scandale, down Caiston and along by Dod Bields. These game lile hounds never thinking to yield. He then climbed Rough Sides, Caudale Moor to Broad How and then turned him in down past Raven Crag to Dod End, he next did try and they turned him out at

Hartsop. Like bees in the spring, when the cry of these hounds made the whole valley ring, both men and women all joined in the chase as true English folk should do, for to see a fox hunt. They killed the fox in Low Hartsop, a grand hunt by the Harriers.

I have given you a little description of my fore-elders. From now on I will give you a little of the history of the Coniston Foxhounds, and how it was started in 1825. Mr Anthony Gaskarth, of Coniston Hall, as well as being a farmer was also a butcher, and as a result of one of his customers not paying a debt, he seized two hounds in payment. These hounds came from the Duddon district and were bred from to form the foundation of the present pack. So Coniston began their history as a trencher-fed pack, in those days there were no kennels, hounds were living on various farms and assembling at a meet on the sound of the horn!

At this time they covered a very wide range of country extending from Black Combe, on the Cumberland coast, to Longsleddale. The kennels at Greenbank, Ambleside were originally built for Matthew Benson Harrison to house the Ambleside Harriers, a private pack of hounds, but when the Coniston Foxhounds moved here in 1881 they still kept the name of Coniston.

My father was made huntsman in 1908 and retired in 1932. He had to give up hunting hounds after he had an accident (injured ankle) when out hunting and left it weak – it was said in one of his last hunts that he finished it bare foot. Ernest Parker (his cousin) had been a whip for the Blencathra Foxhounds under Jim Dalton, the huntsman, and when he gave over with the Blencathra became a farm man at Troutbeck Park Farm for Mrs Heelis (Beatrix Potter). He then became huntsman to the Coniston in 1931.

My father's last meet as huntsman was at Coniston Hall in November 1931 and he had a great hunt, finding a fox in Gray Crag above the Copper Mines and made out for Threadle, before passing Levers Water under Hookriggs and Brim Fell to Low Water. Out over the top of Coniston Old Man, in by Goats Water and up the fearsome Dow Crags but hounds gave him no respite and forced him out and through the Turnels to Blind Tarn, where the 'sly un' (the fox) had not much steam left and rushed him inbank (coming down hill) and caught him at Cove Bridge. It is a custom with fell hounds not to break up their foxes and the fox was given to my father by the Master (head of pack) as a fitting trophy to mark the close of his career as huntsman. At father's retirement he was given a cheque for £105 and a cut glass decanter.

II

My Early Days

A S I HAVE SAID, I WAS BORN AT RYDAL, and went to school at Ambleside. We had to walk there and back, no buses in them days. From my early days I was very keen on hunting and shepherding and whenever I had a chance I would go hunting with my father, I would be about nine or ten. Even when at school me and a few of the other lads that were keen on hunting used to run away from school and run with the hounds. Mr Todd the schoolmaster didn't mind, as he was keen in fox hunting as well. I used to be proud to help my father at nights or weekends.

A few of my first hounds I can remember were: Yew Tree, Chanter (a black and white hound), Hart Head Freedom, Mrs Fleming's – Charmer, Mrs Leck's – Manager and others were Duster and Fetler. Record and Countess were both killed out of Dove Crag, Climber fell out of Raven Crag on Helm, Christmas Eve 1926.

Another incident I recall on 30 October 1929 when ten hounds were badly injured on some spiked railings whilst jumping them into the Thief Hole at Wansfell House, Windermere. This was Miss Wrigley's house and when she heard all about this next day she ordered the blacksmith to put little round knobs on them. How very thoughtful of the lady.

Foxes in those days were not as numerous as they are now, often had blank days. In them days the big houses that had land had gamekeepers and they either trapped or shot them. They lost the keepers during the Second World War and then afterwards it was uneconomic. The most the hounds caught in father's twenty-three seasons, was forty-eight.

A long hunt they had from Grasmere on 21 March 1927, they tried Grasmere fells and got back to Silver How before finding a fox between one and two in the afternoon. Hounds soon left hunters far behind and lost touch as they sped away for Langdale Pikes to Rossett Ghyll, Bowfell to Scafell, to kill their fox in Wastwater Lake at dark and they were kennelled up for the night by a Mr Wilson.

When I came of school leaving age, I worked at Round Hill Farm where my father was in partnership with Mr John Newton, an old friend

George Chapman after a kill in Greenburn

who was also a builder in Ambleside. The quarries up Rough Sides in Scandale are called after him. I remember when they were working there in 1920. I was at the farm about two years, then father had a nervous breakdown and he packed in farming. Johnnie Bell, who was a butcher in North Road, bought his share out, so I had to look for another job in the backend of 1929.

I went to work for J.V. Allen of Hartsop Hall, Brotherswater, a very noted farmer and good sheepman – all Swaledale; a good judge at Sheep Dog Trials far and wide, he was an international judge in his day. I went there at term time, about 11 November . There were two terms in farm work then, 11 November and Whitsuntide – that was when you got hired. The farmers used to ask you about three weeks before the term and asked you if you were 'stopping on' and made a wage bargain with you for the next six months. You only got paid at the end of the term. I remember my first wage was thirteen pounds and keep for six months. Living on the farm was Mr and Mrs Allen and their three children, John, Elizabeth and Ruth. There was a married man at Caudale Beck – Harry Blamire; a shepherd – Dick Dixon, and servant lass – Mary James (now Mrs G Wilson, Glencoyne)

My boss knew I was keen on hunting and whenever the hounds came about I used to 'take off' whether it be the Ullswater or Coniston. Brait Wilson was huntsman to the Ullswater at that time. I used to like to go with him, he told me a lot. Once on High Street, he said, 'If ever you become a huntsman, never let a terrier in Fox Bields or in High Holes Earth in Mardale.' Meaning likelihood be you would never get them out! He was known as the 'Flying Whip' to Joe Bowman (quick on his feet!).

Whilst working there, Mr Allen used to send his hogs away for winter to Staveley-in-Cartmel onto what was known as the Great Planting. At spring time we gathered them up on 5 April, kept them in a field at Sand Fold Farm and set off next morning at five o'clock to walk them back to Hartsop Hall, by Beck Hill, Bowness to Cooks House Corner, up Troutbeck over Kirkstone Pass to home. What a journey, good job there was not many motorcars in them days. There would be about four hundred of them 'what a road full!' We had a pony and trap travelling behind, picking up them that got tired and give them a ride now and again.

In an old diary I have one hunt in it says – Tuesday, 2 December 1930, hounds met at Nook End, killed one in Rydal Hall drive and another at Kirkstone Foot. I well remember the one at the Foot. We had just come out from dinner at Hartsop Hall, J Wilson and myself (he had taken over farm from Dick Dixon as Mr Allen's shepherd), when we heard hounds as we thought, but after a while we could tell there was only one, it was running very hard down the Dod. After a while, a minute or so the 'sly un', was coming across the field towards the farmhouse with Merry (that was the hound's name) close behind. In the corner of the field was an Elderberry bush into which it took refuge but the hound being game forced him out, viewing the fox around by Caudale Beck, up towards the Foot and back in front of Syke Side Hall, into a big stick heap. (Charlie and Grace Dixon lived there, two real old Lakeland characters.) By then Ronnie Porter arrived, he was whip to the Coniston Foxhounds for three seasons, let a terrier in, out Reynard (fox) shot, our Merry after it rolled him over in the field below, a good solo effort!

Another hunt I recall whilst at Hartsop Hall (I had a lot!), was one day the Ullswater were at Cow Bridge, Mr Allen sent me down the Low Wood to clean out the gutters, went home at dinner time, had it, and then I was sent to feed a calf at Caudale Beck. When going across the fields I could hear hounds running, coming down Ghyll Crag bottom, the music (sound of the hounds) was terrific it was coming nearer and nearer. By the time I got to the calf it would not have its milk, so I rushed out and the fox was going up the yard and about sixty hounds coming. They climbed Rough Sides into Caudale Cave turned left under Swine Knotts, pushing the fox hard inbank, to kill an old dog fox in New Close Wood. Why so many hounds? Well the Ullswater were at Dove Crag bor-ran (heap of stones or rocks) when Coniston came in down Huntsman Cove, Fairfield, from Rydal and Ullswater Foxhounds joined in.

III

Whip to Coniston Foxhounds

WHEN RONNIE PORTER FINISHED the season 1931–32 as whip, I got the job in that backend of 1932 for the start of the next season. As whipper-in you are assistant to the huntsman and try to help and learn as much as possible. I was paid £5 for a month, lot of money in those days. I would pay my mother £4 and £1 for myself – fags (cigarettes) were 4d (2p) a packet and beer 5d (2½p). The seasons then were from October to May (now they are longer). Some of my first hounds I can remember were Gadfly, Glory, Freeman, Friendship, Merryman, Matchless, Cruel, Charmer, Crafty and Countess. A noted man – Lint Inman of Lyth, a gamecock man.

The kennels were lit in olden days just by oil candles that were homemade by an old lady down at Nook End – she made them from sheep fat. Then we got paraffin lamps. We got our meat from the farmers, when something died they would let us know and we would go and get it. To begin with it would be by horse and float. If a cow died up Grasmere, we would butcher it there and bring it back. We didn't get as much in the early days as we did later – more loss amongst the stock and of course they kept more.

The first day out was up Red Screes. Foxes were bad to find in those days, not as many about as there are now, nearly all estates had gamekeepers. We had no hunt till we got to Dove Crag, put one off there, holed in Rydal, heard, bolted and killed by Rydal sheepfold. We used to have blank days – when we could not find a fox. As whipper-in I used to have to get onto the fell top right away so I was ready for when a fox was put off on the valley below and take off onto the fell tops. If I had to I could shout to the followers, 'Come this way!' That season, hounds caught thirty-eight foxes.

At the end of the season, hounds were taken out to farms in the Coniston district for a well-earned summer's rest. I used to take them out to the places on a bicycle; the furthest one I had to take, was to Lint Inman's at Lyth.

Anthony – whipper-in – taken when he was 20 years old

I went to work for Teddy Lucas at Oaks Farm, Loughrigg for the 1933 summer months, a very hard man to work for, from daylight till dark, no eight-hour day's, same as it is now. Five pounds for a month and keep, ten shillings extra for a month's haytiming!

October came round again, we did the same as at spring but fetched the hounds back again to the kennels on our bikes. Our Puppy Show at that time was held on the Ambleside Sheep Fair Day, it was always on 13th October, except when that date fell on a Sunday. The show was on the same field as the fair. The first I remember was on White Platts, a golf course and tennis court. Miss Belk gave a silver teapot for the champion hound, all the others got a silver teaspoon.

The first month of the season had a few blank days, then catching five foxes and one outstanding run from Long Green Head Farm, Troutbeck, where the hounds used to stay for the week, catching a fox weighing nineteen pounds. November was a better month killing seven foxes, including a good week at Coniston with three foxes – staying at Ship Inn, with Mr and Mrs Smith. On 30 November we went up Scandale, put a fox off between Brock Crag and High Pike and we lost them completely, it was a day or two before any news about the hunt came to light. The hounds landed back through the night and next day. I've always thought a hound had a wonderful aim. A hound called 'Cruel' came with a piece of string round its neck and on it was a fox's foot! News could not travel fast in them days but it came to light in a day or two that they had caught their fox not so far from Thirlspot. The shepherd did not know whose hounds they were, so put the pad on its neck. One way of finding out!

On Boxing Day that season hounds never were loused (loosed) too foggy, it did not happen very often not having a hunt on a Boxing Day. New Year came, 1 January very bad day, got nowt. On 20 January from Langdale, holed a fox at a place called Cat Lugs (never seen one in that place since), three terriers were let in, did not look a bad place but only one was got out after six days, Spider, belonging to Mrs Duder. It was as the song says:

> 'Then the brave lads of the valley toiled day and night
> to bring the terriers back to God's blessed light.'

In them days we used to stay at Sand Fold Farm, Staveley-in-Cartmel. In my diary I have Bigland Hall, ran bucks (deer) all day, no foxes about, not much good – we had lots of blank days.

In the spring of 1934 hounds went to High Borrans, Windermere, the home of the Holt family and caught two foxes, one at Hartrigg, another at Gavel Crag. Killed forty-three foxes that season. That summer I went to work at Dove Nest for my uncle and aunt, Mr and Mrs Leck, great hunting people.

Season 1934–35, we started hunting 3 October at Red Screes, killing a fox in Scandale. We used to like to kill a fox or two at the start of the season, made the hounds keen to work. Seven foxes in that month.

November 15–16 Cartmel Fell, that was my first time down into that country and stayed at Strawberry Bank, with Mr and Mrs Matthews, two old stagers. When we were boiling porridge, he used to come and pull the fire out. He thought we were going to burn the place down! 4–7 December Troutbeck, awful weather, never found a fox. What would you think of that today?

The following week went to Lowick Bridge pub to stay with Mr and Mrs Wilk Coward. We had a great hunt one day, tried Bell Wood, Arklid Wood, Brockbarrow and did not find one till got to Park-a-Moor and then a very long walk started. They turned down bank to Arklid Farm round the River Crake, up by Tottlebank to Giants Grave and into Woodland. At this stage there was three followers left, Ernie Parker, George Rigg of Hill Park, Colton and myself. We had no idea where they had gone, so we parted. Ernie went towards Gawthwaite Gorge and I went into Woodland bottom. Getting there, we were told hounds were running well and gone out by Woodland Station, Bracelet Hall for Broughton Mills. We plodded on in them days we had to ask anybody we saw if they had, 'Heard owt?' That was how we kept in touch. We landed into Broughton Mills about three o'clock, called at the pub, got to know hounds had crossed the valley and gone into Ulpha. Set off up the road, met a roadman coming down. He told us the hounds had crossed that valley with a good hunt, making for Birker Moor. Got down into Ulpha valley and were told hounds had killed the fox in the wood behind Church House Farm and the people living there had put the hounds in. That put new life into us. Mr and Mrs Stables gave us something to eat and drink. They told us the best way to go, was up the valley and turn off to go over Walna Scar to Torver and down the road to Lowick Bridge. It sounded all right but by then it was dark and we had never been in there before. So we set off with hounds and carrying the fox as well, on a stick.

In them days it was the custom to carry the fox back to where the hunt started from and anybody that did that were proud to do it. We were doing as told, so set off up the road 'plodding on' getting to the bottom of Travellers Rest Hill, saw some lights coming, getting hounds into the roadside, a motorbike and sidecar went by. It had carbine lights, it pulled up and came back and a voice said, "What hounds are they?" We replied, "Coniston!"

"Where are you going?"

"Lowick!" was the answer.

"Not tonight," he said, "you can stay at our house."

We were very thankful. It was Mr Gilbert Hartley from Turner Hall. He fed the hounds and gave them a good bed, a good thing for a pack of hounds. Mrs Hartley gave us a good supper. By then we were ready for bed. There was only one telephone in the valley, at the Water Works, and we let them know at Lowick what we were doing.

After breakfast next morning we thanked our hosts and set off back and carried the fox back to Lowick Bridge pub. Hunts like that one are worth remembering, we only found one fox that week. On 24 December was the 'Jerry Hunt', that is what they called 'The Travellers Rest', Grasmere in them days. Mrs Easton kept it, a grand landlady! If ever we landed there, it was always bread and cheese and pickled onions for everybody – free! A bit different nowadays.

Hounds caught a fox up Easdale, ran it about the village all morning. There was a hound called Sweeper, kept at Brimmer Head by Jos Hardisty, went for the first time. It had been in the kennel all the season before and never ran until that day and then made a 'good un'. Some hounds don't take in as fast as others. It is very seldom a hound does not go at all.

8 January 1935 Rydal Park – got a fox at Kirkstone top, killed one down Hartsop by five couples of hounds. In my diary I put – 'After a grand hunt touching eight valleys!' It was described in the Westmorland Gazette as 'Coniston thirty mile run!' Meeting at Rydal – the pack enjoyed great sport, two foxes accounted for, one after an exciting chase about the home districts, killing at Kirkstone. The pack had split on Fairfield and the five couples drove their game in by Dove Crag but the 'sly un' turned in by the dangerous Greenhow End, held the breast (hillside) of Flinty Cove to cross Deepdale Valley for Gavel Pike, where a sharp turn brought him to Blow Crags. Hounds hunted well in spite of adverse conditions and forced their game past Hayton Crag behind Arnison Crag, they had a bad check with sheep running in front of them, brought hounds to their scenting abilities.

In the meantime Reynard kept going to reach Black Crag but came inbank (downhill) through Trough Head to Glemara Park and entered the pastures at Home Farm, where he received a rousing 'Hallo' from J. Teasdale as he passed Close Cottages, into Patterdale Hall grounds, following Grisedale Beck onto the Penrith road at the Saw Mill. Hounds lost some time on the road, eventually 'Royal' got going again by Ullswater Lake and followed the shores of the lake to the mouth of the River Goldrill. They followed the banks of the river to the Rectory, where they crossed for Side Farm. It now became evident that the fox was far from being done. He started to climb Place Fell at Harrimans Gate and reached Gray Crag with a good lead. This was a severe test of the hounds' stamina but they lost no time in the ascent of the fell. Reynard now chose an easier course, by way of Neat Pike to Scale How, near Sandwick. He turned at the sheepfolds (pens) for Nettleslack but kept left handed for Boredale passing that inviting retreat of Fouls Earth, a noted borran, reached Boredale Hause. The hunt was slow down the bridle path and remained so past Beckstones Crag and Dob How to Angle Tarn Ghyll, at Lingy Crag. A great improvement in the hunt took place when the hounds went forward to the skyline with renewed energy, speed never slackened, passing Angle Tarn to Prison Crag. 'Sly un' visited the Filter House at Haweswater. By now the fox was feeling the strain from this long hunt and hounds knew they were getting nearer to their game as they made Hartsop Valley ring with their music (barking), as they crossed the Wath and over the Pasture Fell. Trying to climb Hartsop Dod, this steep fell was to much for him, turning in for Hartsop Valley. Once again hounds ran from 'scent to view' (scent to sighting fox) and killed the fox in the meadows near the village. Mrs E. Kinnear was first at the kill. She was a servant girl at Grove Farm for Mr Dobel, when I was servant lad at Hartsop Hall. Hounds were all dead beat after their long hunt and immediately lay down beside their victim.

I mentioned a hound called Royal, I think he was one of the finest made hounds I ever saw. He was good at his work and a champion in the show ring. Two other hounds running that day were T. Prestons 'Bounty' and Troutbeck Park's 'Brilly', two sisters.

Foxes were scarce that season. 19 January met at Red Bank tried Wyke Woods, Silver How, Hookriggs, Blakerigg, Codale Head, Tarn Crags, Deer Bields, Asthwaite Carrs to Horn Crag before putting a fox off and killed behind West Head. That was a long 'traipse!'

23 March 1935 Kentmere – running a fox in Longsleddale, standing on Buckbarrow Earth trying to keep him out, it would not be turned and got in amongst our feet. We let four terriers in after it – never heard them again. I had to stay in Longsleddale at Joe Fishwick's at Sadgill Farm waiting for them to come out or hear them. I was there for six days and never heard whimper daylight till dark and hardly ever saw another per-

Bruce Logan – Master of Coniston Foxhounds

son, only sheep and ravens for company. What a job that was. We could not work, as by not hearing them we did not know where to start, must be very deep; I have never let a terrier in since. On the fourth day I had just had my dinner, Mr Fishwick would not let me go home till dark and was standing behind the wall when one came out. I was pleased to see it, one called, 'Turk' a very good terrier, jet black in colour. We had a few black ones in them days. It belonged to a very keen hunting lass – Diana Faraday, who now lives in Australia. I remember I was there on my twenty-first birthday. Three that did not come out were Nip my own terrier, Tats belonging to Mr Jack Nanson – Dallam Tower and Set of Mrs W. Parker, Elterwater (Ernie Porter's mother).

My father once had one in Settle Earth for twelve days. Lakeland working pack terriers have a very hard life, a bit of leg and hard coats to stand the rigours of winters. I always said they were worth their weight in gold. One called 'Mert' fell in Hodge Close Quarry after a fox and was got out alive. I think the greatest rescue was when Patsy, fell down a mine-shaft at Great Wheel Crag. It fell two hundred and fifty feet and was alive and the fox dead. It was got out by RSPCA Inspector Torrence of Kendal.

Another hunt I well remember at Coniston was from the Ship Inn on 6 March 1935. We put fox off on the Scrow, went out Gray Crag, Levers Water, Townson Cove out over the skyline, that was the last we heard of them for hours. When we did hear tell of them again, they were marking (barking) their fox in Stonester Ghyll Borran. Sam Inman and myself got them after a long 'lait' (find). The fox would not bolt and we thought the terriers had worried it. We could not 'grub' (dig) it out, so left it. By now it was getting dark so we set off up the bottom to Hall Dunnerdale Farm where Mr and Mrs W. Boow put us up for the night. Sam Inman married Maggie, one of the daughters, she was keen on hunting and could show a hound in a show ring. Got back next day. A couple of days after a message came to the Ship Inn, there was a parcel for me at Coniston Station. Went for it, little knowing what it would be. Got there, signed for it. It was a sack, I opened it and there was dead fox and a letter from Gilbert Hartley of Turner Hall. He had gone to Stonester Ghyll the next day with a crow bar and dug the fox out. That was the way then, if a fox was worried underground, somebody always tried to get it out. It is an old saying, 'Never count a fox until you have hold of him!'

I well remember a fox at Cofa Pike that had been killed by another pack. I was about there four days later and there it was still running about! I had five hounds with me and they saw it, ran it and caught it in a minute. Another one at Raven Crag on Holme Fell was running about next morning! They also thought it had been killed the day before! So the old saying is right, they'll count anything these days!

In the spring of 1935 the hounds got what we called, 'kennel founder' it is like rheumatism what people get. It was pitiful seeing them trying to move in a morning, they were so stiff until they got warmed up. We had had it before but not as bad as this season. The kennels then were built into the banking, so that summer it was all dug out and a pathway made around them. The loft above where the hounds slept, we kept the bracken in there for bedding. We always used it, grand and warm. This was taken out and vent holes put in so that the steam could rise off the hounds after they had been fed and went to bed. The hounds never had it again.

The last week's hunting that year up Langdale the hounds were kennelled at Elterwater. Ernie and myself stayed with Mr and Mrs Fleming Mawson, at Chapel Stile. We had to walk from there in a morning to Elterwater then get the hounds walked to the top end of Langdale to start to hunt. We were getting up at 3 AM to be there by daylight and hounds in that state – now that was hard going! At the end of the season, hounds had caught forty-eight foxes.

When we stayed on the various farms during the hunting season, for breakfast you nearly always got porridge. Then you got bacon and egg as well. Baked bread in early days – never went to shops. Old black oven in side of fire I used to call them 'black fire spots.' Boiler one side with a tap, cooking over t'other side, lumps of wood kept handy for stocking it. Baking days was all day. Loaves of bread – rub butter over top of it to keep it from going hard – crusty – after it comes out of bread tins. They cured their own bacon and ham.

When you were away for a week you just went in what you were travelling in – another pair of stockings in your pocket and what we called 'a front' – this was what you fastened round your neck to cover your shirt up that you had on perhaps a week and a clean collar and tie. You popped this in your pocket, it wasn't big. (Waiters have something similar called a 'Dickie').

Farmers would dry things out for you. Marvellous people – get you rigged out in something dry. After giving you your breakfast, they would give you a packet of sandwiches to have during the day. Nearly always ham or bacon, when I was a lad I used to be into them within an hour, later I was never that hungry.

There were always articles every week in the paper saying where the various meets and packs were going to be, together with reports of previous hunts. Later on I did it for a spell for the Gazette – a penny a line. Farmers would look out for you and come and have a crack (talk).

Back to hunting and the season 1935–36 came around, it was bad for finding foxes, not many about and lots of blank days. These are some of the hounds, Chanter, Charmer, Comely and Cragsman – they were out of Coniston Crafty got by Blencathra Wynburn. Crafty was out of black and white Charmer (kept at Low Wood) by Cumberland Farmers (pack near Carlisle). Marden used to run with that pack till spring and then it came to us, a very good all rounder. Another litter: Gadfly, Bowler, Briton, Bounty were out of Coniston Bounty by Coniston Royal. Tippler out of Ullswater Brilly (she was a flyer) by Coniston Tippler, (that was got by Joe Gregg's Friendship).

We had twenty-one couples to start with that season. They had all been 'out at walk' kept by the farmers in the district. They are the back-bone of fell hunting. Hounds were sometimes coupled together – they were actually linked by a chain from their collars. Used to couple a young foxhound with an old one and that was how it learned to follow. Took about twelve to eighteen months to learn the job. We had a mixed pack, dogs and bitches and they ran well together.

Back to hunting – the first week or two did not do much, must have been bad weather. 1 November Snarker Moss, very bad day. 2 November Rough Sides – found nowt – shocking weather. 5 November – Ship Inn, Coniston for week, bad week 'got nowt'! That is what I have in my diary. 13 November, Strawberry Bank, had a grand hunt and killed on Windermere Lake shore after five hours. The hounds ran that fox round Gummers How, Blake Holme, Tower Woods, Winster, Lamb How, Bowland Bridge. The pursuit was not always fast amongst the stick heaps (woods), Cartmel Fell, Great Planting they crossed the Newby Bridge road four times and every time to the top of Gummers How. Each time we went after the hounds, thinking a kill was in sight, the 'sly un' (fox) was game, and out it would go again, to the top. The third time down, two hunting men, David Harrison from Lightwood and Billy Kellett from Addyfield, said 'It'll niver clim again!' but it did. Stout foxes in them days but for the last time it did. But after a marvellous hunt the hounds rushed Reynard (fox) inbank again and killed him by Windermere Lake. The same week we had another good hunt from Lords Lot, Winster, ran a fox for two and a half hours killing him on the road in front of Beech Hill Hotel, what a 'harvel' (drink and something to eat) we had then.

This season we were invited to go and hunt in the Sedbergh and Barbon district as the 'Sedbergh Foxhounds' had been disbanded. The

Anthony patiently waiting at the end of the day for the hounds returning. Note his strong 'tackety' boots used by most farmers.

season before the Eskdale and Ennerdale had been on invitation there and as they were going through Newby Bridge they saw a hound walking on the road and it turned out to be one of theirs, it had been short about six months 'they were lucky to see it!'

Hounds lose their bearings sometimes but, not often, as they have a wonderful sense of direction and a marvellous aim back to where they have been kennelled. Getting back to our visit the hounds were put up at Bainsbank Farm at Kirkby Lonsdale, by Mr Tom Robinson, he had been the master and huntsman of the Sedbergh Foxhounds. We were taken from Ambleside to Bainsbank in a wagon, I think it would be the first time in their history that the Coniston Foxhounds had travelled in one. We went on 18 November 1935 and stayed ten days. The first meet on the 19th was at Barbon Hotel there was 'Rum Punch' for everybody! The first time I had tasted it and by it was good! The hounds put two foxes off that day and killed them both on the open, one below 'Combe Scar' and the other at Middleton. We went into a pub there and had some 'home brewed ale.' It was the first time I had had some of that. After killing two foxes Ernie Parker said, 'It was like running on a bowling green for his hounds!' Hunting people will know what that means, at least they should!

The next meet was at Birkhaw Farm, Howghyll, on 21 November, we never found a fox that day. The people had a Hunt Ball for us on the 22nd and made twenty pounds – a lot of money in them days. The following day the meet was at Barbon Manor. We put a fox off and it crossed the Dent road by Bull Pot, Leck Fell House and the fox went to ground in a ghyll bottom – a very bad place called Ease Ghyll, and was worried under ground by the terriers.

On 25 November 1935 the meet was at Low Borrow Bridge Farm, a fine day and a good master of hunters, Ernie tried all the way through Low and High Carton breast out to Black Force, rightly named, what a dark place. We had never had a bark (no foxes about then), got out onto the fell top and somebody said there will be one in Cautley Crag, so off we set. Got there and all hounds put off was an old hare! What a walk for nowt! On the 27th it was Barbon Low Fell, another blank day. After that season I think Mr T. Robinson started a pack again, he had them kennelled at Tebay.

On Boxing Day of that season it was a misty morning so we went to Skelghyll Woods and put a fox off in Dove Nest Wood and made a great hunt out by Kirkstone top and Rough Sides, dropping in to cross into Low Wood out by Dove Crag through Deepdale Head to Grizedale Tarn.

Over Seat Sandal across Dunmail Raise out by Steel Fell to Wythburn Head, back down Greenburn to Helm Crag, where it went to ground (down a hole) off the edge of Raven Crag. 'Sly un' cannot have known of the 'Rush'! It was about dusk when we found them but a terrier was let in and found him after a while, the fox shot out, we could just see him. He was 'game' but done and hounds killed him in Helm Side Garden in the dark. Foxes were tough in them days. I have it down as one of the longest hunts that season. 1 January 1936 Duck Hunt (Drunken Duck Inn). Had a fast hunt and killed at Oak Howe, Langdale.

18–28 January, no hunting as King George V had died, that was to show respect to him. On the 28th we were to go to Sand Fold Farm, Staveley-in-Cartmel, and our master would not let us set off till after the funeral at 3 o'clock, that was a walk after that time of day by High Wray, the Ferry, Graythwaite, Stott Park, Lakeside, Newby Bridge, then to Staveley, between three and four hours. Caught two foxes that week, one on lakeshore and the other at Cann Brow of Yewbarrow.

1 February, White Stone, never found a fox, the younger generation of today would think that could not happen, but it did! 20 February – Mayor's Hunt, Troutbeck – Tom Bland was the Mayor that year. Never found a fox that day and it would not be for the want of trying!

Mrs Leak of Howe Farm kennelled the hounds and sometimes the Ullswater stayed as well. I have it down 23 March to 28th, Coniston, weather very dry and 'hask' no scenting, ran 'wild dog' (tried to find a scent) right round Lingmoor and gave over at Dale End. I cannot remember much about it other than spring lamb worrying was bad at Hart Head.

23 April put one off at bottom of Scar, went round Fairfield into Deepdale Head and returned and lost it at Rydal Hall. 24th put fox off at top of Scar and caught it in Blake Brows. 26th dragged into the Hollins, bolted and killed it behind Hollins House – bitch and five cubs. No lambs worried after that, just shows what a worrying fox will do passing lambs on its way to Hart Head.

Season 1935 finished on 19 May. It had been a season that was foiled by the shortage of foxes but the foxes we did find made some very long hunts. We had some blank weeks. Our total for the season was thirty-six foxes.

1936 season came around, the first day out was up Kirkstone Pass, it was our favourite spot, to get out from amongst the thick brackens and to see what the hounds were doing, whether they had learnt any bad manners when 'out at walk.' We did not find a fox until hounds got to

Pinch Crags in Scandale and it went straight back to Petts Quarries and holed in the big rubbish heap, so was left. The quarries were not a noted stronghold nobody was working there then. We used to try to keep them out but if a fox was determined to get in, nowt would stop it! My father once had 'Crest' a terrier in for nearly a week but came out on its own.

There was a hound running about now called 'Barmaid' was brought up at Hartrigg out of Ullswater Brilly got by Coniston Gadfly, she had a brother Glider and a sister called Glory. Glider and Glory were with the Ullswater, there was a lot of arguments by both sides about which was the best. Coniston followers stuck out for Barmaid she was a very clever hound, a good 'laiter' (looking for), a grand 'marker' (standing by barking) and could catch foxes on its own, it was a very 'kenspecked; a black hind leg. Once when it was a pup the Ullswater came past Hartrigg after a fox, after loosing at Millriggs and it joined in and was at the kill in Langdale Chase Garden, a grand set off (start) for a young hound. There were not many hunters landed (came) to where that fox was killed.

Getting back to the season, had a good day on 28 October at Helm Crag catching three foxes, a notable performance in those days. Then came Kentmere week, one hunt I remember, 3 November, put a fox off in H.P. Planting (this was a larch wood with spruce planted in the middle of it making the letters H.P.) and went out by Green Quarter behind Brockstones, round by Settle Earth (a noted stronghold), crossing Longsleddale, out behind Buckbarrow and came in down Stockdale Banks and on down the bottoms (lowland). The 'sly un' being hard pressed, it took refuge in a farmhouse sitting room! It was set on its way again but did not get far before being bowled over in the open. From that hunt there were three hounds short at night and heard nowt of them. On the Thursday I was sent back to Ambleside kennels to see if they had come back home again, but no sign of them. On Friday morning we loused (let hounds off) into Ireland Wood, put a fox off and went straight to Settle Earth, we followed on and got there and all at once this row struck up across at Buckbarrow, hounds 'gowling' (howling). It was these three hounds fast on a benk (ledge on a crag) and Mr E. Wightman from Grove Farm, Windermere, rescued them – marvellous crag man! (They were lucky hounds, went in there again that week.)

5 January 1939. That season hounds went to stay at Thornthwaite, Woodland for the first time in their history. Mr and Mrs J. Hutchison had gone to live there, before that they had farmed at Low Skelghyll and that is how we got a start going into that district. Three foxes were accounted

for, one at Torver at 7 o'clock at night, not many foxes are killed in the dark. 25 February – Mayor's Hunt, a very bad day, never found a fox.

26 February Howe Farm, Troutbeck, had a long 'lait' that means it took a long time to find a fox and when we did it was a 'straight necked un' (didn't deviate). The fox was found behind Long Green Head and right away set 'his mask' (headed) for the high fells and left hunters far behind. When we got onto High Street we found their footings in the snow and followed them into Mardale, down to Long Top and found the hounds in Chapel Hill pastures. Run out of scent by then, it was coming on a very bad day. There were four of us landed there, we gathered up the hounds, had a drink at Dun Bull and set off for home. By now it was coming dark, raining and snowing, what a job we had getting out to the top of Nan Bield Pass. The four that were there were Eddie Wightman, Ernie Parker, Nick Wilson and myself, who was about 'done in! Went in down Kentmere and across to Hartrigg Farm, intending to go over Garburn to Troutbeck, but on reaching the farm, Mr and Mrs Fishwick invited us to stay the night but Mr Wightman would not and plodded on. He had his motorbike and sidecar at Applethwaite Quarries. Hounds were bedded down and fed and we were given dry clothes, they dried our clothes the best they could, we set off for home the next morning, thanking them for their hospitality, they were marvellous people. We never forgot it!

Have in my diary the season 1937 as being a very bad winter for snow and ice. On Easter Monday, 29 March we could not go up Kirkstone our regular meet, we went to High Cross and loused down behind Coniston Lake, put a fox off and lost it at Arklid, what a walk out that was. Two Meets here 13 April, Brow Head, Loughrigg, put a fox off and lost it in Borrowdale. 15 April, Grasmere – ran hounds out of scent at Wanthwaite. Foxes then were very hard and good runners, nowadays they are about like rabbit hunts. I think a lot off them must be 'kin bred' (inbred). Killed forty-three foxes that season.

Season 1937–38 came around I always looked forward to the start. My wages had gone up to eight pounds a month. We had nothing much to write about. That backend hounds had killed fifteen foxes up till 31 December. 1 January – Barngates Inn – as usual killed a fox at Hawkshead. 17 January – Skelghyll Woods – got three foxes, was always a noted place. 1–5 February – Ship Inn, Coniston, Mr and Mrs Mat Smith used to have it in them days. Caught a fox every day, we had a 'harvel' every night. Mrs Smith did like a sing song, pub used to be packed every night. The quarries were at full strength, Bill Mossop and Jim Birkett used to fetch the slates down by horse and carts to Coniston Station.

31

An early photo of Greenbank Kennels in early 1920 (nothing much has changed)

IV

Pre-second World War

IT WAS DURING THESE SEASONS before the 1939 War (Second World War 1939–45) and after that we nearly always had a spell of the dreaded disease called Distemper. There were no injections at this time and it was a nightmare keeping them alive. At the kennels there is a place called 'The Parlour' with a fireplace in. We had to keep them in there and a fire day and night to keep the hounds warm and they had not to get their feet wet. It was a hell of a job trying to get them to eat a medicine we used to give them called Benbows and Lintox and it was not always successful. Packs would lose two or three or more every year, it was great when the inoculation came in in the fifties, it is a thing you hardly hear about now. 'Hard Pad' was another illness but I always thought that was just another name for 'Distemper'. It is not all a bed of roses being a huntsman or whip to a pack of hounds, you had at times to be as good as a vet to look after them. You could only afford a vet occasionally. I remember we once had an honorary vet and he did it for nothing. I always felt sad when we lost a hound in any way, which could be many. Science has played a big part in any animal's life since those days.

Getting back to my days as whip, I well remember a hunt we had on 15 March 1938, staying in Kentmere at Hartrigg, tried through Ireland Wood, wound above Brockstones into Longsleddale, trying Goat Scar, Settle Earth to Randale Ghyll Quarries, across Gatesgarth Pass, Buckbarrow Crag and never put a fox off when all at once we heard hounds running and coming into our view, they were the Ullswater Hounds and our hounds joined in. What a hunt then, about seventy hounds altogether making the valley ring! He was a stout fox, pressing him down the valley as far as Garnett Bridge, the 'Sly un' crossed the River Sprint to climb back to Potter Fell giving 'Jackie the fox', no rest place or harbour to be found, he once again crossed the river at Longsleddale Church to climb Ankerer Brow, turning a beaten fox down Stockdale, they killed him on Stockdale Bridge. The Ullswater Hounds under Joe Weir and Joe Wilkinson as whip, had put the fox off on the Lamb Pasture at Forrest Hall, Selside, where they were staying for the week.

A great song was made up about it by a good friend of mine called Lanty Langhorn, 'Lile Lant' as everybody knew him, we had grown up together, went to school together and he was always a good mate, out hunting, help in any way he could but always liked his own way if he could get it. He was a noted character in Ambleside. One of the lines in the song about when hounds killed the fox was:

'Before the eyes of the Nation this fox was put away!'

That was quite true because the making of the tunnel from Mardale to Longsleddale was on, the 'navvies' all gathered round and they were English, Irish, Welsh and Scottish men working at that end of the tunnel. Lanty called the song 'The Day these two Packs Met.' It's a song well put together of a good hunt, of a grand fox, by a grand 'lile fellow.' He made one or two more, one I well remember about a hunt from Borwick Lodge and catching a fox at 'Slops Bridge, Langdale'; another song one day from 'Hart Head, Rydal, killing a fox at Fell Foot, Little Langdale – great hunts them!

On 22 April 1938 – The meet was at Kirkstone Top, the pack split about Caudale, one lot ran a fox by Haweswater into Riggindale and caught their quarry at Flake Holme, Mardale, the other section ran their fox into Longsleddale and ran out of scent on Sandbeds.

Lanty Langhorn and Fred Pickett in the 1960s after laying a hound trail

We were up Langdale to finish the season 6–11 May, plenty of hunting but no kills. Up to that time the most foxes killed by the Coniston Foxhounds in a season was forty-eight. When my father was huntsman in the last week of that year up Langdale, they caught six foxes in five days of hunting. He used to tell me what a memorable week it was and they were all caught by 'speed of foot!' So in the season 1937–38 we broke the record.

Thank goodness the summer is over which has been quite a good one, the farmers have all finished hay, good blessing. I have seen some hay timing in October. A new season has come around and we had our Puppy Show on Ambleside Fair Day once again.

Season 1938–39 opened on 5 October – Petts Quarries, not much hunting. In November from Troutbeck a fox holed in Park Quarries, after a while it bolted and went out by Blue Ghyll into Kentmere, when next heard they came over the top of Ill Bell and caught it near the cairns. That was a thing to take notice of because there are not many foxes killed on a fell top, they nearly always make for the bottom to try and throw hounds off their scent amongst, houses, roads and sheep. Old saying, 'It will have washed itself in't beck!' – if they came to a check after crossing a river. Another old-fashioned fox's trick was run along the tops of walls, hounds follow either on wall or both sides of it. There is always a hound or two that can hunt down a main road, or a mile and a half through roads in a wood.

Huntsman, hounds and followers gathered at Hodge Hill, Cartmel Fell in the 1950s. The following are here left to right: Bryan Lishman, Tom Lishman, Frank Atkinson, Anthony; behind him is John Lishman, Stan Faulkener, Gladys Lishman, Jill Woods, Tommy Preston, Barbara (daughter) and Mrs Johnstone, Ann Woods, George Hodgson, May Armstrong and Wilf Nicholson (duffle coat third from right). *Joseph Hardman*

V

Hunting Fraternity

I HAVE NOT SAID ANYTHING about the hunting fraternity in them days, so I will mention a few. There was Birketts; Greggs; Pooles; Mat Walker, from Langdale; Gilbert Smith; Tommy Posty; Jos Hardisty, Brimmer Head, Grasmere; also the Reverend B. Phillips, the Vicar of Grasmere, he liked a hunt. Also another churchman – Canon Townley, who lived at Town End, at Newby Bridge, he was a big long legged fellow, he used to run after the hounds when they were hunting, a great sportsman. The Milburns of Nibthwaite; Neddy Swainson, one time huntsman of the Coniston Foxhounds, of Nibthwaite; Sam Inman; Watson Cheeseman; Johnny Wilkin of Coniston; Tommy Preston; game old Fred – Cartmel Fell, he used to walk there to Ambleside, hunt all day and then walk back, now he was a 'game one!' The Hodgson family from Witherslack; Jimmy Brakewell, Brathwaite, Hawkrigg; the Dixons who used to make 'pop' at their factory, where Ambleside Library is now, and lots more – Miss Belk; Mrs Duder; Mr and Mrs R Clapman, he is a great writer about hounds and hunting. If the hounds were in the vicinity of Troutbeck they always went to Broad How to try and keep foxes out, they would have some weary waits but it showed what dedicated hunters they were.

Every village where the hounds used to stay at had a Hunt Ball to raise money for the upkeep of the hounds and pay the huntsman and whips wages. As I said my first wage was five pounds every four weeks, a pair of shoes and clothing. Our shoes were hand made by Bill Megars of Skelwith Bridge, two pounds ten shillings (£2.50) a pair. My breeches and leggings were made by a Mr Hodgson, of Grasmere; my jacket and waistcoat by Mr Tyson, of Water Edge Hotel, and were made out of Herdwick wool.

The Hunt Balls were great do's. They were supper and dance, three shillings and sixpence (17½p). Ambleside held one in the Assembly Rooms, every year, dance on the top floor and supper underneath. It used to be attended by between six and seven hundred people. I have a cutting about one of such do's up Troutbeck, which says 'In support of the Coniston

Foxhounds, a successful Whist Drive and Dance were held in the Institute on Friday night, 18 November 1929 and Coniston Hunt is fortunate in having some very good friends in Troutbeck and the affair was a distinct success. The room was gaily decorated with evergreens, fox masks (heads) and brushes (tails) being trophies of the hunt. Proceedings began with a Whist Drive for which there were twenty-six tables, some extremely handsome prizes were given by hunt supporters to the lucky winners and were presented by Mrs Leck, which included turkey, hen, a bedroom clock, travelling rug and bag, a flitch of bacon and sack of potatoes. Miss Nicholson's Band from Windermere provided the music for the dance that followed. Supper was a splendid affair and reflected on the generosity of the Dales people. Those in attendance in the company were Mrs J. Hutchinson, Mrs M. Black, Mrs W. Bland, Miss Forrest, Miss Ridley and Mrs W. Leck. The food was donated and the pack was generously given £25.'

We had a day at Coniston that season when our hounds were hunting on Coniston Old Man in November and when they came in down past Bell Borran, there were now two packs together, Eskdale and Coniston, they crossed over by the Gaurds over Fell End to High Cross, out over Hawkshead Moor, no trees on the land then, all good sheep ground. We were left far behind but followed on, only two followers left, George Wilson, who had a poultry farm at High Cross, and myself. When going down Hawkshead Moor for Grizedale, we were inside that estate fence, I was going first listening for hounds now and again, when all at once I saw a fox not twenty yards in front of us watching us, I stopped and spoke to my mate and then set off towards it. The fox still sat there until we nearly got up to it and then it made a jump, when the fox did that, I had four terriers with me in couples. I said 'Scullard' (encourage) and they went after him and caught it. A good job too for it was minus a foot. That was why it was sitting there, in a gin trap, it had been set by a gamekeeper from Grizedale Hall. I took the brush off and buried the remains and then set off on our way again, we collected what hounds we could about Farrer Grain and set off for the Ship Inn.

Willie Porter, who was master and huntsman of the Eskdale and Ennerdale then and his son, Jack, acting as whipper-in, also our Deputy Master Mr R. Logan, were waiting. They started to cross question me about what had been going on but when I pulled the fox brush out of my pocket there was more questions thrown at me, so I kept them in suspense for quite a while before I told them the truth and then there was a laugh about it and they had a 'spree up' (drinks) and all went to the

Hunt Ball in Coniston Institute, a great night, about five hundred people there.

Had two good hunts on the Saturday and two kills, they were both carried back to the Ship and hung up in the pub for everybody to see, great enjoyment then. Then at about three o'clock we all went outside and lined up by the roadside as the funeral of a noted old character went past called 'Buttons'. I think his people's name was 'Barrow', that was how we showed our last respects to him, then Ernie and hounds and myself set off for home kennels at Ambleside.

Another good hunt that season off Holme Fell, it was covered in big long heather, which was very bad to travel on. (Holme Fell went on fire and burnt for days after that, it was better getting about on it). A fox was put off at Raven Crag, put a round or two by Tilberthwaite before crossing at Yew Tree Tarn by Tarn Hows down by Brantwood 'once the home of Ruskin' out over Park-a-Moor, where the hounds had a job to hold the line, but the pace got better in by Ickenthwaite to White Stock. By now this stout fox was feeling the strain as he crossed Rusland Valley out by Thwaite Head back into Satterthwaite and was finally rolled over at Paddy Bank, after four and a half hours. Our Master, Mr W. B. Logan, picked it up and his weight was twenty-four pounds (10.9 kilos), an old dog. A grand Master was Mr Logan, a real old fashioned sort, after a kill, if near a pub he would take everybody in and treat them to a drink, he was very respected by all.

18 January 1939 the meet was at Grove Farm, Ambleside, had a good hunt and killed a fox in Hartsop. We lost a hound that day and it was never seen again, it was one of four in the litter out of Mrs Leck's 'Cruel' by 'Tippler.' Three of them were lost and never seen again from out hunting, you would wonder what happens to them. The fourth was Climber, brought up by Johnny Wilkin at Thwaite Farm, now it was lost from a meet at Winster and ran a fox to Brigsteer Woods. The next morning it had landed back at Thwaite Farm, he had a broken shoulder, now that was a fair stretch. How far it had walked like that, nobody ever knew. That is an example of what a hound will do. Had a very good week at Coniston that season.

20–24 March, killing five foxes, now that was a feat in that county of bad crags and rough borrans and had some starring hunts. End of the season came up Langdale as usual in May – catching fifty-six that season.

Season 1939–40 came and things were looking very bad in the world. Hitler was on the rampage and war was likely to break out at any time and did at the end of September. One thing I can remember was that the International Sheep Dog Trials were held at Calgarth Farm that month and they used our sheep from Dove Nest. They had them for three days, when we got them back home, about thirty of them were wicked, some died. A blowfly will lay its eggs in the sheep's wool and within twenty-four hours they will be alive, it was very bad. It had been very sultry weather. It was a great benefit to sheep when the new dip came out which killed all the 'keds' (tics). They were a parasite that lived by sucking blood and did their business in the wool and made them stink and that attracted the flies.

Back to hunting, I cannot remember much about hunting that season, the country was in such turmoil, ration cards, petrol coupons and black outs. When down Cartmel Fell district we stayed at the Hare and Hounds, Bowland Bridge, with Mr and Mrs Walker, it was a pub with a little farm attached. From one meet we had at Roper Ford, a fox was put off on Rosthwaite Lot and ran it onto Whitbarrow and caught it on the top, a thing that had not been done for about twenty years. Billy Brockbank 'a grand old sort' and his daughters were there from Pool Bank Farm, he used to wear clogs and he could make them rattle!

It was a very hard winter, the frost came in the beginning of December and thick snow, it lasted for about two months. We did not do much hunting, only took them out for exercise. Our greatest job was throwing snow out of the kennel yard. The hounds could look out at the bottom of the railings, they had no need to stand on their hind legs to look out. I was fed up with that job, could not get near the kennels then, had to carry hundred weights of meal from the bottom of the kennel field as there was no road up then, that took doing without a stop. Coals to carry as well!

Ship Inn, Coniston

Identity Card

VI

War Years

I USED TO GO AND HELP MY UNCLE, Mr Leck, to drag sheep out of snowdrifts. There were hundreds of sheep lost that winter and there was no disaster fund for the farmers then. I had a very good sheep dog that could find the buried sheep, never went past one, whether it was alive or dead, it would start and scratch on top of the snow.

In March 1940 my age group had to register for National Service. Lanty Langhorne and myself went the same day to Windermere Drill Hall. I was told I had to go shepherding right away, so I left the kennels and went full time for Mr Leck, as he had got a lot more land up in the Scandale Valley.

The hunt had to be cut down in size, with only one man and less hounds as they were rationed as well. I went once to a farm where they were staying. The farmer was doing his best, he said he would get something for the hounds to eat and as hungry as they were, they could not eat it – that was gay (awful) stuff! The Pack was down to about ten couples but there was some good hounds amongst them, could catch foxes single-handed. One I remember, Ringwood, out of an Eskdale and Ennerdale bitch, got by a Cumberland Farmers dog hound. Mr R. Harker was Master of that pack and he was Mr R. Logan's wife's brother, a great hunting personality, after he resigned there, he went to be Master and huntsman to the Jed Forrest. He once fetched a fox from the top end of Troutbeck, I was putting a wall up on the Boys' Lots, when I heard a hound coming towards me, 'foxy' just in front making in for Blue Hill and Gasworks. I followed Ringwood and he caught the fox, at the blacksmith's all on his own.

Joe Gregg walked Ringwood at Mill Beck and he used to tell me what hunts it had up Langdale in summer, let alone winter. It ended its days with my wife at Huntsman's Cottage, she thought a lot of it, he was fourteen years old.

Stormer was another that could catch foxes on his own. To me it was more of a sport before the war but when that came it changed. The hounds were required more to put the foxes down, as the estates had lost gamekeepers. I remember when Grizedale Hall had five and that is just one instance. One of them, called Jack Braithwaite, was keen on hunting as well. I used to like to hear him at the Hunt Ball get up and sing 'For I tumbled and cut me bum!'

Look at Whitbarrow, there were keepers all round that fell, very few foxes on there then, nowadays they are from one end to the other. My father used to tell about two terriers getting into a limestone clink (split or crack) at Whitbarrow Scar and they could not get them out, they had to put poison down for them on meat and walled the place up.

Boxing Day 1941, Ernie and his little pack met at the Market Cross, Ambleside, and went up Kirkstone and put a fox off. Had a very good hunt after him crossing Scandale Valley, Rydal and Grasmere and killed an old dog fox above Brimmer Head. Jimmy Elleray and his daughters were the only ones in at the 'death'. I still got as much hunting in as I could.

Another day in November 1942 from Low Lindeth Farm, Ernie Bainbridge and myself went onto School Knott, found a fox which made off by Bannerigg up Borrans Lot out to Buck Crag, Rainsbarrow, Ill Bell, Froswick, round Hall Cove to Nan Bield. Good job hounds turned him back down Kentmere, as we were left a bit behind by now. Only three of us walking, we had got to Kentmere Hall Park when we heard them coming back down Brockstones (what a cry there was), we had a grandstand finish as they caught a fine fox below the church.

1942 saw a great loss to the Coniston Foxhounds when the Master, Mr W.B. Logan died, he was an all round sportsman. I think it was great for me to have been a servant to him he had been the boss from 1908–42. He was always looked upon as 'an old English gentleman' he was often called upon to be starter and judge of hound trails at the Lakeland Sports Meetings.

Mr Robert Logan (Robin to his many friends), who had been Deputy Master to Mr Bruce for a number of years, took over, he lived at the Low Wood Hotel, his family had been there in the catering industry for nearly a century. He was keen on farming as well and besides the land at Low Wood he was in partnership with Mr Joseph Kirby (nicknamed 'Darkie') at Rydal Farm. Mr R. Logan was also Chairman of the Rydal Sheepdog Trials Committee and was largely responsible for building up the show of Fell Foxhounds and terriers, held in conjunction with the Trials, to its present position of the principle hunting gathering of its kind in the north. Mr Logan's most absorbing interest was in Fell Foxhunting, which he and his brother John had followed since boyhood days. As youths,

Left: Mr Robin Logan and young son Bruce. *Mary Logan*
Below: Anthony ploughing on the shores of Windermere at Waterhead, Ambleside.

they kept a small pack of their own when at Low Wood and hunted in the Ambleside area. There was a hunting song about them. I will give the first verse and last one.

> When Robin and Johnnie fra Low Wood Hotel
> As keener young sportsman you'll find in this dell
> Rose early one morning on foxhunting bent
> With six couples of hounds into Skelghyll they went!
>
> William Abbot of Hartsop was in at the death
> He was glad that old dog fox had gone to its rest
> For of his ducks and hens he had lost scores and scores
> But he knew that old fox would nivver take more!

The war was still carrying on. Home Guard was on the go and any-body that was able joined. We used to have to go out at night and stand guard over places for fear Hitler might drop paratroops. I don't know what we would have done if they had come because we were a real 'Fred Karno's Army!' (Chaotic! – WW1 Concert Troup) It was some job going up past Nook End Farm to look after the pipes carrying the water to Manchester always at night time, standing on that bridge could hear nowt but water! Thickholme up Troutbeck was another place where the line crossed the valley and was not under ground. Jack 'Pip' Phillipson of Witherslack used to sing a song about the Home Guard. Here is a line or so:

> Some might be a bit weazie
> Some might walk with a stick
> But more John Bull is crippled
> The harder the bugger can kick.

Lile Jack has kept me in walking sticks, he used to get them off Yewbarrow, root grown ash they were, very tough and strong.

1943–4 season – Ernie Parker was having a very trying time, he was having very bad health. In that year he found he could not do the job owing to his health so he retired at the end of the season. I also had had a very bad attack of rheumatism – off work for five months. I could not go at all, I had a month in Kendal Hospital lying flat on my back but from then I have never had it again. I got over it and got back to work at Dove Nest.

VII

Huntsman

IN MAY 1944, I WAS GOING TO AMBLESIDE to do the shopping for my Auntie Maggie on my bike and going past Waterhead Range. Mr Robin Logan was coming out, that was where he was then living, after leaving Low Wood Hotel. I shouted, 'Good Morning!' He shouted back, 'Hey!'

I jumped of my bicycle, I had no idea what he wanted.

He looked at me and said, 'We are wanting a Huntsman for the Coniston Foxhounds, would you like the job?'

Without hesitation I said, 'Yes Sir!'

I did not even consult with my wife but I knew it would be all right with her and that was how I became Huntsman to the Coniston Foxhounds in 1944.

I well remember the letter he sent me to confirm it, on the bottom was in big letters 'BEWARE OF MUTTON' – a very true saying with a pack of hounds – any caught sheep worrying were put down. That back-end there were nineteen hounds in the kennels and some very good ones amongst them. Their names were Briton, Barmaid, Brilly, Cruiser, Crowner, Chanter, Countess, Glory, Gleaner, Gambler, Glider, Fearless, Marden, Gaylass, Ringwood, Rainbow, Stormer, Sweeper and Singwell.

The first three weeks we could not catch a fox, had some long runs but nowt at the end, till we went to Hartrigg first week in November. Tuesday morning I set off for Longsleddale, that was where Stormer was walked at Mr Fishwick's at Sadgill. Going across the fields' hounds took off up Ireland Wood. Hounds were good 'laiters' (finders). I used to like to see them taking a fell breast in front of them they had to do, as foxes were not numerous. Getting back to that day, hounds soon had a fox going straight to 'Tongue Earth' and split, one lot went into the bor-ran the others went out Ill Bell into Troutbeck, the ones at Tongue had Reynard in by the wall. I let a terrier in called Riff belonging to Ernie Towers of Knott House, Grasmere. He was a 'goodun' went about his work quietly. When he 'gave mouth' (barked) the fox was there, he soon found it and out it shot but was soon caught below Tongue Barn. Jack

Early Puppy Show. Included are Anthony and his son Edward, Robin Logan, Mr Rigg, Angus Logan, Norman Shepherd and Mrs Wilkin. *Mary Logan (Sanderson and Dixon)*

Fishwick landed up, only two of us looking about and listening, could hear the other little pack coming down the Yoke for Rainsbarrow and that one went to ground in the old quarry rubbish tip. Off they set, bolted that one, rushed him inbank and caught him. I used to like to see a good clean bolt and 'hoo git away'. Old Jack said 'By gum thoo's do'ng wiell but I'll have to be garn back to wark!' Not many followers about then. There was one hound short, Stormer. I thought to myself, 'He'll be after a fox somewhere!' So hounds and myself set off up the bottom past the quarry house towards the reservoir 'looking and listening' and there he was in the next quarry 'marking' (stand and bark) a fox to ground, we soon had him, that was three foxes for the day. Our luck did not last long as we didn't get another fox that week, it must have been beginner's luck and good scenting.

Went to Winster for a week in November to stay at Low Lindeth Farm with Mr and Mrs Preston, they were a grand pair, used to play 'Halfpenny Nap' at nights, what a grand 'school' it was, Tom Wilson and Anthony Sowerby from Staveley; Tommy Hadwin and Tom Coward of High Lindeth; Sam Hodgson; Jack Ainsworth; John Kirby, Mr and Mrs Preston and myself.

Tommy Preston had a milk round in Bowness and I used to get up and help to milk the cows in the morning by hand, so that he could get back to go hunting. He is mentioned in a hunting song:

> There's Tommy Preston up fray south
> He dreamt he heard a hound give mouth
> So up he jumped and out of bed
> And left his missus the stock to feed!

He was very keen on hound trailing and had a good hound or two in his time and he used to train hounds for Mr Lafone as well. I was always keen on hound trailing as well and have run trails since I was a lad, I well remember noted men and hounds such as Stan Bowes and Kruger; Clarks – Dairymaid and Dairyman; Brait Black and Misty Morn; Albert Dawson with Coldstream and Sweden Lass. Farmer Jack with Plunger, they were hounds kept in Ambleside once upon a time. There was a champion or two amongst them as well.

Getting back to the week's hunting at Winster, we were out five days and did not catch a fox until the fifth day. Saturday put a fox off at Knipe Tarn and away by Gilpin Park, Craghouse, School Knotts back by Matson Ground and forward to Ghyll Head to Beech Hill and Great Tower Woods to Blake Holme and Gummers How. By now we were left far behind but kept in touch by asking anybody we saw, but ran out of news of the hunt's whereabouts. We were on the road at bottom of Ghyll Head when a motor car pulled up (not many in them days), it was a taxi, driven by Tommy Faulkener of Browns of Ambleside and he told us, 'I have just seen a lot of hounds lying behind the wall on the roadside at the bottom of Gummers How.' I said to him 'Have they caught the fox?' He said 'I did not stop to see!' Thanking him for the information, off we went forward again. The hounds were still there when we arrived and were lying around the fox they had caught, they used to do that in olden days, after long runs lie down and have a sleep.

We had no young entry for 1944 but had four couples for season 1945–46. They were a very good lot and we were ready for them as there had not been many bred during the war years. All packs were the same, they were wanting to breed up again and wanting fresh blood and that spring, Sir Alfred Goodson of the College Valley sent three bitches down to our dog hounds, they were Rebel, Charmer and Regal. Jake Robson of the Border Foxhounds had one called Lovely put to Ringwood. Sir John Buchanan Jardine, from the Dumfriesshire Foxhounds, sent two down, they were black and tan colour and had them covered by our Gambler and Ringwood, the bitches were called Vary and Dowry. They all gave us puppies back for the use of our dog hounds. These men were great hound men, whenever you met them the topic was hounds and hunting.

The season 1946–7 came around and we had eight couples of young ones which were ten dogs and six bitches but before the season ended we had lost two couples through a bad attack of Distemper. Also lost two older hounds, Rival and Ranter, whilst away for the week at Heathwaite, Coniston, what a sickening week that was.

My wages for the season were £158, including uniform and boots, had my wife and three children to keep out of it as well, what a contrast now! Ruler was a first season hound that year, its mother was Ullswater Sunshine and its father was our Ringwood – it could hunt, and catch foxes on its own, seen many exciting finishes with him, he was a hound that did not give 'much mouth' (did not bark much).

The weather that season was very bad. Sheep got in a very bad state, very heavy snow and then snow and rain together, there were many weeks lost of hunting. I well remember one week in February 1947 where we should have gone to Woodland but there was too much snow about, it was not fit to go, and was like that for a fortnight. In the middle of that month there was a slight break in the weather, so Mr Logan said I had better go. So I set off next day and walked from the kennels to Hawes

Peter Martin on the left of the car and Ken Shepherd on the right.

George Robinson, on the left, and Anthony and his followers.

Farm, Woodland, a distance of about sixteen miles. Mr and Mrs Fisher lived there. I always used to say, 'It was the coldest house in England!' There was still a lot of snow about. We were out Friday and did not find a fox. On Saturday we found a fox but lost him in Broughton. The weather got worse again, snowing everyday, by the following Wednesday there was about two foot of snow. I told my hosts, I am going back home in the morning. They said, 'Stop a bit longer.' I said, 'No, I am off!' Next morning came, the weather still as bad as ever. I said, 'Good day and thank you!' Off I set back to Ambleside. What a job I had, the snow would not carry me, every step I took was up to my knees. It took the hounds and me one hour to get out of sight of that house but I was determined not to go back. After a while I crossed onto the main road, the snowplough had been and I could get away a little faster then. Now in all those miles, I never met a motorcar!

That spring lamb worrying by foxes was very bad, the sheep were very weak and after having lambed could not look after them, the lambs were easy prey for the foxes. The farmers were very frustrated, the weather was still bad, snow and rain together which is one of the worst things in lambing time. We were kept very busy going from place to place that spring. When the farmers wanted us they got in touch with the Master and then he would get in touch with me. Went the night before and put hounds somewhere safe and bedded them down. The farmers put us up and we would set of at daylight.

Usually though, the mother of the lambs will chase a fox but if twins it is difficult to look after them both. A fox nearly always does a twin lamb. Some will worry for worryings sake, never eat them, just devilment – enjoys it! They chew the tail of lambs they have worried. Nearly always go for throats and if you skin the lamb you can hardly see the teeth marks – their teeth are that sharp! When foxes have been bad, farmers have put oil lamps round a field to scare them of, though this does not work at whelping time – as the fox would have to hunt all night for beetles, mice and frogs and besides new born lambs are easier by far!

The farmers grumbled that much about their losses that they got a 'Disaster Fund' up for them and it was like any other, it was abused. In 1940 the losses of sheep was very bad but nothing was said then about a fund. I remember, when out hunting in 1947, finding a sheep in a snow drift behind a wall, it must have been there two months, was still alive but in a very poor way. How it had lived I do now know.

The fox unites two packs at the Eskdale and Coniston meet. For the Langdale visit of the Eskdale Hounds, they were kennelled at Dungeon

Ringwood and friend

Ghyll Hotel and were cast off for Langdale Pikes. Soon a cheery note warned Reynard of danger and the pack gave him a good send off at White Ghyll, to speed away and set his mask for Wythburn district. A biting wind drove him back by Blakerigg to cross Langdale Valley at Raw Head for Lingmoor. The pack was holding well together as the chase sped past Spout Crag and over Dale End into Little Langdale. They passed over Fitz Bridge to make out for Stang End and Oxenfell, over Holme Fell to Tom Heights. Reynard was hard pushed when he made for the Hawkshead country but a change of mind sent him back down Glenmary to Yewdale. It was here that the Coniston Foxhounds joined in and added 'their music' through Tilberthwaite to Stay Borran and down Moss Rigg. The combined music of the two packs as it echoed and re-echoed from the surrounding fells for miles was a never to be a forgotten experience. The game fox rallied to the challenge and led away out by Oxenfell and Colwith for Elterwater, as though he wanted to be back into home country. His pursuers gave no respite and on went the chase past the Police Station over Red Bank into Grasmere to make for Dunmail Raise. By now the 'sly un' was feeling the strain of a hard chase as he made his way back by the Helm for a last stand and at Lank Rigg he surrendered his brush. What about that for a hunt!

Season 1947–8 came round we had our Puppy Show as usual on Ambleside Sheep Fair Day. We had five and a half couples, a great interest was taken in them because four couples were from other packs for

Edward, Anthony, Annie and Mavis in this family photo in the late 1940s

the use of our dog hounds, including two from Sir John Jardine's of the Dumfriesshire. One was called Venture and walked by a man called Charlie Dixon of cock fighting fame. Charlie and a few mates were once having a cock fight when they were raided by the police but Charlie was also a fell runner in his day and he got clean away! Venture was black and tan in colour, everybody knew him, he had a very good nose. One thing I can always remember about him was when a fox went to ground in a 'borran', he used to stand out on the rocks and 'give mouth' loud and clear and he could be heard for miles around, it's a grand thing in the Lake District, is a 'good marker' (standing back).

The other hound was called Victor, he was brown in colour and was walked by a well known supporter, Johnie Wilkin of Thwaite Farm, Coniston. In October 1949 the hound was unlucky, nobody knew what really happened but he was found on Kirkstone Pass with a very badly smashed shoulder, so he had to be destroyed. So he had not a long life fell hunting.

In March of 1948, it was the week for hunting at Knott Houses, Grasmere and one day when out hunting on Steel Fell hounds ran a fox to ground. When trying to bolt the fox I was standing with my back to the hounds, when one of them set a rock off and on its way down hill, it landed on my hand and broke three fingers. A follower got me down to the main road at Dunmail and from there I was taken in a car by a man called Harry Setford to the doctor and he sent me to Kendal Hospital, where I was kept in for a fortnight. George Robinson, a big mate of mine, was there and he gathered the hounds and took them back home and from there onwards he hunted hounds till the end of the season. He worked for a great hunting lady called Miss Belk and she was very generous in letting him do so and she paid him his wages.

In February of 1949, when the hounds were staying at Woodland, Broughton-in-Furness for the week, they caught eight foxes, something that had never been done before in the history of the pack, we were out four times and got two foxes each day. It was very warm for that time of year. Some of the followers were running about with their jackets off on the Saturday, we lost contact with the hounds and did not find them till Sunday morning and they had caught the fox at Bouth, about ten miles away. They were very stout foxes in them days!

VIII

1950s – Mr Bruce Logan as Master

IN THE WEEK OF FEBRUARY 1952, while hunting in the Woodland district we lost touch with the hounds and passing a lonely farmstead, I saw a man standing in the yard. I did as we had always been learnt when in that predicament to ask anybody we saw, if they had 'Heard owt?' The answer back from him was, 'Aye, King's dead!' Which was right! When we got back home it was true, King George VI was dead, but that was not the answer I wanted. He likely thought he was telling us something!

Another great achievement that season was on 20 March 1952 the hounds caught five foxes in one day, something that had never happened before. The hounds were kennelled at Nibthwaite for the week and I stayed with Mr and Mrs J. Milburn, grand old couple. A start was made in Arklid Wood, where two foxes jumped up and the pack divided, they all went after one fox, except Ruler and he stuck to one. Tommy Milburn followed him and had a good run for about two hours before he killed him single-handed, a great job for one hound. We followed the other hounds over towards Ickenthwaite going on the fell road at 'Three Foot Yat.' Met hounds coming back and they bore signs of having killed, and they had, below Fardy Jackson's farm. 'Trying forward' (going forward) towards Grizedale, another fox was found and was quickly dispatched. Another was soon afoot but he had a bit more stamina and ran about till well into the afternoon, when the hunt came to an abrupt end. We looked for the fox but could not find it until next day.

On our way home the Dickinson family at Force Forge offered me a cup of tea, which was very welcome. Whilst having it, we heard another hunt's two hounds coming, Barmaid and Ringwood that was walked at that time by John Nicholson of the Grove Farm, Ambleside, now the present day Huntsman of Lunesdale Foxhounds. So we joined forces again and after another hectic half hour, hounds rolled him over at Dirty Poodle. Night was drawing fast, as we made our way back to Nibthwaite well satisfied and even more satisfied when Old Tommy told us of his days trailing with Ruler.

Bruce and Anthony on North Road, Ambleside in the late 1950s. Note two of the hounds are coupled. Not sure what is happening.

Another day I well remember from Bryan Beck, Cartmel Fell – 7 AM, loused, put a fox off right away, ran for one hour and caught it on top of Hubbersty. At the same time Tommy Preston 'hallo'd' (anyone seeing the fox will 'hallo' and hounds understand what it means) another fox on top of Pier How Hill, it being about 8 AM. It was spring of the year we 'harked' (telling them to go forward) hounds to him and then began the longest hunt of my career. Sometimes the hunt was fast, sometimes slow but we kept at it. Ran that fox all day in the Cartmel Fell, Winster, Great Tower and Blake Holme district, we had some good hounds for keeping going. Between four and five o'clock in the afternoon, hounds were about out of scent on the road at Hartbarraw Farm. Mr Robin Logan was standing there and said, 'You had better give over as hounds are tired.' I said, 'I bet fox will be tired as well, I'll just try them across this field and into the wood and there he was lying in some briers. Out he jumped and we after him again, a very stout fox but he had done his best to outwit us but did not and from 'scent to view' and 'from view to a kill' on Rosthwaite Lot at 6 PM. The first fox ran one hour, the second hunt was ten hours!

Season 1952–53. The new entry were six dogs and two bitches, four were out of Barmaid by Jed Forest – Falcon, Bowman, Fairy, Bowler. Brilly was lost up Rydal and was found dead in the river at Rothay Bridge. Ranter and Rockwood were out of Rainbow by Bouncer. They were both very good hounds. Rockwood broke its shoulder over a crag at Chapel Stile. Hunters who saw it do it said it was going that fast it could not stop and went over the edge. Manager was one by itself as was Ranter, it was out of trail hound Lawless (which was a champion of its day owned by Mr Lafone) by Coniston Sweeper. Ranter was killed on the railway between Torver and Coniston. There was hardly a season went by without a hound being lost on the line. The train drivers were very good, we always used to let them know when the hounds were at Woodland and Coniston. I have stood helpless many times when seeing hounds going towards the line and a train coming. I well remember once seeing it happen below the Five Arches, Woodland. The train went clean through the pack and not one was injured but some had a near squeak, they were covered with oil and grease, they must have been underneath the train!

4 October 1952 staying at Troutbeck Park with Mr and Mrs Wilson, we were running a fox about Broad How, when hounds of the Ullswater Foxhounds joined in and killed the fox in Dale Head. Lile Joe Wear landed and said, 'It was their fox!' They were always beggars for claiming foxes.

Swan Hotel, Newby Bridge

16 October – High Dungeon – Ruler put one off in Pikes and he killed it in the fields at Middle Fell all on his own, a good hound like his father 'Old Ringwood!' Had a good week up Kentmere catching six foxes. One was caught in the lavatory at the Institute. Another one was caught in the bottom of Ireland Wood. I made myself ten shillings (50p) that day by a bet with Ben Dickinson of Brockstones. I said to him, 'They've caught it!' He said, 'They have not.' But he paid up when he saw that they had.

We had a very good hunt at Coniston, ran a fox four and a half hours and killed him in the Wigwam. What a queer place that is, it was man-made – big clump of trees in the middle with rhododendrons round the outside. Lost a hound called Cruel, it fell down Yewdale Crag.

We used to be away for a month about this time of the season, only home at the weekends. Both huntsman and hounds were ready too. On 29 November the meet was at the Brown Horse Inn, Winster, Mr and Mrs John Kirby were the landlords. John was one of the best singers I ever heard in a pub, he could fairly get things going. He kept a hound for the pack called Barmaid. That night it was missing after hunting and we thought something must have happened to it, so a search was made next day and it was found dead at Lowless Beck in the Winster Valley. She was taken to the vet and he told us that it had been hunting that hard that it had burst its heart. Hardly a season passes but what something happens to some.

10 March 1953 – Knotts House, Grasmere for the week, whilst walking there passing by the Hollins Farm a queer thing happened. There were two donkeys looking over the hedge, when opposite them they both started to 'he haw!' Hounds had never heard owt like this, they scattered in all directions, it was a funny sight! On about donkeys, we have had one or two sent to the kennels and I always said they were the hardest to skin as anything I had owt to do with, no give at all. The hounds had a good week killing five foxes, a red-letter day on the Saturday with three.

30 March – White Moss was the venue for the meet, I have it down we killed one at Stone Cove under Great Rigg, another one at Heron Crag and found one lying dead, died from old age, only one fang left! The fox must have had a lucky life to live that long – nearly always find one now and again. The season came to an end on 15 May by killing a lamb worrier from Millbeck, in Easdale, another record of seventy-three foxes.

1953–54 – after a good summer's rest, hounds were back in action again on 24 September, Petts Quarries. Always liked to go up Kirkstone out of the brackens and could watch the hounds on clear ground, caught a fox in Coniston so that was a good set off (start). We had three and a half couples of young ones. Crowner, Cleaver, Crafty, Countess were out of Cruel by Ruler. Dainty, Dilwyn and Dinah were out of Ransome by Lunesdale Bellman.

28 September – had a good day from High Green, Troutbeck. It is a grand valley to hunt in, you can see so much, a lot of foxes have been caught in it time and again, as was that day killing three foxes, one on Lane Foot Allotments. An allotment is a piece of ground with a wall or a fence right round it. Another fox was killed on the Hundreds and the third was killed in Rydal Lake, what a finish to see the hounds swimming after him and getting hold of him in the water and then brought it back to the side for us. What a grand first month killing eighteen foxes.

19 November – Queens Head, Troutbeck, Shepherds Meet, so called because the farmers come to collect their straying sheep off the surrounding hills and dales. It is a very old custom. If a farmer was not at the meet and there was some sheep for him, they used to charge him so much for them. Coniston Hounds meet there for a hunt as well as the Windermere Harriers. That day we holed a fox in Atty Cove and I crept in to get him out and there was a rush of stones and my mate standing outside, Frank

Travellers Rest, Kirkstone Pass

Duck Hunt in 1954 – a popular date in the hunting calendar! *Sanderson and Dixon*

Atkinson, shouted, 'Come out of there!' He thought the rush of rock had got me fast and he said, how pleased he was when he saw me move. What a good week's sport down Satterthwaite, got eight foxes in four meets, a good effort for that country. I well remember when there was no forest and now there are thousands of acres. We stayed at Eagles Head, a few seasons, then in 1930 went to Adam Dickinson's, (a relation of his housed Coniston Hounds, when kennelled at Satterthwaite), at Force Forge, then we moved up to Ickenthwaite to Fardy Jackson's, they were a great family, used to like a bit of fun!

Boxing Day, Loughrigg all I have down is 'Bad Day'. It had been very mild and open weather that backend and had killed fifty foxes before the New Year.

1 January 1954, Drunken Duck, caught a fox at Park Farm after a very fast hunt it was as the song says:

'The hounds were nearly flying we had never once a check!'

On 27 February – Troutbeck Mayor's Hunt – began again after being defunct since the start of the war. There are records that go back into the 1700s. In them days hare hunting was more popular and at the end of the day if a hare was caught it was given to the Mayor on his election. Nowadays the Mayor for one year nominates his successor for the following year but does not announce his choice until the middle of the evening sing song. The origin of Mayor Hunt's is lost in obscurity but they were not uncommon in this part of England. Besides Troutbeck there was one at Bowness, Ulverston and Cartmel Fell. Troutbeck alone survives.

Mrs R. B. Fleming had been the Mayor Elect since 1939–40 and did not take office till the event was started again in 1953/4. We had a great hunt for the day killing a fox in Troutbeck School yard, an old supporter got the mask (head), Mr Jack Park from Witherslack whose nickname was 'Seagull.' He used to ride a BSA Bantam, there was not many places he could not get, road or trods (sheep paths), they were all alike to him.

14 March had a grand day hunting on Helm Crag, Grasmere, killing three dog foxes all by 'speed of foot.' We were having a wonderful season killing foxes, any district bar Woodland, had a blank week, no scenting, a bit different at Nibthwaite, got seven in four days hunting. Towards the end of the season a great blow was to come to us by the death of our

Shepherds Meet at the Queens Head, Troutbeck in the late 1940s. Mr and Mrs B.L. Thompson are on horseback

Master Mr Robin Logan on 3 May 1954. He was Deputy Master for many years before he took over the Mastership in 1942. He was my idea of a dedicated hound and hunting man.

On 8 May his younger brother John also died, he had been Honorary Secretary for thirty-two years 1908–40, his most absorbing interest was in Fell Foxhunting, it was a sad ending to a wonderful season. They were both told before they died that Coniston Foxhounds had broken all records again by accounting for ninety-six old foxes – a great effort. Another Logan making it a family tradition took over the Mastership, Mr Bruce, the younger son of Mr Robin Logan.

1954–5, the following season a start was made on 23 September at Petts Quarries after a nice hunt, caught a fox at Red Pit. I was always pleased for the hounds catching a fox on their first outing because after their summer's rest they used to come back from their walks as fat as pigs! I always used to say it was easier to take off than put on. The pack was again strengthened by six and a half couples of young entry but we were soon to have some casualties. Tippler died of pneumonia. One got away with couples on and necked (hanged) on an iron gate. Sparkler broke a shoulder and had to be put down on 20 October. Rockwood fell out of Raven Crag at Chapel Stile and broke a leg. He was the father of five in this year's entry. Scenting conditions have been very good not many days lost through the weather.

By now the hounds were having some very good hunts and kills in their favour, got twenty-two brace up till Christmas. Had a red-letter day on 1 January 1955 by getting three foxes on the open before a big crowd of hunters. On 4 February staying at Heathwaite, Coniston with Mr and Mrs Grisedale, they were a very devoted couple, she would not let me go out in a morning without having my boots cleaned and blacked, she always used to say, 'A huntsman should be clean and tidy, you see some followers with dirty boots that have never seen blacking for months!'

Getting back to that day the hounds put a fox off in High Park Wood and had a screaming hunt out Coniston Old Man, passing Low Water into Brim Fell Crag, where one poor hound, Remedy, was too daring and fell out and was killed. It was a great loss. It was one of a litter of six out of our Ruby got by Blencathra Mountain. It was a hound that I used to like to shout to when I heard it 'giving mouth,' it was always true to fox game. I have mentioned this fellow before, 'Lile Lant,' he made a very touching song up about it and here is a line for you to sample:

'Remedy you took one leap too many and that was the way you died!'

Day's hunting in Langdale

Crown Hotel, Newby Bridge

The weather up till now had been quite good but we would be very lucky to go through a season without bad weather and it came the last week in February, even the Mayor's Hunt was off owing to thick snow and ice. These fells can be very dangerous when the crags are full of ice, a fox will go where a hound cannot and that is when the trouble starts.

There is hardly a season passes without we run into our neighbouring packs and this one was no exception because on 5 March the Coniston and the Lunesdale joined up in Barrowfield Woods but had no success. As on 2 April the Ullswater Foxhounds joined in with ours and killed a fox in Coniston bottom. There was only one of the Ullswater supporters there to witness what happened and he had to give way to us. It was that well known hunting man, Johnny Poole of Glenridding, he was a great mate and helper of Joe Wear's.

Salutation Inn, Ambleside on 29 June 1955 – celebrating the Coniston Foxhounds in reaching a Century. Left to right: Harold Hodgson, Ernie Towers, Mrs Harker, Michael Osman, Anthony, Annie, Bruce Logan and Mr Rolly Harker.

IX

A Century for Coniston

W<small>E WERE HAVING A HELL OF A SEASON AGAIN</small>, the hounds were in great fettle and killing lots of foxes one, two, three and up to four a day. That happened from the Knott Houses, Grasmere; one in Hollins; one at White Moss and two in Nab Scar borrans. My terrier Vicky bolted both of them.

Although I say it myself I had some wonderful terriers, you needed them in these big borrans as we call them. Naming a few of them – Riff, Crab, Metz, Tess, Spider, Sting, Gyp, Bodger, Vic, Mut, Rags, Rose and Patsy. I won the championship with one of my terriers, called Crab at the Fell Foxhound Show at Rydal and lost him the following season. A pack terrier has a very hard life. As I was saying we were having a good season, some very good hunts. On 18 April, we were up to last year's total of ninety-six foxes, meeting at Nook End Farm and killing a fox in front of Kirkstone Inn, one of the highest pubs in England. On the 23rd we were in Kentmere, adding two more to our tally on the 29th. We were at Broadrayne, Grasmere, staying with Mr and Mrs E. Tyson accounting for two more, at Black Crag in Rydal, which brought us our century, something that had never happened before in the history of the Coniston Foxhounds and I say I do not think it will happen again. I was proud, that I was the huntsman of those hounds that did it. I have to say here and now that I had some wonderful support behind me both in hounds, terriers and everybody who helped me in any way, to all those I say, 'Thank you!'

Before the season ended the pack had accounted for one hundred and five foxes. One day I must mention was 20 May, Stool End Farm, Langdale, loused at four thirty, struck a drag (scent) right away, went out the Band forward to Bowfell. We were left far behind but followed on, could not find them anywhere. Waiting and listening at top of Eskhause, so set off back for home when a hound came in behind us, did not know what direction it came from. I rubbed my hand over its mouth and then smelt it, I said right away, 'They have caught a fox!' When we got back to Stool End, John Bulman of Dungeon Ghyll Hotel, Master and Huntsman of Windermere Harriers, had a telephone message, to say the hounds had caught their fox at Wasdale Head and all hounds were fastened up bar one and that was how we met. John was good enough to take me round in his cattle truck to collect them from Jos Naylor's farm. It had been twenty-eight years since the Coniston Hounds had caught a fox in Wasdale Head. This is what one newspaper wrote about our achievement: *"The feat of the Coniston Foxhounds in reaching a century has brought the pack into prominence in northern hunting circles and makes the huntsman's latest achievement all the more notable in fell hunting, where most packs have two men and he* (Anthony) *did it on his own".*

This is what a lady wrote when the Coniston had their hundreth kill:

> *Congratulations Anthony, my lad thous done reet well*
> *In killing all those foxes on woodland, moor, and fell*
> *This hundred is a record which adds well to your fame*
> *And is it any wonder, when Chapman is the name*
> *Your forbears they were famous, when they hunted on the fell*
> *But none have caught so many and none been liked so well.*

There was a man in Ambleside called Wilf Nicholson, we called him Lile Wilf from Girt Shirt Shop, he was a great friend of our family and he thought something should be done to commemorate the occasion, by a presentation to the Master, Mr B. Logan and to the Huntsman, Anthony Chapman. He got a gathering of hunting people together on 29 June 1955, for the occasion at the Salutation Hotel, Ambleside. Mr E.W. Towers (who was a well-known farmer and a champion pole-vaulter in his day) presided at the presentation proceedings which followed the dinner. The principal speaker was Mr R. Harker, Master of Jed Forest Foxhounds, who recalled how as a youth he learned his hunting with the Coniston Foxhounds and used to whip-in for my father, when he was huntsman. Mr H.S. Hodgson made the presentation to Mr Logan of a handsome picture of himself with huntsman and hounds on Sweden Bridge in Scandale Valley. For myself an inscribed whip, a pair of binoculars and a cheque subscribed by admirers from all parts of the north and further a field. Nine year old Michael Osman made his own personal presentation of a copper horse brass.. Mr H.S. Hodgson was a well thought of auctioneer from Witherslack. I used to like to be in his company, he used to like to have a good sing song!

1955–6 – After such a very good season before, foxes were scarce and we had a lot of blank days. I had three and a half couples of young ones; four were by Lunesdale Bellman out of our Chorus and three by Ruler

Carrying a fox on a stick are Wilf Nicholson, Albert Dixon,_____ and John Kirby

Rydal Park Sheepdog Trials in 1950s with the huntsmen rowed up.
Left to right: Harry Hardisty (Melbreak), Walter Parkin (Lunesdale), Joe Wear (Ullswater), Anthony (Coniston), Johnny Richardson (Blencathra) and Arther Irvine (Eskdale and Ennerdale).

out of Melody, two of which had accidents that proved fatal. One fell out of Raven Crag, Holme Fell; 'Matchem' walked by Mrs Lishman of Cartmel Fell, broke a hind leg at Park-a-Moor and had to be destroyed. We were soon having some more bad luck on Saturday, 1 October from Troutbeck Park, got one fox in Hartsop and holed one below Broad How. I entered two terriers, Tess and Spider, and thought the fox was boss of them in trying to bolt him, so I let Crab in. Whilst we waited, we heard a rushing of stones and all went quiet. Digging operation was started at once but it took us till Monday to get to them and it was a sorrowful sight when we did, as Tess and Spider were dead and Crab was fast and could not fend himself. The fox was alive and he had given him a bad time. Crab was carried home to my house and my wife Annie looked after him but to no avail and he too passed on, a great blow to me.

Had one good week that backend up Langdale with a tally of five foxes. There were many weeks we only accounted for one 'sly un.' Winster week ran a fox to Whitbarrow, that is a place that is nothing else but limestone, it goes for the hounds' feet. One day when on there, we had a fox holed in a place called Ash Holes, a lady, Mrs Johnson by name, was standing watching when she touched something amongst the leaves and muck and to her surprise it was a hunting horn. It had been there for years, the owner's name was on it, de Courcy-Parry. The lady has it to this day. Mr Parry even made a song up about it.

The Mayor's Hunt of that year must have been a bad day because we never went out. Went to Lindeth Farm on 28 February, all we did was find two foxes lying dead. It was a bad year for our terriers, as on Easter Monday we got one fast in Dod Bields, there was men working for it for nine days before it was got out to God's Blessed Light! Ended the season with sixty-seven old foxes and twenty cub foxes, they were a bad lot amongst the lambs that spring.

Once upon a time all hunters walked but now it's motorised. Biggest part of them ride about in motor cars, and they are not much good. I have often noticed when walking with hounds on the road and a car passes the hounds will start and blow it out of their nostrils, so it just shows. An old hunting man once told me for a good scenting day you wanted a southwest wind and a cloudy sky. I know one or two things that contribute to bad scent, a blue haze, when water is standing like bubbles on the grass when storm is in the air. I think the best of them all be it good or bad, are the hounds!

The accounts for the year 1956–7 were again very good and showed an excess of income over expenditure of £462.10s.4d. Hunt Balls raised

Anthony and his son, Edward walking with the hounds at Rydal in the 1950s. They would be walking to the meet the day before and Edward would get a lift home. *Sanderson and Dixon*

a record total of £975.12.6d. Subscriptions were up to £209 – good efforts!

At our Puppy Show for the season 1956–7 held at the Open Fell Foxhound Show at Rydal, the silver cup given by Mrs Leck in memory of her hound Ransome was won by Ragman, walked by Mrs Ainsworth, and D.F. Cockerton prize for the best walked puppy was won by Steamer, walked by Mr R. Birkett. We had five couples of young entry. Five of those came to untimely ends. I'll just say what happened to them. Ruby lost up Kentmere and was never seen again. Ragman died in kennels 29 December 1961. Royal lost Easter Monday 1961, never seen again. Remedy killed on railway 7 February 1957. Reckless killed out of Deer Bields Crag 11th March 1961. It just shows what losses we have amongst fell hounds.

I will give some days of hunts.

4 October – Bad day snowing, heavy all day, that was very soon in the year.

10 October – Brathay Woods, three foxes accounted for.

27 October – Hawkshead, two fast hunts, one Grizedale Hall the other below Satterthwaite.

3 November put a fox off Diatomite Works, Kentmere and caught it at Gate House, it was a big fox weighing 19 lbs (8.6 kilos).

16 November – Bell Crag, Coniston, catched a fox at Walthwaite, Great Langdale, that was a tidy step.

8 December – Woodland, put a fox off in Thrang Crag Wood but joined up with the Eskdale and Ennerdale and did nowt.

7 January – High Newton, got a fox at Sunny Green, bigger still, 21 lbs (9.5 Kilos) weight.

I have for 29 January, a grand day – fine and warm.

30 January – a bad wild day a big difference from yesterday. It shows how weather can change in twenty-four hours.

Mayor's Hunt, put a fox off at Raven Crag, had a good rattle round Woundale back down Troutbeck, went to ground besides the Queens Head, bolted and never saw him again, as it ran hounds out of scent and came on a bad day. I have a photo of him and what a fine fox he was!

5 March found a fox on Stone Arther, ran him to Wythburn and caught him and hounds left it. When we got there we realised, no wonder the hounds left it as it was covered with tics, never saw a fox like it and never seen one since!

12 April – lamb worrying at High Yewdale, Coniston, went the night before so that we could let go next morning at daylight, it's always grand

Ambleside Sports in the late 1940s. The hound trailing has just set off

at that time of day, strike a drag right away out of the lambing field and away the hounds went right round Coniston Hall at 8 am. Peter Martin, he's a bit of a songwriter, made a song up about that hunt and he sings it at these 'harvels'. Here is a line:

> '*Old Dilwyn* (hound) *told us plain, that fox that night, had been up to his tricks again, he was a good hound that one.*'

The following morning we went off again and put a fox off in Yewdale Crag and caught him on the road below at 7 AM. Got another at Cove Quarries, that stopped them lamb worrying.

Finished the season off at Stool End, Great Langdale, with a good total of eighty-eight. 3 October – Rough Sides Wood, put a fox off but soon lost it, then had a long draw before finding another in top end of Caiston. After a fast run was overtaken in High Pike breast, another one had been disturbed and gave a capital hunt for about three hours. Near the Ambleside to Keswick road his dodges gave the hounds some hard work to puzzle out the line but was seen by Mrs Chapman, who 'hallo'd them on' and this cunning varmint turned back up Nook End Ghyll, where he ended his days after an exciting chase and finish.

On 5 October, hounds holed a fox behind Nab Crags at Wythburn, we did not know it had gone to ground and we were all standing listening when a lot of the hounds came onto the edge of the crag and started 'to sing' as we call it. I had never heard the hounds do that before and I have never heard them do it again, wasn't that a queer way of telling us! We had a great day's hunting from Chapel Stile, accounting for four foxes on the open, one at Brimmer Head, number two at Robinson Place, number three at High Close and number four at Silverthwaite Quarry. What a day that was for the followers!

We used to have a meet at Miller Bridge House, a fellow called Mr Marsh lived there and the hospitality was always great, coffee was had and 'Lile Lant' used to go round with bottle of rum, I liked rum and coffee. Another fellow always came to that meet, I have known him for a long time but I still do not know his proper name yet and he still comes – we christened him the 'Manchester Huntsman!' He was a 'crag rat. ' I once saw him disturb a fox of a 'benk' (ledge) in Tarn Crags I would not have gone in to it. We had a good hunt from that meet.

All kinds of things happen when out hunting. 7 November 1957, Nab Farm running a fox in Nab Scar, we weren't making a great lot out, was not the best of scenting. My wife and Mr Herbert Holmes, a well-known Ambleside man, were standing in the field behind the farm, when they saw the fox coming. 'Birbo' (Herbert) that was his nickname, got excited and started to 'Hallo', he got two shouts out and dropped down dead, what a job that was. He died doing something he liked. When I got to know what had happened, we took the hounds home to show our respects.

1 January 1958 saw the hounds at Drunken Duck, again bad day, nowt doing only supping ale. The inn became known by this curious name because of a comical occurrence about a century ago, when a man called John Wardle was landlord. A careless carter dropped a barrel of ale from his horse drawn dray when delivering at the inn. The cask burst and its contents went down the gutter. The innkeeper's ducks dibbled in the spilled ale and before long all the ducks were lying helplessly drunk beside the inn. The landlord's wife was greatly distressed to find them all apparently dead and they were put into a heap in the orchard but by next morning they had come to their senses and were none the worse for their drunken dibbling! Its proper name is Barngates Inn.

One morning whilst walking to a meet at Woundale Gate on 28 March, I had Keith Clements of Kendal with me and we did not manage to land at the meet for the hounds broke away after a fox and before night, we had got two foxes. One killed on the lawn at Scale How, Ambleside and the other at Hart Head, Rydal. We perhaps did better than getting to the meet.

From the last meet of that season, I went to lamb worrying at Millbeck – caught a 'sly un' in top end of Eskdale, one hound short, Crowner, walked by Mrs Lishman of Bryan Beck, Cartmel Fell. Looked all over for it then advertised for it in the paper and it turned up at Longtown, the other side of Carlisle. He must have lost his direction, better finding it than not at all. It would be fifty miles away but he was none the worse for his travels.

After a good summer's rest for the hounds, backend was upon us once more. We had got all the shows in and as many of the sports as I could. 'Ambleside Sports' was growing from strength to strength, to be in line with the world-renowned Grasmere. We were the boss when it came to Hound Shows, with our famous Rydal which people attend from all over the country. For our own Hound Show held the same day, a lady, Mrs J. Wilson of Dixon Ground Farm, Coniston, gave a silver cup for the best walked entered hound and was won by Rascal walked by T.N. Preston; Mrs Leck's cup for the best looking puppy was won by Driver walked by 'lile Alan Dugdale and for the best walked, went to Wyndham walked by Fardy Jackson. Wyndham did not last long, as it died through an accident the following year. There was a hound that season called Rambler, got that deadly illness, 'Yellow Jaundice'. It started when we were staying away from home, I got him back to kennels but my wife said, 'Fetch him down to the house!' The vet gave him no hope. She kept him in the kitchen and we lived in the sitting room for three weeks and it was through her care and affection he pulled through. That capped the vet! 'Nowt like a woman for looking after a sick hound!'

Mrs Leck (Anthony's aunt) in the late 1950s
Sanderson and Dixon

X

Late 1950s

THE SEASON GOT UNDER WAY 1958–9. 29 September Rydal Park, never found a fox, I thought that was a very bad set (start) off but things mended. Scenting was a bit queer for a bit, I always think brackens have a very strong smell at that time of year. We did not do much until we went for our week at Millbeck, Great Langdale, with Mr and Mrs Gregg.

14 October – White Ghyll, it used to be very dangerous for hounds, it was covered in heather once upon a time, overhanging on the banks but it got on fire somehow and it burnt it all off. Put a fox off in Raw Breast after a fast hunt round Pavey Ark, hounds were foot gaining, hard on his brush at Stickle Tarn, he had to turn inbank and be accounted for below Scout Crag. It being 11.30 am, another fox was looked for and found and we kept at him till he was caught at 5 PM, he had been an old stager! A fellow once wrote a poem about me. I'll put in a verse.

Our huntsman Tony Chapman
Is lanky, lean and tall
He was summat to contend with
To try and please us all
But when they're hunting foxes
He's always full of pluck
He often perseveres
When others would give up!

That's enough lines of prose for now. One day when hunting from Coniston had a good hunt after one and landed at Hodge Close Quarries, a helleva quarry hole. The fox was about done and was running round the edge and Mert, a terrier of mine joined in. Both fox and Mert fell in, they both fell about two hundred feet. Fox was dead, Mert alive and none the worse for it's fall. That place is now full of water.

4 December – Torver, ran a fox to Ulpha. There was only Fred Tyson, that grand landlord of the Blacksmiths Arms, Broughton Mills, got there, they were running the varmint about a wood at Home Cottage Farm. I

Sweden Bridge, Ambleside with Anthony and his hounds in May 1959. *James Jennings*

could tell hounds were hard at him 'so I sowed' (joined) in as well, when there was a woman came out of the house and I could tell by her antics she did not want me or the hounds there but I could not stop them. A good job they caught the fox and I off out of her road! The same week up at Dow Crags running very hard, followers standing guard on the borran. A very bad place when the 'sly un' came again and tried to get in, we turned him out again. This is what we saw, Cragsman leading the pack by about a minute, ran to view and killed him on his own. A grand effort not many hounds will 'yorke' (attack) a fox on its own but he did not stand back and wait.

We were having some long hunts. 17 December, Ickenthwaite, hounds killed a fox at Black Beck, Bouth, lasting five hours. Had the usual hunts at Christmas time and had good sport. 1 January from the 'Duck' put a fox off and lost it in Skelghyll Woods, that night I slipped in the kennels and cracked two ribs. From then on for about three weeks the Master, Mr Bruce was the Huntsman, I think he found that the days were long and hectic with not much time inbetween. That year hounds did not go to Newton-in-Cartmel, that Committee went defunct but supporters were not going to be done out of a week's hunting so Mr H.S. Hodgson, Jack Park and Frank Atkinson got a Hunt Ball going in Witherslack. It's a country that's nowt but limestone, briers and stickheaps (woods) but has a good hunting fraternity. The hounds caught one fox after a very long and local hunt. Frank 'Ack' as he is well known, made a hunting song up about it and sings it at these hunt suppers as they call them now. The first lines of the song set off like this:

> When back in 59 to Witherslack did come
> Those gallant Coniston Foxhounds and didn't we have some fun
> The Master, Mr Logan was hunting hounds himself
> As Anthony had cracked some ribs and wasn't feeling well.

It finishes of something like this after the kill.

> And back to Slate Hill Farm we set
> Where missus says 'by gocks'
> All ye folk and all them hounds and 'all yer git is yan' fox

I don't know how many foxes the farmer's wife thought hounds and hunters should have got!

We were having a good season, very open, and having some great hunts. I was back in action again and I must put this day in, 6 February 1959, Coniston went to Guards Wood, was not fit to go to the high fells,

Kirkstone in the 1950s.
Left to right: Sammy Garside, Anthony and his daughter Mavis, Michael Osman and Tommy Armer

snow and ice at Fell End. Cragsman roused two foxes and whilst hark-ing the rest of the pack to him, they all got after one bar him and he went after the other solo with Bob Birkett, he was as good as a hound. Myself and all other hunters went after the larger pack and had a good hunt and kill behind Coniston Lake.

Did not know what had happened to Cragsman until nightfall, when he and his hunter landed back and told us what had happened. The gal-lant hound had run the fox hard on three hours and somehow Bob had kept in touch and the astounding part about the outcome, was that he caught the fox on his own, within a quarter of a mile from where he was walked in the summer months at Mr and Mrs Benson's, Skelwith Fold Farm, Ambleside. It was a great credit to the hound and of course Bob for keeping up!

On the 7th it being Saturday we had another go, we had only eight-een hounds left for that morning, the others being short somewhere. It a bit frosty, scenting was not great, it was a long hunt, not always fast, sometimes very slow but hounds and fellows were game and 'braided on' (encouraged) with the hunt, till they put the fox off again in Grizedale Forest, after that it was a different go. It was said, 'The fox and hounds crossed Coniston Football Field and in the excitement, the referee had to stop the match, till the fox and hounds got away!' The hunt went forward through Coniston village but with all his dodges, he could not shake off his pursuers and they bowled him over at Coniston Hall, not far from the farmhouse door. To my followers and me, these were great hunts worth talking about.

That weekend, hounds and myself went forward to Woodland for their week of enjoyment, it was like a week's holiday when hounds were about. Back in the Hawkshead district that was the third week away from home, one day after receiving Mr and Mrs Manzie-Fe's hospital-ity, a start was made from Borwick Lodge. We had a good drag and put off on Tom Heights and proved to be a stout fox covering the districts of Coniston, Wetherlam, Little Langdale and the Three Shires Stone (where the counties of Cumberland, Westmorland and Lancashire meet). He crossed the valley to Oxendale, Mickleden, out towards Langdale Pikes. By now he must have been feeling the strain of this long hunt, he dodged about these mighty crags to baffle these hounds it was his intent but they forced him out into the open fell again and raced inbank, where he met his end at Slops Bridge, Great Langdale, a fine old dog fox!

The winter had been very open, not many stops through bad weather, that keeps hounds in fettle if no lay offs. Nibthwaite, week's hunting 3–

7 March – out four days getting six foxes, all by 'speed of foot.' We were suiting the farmers then just before lambing time. I am trying to recollect hunts but there are many more I could do, but it is time and space.

On 7 April we loused at Hart Head, put a fox off at Heron Crag, he was lying on a benk, it was a bit before hounds could force him out. He went away from Rydal fell head into Deepdale but we found hounds out of scent at Cofa Pike, so nothing more was done that day. We were one hound short that night but thought he would land back to the kennels but did not return after three days. I thought the worst and set off to look for him in Deepdale Head, some of the roughest ground in England and there I found him lying dead. He had fallen out of a place called Greenhow End. It was better that way than not finding him at all. He was called Briton and was walked by Jimmy Bewley of Grasmere, he was out of a North Tyne bitch got by our Miller. That was another one gone!

A report of lamb worrying at Rydal Farm, so loused at daylight to get a drag away from the lambing field if possible, you then know you're after the right one as it was this morning. The drag took us into Buckstones where an old fox was on the move and went away for Fairfield back to Nab Scar, crossed White Moss over to Elterwater and Little Langdale, the full length of Lingmoor, crossed out Blakerigg, turned him in down Wrynose Pass to the kill at Fell Foot Farm, a fine dog fox in his prime.

We ended our season on 13 May at Stool End, Langdale by bringing a fox to book in Eskdale. Our tally for that season eighty-four old foxes and will be remembered for a lot of excellent hunts and such a large number killed in the open.

At a meeting of the hunt in the summer of 1959 the Committee felt it was time a paid whipper-in was had and a young man, Robert Nelson, got the job. He was a very likeable fellow, got on well with our supporters, good mannered which I think is one of the first things in hunt service. He took up his duties with me in October 1959–60. It had been one of the hottest summers on record and still very hot that backend and it was not much scenting for a bit and did not do much till the end of October at Hawkshead, when we had two good hunts and got both on the open, that set us up a bit. The young entry of which there was four and a half couples, weren't having much fun but thought hunting would mend.

9–14 November – Coniston – a bad week, a lot of snow about but it was a better month hunting wise but still only got seven for the month. Had good sport on New Year's Day. One fox ran a long way from the meet to be caught by the side of Goats Water under Dow Crags. Scenting

Difficult times – in a borran

was still very bad, as seen by my stay at Witherslack, out four times but did not catch a fox, as was the same at Sawrey where we never got a brush. From 14 February to the 25th heavy snow, went down low country out of it, Witherslack for a day, two hunts and kills, one ran two and a half hours and the other for four hours

The Mayor's Hunt up Troutbeck, the weather was that bad, thick snow, it was no good up there, so took hounds down to Lindeth Farm, thick snow down there but we knew hounds could not hurt themselves, as no crags to tumble out off. Had some sport, got after two foxes, found them both 'lying in' (in hole or earth), both bolted and were caught. For one week up Kentmere, had a nice hunt or two but the foxes were boss of us.

From Hawkshead on 22 March, a bitch called Lavish, ran a fox all on its own and caught it at Colwith Bridge, a good solo effort by itself. Foxes were bad that spring amongst the lambs, I well remember one morning from Pool Bank, Jack Ainsworth and family lived there and we were called to deal with one. We ran him about and holed in a drain and thought, let him out down a big open field. He shot out like a bullet and away, left hounds standing still. By now Mr Ainsworth was going mad for letting it out. 'They will never catch it!' he said. I thought we would get a good cursing if the hounds didn't but they showed their fettle and ran him down. Jack was all smiles then and no more lambs went after that. So we did some good for that farmer.

2 April 1960 at Torver, staying with Mr and Mrs Wally Stilling, he was a fellow who liked the old fashioned type of Lakeland Sheep called Herdwick, a very hardy kind, that can stand rough winters, always has a very good coat on it. They have brought up some good hounds for us time and time again, Mascot, Rockwood, Dalesman are some. Well that morning Wally said, 'Try for a fox on Back Common?' We did and drew a blank. So we went out High Park round by the Bell also blank. I thought this was a bit of a devil but not to be outdone, we went into the Guards Woods by Coniston, by then the hounds were fit for the fray when they put a fox off and away they went full speed, we were left far behind but followed on. He made straight for the high fells. When out Hookriggs, it was getting late in the day when I met a hound coming, it was one I have mentioned, Mascot, he bore the clue to having killed a fox. We had to about turn and nearly all the hounds came, we were told after that they had caught Reynard down in Greenburn Valley. What I am getting at about this hunt, was the long draw to find a fox, we were never faint

hearted in them days. That spring we had a fortnight's stay up in the Langdale Valley and enjoyed it.

During the summer of 1960 our whipper-in was taken into the army, a great blow for him, so we got another Dennis Barrow, to fill this position. We also lost one of our hunt's oldest supporters, Mr D.F. Cockerton from Cartmel Fell, he had supported the pack for fifty years and he left the hounds a legacy of £25.

That backend we had a bad October, not many young foxes about, that's what you want to get the hounds into fettle. For the first month only accounted for five foxes, some old foxes about, we could make nowt of them, they could run all day. They say foxes are good to catch at black bum (blackberry) time. Had quite a good week up Kentmere accounting for four. It had been our week for November, the Ullswater also go into that valley, we change about, one Hunt goes in the backend and the other in the spring and vice versa.

Whilst at Torver, the Eskdale and Ennerdale were at Broughton Mills and on the Saturday morning both packs got joined up together and had a successful end in Stevenson Ground Ghyll. On about packs joining up, once from Knott Houses Farm it being a Sunday morning, that was because a fox was doing a lot of damage amongst the lambs. The Blencathra were in the next valley on the same job. We loused four thirty in the morning, struck a good drag and began running him hard. The other pack in the next valley was doing the same but their hunt was coming towards ours, we could hear both packs at one time. The Blencathra got a check amongst the flock of sheep, they then heard ours and was not long before the hounds were all together, then what a cry, it would have wakened the dead! It was not long before they had a successful ending to a joint meeting.

It was getting better scenting as the season went on, had some grand hunts about. At Christmas time, Cragsman was still showing his ability at catching foxes on his own, by getting a fox at Satterthwaite School. On the last day of 1960, put a fox off at Skelghyll, what a route it took, first nearly to Grasmere, then back to Troutbeck then into Kentmere, to go to ground at the Diatomite Works. We stood well back and after a terrier was let in, he was game and out he came. There was hounds and folk and with shouts and sounds, from both hunters and hounds, his end came in the River Kent after a great hunt!

Clipping time at Knott Houses, Grasmere in the late 1950s.
Left to right: Johnny Holmes, Jack Thackray, Ernie Brownrigg, Dennis Batey, Tommy Graves, Jos Hardisty, Tom Swinburn, Lant Constable, Mrs Towers, Joe Thompson, Ernie Towers, Anthony, Connie Thompson, Norman Shepherd, Alison and daughter Jill ....?.... Philip Powell and Roy Dixon
Sanderson and Dixon

XI

Early 1960s

IN THE FIRST WEEK OF JANUARY 1961 we lost our Chairman, Mr George Grundy, he had been a staunch supporter since 1908. After the Reverend E.M. Reynold's death the Coniston Foxhounds were kept on by Mr Grundy for a time, until he and the Logan family reorganised the pack on a subscription basis and has been since.

When at Coniston we had a fox in Bell Borran, a terrier called Pip went in and we never heard it again. About a week after, a shepherd was going past and he found it dead. I did not like to lose them they were my true pals. Following week up Grasmere ran a fox into Deer Bields Crag and one hound called Reckless got too venturesome and fell out and was killed outright. An unfortunate name!

We finished that season a bit earlier because the foxes had kept quieter during lambing time. In November 1961 for our week up Troutbeck, we had a good week getting ten foxes in three louse's. From the first meet at Long Green Head Farm, hounds got broken up, one section ran a fox to Lamb Fold Quarry in Kentmere, now this is a very bad place and very rarely bolt or can be worked out but we were lucky and the fox was got without a great deal of trouble, a unique experience for me. I had never seen one get out before and I have never seen once since. Whilst we were there two hounds, Bounty and Lavish, had been running a fox on their own in Troutbeck and ran it into a shallow hole and 'scrated in' and got a bitch fox by themselves. On our way back to our quarters, the hounds struck the line of another and ran it into a badger set. It was getting dusk but we were game to let him have a go and out Reynard came and after a fast spin, a dog fox was accounted for in the twilight. Next day hounds had a rest.

The Shepherd's Meet was held at the Mortal Man Hotel that year, now it is always held at the Queens Head Hotel. As mentioned before the farmers gather up their sheep on the surrounding fells and if they have any strays, they are sheep that don't belong to them, they are brought to the Meet for farmers to claim and in among hands, they'll have a hunt with the Coniston Foxhounds or the Windermere Harriers. The hounds had a good drag and roused their fox in Skelghyll Woods and after a good long hunt claimed their fox near the Kirkstone Pass Inn. There was much sampling of ale that night at the pub and a good sing song!

On Saturday, 18 November the morning was fine and clear and after hen worrying had been reported, a start was made in Thickholme and found a fox almost at once and after a fast circle out to Hagwood, he was turned inbank and bowled him over. Next hounds were 'marking' at some big holes up near Holbeck Ghyll, terriers were entered and soon were 'marking.' It being such a fine day and good scenting I took hounds forward and left some mates at the holes, never thinking how many foxes there were in them but never mind, it was not long before the hounds were again going full out. We had some grand 'laiting' hounds, that was what I used to like them to do, find a fox for themselves the 'hoo git away' (sending hounds on). Well they did and had another rousing hunt both sides of the valley and was overtaken near Troutbeck School. By now it was late afternoon, the followers I had left at the holes had never landed to us, so we went back to see what was going on. In the meantime, they had got tools and told me the terrier had 'yauked' (attacked) something but also said, 'There is a fox wanting to be out.' So I said, 'Come on stand back and let it be going!' Hounds viewed him for about a mile and caught. While that was on, another shot out and it got a good start but we 'hallo'd' them on again. By now it was getting dark, could not see the hounds going but the cry was enough to waken the dead. The hounds bowled that one over near the main road at a place called 'Ill Step.' It was found that the terrier had accounted for two more in the holes, that made six for the day. That was a record for the Coniston Foxhounds. It made a tally of ten for the week, another record!

It was not all plain sailing, five meets before that week had all been blank. I am getting a bit in front of myself. I should have told you about that one on 11 October 1961. We had our first eve's 'Opening Meet', we had never bothered before, it was held at the home of our Master, Mr B. Logan, at Waterhead Range. The week before we were at Skelghyll Woods and that night a hound was short and was missing for a week but landed back at the kennels minus its stern (tail), everybody knew it after that, it was 'Magic.'

Passing on through the season, on 13 December at Force Forge in the Rusland Valley it was a bad morning but we had a go and ran a fox about the woods and was soon overtaken, so would try on again for another and going through a wood (there was myself and Ossie Dickenson, a keen hunter) when Spanker started to fly around and 'give mouth' under

Frank Atkinson and Anthony watching the hounds having a well-earned feed at the end of a hunt. Usually consisted of flake maize and boiling water. Note the turnip cutter in the corner of the farmyard.

a yew tree with branches about eight feet off the ground. None of the other hounds was getting excited but he was true, when all at once a fox jumped out and away. We both stood there with our mouths open, we never knew what happened to that fox as we found the hounds just walking about but it was never picked up. That's something to remember!

Round about Christmas the weather was very bad one meet at Braeside, worst of the winter thick snow and bad drifting from 24 December till 11 January 1962, never caught a fox. On 20 January from a meet at Chapel Stile, got one fox at White Ghyll and another went into a drain. A hound called Caution must have followed it in before anybody got there, a lot of water in and when it was found it was dead through drowning. They come to some untimely ends!

We were having a lean time, not as many foxes about, going to places for a week and should have been getting three and four foxes but were only getting one and sometimes none. Should have gone to Kentmere but too much snow and ice in the crags, dangerous for hounds. One day a fox lying in on top of Helm Crag I let two terriers in, wished after I had not, as we had to work them out. One was in two days the other six, so that made a lot of work for the brave lads of the valleys.

Had a very busy spring amongst the lamb worriers, I thought it was with having so much bad weather and with not being able to get out as much but after that the number of foxes dispatched was seventy-five old foxes.

The young entry for 1962–3, five were out of Welcome got by Eskdale and Ennerdale, Rockwood and proved to be an outstanding lot. There was Brilly, Bounty, Barmaid, Bowler and Chanter, two of the litter came to bad endings. Brilly got fast in a fence at Hoathwaite, Coniston, her hind leg was nearly off when found by a farmer next day, what a job that was. Bounty, another outstanding bitch, was killed out right by a lorry at Grasmere. Hounds had been running hard at a lamb worrier, when they forced the fox inbank and were going down a driveway onto the main road when it happened at six o'clock one morning. Cruiser and Cragsman were out of a bitch called Cora by Ullswater Winston and an odd one called Rompish.

On 27 September – Kirkstone, not much scenting, very hot, tired after a very hard first day. Our opening meet day at Waterhead Range, when everybody enjoyed the Master's hospitality, had a very good hunt off Loughrigg round by the Drunken Duck, back again onto Loughrigg and was overtaken at Tarn Foot. It's rather a unique job how some packs in our country always have plenty of foxes. It must be that the foxes get away with breeding and are not noticed, such as up Kentmere, we very seldom have a bad week up there unless, it is bad weather, and it is always the boss. Our count that week was five.

One day from Hawkshead we were having a very good hunt and killed a fox in the churchyard just as a bride and her father were walking up the path. I bet she will always remember that! Christmas Eve Jerry Hunt, never found a fox, it would not be for want of trying.

Crosthwaite Hunt Ball on 5 January 1963, that was always very bright and cheerful, afterwards we used to go and sample Sam Hodgson's whisky for about an hour, and have a crack. Next morning the hounds met at Crosthwaite House and after everybody had sampled Mr and Mrs Hodgson's rum and coffee, a start was made and it was not until 3 pm a fox was found and ran about five minutes and was caught, not much excitement that day. It had been very frosty weather for about a month. Windermere Lake was frozen but not bearable for skating. What I am getting at is this, from a hunt at Wray, a hound was lost and never seen again and we always thought he had gone through the ice.

Another time a fox crossed the ice at Tarn Hows, hounds followed, swum, went through and a great rescue took place by hunters who were following on, a good job they were there. Once when hunting in the Hawkshead district, a hound called Witness went across the ice on Esthwaite Water and fell through, a brave attempt to get her out was made by two men who got a boat to push across but was to no avail. The hound disappeared under, it was found after the thaw came by the local gamekeeper. It just shows the many hazards fell hunting is under. We were still having a very hard winter, January, February and into March, before there was any kind of a thaw came. On our Mayor's Hunt Day the high fells were not fit to let hounds on, so hounds were taken to Winster onto lower ground and had a nice hunt and killed a fox, the first for a month.

9 March 1963 was my daughter Mavis's wedding day at Rydal Church where I was once in the choir. That day Dennis Barrow hunted the hounds for the first time from Brathay Woods and had beginner's luck, by accounting for two foxes of all places, Latterbarrow. From my early hunting days, I never liked the place and it's worse now, as it is nearly all forestry. The weather by now was showing signs of a thaw.

The season finished on 18 May at Stool End Farm, had a nice hunt and Eskdale and Ennerdale joined in and a fox was overtaken at Chapel Stile. The severity of the winter resulted in some of the country not being hunted as much, with the tally of foxes being below the average of recent years, being fifty-nine foxes.

We lost a very good supporter and a great friend of mine in the death of Mr H.S. Hodgson of Latterbarrow Farm, Witherslack. He was a member of the auctioneering firm M.B. Hodgson & Son. A familiar and respected figure, particularly among the farming community, he had conducted sales on almost every farm in the county. Mr Hodgson was also a sporting man and had a life long connection with hunting as did his family and was a former President of Ambleside Sports. He enjoyed an unrivalled reputation as a chairman at social gatherings in Lakeland and his presence at the annual Hunt Supper of the Coniston Foxhounds was greatly missed.

We lost a young hound killed on the road at Ings Garage. From a meet at Rosthwaite, Woodland, two foxes were got, one was run by Magic all on her own and caught the fox by herself. She had two brothers, one wasn't so bad but the other was good for nowt, same as scenting is sometimes!

One day up Langdale, two hounds did not return to the kennels and they were found by some fell walkers crag fast and were there for five days but at the finish they got out themselves, they were Dinah and Cruiser.

Anthony and Bruce Logan at Greenbank Kennels

XII

Hounds, Foxes, Badgers and Otters

Irst of all about the hound:

> *He's strong and he's straight lads, his tongue like a bell*
> *And the stout heart that's in him lads, tongue cannot tell*
> *For to breast the steep hillsides whose faint hearts must fail*
> *And to sweep the wide moors in teeth of the gale.*

The fell hounds, are not much different in appearance than what they were fifty years ago but the down country hounds, are not as big and as heavy as they were. A pack of hounds is got together with the object of showing sport and killing foxes.

A fell hound should have a good nose, plenty of tongue and plenty of speed. It should have a good frame. Hare footed, good neck. A fell hound should stand under rather than over 22½ inches (57 cms). Many people consider a big hound more suited to jumping high walls, a smaller hound crosses them as it jumps, a light built hound will show less signs of fatigue than a heavy one at the end of a long hunt and will return to kennels with its stern (tail) gaily carried.

A great craze in summer is the Hound Shows which I think is good, as it keeps hound men interested as long as the object is breeding for sport, and if he crosses workers with workers, nature will see to it that beauty and good looks suited to the particular type will eventually accompany that ability. It is much better to do this than allow beauty to come first.

Hunting on the fells necessitates practising the 'let 'em alone principal' because throughout the majority of runs, hounds do all their own work unaided. Thus they learn perseverance, which enables them to carry on when scenting conditions are not good. In the 1930s and 40s hounds had to persevere with the line as foxes were not as numerous as they are now. If they lose the line of a fox now they lift them and go and find another, it's that easy.

Nowadays hounds nearly always break up their fox but in by gone days they did not, they were content to kill it and leave it at that. Fell hounds are owing to the roughness of their country far more likely to

95

have accidents than hounds which hunt low ground and in the dangerous nature of their work it is surprising there are not more accidents.

Our hounds were walked as I have said by local farmers during the
summer months and went back to where they were fetched up at the end
of each season. Farmers whelped them and brought them up to eight
weeks old and then they go out to various farms. We did not keep all
the pups, they maybe had eight or nine. There was maybe one wrong
of the leg or deformed – we only kept the good ones, the others were
done away with. Ours are different from the lowland packs – bit of fell
blood in them and they are lighter in colour so we can see them easier
on the fells. We sometimes would get a pup from another fell pack – they
maybe used one of our dogs to cover one of their bitches and we would
get a pup back in return. All the huntsmen knew one another and what
hounds' we had – no money changed hands, just the arrangement and
you got a puppy.

We coupled them together to start with. The young ones would learn
from the older ones and they would learn to follow in this way. Some
of them take to hunting straight away. Odd ones are a bit late to start to
work but I have never known a hound that did not. Some are lazy ones
that cut corners, not all alike, takes all kinds!

The hounds are invaluable animals to us, take a bad season and you
maybe lose five or six, it takes a lot of replacing, you can't buy one in and I
have never sold one. You get very attached to them, they are very friendly
to a certain extent and are very intelligent. You could set of moving and I
would say, 'Try away up. Hark to' – sending them out looking for the fox.
Then 'after a hound giving mouth' – sending the others hounds to it. I
would know which hound by its mouth (it's bark). I would maybe have
twenty couple and all have a different tune, some squacky, some deep
mouthed and some inbetween. That's what it means being a huntsman.
Some hunt all their lives and don't know one from another. Others can
recognise better by mouth than by look! I had about half a dozen terriers and would take three or four out in a hunt and they stayed with me.
Didn't like to see terriers running with hounds.

All the other fell packs have had houses next to kennels, I used to
come on a bike from Rydal. On the various hunts or weeks away I used
to walk the hounds to the various places, Coniston, Strawberry Bank or
High Newton. Further hounds go, further you go, twenty miles easy on
a day, walking from here to Lowick Bridge took four hours and hunted
the following day.

Losing lambs to a fox can be a serious business to a fell farmer who depends for his living entirely on sheep. Once a fox has acquired this habit of going off with a lamb or two every night, the only thing to do is to find and kill it. Michael Black when he farmed Nook End, at Ambleside (just next door to the Kennels) had a rough time with a fox at lambing time in 1952, it used to worry two or three a night for nearly a week. We were loosing hounds every morning at daylight, it was a bad fox and used to take a hunt right out to the fell head every time. We let go one Sunday morning something we did not like doing but we were desperate to get him or her and this morning the same thing happened again but we were in luck's way, hounds were found marking to ground at Dove Crag borran, terriers found him and destroyed him underground and he was grubbed (dug) out – a very old dog fox.

Hartrigg at Kentmere was another place foxes could be rough at lambing time. I have a cutting out of the paper about a fox that killed nineteen lambs at Hartsop Hall and the Ullswater ran the same fox for five mornings and had some good hunts after him but always ran them out of scent, till the fifth morning when he was caught. Hunters got to kenning it by its colour and when caught its feet were red raw.

At his own pace a hill fox can go forever and it is when scent is rather permanent than strong that extra long runs take place. Even on the roughest fells there is always some ground where hounds can press their fox and so by degrees, get on good terms with him. It is the pace in the first half-hour that kills. If a fox has gorged himself overnight, and hounds find him early in the morning, he is not in condition to show them a clean pair of heels for he cannot, like a heron, lighten himself by throwing up his food. The consequence is if hounds get away on good terms, they burst him in a very short distance. If a fox travels a long way in search of a vixen he will perhaps have an empty stomach and when found he will make a beeline back to where he came from. The pace of a fox is very deceptive. He moves with a gliding action. From a bolt you would think hounds were going to catch him right off, give him a hundred yards, he will be two or three hundred yards (250 metres) ahead in no time. I have heard people say fox is jiggered but he is never done till you have hold of him.

The fell fox does not get his first experience of being hunted until later in the year than the date set for cub-hunting in the Shires. Odd ones might as the farmer, gathering in his sheep, could have his hound with him and it will always have a go at hunting. Once they have been run, foxes gain confidence. I have heard it said that a fox dislikes travelling downwind when the latter is strong, because it blows its brush about but from my own experience I have known foxes travel both up and down wind. One thing I always noticed was that hounds could go faster if going with the wind. A fox, like a hare, or any other hunted animal for that matter, if forced beyond the limit of his beat will run in an aimless manner and seek refuge anywhere. I once remember the Airedale Beagles hunting in the Patterdale area when a hare swam across Brotherswater Lake!

From the meet at Miller Bridge House on 9 November 1963, ran a fox off Loughrigg, crossed at Rydal went into Scandale Valley and we bolted it three times and was killed at Brock Crag. Mentioning Brock Crag reminds me of the first time I ever saw a badger, it was in Guards Wood, under Rainsbarrow. Hounds started 'marking' under a large rock there. So I let a terrier in and it started 'baiting' (barking at fox) right away. So we got some stones out and I crept in myself and with the aid of a flash light, I could see this animal which had a white mark down its face, it set off towards me and I had the presence of mind to put my arms up to my face and it brushed passed me and bolted. That was the first badger I had ever seen, there were not so many in them days but now they are everywhere. The date was November 1948.

Badgers, now I have had hens of my own worried by them. I well remember one early morning from Stool End Farm, Langdale, went through the Band trying for a drag of a fox that had been amongst the lambs, on reaching the Green Tongue, hounds struck a line making out for Bowfell. I thought there was something queer about it, some of the older hounds would not have a go, but we followed on and on reaching Broad Borran towards three thousand feet up, hounds started 'to mark' and I let a terrier in and out a badger came. I have never heard of one being found so high on a mountain like that before or since.

I have told you about badgers, I will tell you when my father was a huntsman he found otters on 2 February 1921 whilst hunting in Troutbeck Fell Head. He found an otter lying in Broad How Borran, it bolted and hounds caught it. I have the otter's head in our bungalow. Another time at Pavey Ark, in the Langdale Valley, he bolted one and hounds caught it just before it got to Stickle Farm. The only one in my hunting days was found in Banaside Quarry. It just shows how far out they used to travel, they are few and far between now, I think the mink have taken over.

XIII

The Master Marries

ON 28 JANUARY 1964 OUR MASTER GOT MARRIED to Miss Mary Woodhouse of Low Wray Farm, Ambleside at Wray Church. We took a few hounds and Dennis and I were guard of honour with our whips when they came out of Church and then we went to the reception at Newby Bridge Hotel and had a good do!

The day before, the meet was at Wray village and a fox was put off on Latterbarrow and ran him at great speed by the Spicker, Dan Becks, Holmes Head to cross the River Rothay onto Loughrigg and was despatched on there whilst running there. Another fox got on the move and was also accounted for. That should always stick in them two people's minds.

On 29 February it was Troutbeck Mayor's Hunt. The Mayor for that year was Mr John Wharton of Town End Farm and had two rattling hunts round the dale. It shows how you remember some things, the hounds were running in Park Fell and we were standing guard at Park Quarries, a very bad place, when Winsome brought a fox towards the quarry, we got it turned out and inbank, she was running it hard, we could see both fox and hound going, I thought by gum it'll catch it but disappeared over the Tongue out of our sight. Some more hounds came but they could not hunt the line as she was, so we followed on. Before going far we met the hound coming back wet and dirty and smelling of fox, so we kept going and we walked right on top of the fox. She had tried her best to worry it but had not quite finished Reynard off. When arriving on the scene, it made another desperate attempt to get away but the other hounds soon finished the job off. She was running her third season and a grand fell bitch. They have a hard life has a fell hound and that one came to an untimely end, as she fell out of a crag in Deepdale Head on 6 May 1967.

Had another grand week's hunting up Kentmere accounting for five foxes. Mr and Mrs Swinburn were our hosts for the week they were both mad keen on hunting. Tom as we all knew him by, had been whipper-in to the Melbreak Foxhounds in his early days with Billy Irvine.

The wedding of Bruce Logan to Miss Mary Woodhouse on 28 January 1964. Anthony and Dennis Barrow were guard of honour. The foxhounds were kept behind the gate in fear of the odd accident! *Sanderson and Dixon*

In the summer of 1963 a lot of improvements were done at the kennels and a lot of labour in preparing the site for the builders was done by our supporters, which was a considerable saving for which the hunt was very grateful. Four of our village Hunt Balls deserved special mention because they all topped £100, a very notable achievement.

Back end of 1964 came and a start was made in the usual way, we had only a small entry of two and a half couples, we had not bred any of them ourselves. One was called Melody it was got by the South Berkshire 'Brig.' That pack is now defunct (gone). Another two of them were from a North Wales Pack. None of them was in any way outstanding but they were all workers.

We had very good sport and one outstanding week was at Winster, which was a record for the pack, when on 23 November the hounds caught five foxes. That was a record in itself, never happened before in that country. Foxes were accounted for from Lindeth Farm to Witherslack, the last one was caught at Beck Head. Wednesday got another two, Thursday got one and had a hound killed, called Dainty, on the road and to finish the week had another kill on Saturday. Nine in all which was another record.

About that time we had a Hunt Ball at Newby Bridge and then loused from there next morning. Used to go onto Gummers How. This particular day, we put a very short tailed fox off and it went straight to Whitbarrow but ran hounds off on the limestone.

On 1 January had a good hunt about the Drunken Duck and caught a fox. Next day the meet was Braeside, nice day's hunting from Skelghyll Woods, holed and had a grand bolt and kill.

On 9 January we were at Crosthwaite House and was a very wet day, did not do much. 28 January went to a place called Low House, Ings, found a fox lying in on Charnleys Lot, bolted but did not go far until overtaken. Put another off about 10 am, we had to stop them about five at night at Kentmere Hall. The same day a hound called Cragsman got crag fast and was not got out until next day. Some rock climbers staying in the Quarry hut under Rainsbarrow got to him with ropes.

On Saturday 30 January we were at Langdale and went onto lile Loughrigg, a fox was 'hallo'd' but got a bit of a start and hounds had a job to hunt him but stuck to it and put off afresh at Skelby Crags. Got on better terms and went out over Loughrigg to cross the River Brathay. After putting a round in on Brow Fell, came inbank to the shores of Lake Windermere, out again by Wray to Brathay Quarry, where hounds were run out of scent. Another put off was made and went away by Bull Close to Elterwater onto Lingmoor where the hunt was poor and slow and that hunt came to nowt.

Two hounds that month came to grief through being fast in wire fences, Wisdom and Climber. The first week of February was spent with Mr and Mr Bob Birkett, he was a cousin of mine so he had plenty of hunting blood in him. My father always used to say he should have been a fell huntsman but he was a sheep farmer and a 'good un' at that. The high fells were a bit tricky so kept down in the woods. The weather being like that, we loused up Carron Road behind Coniston Lake. Soon had a fox going on Brantwood Intakes (Brantwood was the home of the poet Ruskin) and made out for Carron, the hounds' 'chivved' (chased) him about in Grizedale Forest for an hour and a quarter. A grand hunt was had by all before he broke cover out into the open (you can't see much in the forest but always hear grand music) at Dugdale's Intakes and crossed by Lawson Park into the grounds of Brantwood, he dodged about the laurel beds before hounds pulled him down, a grand two hours! Thirty-one hounds out, same number in at the kill – Countess, Lavish and Careless running well that day.

On Saturday morning one of lads went to feed hens and came running back and said he had seen two foxes. We did not wait for time off, we went in a hurry, got all hounds laid onto one (chase one fox), which took by Fish Tarn back by Yew Tree, Craghouse out Raven Crag, a grand hunt now. Over the top, in by Ivy Crag crossed the main Ambleside to Coniston road down to Low Yewdale, crossing the road again, out by the Stirrup, a very fast hunt now, never a check by Far End Fell passing Blue Quarry onto the Scrow, going to earth in Bell Borran, we landed there after a while hounds had been going that fast, they'd left us behind. A terrier was let in and he soon bolted out, he gained on the hounds down the rough ground but when he got onto plain, hounds soon overtook him.

That was the finish of Coniston week so packed up and went onto Woodland for a week. The weather was still a bit wintry, got one fox that was roused in Broughton Moor forest out by Walna Scar, Dow Crags, Goats Water and was caught under Brossen Stone, a fine dog fox of 18 lbs (8.18 kilos) weight. On 27 February it was Mayor's Hunt at Troutbeck. The Mayor was Mrs C. Clark, another of the Chapman breed!

The morning was fine and clear, hounds were loused up Green Lane for Robin Crag when somebody 'hallo'd' a fox away up Hallilands which was too far away and should not have been done because before the hounds got to the place, they got split up. Two hounds got well away after

Hounds hitching a lift

foxy and the others had to follow on after their cry, across Woundale bottom, over the top of Broad End to the top of Caudale passing Old Mark Atkinson's monument. His ashes were buried there, he was owner of the Kirkstone Pass Inn. The hounds pressed on, there were more hounds together by now. Black Crag and back through Sadgill to go to ground at Hart Crag borran. After a while and some hard work, he shot out like a bullet and away. A hell of a chase then took place with a hound called Wynburn taking the lead over into Dale Head. The fox cannot have known of that notorious borran of Broad Howe, as he turned inbank down Hollilands and was caught in the beck at bottom of Herdwood. After a finish and a hunt like that, off we set for the Queens Head Hotel for tattie pot and a few pints of ale. Mrs Clark was only the second lady 'Mayor of Troutbeck Hunt' which was held annually, a lady called Renee Atkinson being the other she was the landlord's wife of Kirkstone Pass Inn.

On 14 March 1965 a well-known hunting lady, Mrs Leck, passed away. She came of the Chapman family, being a daughter of 'Auld Anthony'. She brought up some good hounds for the Coniston in her time, I can remember, Manager, Cruel, Royal, Tempest, Careless and Ransome being some. She had given a silver cup to the best looking puppy at Rydal Hounds Show for a number of years. The Hunt Committee was grateful to her for she left them a legacy of £100.

On the Saturday of the hunting week at Grasmere a start was made at Ghyll Foot Farm. Hounds were soon 'laiting' a fox and struck a drag which went forward through Raise Breast to Rake Crag, where everybody thought the 'sly un' would be lying, but no, he had gone on and into Steel End Wood where they put him off. Scenting was not good but the Coniston Hounds were a persevering lot, like their huntsman and followers. Running in for Thirlmere Lake, crossing the main Keswick to Grasmere road, he twisted about the breast going out for Helvellyn but he had stopped too long in a little crag, as the hunt fairly mended and was forced inbank above Wythburn Church and then a good twenty minutes was had by all, as he was chivved about the forestry. Chanter and Rockwood running him well, the others joining 'chorus' as he was turned inbank for the last time and caught ready at my feet. A good hound hunt showing what hounds can do – fell hounds of course!

It was a misty morning on 27 March, so Loughrigg was tried for a fox. A long 'draw' (time finding) before any signs of game, when a fox jumped up in Howe Breast and ran about that side of the fell, up hill and down hill and when Traveller got 'to viewing' him he took refuge in a drain. Tinker was let in and found him right away and forced him to leave his hiding place and after another sharp burst was pulled down by Loughrigg Tarn. While this was going on, another fox was seen, so hounds were laid onto it. This fox had rather more guts than the first, as we were kept going till 5 o'clock and hounds had to give him the best as the line was lost. Bounty, Brilly, Marden, Tempest running well, we were having a great season.

On Saturday 3 April we had been at Torver for the week, a very foggy morning visibility about nil in the bottoms but top clear. A fox was run into the Spring's drain, near Coniston Hall. Tinker was let in but fox was boss of it, got a bit of a mauling, got her out and Maysh was tried and soon mister fox was out. Hounds coursed it across the fields and into Low Park Woods before a fine bitch fox was pulled down.

I tried on again and another was unkennelled (good put off) and gave a great hunt round about Coniston and the village. Hounds were lost on the railway line, when a welcome 'Hallo' from above the village got hounds away again, after another sharp hunt, ran him down at High Ground Farm on the main road.

The following week was our visit to Bryan Beck, Cartmel Fell, the home of Mr and Mrs Lishman. The Hunt Ball on the Friday night was a very good and lively dance and the profit from it was £125 for the hounds, not bad as it was held in a little village schoolroom. The meet on the Saturday, 10 April was at Birkett Houses, Mrs Burgess lived there and she provided rum and coffee for the followers. She always gave me a glass of whisky, a packet of fags and a box of matches. A good old country lady, not many left!

Hounds tried round Rosthwaite Lots, Fox Crags, Blake Holme and Gummers How, before there was any sign of game and a good unkennel and hounds got a flying start after it inbank to Great Tower, back by top of Blakeholme in by Addyfield to Bowland Bridge and a bitch fox was caught at Woodside, after a very fast half hour. Five foxes that week.

There was quite a lot of lamb worrying that spring. From 10 April till 1 May hounds accounted for nine old foxes, it showed that the hounds were in good fettle. On 1 May we were at Barkhouse Bank, Satterthwaite, home of the Dickinson family, on a lamb worrying 5 AM call. It was a fine morning, hounds struck a drag into the forestry, it was moderate but they stuck to it and put a fox off on Satterthwaite side. A good hunt crossed for Dale Park and ran the plantings there for an hour before crossing back at Moor Lane, passing through Great Knott Wood and round above Force Forge and into the lambing fields at Bankhouse Bank. Foiled up amongst the sheep the hunt slowed down a lot but hounds were game and brayed the line out onto the fell, where it mended and were soon away again by Bethecar below Harnsbarrow and in for Park-a-Moor. We were getting left behind by now but kept going. They were next heard crossing Heald Basin out to top of Carron. The hunt now had fairly mended and was running him strong across Grizedale bottom and out for Brock Crag in Dale Park, after another big round as far as Force Forge back by Bowkerstead, he was forced to ground below Brock Crag. Lile Tess was put in and soon had him out into the open again, another ten minutes of 'speed and music' enough to lift your hat off your head, he went to ground again. Jet and Rags were tried and he was accounted for, we had had five hours of the best, a game old dog fox!

Went up Langdale to finish the season at Stool End Farm. On 15 May had a nice hunt round Crinkle Crags and killed a dog fox under Kettle Crag. Had a grand season, some very good hunts, hounds running well and caught eighty-six foxes – a very good effort.

Opening meet at Waterhead Range with Bruce Logan, Mary and Anthony together with their many Coniston hunt supporters. *Paul Allonby*

XIV

Mid 1960s

AFTER A GOOD SUMMER'S REST we were again fit for the fray for the season 1965–6. I was having a lot of trouble with an ankle. If I was going through a fell breast one way it didn't hurt but going the other way it gave me hell, but I was determined to keep going. There was only myself knew what I was going through. We got all the Hound Shows in. At Rydal our annual Hound Show was held in August. For the Mrs Wilson Cup for the best walked was T.N. Preston's 'Bashful'. A new Challenge Cup given by Mrs E. Steele of Newby Bridge Hotel in memory of her late husband for the best walked was won by 'Trusty' walked by Mrs S. Jackson of Hawkshead. A silver cup given by G. Gregory for the best looking puppy was won by 'Lawyer', walked by Mrs B. Logan, a cup given by the Master for the best looking puppy was won by 'Tippler' walked by Mr J. Elleray, Grasmere. The Hartley Challenge Trophy given in memory of a Lakeland landowner, for the best working hounds of last season was won by 'Workman', walked by Mr D.Tuer, High Wray. It just goes to show how well these hound walkers look after their hounds in summer. I have always said you can take flesh off a hound faster than you can put it on. They are the backbone of any pack are the walkers.

Our opening meet was at the home of our Master and his wife in October. After partaking of refreshments by all and sundry, we loused on Lanty Scar, a helleva spot for brackens. We soon had a fox going and did not run long before he was caught at White Moss. He must have been feeding off Black Bums (blackberries!). Another was found at High Close and went out Silver How, out Maslet a time or two before going to ground in a drain at Jams Quarry. Tess and Rags forced him out and ran 'from a view to a death', a fine dog fox. A few of the young entry got to doing, nowt like catching foxes at backend, does hounds a power of good.

On 30 October after last Ambleside Sheep Fair the meet was at Hawkshead Square, a fox was put off near High Barn in Grizedale Forest, they were getting to be bad to make out of in the forestry now, too much of it, and too many foxes bred in it. (For a few years when the trees were eight to ten years old, vixens had their cubs on top, no need for a hole, trees were that rank to keep them dry). Within five minutes there were hunts going everywhere and all came to nowt. Gathered hounds up and had a fresh start behind Esthwaite Hall but we did not run that one before the line was lost. I think I have said before in these notes, I remember when foxes were scarce and hard to find, not like nowadays, it shows the 'keepers' have gone.

We have blank days as well as good ones but you take the good with the bad, some people think you should be catching foxes every day, two and three at a time! Well we did this day, 9 November 1965, at Coniston, it was a fine clear morning, a drag was struck out from Heathwaite and a fox was unkennelled at the Bell Crag and sped away out to Low Water and back though Brossen Stone. A very fast hunt forcing him in for the Green Hills across Banniside and went to ground in the quarry tip by the sheepfolds. He would not bolt, so he died underground by the work of Grip and Jess.

An old dog fox was got out, he had no little teeth left and his fangs were nearly worn down to the gums, his weight was 18 lbs (8.18 kilos). While the lads were getting this fox out we went and tried for another fox and soon found one in High Park Wood and another fast hunt was had. It tried two or three times to get in the quarry tip where the lads were working but they gave him a loud cheer as he turned up Addy Scale fell, turning back down Hare Hill into Dickinson Wood, where he tried to hide in a blown down tree but to no avail and was forced out and killed in the open. Both foxes killed were old dogs.

Next morning a start was made from Heathwaite for the Scrow and soon had a fox away and Charm for Blue Quarry, out to the top of Lang Crag, back again by Mouldry Bank, across Mines Beck and into Brandy Crag Quarry rubbish tip, a noted strong hold Bracken, Turpin and Jess were tried and found him and he was got out by Dennis the whip. That was the first time in living memory that a fox had been got out of there, so that was something to shout about!

A lot of ground was tried again for another fox but no game was found until we got to Hookriggs, another bad borran, about two to three acres of it but hounds marked a fox to ground and Jess was let in. She was a grand finder and soon foxy bolted and ran down the borran with hounds in pursuit. He put in a circle about twice, we kept him out but after a while when hounds were 'viewing him' and getting near to catching him, he got back in again, in spite of a hell of a row from the hunters hounds. Hounds Mercy and Peggy, Bracken and Jess soon had him.

Brilly was found fast in a fence that day, had been in since the day before poor thing, what a state she was in. She was a hell of a good hound, what a finish for her.

We had the Shepherds Meet at Troutbeck, met at 9 am and the Windermere Harriers at 11 AM, that had always been the practice. I took hounds to try Robin Crag, a smitle spot (usually find a fox) but no hunt about, till we reached the Hundreds and put a fox off on Hind Cove crossing the Stock Valley onto the highway. The echo then told him he had no time to stay and over into Scandale Valley where another fox must have got up, as by now hounds were running in two directions. One lot of hounds were next heard coming down Red Screes to go to earth at Round Hill in a badger set. He was bolted by Tinker and after a short run was bowled over.

The other portion were having an excellent hunt by way of Brock Crag into Rydal Park, passing our kennels and crossing Stock Ghyll through for Skelghyll Woods and away to Holbeck and into Briery Close gardens, where he tried to shake off his pursuers, by dodging about in the big laurel beds but it was good scenting and hounds pushed him out to cross behind Low Wood Hotel at a great pace. He had laid down under the road and after a fresh 'put off' coursed him across Holme Crag and was run into on the shores of Windermere Lake.

When this was going on a few followers and me was looking for another fox up High Grove, trying through the breast hounds started 'to mark'. I stopped and watched and thought that's a queer spot, as it was only a wall broken down but hounds were going mad, so went and had a look and pulled some stones out and there he was. He soon came out of there but with hounds viewing and good ground, they soon had him. I had never seen a fox in a wall before. Three foxes for the day and a 'lile harvel' at the pub.

On the Saturday my wife and I had been invited to a wedding, so Dennis was in charge and what a good hunt he had. He took hounds from High Green across to Limefit and struck a drag right away. Ransome was first to 'give mouth' and out to Applethwaite Quarry where the 'sly un' was lying in the quarry face, he jumped up as Rockwood got nearly to him. Magic tried to catch him as he sped away for Thickholme to Holbeck, through Skelghyll Woods above the Grammar School and over Stock Ghyll. It was a fast hunt above Nook End and into Rydal Park, he turned at Rydal Hall, once the home of the Le Fleming family, down into the fields which he followed to the housing estate, across the River Rothay out to Brow Head, once the home of the Windermere Harriers.

Crossing Loughrigg by Ivy Crag and in by Tarn Foot at a hell of a pace. They had a check on the road but Sweeper struck the line into Neaum Crag Caravan Site, a tricky place for them to be in and followed the road towards Langdale. Sweeper was still doing a lot of work on the roads, many of which it crossed in its travels, for this fox had come a long way. The motorized brigade kept up!

Passing Oaks Farm out to High Close, across Langdale Fell to the village of Chapel Stile, he sought sanctuary in the Church Yard but there was none and was pulled down by the Church door, just as it was chiming twelve. A good three hours of the best, not always fast but good all round hound work. I saw part of the hunt when on my way to the wedding and I cheered them on when passing. Dennis Barrow will never forget that day, nor will our followers. We were having quite a good season, hounds had accounted for forty-one foxes up to 31 December so we were all set for 1966 New Years Day at the 'Duck.'

A dark morning, misty on tops, hounds soon had a fox going in the woods below and went by Field Head and Barbow Scar, above Hawkshead Church, with a good hunt now in progress. Crossing Grizedale road to top of Esthwaite Intake, fairly shoving him on now, as he had to turn inbank and was overtaken in Esthwaite Hall Farm yard. All hounds not there, so hounds transported back to Sunny Brow by van, where Bounty, Tempest, Trinket were having a helleva hunt and so we laid all hounds on and another chase. But after putting another big round in, hounds were badly baulked by cars, and after the hunt worsened and the line was lost, came on a bad day. One hound short, Bouncer, looked for it all over, could never hear out about it. Three weeks later it turned up at Hill Park where it was brought up!

I had better put something in here I had just forgot about and if the fellow reads those stories, will think I'm a bright beggar. It's about that hunt Dennis Barrow had when I was attending a wedding. Peter Martin made a great song up about that hunt, worth listening too. I think it was a battle between him and 'Lile Lant' who could make the best one up, they were both good and they had another competitor in Mrs Sylvia Shepherd who was very good as well.

Hunting is not all plain sailing, we have our ups and downs same as everybody else, like the morning from Bryan Beck, Cartmel Fell on 3 January 1966. A clean morning but frosty, hounds were loused into Heights and Rankthorn, struck a cold drag out towards Sow How. Some folk back above Rankthorn thought they saw a fox and 'hallo'd'. I sent hounds to them but could not take a line anywhere, so when all came to

Anthony with his foxhounds *Paul Allonby*

all what they had seen was a hare. I used to say if you are not sure keep your mouth shut! The old saying, keep your eyes open, keep your ears open and keep your mouth shut! We 'laited' all day after that and never found a fox.

Hounds had a good hunt again from the Mayor's Hunt, ran a fox from Troutbeck as far as Grasmere and back into Scandale when he went to ground at Brock Crag. A terrier called Grip was let in and after a while he came out but did not get far. Mr John Atkinson was Mayor. The following week was at Hartrigg. Tuesday morning, showery but good scenting, got two foxes, one up at 'Nan Bield Pass,' the other in Riggindale.

A terrier was in Tongue Earth and did not come out. Worked all week but could not get it. On the Sunday, never heard owt of it, so thought it must have perished. Sixteen men there on Sunday, they were: Jack Talyforth; Dennis Barrow; Bill Armstrong; Ted Allan; George Thompson; Gordon Gregory; Tom Bland; Peter Ainsworth; George Crowe; John Cousins; Bob Crawford; Shep and Hutch; Fred Prickett; Sid Dixon and Peter Martin – a bad ending to a good week accounting for four foxes. Good men!

On 29 March, my birthday, we were at Park Ground Farm, Torver. Hounds struck a drag out of fields and onto Low Fell and put a fox off near the tarn and away out by the moor to Dropping Crags. They fairly flew through Brown Pike and under Dow Crags in by Gates Hause, Ash Ghyll, Cooper Quarry and back into the Plantations. More hounds joined in here and made out for top quarry bank and laid down near sludge road and then put him off again. He followed the road down to Middle Bank and down the rubbish tip. He was a game fox because he could have gone to ground and been safe, can't make owt of them in there, but kept going for Dickinson Wood at a hell of a pace. Bounty and Tempest (liggin into it) they went by Torver Railway Crossing, past Moor Farm. The hunt now was not as good as it had been as they passed by Hoathwaite, Broom back across the old railway line up Blaithwaite Coppice, crossing Smart Field, to Out Rake Intakes, out to the Bell passing this bad borran, he set off to climb and at Cope Crag, put him off again and got topside of him and inbank was his next route at a very fast pace by Scrowbeck and Level Field down Ghyll and followed the line to Hoghouse Park and was pulled down in Low Park Wood. He was a big leggy dog fox. Bounty running well that day – great birthday present for me!

Easter Saturday our meet was always at Grove Farm, Ambleside. This day put a fox off at Wark How and went out over Wansfell top and in at Bank End, crossing Kirkstone Pass road and up Hallilands over Blue Ghyll (where the old Roman road goes out). Down the top of Yoke, down Quarry Lot through. Above Troutbeck Park, down Herd Wood, crossing the valley again and out Lowther Brow to go to ground at Park Quarry, a very bad place but will bolt if you stand back. I was once there and my pocket watch fell out of my pocket, it rolled underground and never saw it again. So if anyone ever digs there again and comes across it, it is mine and will be worth a lot of money because by then it will be an antique!

Jess was entered and was not long before he bolted and sped in down the rubbish in a hell of a hurry. Hallos and shouts made him fairly go inbank and through Troutbeck Park sheepfolds, still had plenty of life left in him, yet as they went about Bank End and Broad End to cross Kirkstone road making for Petts Quarries tip but was killed below. The best of scenting but bad seeing – the terrier 'Jess' went into Petts Quarries tip on 28 April 1966 and was never seen or heard again.

The last day out was from Millbeck, Great Langdale, a fine but misty morning. Struck a cold drag out White Ghyll to Blakerigg, out Sergeant Man, they were next heard at Dungeon Ghyll borran, marking to ground. A terrier was entered and was not long before foxy was out and away in for Millbeck, out Raw Head breast and over the skyline, in by Blind Tarn, passing Brimmer Head at a great pace, over Helm End down Easdale and ran her to a stand still and was caught in some gardens at Butterlype Howe. A good finish to a good season – all hounds doing their best, some better than others. No man alive bred a perfect pack yet!

Hounds ready for their summer holiday. Me as well as my ankle was no better, so that was the end to season 1965–6. I think all hound walkers are pleased to see them back again. The tally for the season was seventy-eight old foxes.

I went to my usual job for summer at Nook End for Mr Logan. I always enjoyed shepherding, I nearly always broke a young dog in for Mr Constable who lived at Broughton-in-Furness – he had a good breed. I used to get in as many shows and sports meetings as I could – it was something I had always been interested in. I was a founder member of the Ambleside Sports Association and had laid the trail for the old hounds ever since they started up again after the war. I also laid the trail for the old hounds at Applethwaite Sheep Dog Trials, also Hawkshead Show, and was neutral trailer at Grasmere Sports one year and for Kendal Show. So I enjoyed summer as well as winter. My ankle was still giving me hell making me very bad tempered!

Dennis Barrow and Anthony in the 1960s *Paul Allonby*

XV

Hospital – Foot And Mouth

THE 1966–67 SEASON CAME ROUND and started in September and we collected hounds in again. It used to take us about three days to get them all in. I did not like to keep hounds in kennels too long after they had just come in, so we went out Thursday and Friday of that week and then went to Eskdale Show, it was always the last Hound Show. We had two litters of pups for that season. One lot was out of Trinket by Melbreak Foxhounds 'Bowler'. Three bitches, two dogs namely Truant, Tulip, Tipler, Trueman and Dainty. Next litter was by our own Rockwood out of Melody. There was Cragsman, Stormer, Steamer, Singwell, Starling and Wisdom. 8 October 1966 opening meet at Nook End Farm, went onto Loughrigg, had a nice hunt and caught a fox, it was a beautiful day. It was our turn to be first up Kentmere, my ankle was getting worse. We had not such a good week. The first day was cold and snow showers. We tried all round top of the valley and never put a fox off. The hunters guarding Tongue Earth were there five hours poor beggers!

A big contrast next day, better scenting altogether. Two good hunts and kills, one at Gatehouse and the other up Garburn. One of them fell out of Raven Crag and two hounds as well and none were any the worse. On Friday, Hunt Ball day, loused out of the yard, struck a drag through the Grassings, across to Tongue up around LingmelL and finished up in Troutbeck. Saturday was fine but cold and set off from Kentmere Hall, put a fox off and lost it in Skelghyll Woods, not a very good week up there.

My doctor sent me to see a specialist at Lancaster. (I had tried all kinds of quack doctor's!) He told me the bones in my ankle were working out of their sockets with the wear and tear of my job. Dr Purser said he could operate on the ankle, it would not be quite the same again but I would be free from pain and I would be able to carry on as a huntsman. I thought that would be great, but said I would be off work six months – I was a bit windy about it! He said, 'You are not frightened are you?' I replied, 'No!' He seemed confident, so I went to the Garnet Clinic at Lancaster to have the operation and was glad I did. I could not praise that man too highly.

115

I was there a week and then I was sent to the St. John of God's Hospital, Silverdale and was looked after by monks, they were great men. The doctor had sawn right through the middle of my ankle, then clamped, and pinned it together, so that it is now all one piece and now it all moves together. I am now free of pain, never had any since it was done and for which I thank that Dr Purser again, also the nurses and the monks, they were great men. I spent Christmas in the hospital with them. That year the Christmas number (edition) of the 'Field' had my picture and the hounds on the front cover, taken at High Close just above Elterwater. They sent me a get-well letter with a five-pound note to get a drink with, when I was able to, as the picture had brought so much pleasure to so many hunting people all over.

Another queer thing happened to me that backend, we were at Torver and were walking down the road towards Church House Inn, Bruce Benson was walking with me when he said to me, 'Would I do something for him?' I said, 'Aye, if I can!' 'Would you scatter my ashes on the fell after I die? What could I say, but 'Yes.' Then said, 'Yer net garnt to dea yert!' and left it at that.

From when I went into hospital, Dennis Barrow was hunting hounds himself, with help from the Master, Mr Logan. On 12 January 1967 I came home and I had my leg in plaster till May, so Dennis finished the season off. He also got married on 18 March 1967, to a girl called Carol Stables who was quite keen on hunting. I never got a start at the kennels again that season. Lilter, Bounty and Rompish were all killed on the roads and Winsome and Countess were both killed the same day out of the crags in Deepdale Head, on 6 May 1967. It was a good job that we had a breed of Winsome. What a loss they were, five great bitches. The hounds accounted for sixty-four old foxes.

The season 1967–8 came round and I was again 'fit for the fray,' no pain and my ankle as sound as a 'a brass bell!' We had another two litters of young entry bred of Trinkett again. Her previous litter had all been good ones, and we had a breed of Winsome. The hounds all looked fit when they came back to the kennels, some fatter than others. Caught four foxes up till the opening meet at Nook End Farm, went on to Loughrigg, what a place at that time of year for brackens, two or three feet high, good cover for foxes. Had a merry hunt around the fell and was dispatched at Lanty Scar. Scenting not good in brackens and woods at this time of year but fetches hounds to their noses.

From 17–21 October had a very good week up Langdale, bringing four foxes to book. We just got another week's hunting in when Foot and

Mouth broke out about 1 November 1967 and we were in the area and all hunting stopped. We did not louse again until the end of January. Now that was a lot knocked out of the year! We had to exercise hounds every day. We used to take them as far as Sweden Bridge, by then they were getting worked up and wanting to go. They only broke away once and soon had a fox going, but got them stopped after an hour or two, they enjoyed it but was a very stowing job (hard).

Hunt Balls were all down, for it affected the attendance at them. A great appreciation was to Mr and Mrs Jack Phillipson, 'Pip' as we all know him by, they held a rafle which helped to compensate for some of the reduction in Hunt Ball proceeds, we had a loss that season of £113, so it showed the effect.

After we were allowed to start hunting again, never did seem right. I remember one day 2 March 1968, we loused from New Hall, Staveley, we put a fox off and went by Crook to Cunswick Hall, to Barrowfield Woods, about turned and nearly went the same way back, when Reynard got back to about where he was found. Hunting was not too good but mended about Firbank and set his mark for Kentmere. We were left far behind till somebody came along and gave us a lift as far as Croft Head. By now it was getting late and hounds were stopped up Garburn, you would have thought the fox would have been done but he likely was not. There had been many a fox been caught that had done a lot less running than that one, he must have been tough!

Some foxes are a lot harder than others. An old hunting man once told me that the softer ones were a bit kin-bred (in bred) and I quite believe it so. We had a lot better luck with our hounds than last year, lost one with what we did not know. It had been lost a month before anybody found it – was called Workman, walked by Mr Dennis Tuer of High Wray Farm, it was out of the good bitch Bounty and got by Blencathra Bendigo. When it was found, it was at Dan Becks lying dead in a bracken bed. I was rather pleased when the season came to an end, it had not been a good one.

The young entry for the following season was all from other Fell Packs, as with our bitches we had not had any success. The Eskdale and Ennerdale were good to let us have two couples, all one breed out of their own bitch Duchess by Hardy, so called after Harry Hardisty of the Melbreak from whom they got it. We gave them the names of Dexter, Dalesman, Lilter and Remedy. We also got one and half couples from the Blencathra, they were out of a bitch called Nipper by Mountain and we

All in a day's hunting

called them Climber, Dinah and Mischief, they all made useful hounds for which I thank them.

Two of them did not last long. We had a fox holed in Park Quarry and whilst trying to get to the fox, there was a rush of rocks and Lilter was in the way and got a hind leg almost cut off. Quarry stones are very sharp, she was got to the vet but was to no avail. Poor Remedy was killed on the road at Bowness. Hounds come to some untimely ends. But still here is something to remember, a memorable day from Chapel Stile. Hounds soon struck a drag at Wallthwaite as soon as they had left the road and went out Megs Ghyll into the Savins (gorse) above Wyke Woods, where he was lying. With a 'change of music' they put him off. Hounds got a good go at him, went out over Silver How and forward to cross Sour Milk Ghyll, as if making for that stronghold of Deer Bields, but when climbing hounds were the match for him and turned him inbank to cross by Easdale Tarn into Blind Tarn Moss, to go to ground in a drain at Brimmer Head, from which he was soon evicted and rolled over in the open.

Meanwhile another four couples were running a second fox in the Langdale Valley and went the length of Raw Head Breast and turned the 'sly un' back amongst the houses and ran him down at Robinson Place. Both sections were got together and taken forward to Hookriggs, where number three was put off but had no thought for climbing, went inbank and hounds, in good fettle, pressed hard as he set his mask down bank and what a race by Copt How, Lingmoor View to seek refuge in a drain in Wallthwaite fields hard by our starting point. This is a bad place from which a fox has not been bolted for years but on a day when everything was going right for the pack, out foxy came and crossed the road for Chapel Stile, where men, women and kids were all running after the hounds as true as English folk should do, to see a fox chase, and this was one. As we all sped away, re-crossed the road the other side of the village crossing 'Honeypot' behind Langdales Hotel, into the Langdale Estate which is now a holiday complex but in years gone by was known for the making of gunpowder, the music now was fit to waken the dead but did not stay in there long amongst the rhododendron and waterways, pressing forward to cross Elterwater Common for High Close, but hounds caught sight of his brush and a game fox was overtaken.

As it was still only 12.30 after all that lot, we tried a bit of fresh ground and then behold was number four, quickly on the move on Little Loughrigg and another good rattle up was taking place by Tarn Foot, Oaks Farm back to Robs Rash. Hounds were taking everything in front of them and putting the fear of God into Jacky and pressing hard, entered a drain in the main road. I said, 'We must not break into it!' I then took hounds into Silverthwaite Quarry and a terrier let in.

Although I say it myself, we had some good real working terriers, our pack terriers had to be hard to stand what they went through, in couples all day. I did not like them running about they could easily make trouble. I liked a noisy one when it had gone to ground, 'give mouth' as soon as it found the fox. These yapping beggars outside and always looking for a fight, I don't reckon much of them. I liked them nice on the leg for the miles they have to travel and could get over the rough boulders when at work because we have some very rough borrans. But on the day I have mentioned three foxes entered drains and that is another place where you want a terrier that will give 'plenty of mouth' because drains are often two feet deep and more (they liked work in older days) and bad to find sometimes. I have said a terrier was let in and everybody stood back, it's something if you have a little bit of patience because a fox will nearly always bolt if all is quiet and spares a lot of work, as it did that day and was not long before it bolted and away back towards Elterwater and after another fast spin was bowled over in the open. Scenting was good, hound work of the best, not forgetting the terrier work, a fine day and followers had something to talk about.

Hunting time was coming around again. The last of our Hound Shows was Eskdale and Mrs Sid Dixon's birthday and she took us into the beer tent and treated a few to a birthday drink – good of her!

Our opening meet was again held at the Master's farm, plenty to drink – gin, whisky, rum and coffee was had by all and then we went to Loughrigg by way of Pelter Bridge. It was a very fine day, scenting was not so good, brackens very strong and smelling, but hounds managed to get a fox, a good blooding for them. There was a Hunt Supper at Kirkstone Top at night and had a raffle and a sing song.

It was our turn to be up Kentmere first, it was a very bad week, rained and stormed all week. Mrs Fishwick, with whom the hounds had stayed at Hartrigg Farm for so long, died the same week. She had been a good sort to me.

On the Christmas Eve annual hunt from the Travellers Rest Hotel, Grasmere, had a good hunt, ran a fox into top end of Langstrath to where he went to ground, we were left behind, but could hear hounds 'marking', that is a good thing in the fell country. There was some hunters got to the place before me and I was crossing Stake Pass with Mr Logan when the fox bolted and we had a grandstand view from the other side of the valley, as hounds ran from 'scent to view' and caught him in the beck, a fine dog fox and what a fine clear day it was, very often 'hitty missy' weather about that time of the year.

Boxing Day on Loughrigg very cold and wet was not much scenting at all. We lost a good supporter 'Lile Teddy Casson' from Hawkshead, he had walked hounds for us for a long time. I well remember one, Dinah, if I was not there at the finish of the hunt, that hound would always go back to Hawkshead from anywhere. Another fella, Ernie Knipe of Coniston, worked for Josie Grisedale at Heathwaite and always looked after the hounds that were walked at that farm and were always called Sweeper. He was a great hunting mate of mine. He had left that farm and had just got a farm on his own account, Dixon Ground Farm, Coniston, with his wife Margaret. Went to gather sheep that backend on the Coniston fells and whilst in the Brim Fell/Townson Cove area had a heart attack and died. Peter Martin also shepherding in the same area wondered why he was not coming forward, saw his sheep dogs standing about and went back to look and found the poor fella dead. What a sad ending to the hunting man.

One day when out hunting from Hawkshead Hill, home of Mr and Mrs Sid Jackson, it was a very frozen time, it being 24 February 1969, loused down Hawkshead Moor in the forestry and hounds had got broken up as often they do in forests. North Lonsdale Foxhounds were at Sawrey, some of our hounds heard theirs and went towards the 'cry'. One called Waitress was taking a short cut across Esthwaite Water that was frozen over but did not reach the other side and went through the ice. Two men, Mike Pattinson and Jeff Storey made a gallant attempt to reach her but she disappeared under the ice and was found by Graythwaite Hall gamekeeper after the thaw, on the lakeshore. She was from a very good litter, four bitches and one dog out of Winsome by Melbreak Bowler. Waitress was lost when hunting in the Kentmere district 31 October 1972 and was never seen again. I used to worry about the hounds when they were lost, wondering what could have happened to them. The dog hound Warrior was lost in the last week of the season up Langdale on 11 May 1972 and was found dead at the bottom of Crinkle Ghyll by Mr Harry Cowman, Stool End Farm, where we had been staying for the week. What untimely end some hounds come to.

121

Joe Weir judging after he retired

XVI

Hunting in the 1970s

DURING 1969–70, HOUNDS CAME BACK to kennels looking quite fit, clean and tidy. It was decided by the Committee to have a hunt tie, which was very nice. Despite an increase of £198 in the cost of running the Hunt, the accounts this year show a satisfactory excess of income over expenditure of £78, mainly due to the untiring efforts and the very great enthusiasm shown by all local committees towards the Hunt which is very good. Mr Logan also ran a Hound Trail from Nook End Farm that brought in about £50, so it shows in these days every little helps.

Our season started with three and a half couples of young entry, all one litter out of Trinkett by Melbreak Foxhounds 'Traveller' and soon lost one, Towley, that was killed on the main road. Trinkett is walked by Mr and Mrs Hodgson of The Grove, Witherslack and when a walker's hound's is to be bred off, the people are only too pleased to have them whelped at their farms with a great interest and keep them till they are about eight weeks old and ready for going out to walks.

At our annual Hound Show held at Rydal Hound Show, one of the best in the North of England people come from all parts of the country to it. Our show is always before the Open Hound Show. We always get one of our Fell Huntsman to judge our hounds and this year, the silver cup given by Mrs Wilson of Coniston, was won by Wonder, walked by Mr J.N. Preston. A silver cup given by Mrs Steele in memory of her husband Bob was won by Tempest, walked by Peter Mark. Comrade, walked by Mrs Boyren, won a stirrup cup given by G. Gregory. A cup given by the Master for the best walked puppy was won by Ruler, walked by Allan Dugdale, and the Hartley Silver Challenge Trophy for the best working hound of last season went to Ransome, walked by Duggie Milburn.

From a meet at Wray, Latterbarrow was tried and soon had a fox on the move but after putting a round in by High Wray, was lost rather mysteriously at Town End Farm, Hawkshead and when followers arrived, hounds were completely finished. Another was found which made up for the loss of the first one. Found this one above 'Beyond the Field', put a round in by way of Dan Becks, Wray Castle, back to Belle Grange by the shores of Windermere as far as the ferry. The hunt now was in the woods by the Lake and going at a cracking pace, making the woods 'ring with the music' of the hounds and now and again a follower cheering them on. After a fine hound hunt of two hours, was caught by 'speed of foot' at Strawberry Gardens by the lake shore.

Then from a meet in Hawkshead village square and an enthusiastic crowd, hounds were loused into the forestry, a fox was soon away and after a fast hunt for an hour was overtaken at Ormandy Farm. A second fox was hunted in the Dale Park area and when hounds changed onto a fresh fox at Sawrey they were stopped as it was getting late in the day. Poor Bouncer fell out of Yak How Crag and was killed outright. He was out of Bounty and got by Blencathra Bendigo.

It had been one of the wettest Octobers on record and the opening meet of the Ullswater Foxhounds was cancelled and as far as records show this has never happened before in the ninety-four years since the pack was founded in 1873. The day was same with us at High Nibthwaite but we made a start at about 11 AM, hounds got a flying start at a fox out of the heather at Brockbarrow but soon after were struggling to hold the line, that much water about and the weather was deteriorating and after about three hours, hounds were stopped at Rusland Church. In the hunting notes about the Lunesdale Foxhounds the followers said, 'The weather was vile!' So it must have been the same all round.

On 29 September 1969 we were up Kentmere, a fox or two on the move, one with a short tail and were still running at 8 o'clock at night. Hounds were tired after that it was like for fetching flesh off them. After a day's rest they were fit again and caught a fox at Gate House, Kentmere. 1970 came in with a vengeance, snow and ice, we went to the Duck Hunt, but did nowt!

Then on 29 January met at Low House Farm, Ings found a fox 'lying in,' Bodger a little terrier I had, bolted him, she was only small but a good un' (one). I got her from Stan Mattinson of the Blencathra. It was behind the Diatomite Works at Kentmere, a fast run then took place but went to ground again at Broadgate. It took us about three hours to find and bolt again but hounds were rewarded in the end.

Our stay with Mr and Mrs Park at Witherslack was from 9–15 February, we had some good hunts and kills. The best was on the Saturday, 14 February. The meet was at Halecat House, the home of Mr and Mrs Stanley, a great crowd of hunters. There were lots of children,

I used to like them following me, encourage them they are the hunters of tomorrow. Coffee and eats, Mr Stanley went round with rum bottle, when one was empty, he got another and then we set off round the 'Mosses', could not find a fox, so crossed onto Yewbarrow, we were having a job to find one on there. I was thinking what a bad go for all them folk and kids when about 1 pm hounds 'feathered about' (smell but can't find) a badger set. I let a terrier in called Tinker and stood well back and after a while out a big fox came and with a 'Oop git away!' he soon set his mask for Whitbarrow, that limestone mass, but hounds and followers were ready for the fray and gave him no peace and ran him into a grike, where a fine dog fox was accounted for. Then we had a sing song at night at the Derby Arms. Frank Atkinson was the Chairman. After the pub closed we were invited out to supper at Mr and Mrs Peter Mark's, twenty-five of us that night!

That year it was our turn to go to Kentmere in March but there was that much snow it was too dangerous on the high fells, so we loused at New Hall, Staveley, but no scenting. We went for a week in April, still a lot of snow about on fell tops, caught two foxes, both bitches.

In March – Nibthwaite and Blawith. Torver, Coniston and Woodland Hunt Committees held a sponsored walk and it was a great success, made £471.50 for the Hunt, a great credit to all concerned. I wrote earlier about a man called Bruce Benson and what he said to me, about scattering his ashes. Well it came as a shock, he died in March 1970 and this is what he had left in a letter. 'To my Executor – It is my wish that the ashes resulting from my cremation shall be handed to Anthony Chapman, Huntsman of the Coniston Foxhounds who shall be asked to scatter them on the fell when convenient. For this service, it is my wish that you give the sum of five pounds. Bruce Benson.' I did as I was asked and took them to the highest point of Loughrigg Fell overlooking Ambleside. I never thought that job would come so soon.

By the middle of April each season advertised meets were finished and from then till the middle of May hounds are 'on call' to go anywhere that lambs have been worried or taken and then the farmer sends for us. This season will be remembered for its Artic weather with early snow in November and then unusually late falls keeping the fells white for the whole of March and into April. Our last advertised meets were at Torver. We had to leave two foxes when they went to ground in Broughton Moor Quarry rubbish tips. They are unsafe places for terriers. These tips cover a great area of ground and foxes are not daft, they know where they are safe. The bad luck of the week continued. On Saturday 10 April 1970 when a good hunt from Tranearth Quarries went out Coniston Old Man, Brim Fell, Hookriggs to cross Wrynose Pass but nothing more was seen of them again that day.

All the other Fell Packs have a man in each of their districts going about with a Subscription Book, but the Coniston never have had, but for this last season we had two hundred subscribers, not bad that, as they are all voluntarily given.

For 1969–70 season our tally of foxes for the season was sixty-three, rather below our average. The weather had been against us. After it all we were ready for our summer holidays. I went back to Nook End for summer, I enjoy it shepherding up Scandale and Rydal and running Hound Trails for sports extra. Five Hound Shows to go to during September: Hawkshead Show, Lunesdale Foxhounds Open Show, Kendal County Show and lastly Eskdale Show.

We had a hound about that time doing a lot of winning, Tempest, walked by Mr and Mrs Mark. We had four couples of young hounds came in. Foxes were not quite as plentiful, caught three in Langdale week and three for Kentmere week. On 29 November 1970 'Lile Lant' as we used to call him, Lanty Langhorn, had a heart attack on his motor bicycle and died. It came as a shock to us all. He had been a mate of mine all our lives, a very well known character. I always thought he was a lile wiery fellow but one never knows. He had always been keen on hunting.

George Tansey, a correspondent for the Daily Mail, once visited Troutbeck Shepherd's Meet and wrote this.

> *'Anthony Chapman, huntsman to the Coniston Foxhounds, his fantastic physical endurance and intense devotion to chasing the fox has made him a legendary figure in Lakeland. Like John Peel who had John Woodcock Graves to immortalise his exploits, Anthony Chapman has his own poet Lanty Langhorn of Ambleside, his old school friend and hunting companion who sings multi-verse hunting ballads about Anthony and his hounds out on the high fells. And there is plenty to sing about as his hunting is out of this world kind of hunting and is dominated by perilous crags, screes, bracken covered slopes and forests. 'The day that two Packs met'. 'Coniston and Ullswater'. 'Borwick Lodge Meet'. 'Remedy'. 'The thin white line,' are of his writing.*

Then on comes a man and makes one up about Lanty's escapades by 'Derek Woods'. It has twenty-six verses in it. I'll put one or two in here but they are all that good I'll have to choose. He was a timber faller dur-

ing the war and worked for Croasdale's Wood Merchants. He was working about Haverthwaite and one morning he was late so took a short cut
across an army camp. He was soon spotted by a sentry:-

> *The sentry for a foreign agent 'Lile Lanty' mistook*
> *So straight into t'guard room he was quickly took*
> *Foreign agent be buggered Lile Lanty did say*
> *I work for George Croasdale down Haverthwaite way*
> *Four men guarded Lant when they got him outside*
> *Into a Land Rover which the officer did drive*
> *Straight for George Croasdale away they did steer*
> *Poor Lanty was hoping his good name to clear*
> *Now George at the sight of the Adjutant's face*
> *Denied all knowledge of Lanty for fear of disgrace*
> *He's a queer man to vouch for as you'll plainly see*
> *By the look of friend Lanty he'd been stung by a bee*
> *You silly old bugger, go on tell them my name*
> *They think I'm an agent from Italy or Spain*
> *At last George calmed down and cleared Lile fellow's name*
> *And our friend Lanty did breath freely again.*

After the war Lanty got a job at the Gas Works and worked at
Windermere and went to work on a motorbike. I had some land down at
Waterhead and he passed by everyday and a few campers used to go into
the field and this verse is about them.

(I used to get a shilling each (5p) from them)

> *Early one morning on his way home from work*
> *He spied 'Chappie's' campers and thought he'd play a quirk*
> *He quickly popped round them and collected their rent*
> *When Chappy landed they said, 'Nay we paid a funny like gent!'*

Lanty Langhorn was very keen on terriers and kept and bred a few. He
was known by everyone in the Coniston country and was a member of
H.T.A. and R.A.O.B. Sports Committee. He left a wife and three girls.

It was about now that word was getting around that Joe Wear, huntsman to the Ullswater Foxhounds, was going to retire at the end of the
season 1970–71. He had held the position as huntsman for thirty-seven
years and was whipper for nine years.

At our Christmas Eve hunt at Grasmere a fox from about Brimmer
Head ran the Silver How area for a time trying to shake off his pursuers to no avail so then took off across Red Bank into Elterwater village

Terriers waiting patiently

where a lot of time was lost before hounds struck off the line. Crossing the River Brathay out by Park Farm onto Brow Fell. Then through by Iron Keld and the Tarns the hunt by now was getting slower and slower. Foxy must have had a good lead as no hunters could see him to give hounds a helping hand and lost the line completely on the frozen fields at Hawkshead Hill. It was rather an unusual route for a fox off Helm Crag to take. There was a good crowd out on Boxing Day and so plenty of sport on Loughrigg Fell.

Hounds roused a fox in Cookson's Woods which took two rounds in of the fell by way of Foxghyll, Skelby Crags, Ewe's (Yews?) Crags, Tarn Foot and Ivy Crag, through the Howe Breast and forced him inbank and was overtaken on the shore of Loughrigg Tarn. It was a grandstand for both foot followers and car followers so back we went home for a drink and hot pot at Golden Rule Hotel.

New Year's Day 1971 was a beautiful day we had a grand hunt, gave followers something to talk about and hounds killed a fox at Tarn Foot of Loughrigg. There were a lot of youngsters following me from start to finish, to my delight, and they all wanted the brush. Too keep them happy I put all their names into my hat and drew one out. The young lad was set up that got it!

On 4 January 1971 we lost our oldest subscriber who had been since 1917. Miss Belk was a real country lady, not many left now. She first lived at Bridge House, Grasmere and lived in the vicinity since. She was a great friend of the Logan and Chapman families. She was lean and lanky, a good walker. Walked many hundreds of miles with my father and did do after I became huntsman. Very often had a good terrier and used to let them work with the pack, one 'Crest' was in Petts Quarries for a week. I had one of hers called Grip. When Ernie Parker was lying dying from an incurable illness, she had George Robinson going to sit with him at night. George Robinson used to work for her at Titteringdale, Grasmere. Miss Belk was a very good sort to me as she gave me the bungalow Brae Holme, in which my wife and I live and left me quite well off, for which my family and I thank her.

On 26 January 1971 hounds were loused from Low House, Ings after receiving the hospitality of Mr and Mrs Swindlehurst. It was a very bad morning, very misty but good scenting. Put a fox off at Reston Scar, fast hunt round by High Borrans and back and went to ground up above Scroggs Bridge. It was still very misty but gave him another chance, stood well back, could not see fox when it came out. Hounds were soon on him again and killed in the open. We had to follow that hunt by sound!

Had fine week at Witherslack, there 8 February till 13th caught three foxes, not bad for that kind of country. We had two good sing songs that week and on the Saturday night twenty of us went back to Mr and Mrs Peter Mark's for supper. Mrs Sid Dixon made three pound ten (£3.50) for hounds.

The Mayor's Hunt that year was on 27 February, Mr Douglas Freeman of Town End Farm was the Mayor. There was a big turn out of followers, a fox was put off on Wansfell End and made out Broad How and Caudale Moor, we were left far behind. When we got out to the tops could hear nowt and dropped into Kirkstone Pass at Brotherswater. Were told by car followers that hounds had gone through Hartsop and into Martindale, that was a long way. So the Master, Mr Logan said he would take me and some more round in his Land Rover and a lot more followers besides followed on and what a reward when we got there. Going up Martindale Hause met some hunters who had followed when hounds were heard running hard on top of the valley. The Cookson family was one of the families that had joined in, when the cry of those hounds made the valley ring, told us what was happening. We had not been there long when we heard them coming in off the fell top just about 'viewing' their quarry

129

and brought him in right past us now running 'to view' and killed a fine dog fox at Sandwick. A hunt and finish to remember.

It was right about Lile Joe Wear retiring at end of season 1970–71. Joe had become one of Lakeland's characters during his long association with the Ullswater Pack. Strong, ruddy-faced and sturdily built he was only the fourth huntsman the pack has had since it was formed in 1873, by the amalgamation of the Patterdale and Matterdale Hounds. There was a bit of ill feeling about it, which was a sad thing. It even got into the daily papers – I have a cutting out of the *Sunday Express* which starts off in big letters 'Huntsman fall out over retirement of John Peel of 1971.' In it said, he did not retire on his own, but was asked too to make way for a younger man and in that language it seemed he was sacked. He had as a whip a man called Maldwyn Williams and had been there for ten seasons, he finished as well. A new huntsman was appointed and Dennis Barrow got the job. He had nine seasons as a whipper to me with the Coniston Foxhounds, so had a good schooling!

Chris Ogilvie

Our opening meet in 1971 was the same venue on Loughrigg but was not much scenting amongst the stinking brackens, so we had no luck. In the season 1970–71 I lost another good friend and supporter, Wilf Nicholson, he did a lot for me. It was through him that a small Committee was put together and eventually got Ambleside Sports started again which has grown to be one of Lakelands great attractions, it was all started from nothing, we hadn't a penny. He got the Hunt Ball going again in Ambleside and was held in the Assembly Rooms, a great effort for Coniston Foxhounds in 1945. He had been keen on hunting all his life and hunted with my father when he was a lad. When the hounds went to stay for the week at Mr and Mrs Preston's, Low Lindeth Farm, Winster, he used to come as well and have his week's holiday with me. He had ill health for a number of years and gave up all commitments.

On Saturday morning following a successful Hunt Ball at Troutbeck, hounds met at High Green, the home of Nell and Charlie Clark. There was a good gathering of hunters. The weather was fine and nice scenting. A drag was struck in the pastures above and led hounds out to Poole's Lot a very 'smittle spot' when Reynard broke cover to the Hundreds with a great burst of music. After putting in a circle they then made out Wark How for Hind Cove and Wansfell Pike. Hounds had now settled to their game and pressing hard through Side Lot and 'little Hundreds' and set his mask for Skelghyll Woods out onto Boat Hows. Dropping back into the wood again down Stencher Beck no doubt thinking he might shake off his pursuers in the thick undergrowth under Kelsick Scar but with Bondage, Dalesman, Waitress and Wonder forging ahead forced him past the stronghold of Brock Crag borran and out at the bottom of the wood. But having no time to tarry, sped on through the fields at Low Wood to Holbeck Ghyll and out Green Thwaites into Martins Planting. Hounds were now fast gaining on their quarry. Crossing the road at Cringlemire down the meadows at Castle Syke to Troutbeck Bridge, crossing the Kirkstone road into Thickholme where a beaten fox was overtaken, after a very fast hunt – a fine young dog fox!

After Troutbeck Hunt week, Winster week followed. There were two fellas who always came to hunt with us that week, George Graveson and George Bassett from Newport, South Wales, one was a farmer and the other a fell monger and both liked a game of Nap. George Graveson had left his native Crosthwaite. He started out as a mole catcher and then started farming on his own account and had one of the finest herds of Shorthorn cattle in the country. His sideboards in his farmhouse were covered with silver cups won with his cows, one of them was the biggest silver cup I had ever seen, three feet high! Another thing I noticed in the house (he had invited myself and Chris Ogilvie down for a weekend) was a bath seven feet long and four feet high, you nearly wanted a pair of steps to get into it! It was used for two purposes – as a bath and also to salt bacon in. He also had some very old farm implements.

There was another fella always came for that week, Lile Jack Leake, a bank manager from Huddersfield. They were a grand hunting crowd in Winster Valley. We did not do much that week, 22–27 November 1971, caught two foxes and lost two – baulked by motorcars. When the fox runs the road and then the cars come along and get in front of hounds, what else can you expect, they used to make me mad but nowadays I have joined them. It takes a good hound to hunt on a road. I have noticed while walking hounds on the road and a car goes past, as soon as it has gone, hounds start sniffing and getting the fumes out of their nostrils. The week ended with a sing song at the Brown Horse Inn, Jim Whetton was Chairman and an enjoyable evening was had by all!

XVII

Broken Leg

O N NEW YEARS DAY 1972 we had the traditional Duck Hunt and had two kills on the open. The first fox put off in Pull Scar Crag made out to Iron Keld plantations round by High Arnside, through above Skelwith Bridge and was overtaken near the road under Pull Scar after a fast hunt. I tried hounds forward onto fresh ground and found another on Borwick Ground Fell, he was rather a tougher one and a bit more run in him as was soon to be seen, as Warrior viewed out of some Savins. The others joining in for Tarn Hows that great beauty spot, Sawrey Ground, Hawkshead Hill, passing Hawkshead Hall to Rampsteads and Dan Becks and onto the road below the Drunken Duck, where he got a breather as hounds had a bad check amongst the folk and motor cars. But trying forward themselves, that is an art the fell foxhound has, put him off again amongst the slate heaps at Brathay Quarry, foxy went straight away for nearly ten miles by way of Sunny Brow to High Cross, crossing the road into the Grizedale Forest passing Tent Lodge above Brantwood into the Heald, passing Park-a-Moor and into the road by Coniston Lake. He kept going into the lake and back onto the road, he did this several times to shake off his pursuers but to no avail. By now the foot followers were catching up by getting lifts in motor cars (sometimes useful) and were there to witness the end of a good hunt by a good fox as a last resort set his mask to climb Broad Hollins but had no steam left and forced a game fox inbank to be overtaken above Water Park, once the kennels of the Coniston Foxhounds years ago and are still there. A grand day's hunting, two good finishes and a credit to the hounds!

On 2 January I had the misfortune to slip on a piece of wet board and broke my leg above the ankle so was out of action for six weeks. Chris was in charge but had a lot of bad weather to contend with. He had a tremendous good hunt from New Hall, Staveley.

27 January at the Mayor's Hunt at Troutbeck – it was a very bad misty day and tried a lot of ground before a fox was found and hounds soon caught an old dog fox.

Loweswater Show (Lorton)

It being a leap year, we were up Kentmere on the 29th and was a grand day and had a good hunt killing a fox, 18lbs (8.1 kilos) but did not do much again that week, bad weather, snowing. We were soon in action after lamb worriers at Howe Farm, Troutbeck, and got the culprit. Out next day also and again got a fox and six cubs at Buck Crag in Kentmere, so that was like stopping them.

It was a very cold day one morning in February 1972 when the meet was at High Yewdale, Coniston the home of Mr and Mrs J. Birketts. That family had always been keen on hunting. I was still riding about in a motorcar with my leg in plaster. George Thompson from High Wray was there, a great hunting mate of mine he always walked with me. He came and had a bit of crack to me and when hounds set off he said to me, 'You'll soon be back in action!' and set off after the hounds. I could see nothing wrong with him health wise. My daughter took me round into the mines valley and up towards the Blue Quarries, we had been there an hour or two with a hunt going on and then noticed a fella running down old Isled road down past Mines Cottages for Coniston. We wondered what he was in such a hurry for, after a while a hunt follower came to me and said, 'There has a sad thing happened on Yewdale Moor!' I said, 'What's that?' His reply was, 'George Thompson has dropped down dead!' What a shock that was. That finished our day and we came home. I know it was a great shock to hunt followers and to his family and I had lost a true friend. His uncle was one of my father's best hunting mates and had walked hundreds of miles with him (same as George had with me) he had a nickname of 'Spiduks! How he got that name and what it meant I do not know.

On 10 May we went to Hartrigg and a bitch fox was accounted for, also that day Bondage had pups, three dogs and three bitches. At the end of the season we had caught sixty-five old foxes.

Due to the Brucellosis Eradication Scheme it became necessary to build a slaughterhouse at the kennels to avoid butchering in the open, which had been an awful job when it was, bleak, frozen or snowing. The cost of the building was £1,048 that was well spent. We had a very good balance sheet, I always tried to save them every penny I could.

We had a good summer amongst the hound shows our Tempest was outstanding on several shows. We had two hounds given by Captain Wallace of Heythrop Foxhounds, they had fancy names so I rechristened them Dally and Freeman. Freeman wasn't any good and did not last long. Dally was rather better but was not outstanding, she was like a lot more of the Heythrop Hounds, squarkey mouthed. My wife and I kept her and she ended her days at Brae Holme, she won a couple of cups for us at Rydal Hound Show.

At Lorton Hound Show 'Tempest' got a third for Mr and Mrs Peter Mark. Welcome was second for Mr and Mrs McCrone. Tempest won at Cockermouth Show, also Welcome. At Sedbergh Show 'Coniston' won the Group. Tempest had a first at Hawkshead and we again got Group two days later. She won again at Grayrigg Show and was second at County Show at Kendal and at the last show of the year at Eskdale won a first prize again. Not a bad summer for her!

On 20 September 1972 a new season started with a louse up Kirkstone, fine day not much scenting. We had a young entry of four and a half couples, Comrade, Carver, Cragsman, Trinkett and Crystal out of Bondage, by our own Comrade. Then Lawyer, Leader, Lancer and Lightening out of Coniston Lilter, Melbreak Glider.

On 20 November 1972 which was also the Queen's Silver Wedding Day we had a very good hunt down Winster and caught a fox and on the Saturday, we holed one twice and then lost it, must have been a good fox. Only got one fox for the week, a big contrast to some weeks we've had down there. My father used to call that country a 'blurdy' stickheap (woods) and was not far wrong!

New Years Day 1973 thick fog all day, put a fox off in Iron Keld Planting, a 'straight necked un' but lost it at Oxen Park. I well remember a fox going off Loughrigg when Ernie Parker and I were together and losing it about the same place, but we had to walk back to the kennels at Ambleside, no vans or trailers them days. It was a fair walk that after finishing hunting.

On 4 January we went back to Ickenthwaite as we did not do much when we had been there before Christmas. We had a good day and caught a fox beside the Duck Tarn in the forestry. It was good scenting the 'music' of the hounds had been great in the woods. They stuck to one fox and that's something in places like that.

On 5 January 1973 my Uncle Bob died, he was the last remaining son of old Anthony. He had been a hunting man and a farmer all his life. I well remember a hound he walked whilst farming at Sunny Brow, Hawkshead, called Bowler. It won Miss Belk's silver teapot at the Puppy Show held on Ambleside Sheep Fair Day in White Platts, in Ambleside.

During 7–14 of January we were staying at Cartmel Fell with Mr and Mrs John Lishman, had a good week killing four foxes. Also had a good week for meat, getting five sheep, one ram, two calves, one stirk and one cow, so hounds would have a good feed.

I'll have to mention this hunt from Skelwith Fold, had a good hunt after a fox and killed at the Brow. That night a hound was missing called Rival, the day being 15 January we never heard anything about it until she turned up at Mr and Mrs Lishman's on 27 January, where they had been kennelled the week before she was lost. She must have lost her bearings and then found them again when it got into that countryside.

On 25 January we were at Woodlands and found a fox on the fell and made out to Broughton Moor. When we landed there it was very misty, could see nowt but could hear, could tell there was a hunt coming towards us and very fast when all at once the 'music' stopped and we walked one hundred yards, and there, four hounds were worrying a fine dog fox. The four hounds were Tenant, Chorus, Chanter and Treaty. It just shows if we had not been there we would not have known anything about that kill.

Went to Yewdale Crag on 2 February and a fox was lying in the crag and sneaked out up White Ghyll and Tilberthwaite Ghyll to Hodge Close Quarries, where he was accounted for. But one hound Sweeper was found lying dead on the road, did not know what happened to it. We had had quite a good week accounting for four foxes last one on Saturday, 3 February and had a tremendous fast hunt and holed in Tarn Hows wood after a bit of digging. There's a few fellows about there likes a good grub! He came into sight and stood well back and out he came and what a sight, hounds and folk going down that wood, old and young alike, after another gay crash they bowled him over in John Oliphant's garden – a good end!

The funeral of Joe Wilkinson took place on 17 February 1973. He was a born Patterdalean. He was once over whipper-in to Joe Wear, same time as I was whip to Ernie Parker, the war came and he was same as me, he had to take up farm work. After the war he did not go back into hunt service but got a farm, Crosslands in the Rusland Valley, where he and his family farmed with great success – Gordon and Donald his sons are still there.

A great crowd of hunting people turned out for the Mayor's Hunt. Mayor making had been held on the Friday night and the Mayor had nominated Mike Cousins, a farm worker at Troutbeck Park, once owned by Mrs Heelis – Beatrix Potter to a lot of people. We loused down land that morning was not fit to go upbank (let hounds off in the valley bottom). We had a very good run and came to a bad check about Dove Nest. I was a bit disappointed and could not strike a bit of hunt anywhere, when a young hunter Freddie Garside came to me and said 'There's an

Rydal Sheepdog Trials – 1970s
Left to right: Tommy Preston, Chris Ogilvie – whipper-in, Anthony, Ella McCrone and Tom Mark.

auld fox digging behind wa' up there!' I said to him, 'Goa and haller!' and he did and hounds were soon on Reynard's track again. That was sheer luck and there is a lot of that in hunting, as hounds soon overtook him with a grand burst of music again in Grains Ghyll.

We were at Troutbeck Park on 10 April and got two foxes in Park Fell Head, a dog and bitch and then coming back by Broad How a big dog fox was lying dead. It only had a tooth or two in its back gums, so must have been very old. There is seldom a season goes by but what an old dead fox is found.

Troutbeck Park sent for hounds again lambing time 18 April – struck a drag out of fields and mended in Hallilands and went out Park Fell head into Hayeswater and the fox went to ground at Fox Bields. This place is a noted stronghold not fit for terriers. This inscription is chiselled into a rock – Oct 30th Fox Buller 1908 J.B. T.D. P.T. – so there must have been terriers lost there. Had lots of 'lamb worrying' calls that spring and finished the season up Langdale, at Millbeck and Stool End. We had a poor season.

It was a very hot day for 'The Rydal Hound Show' on Thursday, 16 August 1973. We had as judge for the Coniston Foxhounds Entered and Unentered Mr Edmund Porter of the Eskdale and Ennerdale Foxhounds, first prize in Entered dog hounds was 'Banker' walked by J. Mark and 'Welcome' the bitch class walked by Mr B. McCrone. In the Unentered

'Lawyer' walked by V. Gregg and 'Trinkett' won the bitch class for V. Hodgson. In the Open Show the judges were Mr A. Douglas, M.F.H. Liddlesdale and Captain S.T. Clarke (M.F.H. Cottesmore). The Group Class was judged first and won by the Coniston. We gained first and second in the Open Entered Foxhounds for Dogs with Banker and Belman in that order. The Blencathra won the Championship with a hound called Cruiser and Melbreak reserve with Ransome. Every backend hunting people from all over the country come to the fells for a day or two's hunting generally September, October and beginning of November. The country then is in the change of autumn and I think I will have to put in here a couple of verses from a song 'Lile Lant' made up and I know is quite appropriate:

They keep a welcome on the hillsides, they keep a welcome in the dale
There'll be a welcome from the dales folk it's September once again
The bracken changing colour and the leaves come tumbling down
And the fox glides from his cover, no time for lying down.
The summer months are gone and harvests gathered in
For some there will be plenty and others a wee bit thin
All the woodlands ly a sleeping and the connies (rabbits) *gone to rest*
The cry of hounds ring sweetly thro the mountain breast.

There's a few more verses well put together just as good as 'Auld Wordsworth!'

Our opening meet was on Loughrigg, loused at Pelter Bridge and up Lanty Scar we had a nice hunt and kill and trampled a lot of brackens down. On Saturday, 27 October after the Hunt Supper at Tarn Hows Hotel, Hawkshead, ran a fox about Duck and was caught. One hound short, Welcome, walked by Mr and Mrs McCrone, a very promising young hound and a few days later was found dead by Mr Logan, it had got fast by its hind legs, bad things these forestry fences for hounds to jump.

Whilst staying at Allan Dugdale's at Pepper House, hounds were loused into forestry, well before long there was hunts going all road, nowt fresh. Ran one to ground at Pack-a-Moor, bit of snow on and cold, let a terrier in called Blackie. Had to dig up to him and fox was fairly mauling it. Fox always has an advantage in a soil hole as it had this day, when we got Blackie out the fox had broken its jaw, so let hounds in and pulled him out and worried it. Took poor Blackie to vets but could do nothing for him, so had to have him put to sleep. That was the end of that good terrier.

New Years Day 1974 was a very cold and raggy morning, ran foxes all day never saw much, but ran all day and had to stop them at dark. We've seen days like that when hounds could not push their game. We put a meet in at Langdales Hotel on 5 January, it was a bit misty and wild weather but soon found a fox in Megs Ghyll and scuffed it round a bit and soon went to ground. Hunters soon on the spot and had him out before I got there. I was very mad because they did not give it a chance to run and hounds soon bowled him over. It was a good job we soon found another and had a fast run by Blakerigg, Codale Head, Ashthwaite, crossing the valley out to top of Carrs and turned down bank for Helm by way of Hows Crag but could not reach the stronghold, 'The Rush' and was pulled down in the open at Bracken Hause. That made up for the hunt we should have had.

It was an open January – snow sometimes but mainly wet. On 19 January was Crook Hunt Ball, this had been a new venue started by Mr and Mrs S. Jackson who left Hawkshead and went to live in Crook, it was a very 'good do' that night. Next morning we met at New Hall Farm, Staveley and had a long lait but found two foxes lying in at Crag House Lot. We had not much sport with either of them, one went about one hundred yards and was overtaken, the other was dispatched by Scamp a Jack Russel and a good one at that was given to the hunt by Mr and Mrs A. Logan.

On 25 January 1974 Nan Brockbank died, she and her sister Peggy and their father, were some of the first people I got to know in the Cartmel Fell district as a lad. They were farmers at Pool Bank. Father was very keen, used to wear clogs, by gum they did rattle when he got to running! We had a nice hunt or two Cartmel Fell week and a good old sing song at Strawberry Bank on Saturday night, packed out it was, what people came for. Frank Atkinson was Chairman, everybody had to sing a song when called upon.

Mayor making had been changed from the Saturday night to the night before, on account of the do getting a bit rowdy and fighting. Now you cannot get in without a ticket that keeps them kind of people out. Once upon a time beer was free but not today. It was Mike Cousin's turn to pick the Mayor and it fell upon 'Lile Dick Black.' He has Chapman blood in him, his grandmother being one of auld Anthony's daughters. After the meet at the Queens Head Hotel, it being a very warm barmy day, a fox was 'hallo'd away' by Peter Martin above Bank End, one fox being accounted for in Rough Sides. Hounds got a bit broken up – not good!

One day, 16 March – Nibthwaite, a long day and never found a fox. What would they think of that today? Hunters I meant! A Hunt Supper was held at Low Wood Hotel on 21 March 1974. After a meet there that morning, a fox was found and after a nice hunt, went to ground near Long Green Head. 'It was given law' (freedom or space) but gave us the best, as 'Sly un' was lost in Troutbeck village.

On the Saturday of that week had a good day's hunting in Rydal Park, three foxes were had, the last made a good hunt and went to ground at Raven Crag at Kirkstone, at 4.30 PM and would not bolt, so paid the penalty underground and was drawn at seven that night.

It was getting near lambing time so went to Yewdale early one morning, found a fox at Gate Crag and hounds pressed hard by White Ghyll, rightly named, into Far End Breast. A rough place, by passed Blue Quarry and was killed on Threadale Road. Another in Hookriggs and fell to the terriers, a terrier called Rose worked well that day for a 'young un.' Roger Bigland the terrier man from the Heythrop Foxhounds was staying on his holidays. One hunt he was at from Troutbeck Park, had a fast hunt into Kentmere and holed at Tongue Earth, a bit different place to what the Heythrop foxes go into.

During the season Mr B.L. Thompson resigned from the position of Chairman of the Hunt Committee owing to recent illness, he had been in since 1961 and had been a Committee Member from the 1940s. During the latter part of that season we had an inter-hunt quiz at Santon Bridge Hotel between the Melbreak; Eskdale and Ennerdale and the Coniston – a very happy evening was had by all! The Coniston came out on top at Quiz

Hunting season was finished and it was back to shepherding for me at Nook End Farm and waiting for our summer activities to start. There were getting to be more and more little Hound Shows about in Lakeland, another big one has got off the ground at Lowther. The Judges at the Rydal Hound Show were Captain C.G.E. Barclay M.F.H. and Mr A. Jackson M.F.H. South Dorset and we had Mr R. Bigland, Chipping Norton, judging terriers. The Visitors Challenge Trophy for the best Group went to the Eskdale and Ennerdale. Coniston got a first and third in Unentered Dog Hounds.

The season 1974–75 came round and got a start in the middle of September, soon enough, them many brackens good for hiding 'lile foxes.' On 26 September up at the Kirkstone Valley a young fox or two about, got two – were lucky. A fella said to me, 'Them dogs ran well!' I spoke sharp at him and told him they were hounds. I used to hate hearing hounds called dogs – it is not English!

On 5 October we were at Knott House Farm, Grasmere loused into Planting behind the farm, very thick place, only hounds could get in but soon gave tongue and two foxes came out. Foxes out of that wood, always took off out to high fells, Great Rigg and Fairfield. If they did that hunters were left far behind, it was a long way out that top, as hounds got after one fox and away they went and the hunt came to an unsatisfactory end, bad scenting.

On the opening hunt 12 October 1974 went onto Loughrigg, put a fox off at Fox Ghyll, went down into Rydal Farm meadows, crossed the main Ambleside to Keswick road, it was the start of a very unusual route. The hunt was never fast but kept going, very raggy morning out Rydal, Scandale, Dod Bields crossing Kirkstone Pass onto Rough Sides, scenting very catchy amongst them stone beds out past Old Marks Monument over Caudle Moor to Black Crag, where scent gave out altogether, no reward for hounds. He must have been an old stager!

Harry Hardisty retired from being huntsman of the Melbreak Foxhounds and on 24 October 1974 the followers of that hunt had a Testimonial Do for him. A busload went from out of the Coniston country to help to give him a good send off. Pritchard Bland, who had been whip to Harry, stepped up to huntman.

On Saturday, 23 November at High Green, Troutbeck after having the hospitality of Nell and Charlie Clark, we went onto Wansfell, holed a fox twice and was bolted by 'Maysh' who did well for a young terrier. Caught fox below Queens Head Hotel, the terrier got a bit of a mauling, a very savage fox. I don't know what we would do without these good terriers.

The following week from Winster had a fast hunt onto Whitbarrow and off again (which was not so very often) to Low Gregg Hall, Underbarrow and went to ground in a big badger set in a dyke back. Peter Martin's terrier Rose, worked well, bolted one fox and caught it and grubbed another out, so must have been one lying in. After that hounds were running on Whitbarrow till dark, that made them footsore on the rough limestone.

Hounds had a very rough week and I'm sure they were glad to be back at Ambleside Kennel at the weekend. Some hounds had a wonderful homing instinct. If they were missing at the end of a hunt, they perhaps would not go to the Kennels but go to where they had been summered or brought up at. There were two from Kentmere, Ruby from Hartrigg; Gambler from Rook How; Dinah from Hawkshead; Teddy Casson's

Music from Mrs Shepherd's at Sawrey and Brandy from Brian Garsides. If they were missing you always knew where to find them, wonderful how they did it.

Christmas Eve, Jerry Hunt when we were going to louse, a fox was walking about in the fields under Helm Crag, so we after him, hounds pushed him hard round the fell and down onto Loughrigg and went to ground at Tarnfoot Farm. After a bit of good terrier work he bolted. A grandstand view was had by all, as they raced him around Loughrigg Tarn, we thought he was going to boss them but the flyers caught sight of him and rushed inbank and was rolled over in the open, a good finish!

On New Years Day 1975, after being at Sammy Garsides to let the New Year in had a good party the next day, 'Up to the Duck to join the fray,' but the day wasn't much good – no scenting all day – could not fairly get on terms with a fox all day, useless.

On 10 January 1975 we had a Hunt Ball at Crosthwaite at which £70 was made and went into the Hunt Funds. Next morning the meet was at Crosthwaite Green and start was made out Lords Lot. Soon had a fox on foot and did not run long before being caught in pigpens, used to be an awful spot once upon a time. Pigs and stink, lost many a fox in there, but nowt in it now all gorse and briars!

Had a 'long lait' for another, found another lying in, stood well back and out it shot like a bullet. I used to like to see Jacky (fox) trying to get away, putting some queer turns in, he did not seem to be going fast for the first hundred yards, but always had his wits about him, if he came to a wall he always knew where there was a smoot (hole). Hounds would always rush for the place, find out they could not get through and would then have to jump the wall, by then he was out of sight and then would have to hunt. As it was this day, after that hunting was sometime fast and also slow in the Crook, Underbarrow countryside. Hounds put him off afresh on Bell Hill back by Bonfire Hall, it was a breast high scent as night was falling and he tried to out wit his pursuers by climbing onto a garage roof but that was no place to hide and hounds soon had him – the end of a perfect day! The gamekeeper fetched out a bottle of whisky – was good! Had a good crack and sing song that night at Strawberry Bank.

On the last day of January 1975 found us at Bark House, Witherslack, wet morning, got wet through but dried out before dark, ran foxes about on Whitbarrow all day, just dodging about in front of hounds till late on in the afternoon when scenting seemed to mend (as it often does) and one fox took off and out to Underbarrow. When hunters arrived daylight had gone but found hounds walking back finished and wondered what had happened at Scar Foot. Too dark to start and look but the fox was found next day, hounds had caught him in the dark. As I said before there are not many foxes caught in dark.

On Saturday from Woodland we found a fox in the old Pits at Ash Ghyll, let two terriers in both belonging to Peter Martin – Rose and Maysh, he would not bolt and died underground. Peter Martin, Johnny Birkett and Nutey dug him out, seven feet down in soil hole, so they had a good grub till ten o'clock at night. Rose got a bit of a mauling – bad fox!

One meet we had at Keen Ground, Hawkshead, home of Mr Heaton whose father had been the Master of Oxenholme Staghounds, when they were on the go, now gone, defunct! Put a fox off right away from his little planting, after a fast hunt round about, hounds bowled him over. I said to the followers, we would try a bit of fresh ground, so went to Spika Wood at Outgate and held a good fox, had a great hunt and a very unusual finish at a place called Sawrey Ground. The 'Sly un' was hard pressed, he climbed onto a peat house roof and went down the chimney but could find no hiding place in there, as hound got in after him and finished him of in the peat house – a queer place to finish!

During the season we lost two good hunt supporters. One, Jack Park, who with his wife had put up huntsman and hounds when in the Witherslack area, and Joe Gregg of Millbeck Farm, Langdale. He had walked some very good hounds for the pack, including Friendship, Ringwood and Rival being some of them. He was a very noted sheep farmer. When I first knew him, he was at Baisbrown Farm, Langdale, he then went to Jaw House, Eskdale and returned to Millbeck Farm, from where he retired and the farm was taken over by his son Victor. We used to go there towards the end of each season. Him and I walked miles looking for cubs with old Ringwood, he was a good hand at finding them, he used to look all the borrans, never went past one. During the war years he had a dog of Mr Gregg's called Bob, caught many a fox. He used to delight in telling the tales about the hunts and kills they had.

One lamb worrying call that spring at High Yewdale Farm, put a fox off in Far End breast, went out Coniston fells, split out there, one half went out over the skyline, the others benked their fox in Brim Fell, a very bad place, we could see him curled up watching us below. Hounds were got back out of the place. After a long wait he peedled (sneaked) out. Ran back with hounds and got after him again and had a great hunt after. The hounds that were there were Ruler, Budget, Magic, Sweeper, Bridgeman, Mischief and Treaty. I'll just mention the places they past. Hookrigg,

Jack Park and Anthony having a laugh

Threadale, Ladstone, Yewdale Crag, White Ghyll, Lime Kiln where two more hounds joined in. Truant and Rachel, a bit more weight cross-ing the main Coniston road out Guards, Fell End, High Cross to Sawrey Ground, where they chivved him about the plantings and was caught by 'speed of foot' – real good finish!

Called out to lamb worrying at Brimmer Head, Grasmere on 19 April, struck a drag out of the lambing field, the fox had never (laid down) as the music of the hounds soon changed to a gone fox – out Sour Milk Ghyll (a ghyll right named because it always looks white) out Blakerigg into Langdale by way of the Pikes. Hounds were now giving foxy some-thing to do, as they pressed inbank to Dungeon Ghyll across and caught before reaching Oak How Borran, a noted stronghold on Lingmoor.

We found another fox and holed in a badger set at Lancrigg. Now from 1930–40 we had never heard tell of a badger in this countryside. The first I heard about was when Ernie Parker was hunting hounds dur-ing the war, when hounds marked in a borran in Forest Side in 1942 and out this thing shot, gave everybody a shock because one had never been seen before. What a 'helluva' carry on then, there was also two young badgers in the same place, from then on they are all over the country, ranker than foxes. There is nobody who will tell me they do no damage!

To finish the season 1974–5 went to Millbeck, Great Langdale, very dry weather but ran a fox about the fell tops and lost the scent at

Gimmers Crag. Quite a few Heythrop people up. Chris Ogilvie left the Coniston to go and hunt the Lochaber Foxhounds. I did not think it was a good thing on his part, as he was a single man and would have to look after himself and the spot would get a bit lost but he went and that was it. The fellow who had been there Mark Forster, who had been hunting those hounds for four seasons came to be my whipper-in. Another thing I did not like about the job was they used the hounds to put foxes out of the forestry that would be surrounded by guns, all they could call them was a 'Vermin Pack'. I was one of the people that went up there the first time there had been any hounds, that was when the Melbreak went and all the farmers thought the hounds would worry all the sheep. That was the idea they had about the job.

Getting back to Heythrop people, Captain Wallace was up one morning when we were at Millbeck Farm and set off with me out toward White Ghyll but could not keep up and I looked around and he was going down a scree on his backside, I bet he was blurdy frightened! The hounds had put a fox off and run him to ground at Chapel Stile after a fast hunt. I could hear them marking from the top of Megs Ghyll and whilst making my way down to them, I thought to myself, I wonder where Captain Wallace is and to my amazement he was there with the hounds, a huntsman of instinct.

Snow on the fells

146

XVIII

My Last Season as Huntsman

That spring I told Mr Logan I would only hunt hounds another season and would finish at the end of next season, 1976, and Mark Forster would take over. We had one casualty when out hunting, Rascal fell out of Raven Crag up Langdale and died soon after. We had two litters of puppies that backend, one lot out of Remedy by Lunesdale Trimmer, a good job we had, as she got killed on the road at Bowness on 27 November 1975. The other litter were out of Brilly by our own Leader.

We had started hunting again towards the end of September. On 6 October 1975 we went to Jack Inman's, Crook Farm, Torver, his grandfather was a great hunting man in my father's days. Struck a drag out towards High Ground, not fast but persevered with the line and a fox jumped up out of the brackens. After a good round, out Coniston high fells the hounds brought him back into the bottoms and ran from 'scent to a view' and was rolled over at Park Gate. There was a fox or two about, so tried on again, bits of hunt here and there, till we reached 'Lile Arrow Intake.' Another grand hunt took place for one and half hours and was killed in Blaithwaite Coppice, he went as stiff as a tree right away which shows hounds had run foxy very hard. A bonny day and a good show of foxes, that's something!

Our opening meet was again at the home of our Master, Mr B. Logan and his wife Mary. There was a good gathering of hunting folk. After a drink and a lile crack we made our way onto Loughrigg by way of Pelter Bridge. It was a very bonny day, sun shining, put a fox off but could never press him, as scenting was very bad amongst the brackens and woods, so the fox had the better of us, good job they do sometimes.

On Monday 10 November at Coniston Hall and for remainder of the week. I was looking forward to staying there as we had always stayed at either the Ship Inn or Heathwaite Farm, as my father, when he was huntsman always stayed with auld Willie Inman. But it was not to be for me, as I was struck down with flu and Mark Forster was in charge and had plenty of hunting. I was back again after about a week, blurdy hard work. Hounds by now were running into fettle again. We were getting more and more meat every season, so the farmers must have been loosing more stock, that was our gain and good for hounds. We were nearly always able to take boiled flesh away with us when we were hunting our respective district each week.

4 December – Park Ground, Torver went to louse at Crook Farm, very misty but scenting was good, Leader found a fox in some whins and others joined in out Banniside, Walna Scar, hounds were now running in the mist so had to go by sound as they climbed out Coniston Old Man. I thought that's it for today, as they went out of hearing but no luck was with us, as we next heard hounds coming in at the 'Pernals', been right round behind the notorious Dow Crags. Could tell a very fast hunt now and coming inbank all the time, down Ash Ghyll, when they came out of the mist to my delight and giving foxy some stick across Bullham Moss into Torver Park Woods. Could tell there was a beaten fox in front and after twisting and twining about was caught amongst some briers. A bonny day now, mist had gone, so tried onto some fresh ground and found a fox lying in at White Hoghouse.

A terrier called Toby gave him a bit of a shake up and then stood well back, came out like a 'bat out of hell.' 'Hoo git away' right inbank to Coniston village, had a bit of a check but cast forward and struck the hunt again and out Mouldry Bank. A good hunt was seen by the villagers' inbank to Holywath Gardens where the hunt worsened and fetched hounds to their noses. (I'll have to put a bit in about Hollywath Garden. Once caught a fox in there. Lile Lant was there, picked the fox up but soon dropped it, as it bit his backside!). Foxy climbed out Mealy Ghyll and Dixon Ground fields. Brilly and Leader doing some good work up the fields and Scrow to Bell Borran. He'll have thought 'I will be at home now, a strong place.' I had a little terrier, Jack Russell type, belonging to Mrs Logan. Let her in and out foxy bolted again. I used to tell followers, when a fox bolts from a strong place, keep quiet and don't shout until it gets out of the borran because if you do nine times out to ten foxy will dart back in again and that's the last you'll see of that fox, but everybody kept quiet this day and when he struck green ground we gave it a loud 'Hallo!' What a chase then inbank passing Heathwaite Farm crossing Coniston to Torver road into the fields by the school where he was 'hallo'd' by the school children, good for them, to Waterhead and to the Wigwam (green spot but rightly named), over the Guards to Low Yewdale, crossing main road again into Scroggs Wood where he began to creep about in the undergrowth but was to no advantage, as he was

Opening meet at Nook End

forced to leave and then spent a bit of time about Curdale Dub but Brilly, Brandy and Bridgeman forced him out and into Scroggs Wood again. By now hounds and followers looking for him just in front and was pulled down behind Old Melly's House, what a great days sport was had by all!

We had some grand Christmas and New Year's hunting, I used to like it then, always plenty of followers. I can't put them all in but Jerry Hunt 1975, an inch of snow on fell tops, put a fox off on Helm Crag and ran it out Green Combe, along the top of Langstrath, High White Stones to Gimmer Crag in Langdale, down Dungeon Ghyll to Raw Head Breast, the hunt had only been moderate through here to Speddy Crag where the 'sly un' got up again. A fast hunt back to Thrang Quarries where old Magic fell to her death. Soon after hounds were run out of scent, walked a long way that day.

In April 1975 I lost an old school friend, Jack Abbot, an Ambleside man, who got to the rank of Chief Inspector in the Police Force. His parents kept the Royal Oak Hotel at Ambleside whenever he had any time off he was back at home and out hunting. When we had any do's he did his part by singing that old song 'Under the spreading chestnut tree the village smithy stands!' He was killed in a car crash outside Ulverston – tragic!

I must put this one in, as it was my last Boxing Day as huntsman, caught four foxes, good day for a large crowd of people. First fox found in Cooksons Wood but soon went to ground, stood back and a good bolt – a fast chase after that round Loughrigg. He must have been feeling the effects of the fast run as he 'clapped' (lay down) on the top and stayed too long as hounds then 'viewed him' and caught an old dog fox. We then tried on above Tarn Foot when another jumped up out to the brackens, what a carry on, then right inbank through the woods and went to ground under a tennis court at Brathay Fell. We had been there before but did not bother to let a terrier in as I thought if the terrier got fast under it, we would have had a big job to get the terrier out.

It being Boxing Day I thought I would let a terrier in at the top end and kept everybody back from the then outlet, the drain running under the tennis court was six foot down but hoped for the best and within minutes of the terrier being let in, out two foxes came 'bang on' together. Hounds got after both and split one with Lawyer and a few more (but he was boss of the lot). Ran one about the gardens viewing it quite often, amongst all the excitement nobody went after the others till after a while, hounds and fox was trying to get back into the drain but was turned away and was caught on the main road at Brathay. Another fox was

Anthony and the next generation of hunt followers at an opening meet at Nook End

caught at Halfway House and another fell to Scamp a very good black and white terrier. So a good time had by all young and old!

20 February 1976 on, Cartmel Fell, was a very misty morning and on a day like that you have to trust your hounds as in that country there are also hares, roe and red deer, so when I heard Chanter give mouth, I knew a fox was on foot so we 'harked hounds' (supporters shouted them on) to him and away they went by Gummers How crossing to Ashlea Plantation forward to Tow Top, where the hunt had slowed down to walking speed. Peter Martin a keen fellow caught up with them by help of a lift and he kept hounds going as far as Lindale, with perseverance by hounds and man put the fox off again. In by Sunny Green, Halecat Woods onto Yewbarrow, Whitbarrow to Lords Seat, hounds split up as other foxes got to stirring. Fifteen kept together after running fox in by High Low Wood Farm crossing the Winster Valley and onto Kit Crag he must have had a rest as hunt mended and about turned onto Whitbarrow again. Whitbarrow is six miles long and two miles wide – all limestone and goes for hounds' feet! Round the top end by the old lime kiln back by Black Yews, Witherslack Hall onto Yewbarrow, off again to Jack Phillipson's at Beck Head across the bottoms again and was 'pulled down' at Kirkett

Queens Head

Nook, an old dog fox and knew a lot of ground, twenty-five miles as hounds ran, six hours – good for them to stick to it!

28 February 1976 Mayor's Hunt, Troutbeck, an all ticket do now to keep out the so and so's. Mike Pattinson was the Mayor, a very bad misty morning but hounds put a fox off at Robin Crag, crossed Kirkstone Road out Woundale and lost them for the day.

30 March, Low Wood Hotel, a long draw to Robin Crag and unkennelled (good put off) there Lightning and one or two more, ran a fox into a grike on Kirkstone Pass and was accounted for. Lost another fox at Beckstones, Patterdale. Mr Dermot Kelly and friends with us that day.

On Saturday 27 March staying with Mr and Mrs Stilling, went onto Back Common, Torver, tried through above Roselea Thorn and crossed the road Coniston to Torver at Little Arrow. Had no touches of any hunt till into Blaithwaite Coppice when a fine dog fox jumped up put a circle of the wood before going out Smart Field and outrake (near the top) ground by Long Ouse in by Cat Borran, hounds by now had found their stride and gave him no peace by Blaithwaite across to Brackenbarrow fields passing Hoathwaite Farm through Low Park Wood. Brandy, Bridgeman, Brilly, Winsome, Wonder, Leader, Lancer being some of the hounds pressing him hard, passing Spoon Hall and Heathwaite meadows out Stonegate down Scrow and Mines Ghyll, by now they were making Coniston ring with the music of the hounds, as they landed in the Station yard and into the village and overtook their quarry in Waverley House garden – good do!

It was now getting to the end of my last season but there was still things to happen that had never happened before in my fifty years' association with Coniston Foxhounds. It happened on 1 May 1976, lamb worrying call, to Heathwaite Farm, Coniston. Loused out at Level Field, struck a drag right away and after a fox out Bell Crag, out Old Man Breast and back into Brandy Crag rubbish tip. We have had many a fox in there and let terriers in and could never hear them but this day a terrier called Rose belonging to Peter Martin was tried. Kept hounds and folk well back same as we had always done. After a while could hear Rose baiting and then all went quiet, though same things happened again. Then after about an hour, in that time never heard it again. When all at once a fox bolted, never been known before, nobody alive could remember one bolting before, but it was to no avail as the fox saved its brush by going into Brossen Stone rubbish tip and had to be left. A great credit to the terrier it came out two hours later, owner real set up with the terrier.

Once whilst walking down the Old Man road a car coming up, it stopped and a lady started talking to me. I thought I knew her face and lo and behold it was Thora Hird, the actress, had a good crack with her, she thought what a wonderful job it must be hunting on the Lakeland fells.

On 12 May we were called out to Wallend Farm, in Langdale, loused out Kettle Crag and put a fox off and went to Blakerigg and out by Red Tarn through Crinkle Crags, rough going through there. Hounds were running foxy hard by Three Tarns and the Chains of Bowfell, very rough going out there, access of nothing else but stones and boulders. Very rough hail showers that morning but they did not bother the hunting, so hounds pressed on. Next hounds were heard coming in off Bowfell.

Mayor making in the early 1970s – Bruce Logan with Dick Black

Rattling hunt through Bleaberry Coves and into Crinkle Ghyll where the 'sly un' benked in the crag in the ghyll side, a very steep and rough place but was forced to leave after a while and was rushed inbank and was caught at the footbridge at bottom of 'L Ghyll' (L-shape D) a fine old dog fox. They were always fine big foxes out there.

It was getting to the end of the season but on 18 May 1976 we were called out to Low Wood, losing lambs, a slow 'drag' in the fields and into Skelghyll Woods put two foxes off together and hounds split one lot, ran a fox to Brotherswater, a six and a half mile point, but were unlucky not to catch him. The other half pack ran a fox to ground in Dove Nest Fields and so it being a lamb worrier it got no mercy and was accounted for, had a grub to get it out, very deep. CaptainWallace of the Heythrop was about that day and always tells people that he was there on my last day as Huntsman to the Coniston Foxhounds, and so he was!

I had had a good innings from 1926 when I used to help my father to 1932 when I became whipper-in and 1944 when I became huntsman. I have enjoyed my life through three animals – the fox, foxhound and the working terrier. I had 325 hounds the time I was huntsman. I used to try and make them all alike, some was good at one job and some another.

Mark Forster took over from Anthony as Huntsman

Coniston supporters and many others gave to my Testimonial and I was presented with a colour television, a silver rose bowl, two pictures, a table, a cheque and a silver hunting horn from my Master, Mr Bruce Logan, for which I am most grateful to everybody.

In 1983 – Anthony's coat, whip, boots, were put into a glass frame, with a plaque and presented to the Golden Rule in Ambleside and hung there on the wall. It has recently gone to the Armitt Museum to be on display.
Left to right is the family: Mavis, Ann, Nicola, Annie (Anthony's widow), Michael, Helen (kneeling) Mr Bruce Logan and Edward.

156

XIX

Farewell and Tribute

IN 1977 I WAS MADE MAYOR OF TROUTBECK at the annual Mayor making ceremony at the Queens Head Hotel taking over from the retiring Mayor, Mr Mike Pattinson. This was a break with tradition, as it was usually somebody from the village. I had been chosen by the retiring Mayor, Mike Pattinson and the hunt followers were suited with the choice.

I was a founder member of Ambleside Sports and had laid half of the old hound trails for thirty years without a break, so retired from that job as well and was presented with a silver tray by the Association. It was a bit of a wrench giving over but I have enjoyed life since, hunting with all the Fell Packs and others in England, Scotland and Wales. Always have a great week's hunting with the Border Foxhounds, Frank Atkinson and myself staying with Mr and Mrs Angus Logan, at South Riccalton Farm, near Jedburgh, a great hunting country – foxes have to have plenty of stamina to get away from them hounds. Mark Foster took over as hunts-man.

The above paragraph was the last that Anthony wrote when writing his memoirs so I must finish where he left of. Anthony continued to enjoy life as much as possible and had a smallholding at Waterhead, Ambleside called Wansfell where he kept over seventy Swaledale sheep.

Anthony sadly died on the night of Monday 27 December 1982 after attending the Boxing Day hunt over Loughrigg with his own Coniston pack. He was buried at St. Mary's Church, Ambleside on Friday, 31 December 1982.

There is no suitable or better epitaph than to finish with the one Anthony received from Mr Bruce Logan, Master of the Coniston Foxhounds from 1954 to 1976 and was published in the paper for all to read and acknowledge.

'St Mary's Church, Ambleside, was filled to capacity last Friday to witness a moving scene when to the strains of John Peel the late Anthony Chapman was borne shoulder high by the six scarlet coated fell hunt-men and finally laid to rest with the sound of the horn from Johnnie Richardson, the senior fell huntsman.

This very large congregation was proof of the high esteem in which he was held. His cheerful, vivacious personality and great natural charm, which has always been a strong characteristic of the Chapman family, endeared him to everyone he met. His great enthusiasm for life was transmitted to the hounds he hunted and also to the hunt followers; and often after a long hard day his resilence and wonderful voice instilled new life into both.

He excelled at public relations always having time to stop and talk to people of all walks of life and of all ages. He was extremely fond of children and nothing gave him greater pleasure than to be accompanied by them during a day's hunting, always making sure that none of the younger ones got left behind. He was a great believer in encouraging the young to hunt knowing that the future of hunting would lay in their hands.

To me he was a life-long friend, loyal huntsman and mentor. The long family connection between the Logans and Chapmans, which must be unique, started in 1892 when my great uncle, the late W.B. Logan, became Master of the Windermere Harriers and Anthony Chapman's grandfather, also called Anthony, was huntsman. This connection stretched continuously through three generations until his retirement in 1976.

'His deeds they will oft be related in song
And though he has gone to that haven of rest
We will cherish his memory as one of t he best.'

Sadly Annie, Anthony's widow died five years later on 2 May 1987 and this year on 7 June 2004 Mr Bruce Logan sadly died of cancer.

Anthony and Annie's three children all married. Edward married Christine and lives in Kendal and has a daughter called Hayley. Mavis married Gerald Nicholson and lives in Ambleside and has two sons, who are both huntsmen. The oldest Anthony is with the Derwent Foxhounds, in Yorkshire. Their second son, Michael is huntsman with the Coniston Foxhounds. Ann married Malcolm Parsons and they have two daughters, Nicola and Helen. Ann was Master of the Coniston Foxhounds from 1990–99.

So a chapter in our hunting history has concluded but nevertheless hunting is still continuing as strong as ever in the Lake District fells and the Chapmans are still carrying on in the family tradition.

Fred Nevinson in his book *A Westmorland Shepherd*, his life, poems and songs' dedicated a poem to his memory and I think it is only fitting to end Anthony's book with it as it shows how well thought of and loved he was.

Tribute to a Huntsman

I sing you a song of a Huntsman
A man we all thought so grand
When he hunted the Coniston Foxhounds
He was the best in the land
Round Scandale, Rydal and Grasmere
He hunted with many a friend
And on every fell that he hunted
He knew every rock and hill end.

So we'll all bid farewewll to our Chappie
No more a hunting he'll go
But as long as we live we'll remember
The sound of his view Tally Ho!

Those Coniston Foxhounds they adored him
In his terriers he took great pride
When he set off to hunt in the morning
Everyone would be at his side
Through all the years we have hunted
Our pleasure it knew no bounds
When we hunted with Anthony Chapman
And his gallant Coniston Hounds.

Chorus

He was one of Lakeland's great Sportsmen
Like those whose songs we have sung
But the songs that we sing about Chappie
Will be in our own Lakeland tongue
He was respected by each one who knew him
And where he'll be now is quite plain
I know I will give a great 'Hallo!'
If somewhere I meet him again.

Chorus

159

Glossary (Hunting terms and dialect)

After a hound giving mouth	sending the other hounds to it
Allotment	a piece of ground with a wall or fence right round it
Baiting	barking at fox
Benk	ledge on crag
Borran	rocks/stone heaps
Bottoms	lowland
Braided on	encouraged
Brayed	continued
Breast	hillside
Brush	fox's tail
Charlie	fox
Chivved him	encouraged
Clapped	fox layed down
Clink	split or crack
Couples/coupled	hounds or terriers coupled up when out (chain attached to collars)
Connies	rabbits
Crack	talk
Cry	noise of hounds
Drag	smell of the fox
Draw	go on to find a fox
Duck Hunt	Drunken Duck Inn (near Hawkshead)
Earth or settle earth	foxhole
Feathered about	working it out
Fred Karno's	chaotic concert troup during WW1
Fettle	fitness
Fox off	set it running
Gay stuff	awful food
Give mouth	hounds bark

Given law	freedom or space
Gocks (by gocks)	exclamation
Gone to ground	fox gone done hole (holed)
Good do	good party or whatever
Good marker	hound will stand and mark
Good unkennel	good put off
Gowling	hound howl
Grand school	group
Grike	opening – where rock has split open
Grub it out	dig it out
Hallo/Hallo'd	anyone seeing the fox will shout and hounds understand
Harking hounds	telling them to go forward
Hark For'ard	same as above
Harriers	between a foxhound and a beagle
Harvel	drink or celebration
Hask	dry and windy
His mask	fox's head
Hoo git away	sending hounds on
H.T.A.	Hound Trailing Association
Huntsman	Person in charge of the hounds
Inbank	coming down the hill
Intakes	area of low ground surrounded by wall
Jacky	fox
Jerry Hunt	Travellers Rest, Grasmere
Joining chorus	all hounds joining in singing
Lait/laiting	looking for
Laiter	good finder
Lile	small
Loused (loosed)	let the hounds go
Long draw	long time finding fox
Long lait	long time looking for the fox
Lying in	fox in hole or earth
Marker –Good marker	hound will stand and bark – gone to ground different sound
Mart	Pine Martin
Master	person in overall charge of the hunt – head

Meet	organised gathering of hounds and followers to go hunting setting of from a named location
Mended	got better
M.F.H.	Master of Fox Hounds
Music	hounds speaking
Not much mouth	not much of a barker
Nowt	nothing
Outrake	near the top
Plantings	trees
Pussy	hare
Quarry	prey or game – stone or slate excavation
Reynard	fox
R.A.O.B.	Royal Antediluvian Order of Buffalo
Savins	gorse
Scent to view, view to kill	follow the scent until the fox is seen and from seeing – catching and killing
Scratted in	dogs dug with their paws
Scrow	mess
Scullard	encourage
Shanks pony	on foot
Sheepfolds	pens
'Sly un'	sly fox
Smittle spot	usually find a fox
Sowed in	joined in
Smoot	hole
Spree up	drinks
Squarkey mouthed	Squeaky
Stern of dog	tail
Stickheaps	woods
Stowing job	boring job
Straight necked un'	does not deviate
The band	across the hillside
Testimonial	expression of appreciation/ gratitude
To sing	hounds all sing together
Traipes	long walk

Trencher pack	Out at farms end of May to September Not permanently kennelled for hunt
Tried	try
Trods	tracks/narrow footpaths worn away by sheep
Try away up. Hark too	sending them out looking for the fox
Trying forward	going forward
Unkennelled	good put off
Viewing	to see
Went to ground	fox in a hole
Whins	gorse/thorns
Whip/Whipper-in	assistant/apprentice huntsman
Yauked	attacked

SELECTED ESSAYS OF WILSON HARRIS

The Unfinished Genesis of the Imagination

Expeditions into cross-culturality; into the labyrinth of the family of mankind, creation and creature; into space, psyche and time

Introduced and edited by A.J.M. Bundy

London and New York

*For Margaret
and to my daughter, Denise*

First published 1999
by Routledge
11 New Fetter Lane, London EC4P 4EE

Simultaneously published in the USA and Canada
by Routledge
29 West 35th Street, New York, NY 10001

© 1999 edited by Andrew Bundy

Typeset in Baskerville by RefineCatch Limited, Bungay, Suffolk
Printed and bound in Great Britain by
TJ International Ltd, Padstow, Cornwall

British Library Cataloguing in Publication Data
A catalogue record for this book is available from the British Library

Library of Congress Cataloging in Publication Data
Harris, Wilson.
[Essays. Selections]
Selected essays of Wilson Harris / edited by Andrew Bundy.
p.   cm. – (Readings in postcolonial literatures; 1)
Includes bibliographical references and index.
1. Bundy, Andrew, 1962–   . II. Title.   III. Series.
PR9320.9.H3A6   1999
814–dc21   98–38477
CIP

ISBN 0–415–19565–9 (hbk)
ISBN 0–415–19566–7 (pbk)

CONTENTS

ACKNOWLEDGEMENTS

Five essays appeared in previous collections by Wilson Harris: 'History, Fable and Myth in the Caribbean and the Guianas' is the revised version edited by Selwyn R. Cudjoe and published by Calaloux Publications, Wellesley, Mass. in 1995. It first appeared as a monograph published by The National History and Arts Council of Guyana in 1970, and subsequently in *Explorations, A Selection of Talks and Articles 1966–1981* edited by Hena Maes-Jelinek and published by Dangaroo Press in 1981. The three essays from *The Womb of Space:* 'Reflections on Intruder in the Dust in a Cross-cultural Complex', 'The Schizophrenic Sea', and 'Concentric Horizons', appeared with Greenwood Press in 1983, an imprint of Greenwood Publishing Group, Inc., Westport, CT, USA. 'Tradition and the West Indian Novel' is the monograph version published by the West Indian Student's Union in 1964. It also appeared in the essay collection *Tradition, the Writer and Society* published by New Beacon Books, London and Port of Spain in 1967 and reprinted in 1973.

Three essays appeared in previous essay anthologies on Wilson Harris: 'Quetzalcoatl and the Smoking Mirror: Reflections on Originality and Tradition' was an address to the Temenos Academy, London, delivered in 1994 and published in the Wilson Harris issue of *The Review of Contemporary Fiction*, Summer 1997. 'Literacy and the Imagination' comes from *The Literate Imagination: Essays on the Novels of Wilson Harris*, edited by Michael Gilkes and published by Macmillan in 1989. 'Benito Cereno' was published in *Wilson Harris: Enigma of Values* edited by Kirsten Holst Petersen and Anna Rutherford and published by Dangaroo Press, Aarhus, Denmark in 1975.

The following are transcribed addresses: 'Merlin and Parsifal: Adversarial Twins', an address to the Temenos Academy, London in March 1997, published by the Temenos Academy in November 1997. 'Aubrey Williams', the transcript of a seminar on Aubrey Williams held at the Institute of International Visual Arts (inIVA) in the October Gallery, London in January 1996 and published on pp.79–82 of *Third Text*, Spring 1996. 'Apprenticeship to the Furies', the keynote address for Festival Week at Cave Hill Campus, University of the West Indies, Barbados in March 1996. It appeared in *River City: Journal of Contemporary Culture*, Summer 1996 published by University of Memphis. 'The Unfinished Genesis of the Imagination', an address to the Temenos Academy, London in March 1992, transcribed on pp.69–85 of the review *Temenos* (No. 13), June 1992.

'The Music of Living Landscapes' is the original typescript from which the BBC Radio 4 broadcast of 12 November 1996 was prepared.

'Creoleness, The Crossroads of a Civilization?' appeared on pp.23–35 in *Caribbean Creolization, Reflections on the Cultural Dynamics of Language, Literature and Identity*, edited by K.M. Balutansky and M.-A. Sourieau, published by University Press of Florida and The Press, University of the West Indies in 1998. 'Profiles of Myth and the New World', on pp.77–86 of *Nationalism vs. Internationalism, (Inter)national Dimensions of Literatures in English*, edited by W. Zach and K.L. Goodwin, published by Stauffenburg Verlag, Tübingen in 1996. 'In the Name of Liberty', on pp.7–15 of *Third Text: Beyond the Rushdie Affair*, Special Issue, Summer 1990. 'Jean Rhy's "Tree of Life"', on pp.114–17 of *The Review of Contemporary Fiction*, Summer 1985, published by the Dalkey Archive Press.

The extracts and quotations from Wilson Harris's novels appear by permission of Faber and Faber: 'New Preface to *Palace of the Peacock*', from the re-issue of *Palace of the Peacock* in the new Faber Caribbean series edited by Caryl Phillips and published in 1998. 'Letter from Francisco Bone to W.H.', from the novel *Jonestown* (1996).

Quotations from Emma Jung are taken from p.377 of *The Grail Legend*, edited by Marie-Louise von Franz, translated into English by Andrea Dykes and published by Sigo Press, Boston, Massachusetts in 1986. Quotations from C.G. Jung come from p.3, and pp.102n–3n (para. 123, footnote 54) of *The Personification of the Opposites*, in the Collected Works Vol. XIV: *Mysterium Coniunctionis*, translated by R.F.C. Hull and published by Routledge, London in 1963; and from pp.3–4 of Lecture 1 (7 November 1928) in *Dream Analysis: Notes of the Seminars given in 1928–30*, edited by William McGuire and published by Routledge, London in 1984. Extract from Claude Lévi-Strauss is from *Saudades do Brasil*, pp.19–20 of *New York Review of Books*, December 21, 1995 and reprinted by permission of The University of Washington Press, Seattle. Quotations from Hena Maes-Jelinek come from the essay 'Charting the Uncapturable in Wilson Harris's Writing' which appeared on pp.92–3 of *The Review of Contemporary Fiction*, Summer 1997, published by the Dalkey Archive Press in 1997. Quotations from Stuart Murray come from the essay 'Postcoloniality/Modernity: Wilson Harris and Postcolonial Theory' which appeared on p.55 of *The Review of Contemporary Fiction*, Summer 1997, published by the Dalkey Archive Press in 1997. Extract from C.L.R. James comes from pp.12–14 of *Wilson Harris – A Philosophical Approach*, reprinted by permission of The Press, University of the West Indies, Port of Spain, Trinidad in 1965. Quotations from Arnold Toynbee are taken from *Chapter 13: Challenge and Response* on p.97 in *A Study of History*, abridged edition, published by OUP in 1972. Reprinted by permission of OUP.

Especial thanks are due to Professor Hena Maes-Jelinek for her preparation of the essay bibliography which appears here.

ACKNOWLEDGEMENTS

I am indebted to Sophie Powell, formerly at Routledge, for her invaluable steering of the publication, and to Kate Chenevix Trench at Routledge for bringing it to completion.

Map of Guyana with locations appearing in Wilson Harris's dream-territory of novels.

Note: the novels are numbered in the chronological order in which they appeared. Parentheses show dream-locations in the territory of Guyana. Nos 7, 12, 13, 15, 16 possess allusions (however hidden or indirect) to the dream-map and one might consider these novels to be instances where the dream-map of Guyana has been raised into other places.

1. *Palace of the Peacock*, 1960
   (1) Confluence of Essequibo, Cuyuni, Mazaruni Rs. and associated landscapes
   (1) Sorrow Hill, *Bartica*
   (1) Rupununi R. ('river of the savannahs')

2. *The Far Journey of Oudin*, 1961
   (2) East Coast, Demerara R.

3. *The Whole Armour*, 1962
   (3) Pomeroon R.   (3) Jigsaw Bay
   (3) Moruca R.   (3) Moruca

4. *The Secret Ladder*, 1963
   (4) Canje R.

5. *Heartland*, 1964
   (5) Cuyuni R. with intimations of the landscapes in *Palace of the Peacock* (1960)

6. *The Eye of the Scarecrow*, 1965
   (6) Georgetown
   (6) Raven's Head (intimations of Potaro and other interior landscapes)

7. *The Waiting Room*, 1967
   Transformations of substance into subtlety

8. *Tumatumari*, 1968
   (8) Tumatumari Fall in the Potaro R.

9. *Ascent to Omai*, 1970
   (9) Omai on the Essequibo R.

10. *The Sleepers of Roraima, A Carib Trilogy*, 1970
    (10) Mt. Roraima and landscapes of the Caribbean

11. *The Age of the Rainmakers*, 1971
    (11) The axis between the Kaiteur Falls and Mt. Roraima

12. *Black Marsden*, 1972
    Mostly Scotland and an element of South America

13. *Companions of the Day and Night*, 1975
    Mexico – ancient and modern
    New York

14. *Da Silva da Silva's Cultivated Wilderness* and *Genesis of the Clowns*, 1977
    London.
    (14) The Arbary R., East Coast, Demerara, and interior landscapes

15. *The Tree of the Sun*, 1978
    London seen through other 'eyescapes' and backgrounds, South American and Caribbean

16. *The Angel at the Gate*, 1982
    Mostly London, intimations of Jamaica

17. *Carnival*, 1985
    (17) Stabroek Market, Arawak clock: Georgetown

18. *The Infinite Rehearsal*, 1987
    Cosmic theatre is the magic word
    South American coastal landscapes of Guyana

19. *The Four Banks of the River of Space*, 1990
    (19) Potaro R.

20. *Resurrection at Sorrow Hill*, 1993
    (20) Sorrow Hill, *Bartica*
    (20) Confluence of Essequibo, Cuyuni, Mazaruni Rs. and associated landscapes
    (20) Rupununi R. ('river of the savannahs')

21. *Jonestown*, 1996
    (21) Albuoystown, *Georgetown*   (21) Port Mourant
    (21) New Amsterdam   (21) Jonestown (nr. Port Kaituma)

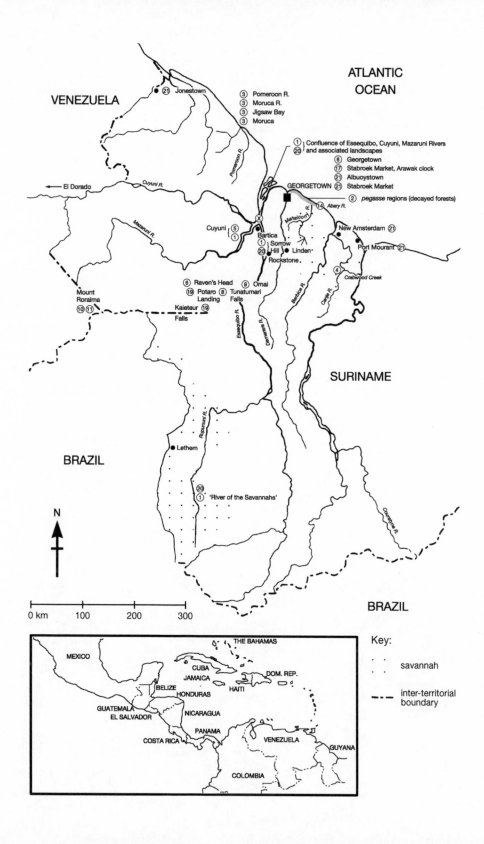

ATLANTIC
OCEAN

VENEZUELA

③ Pomeroon R.
③ Moruca R.
③ Jigsaw Bay
③ Moruca

① Confluence of Essequibo, Cuyuni, Mazaruni Rivers
⑳ and associated landscapes
⑥ Georgetown
⑰ Stabroek Market, Arawak clock
㉑ Albuoystown
㉑ Stabroek Market

② pegasse regions (decayed forests)

㉑ Jonestown

El Dorado ←

Cuyuni R.

Pomeroon R.

Mazaruni R.

GEORGETOWN

⑭ Abary R.

Mahaicony R.

Cuyuni
⑤
①

Bartica
① Sorrow
⑳ Hill
Rockstone

New Amsterdam ㉑

Port Mourant ㉑

Linden

⑥ Raven's Head
⑲ Potaro Landing
⑧ Tunatumari Falls
⑨ Omai

Berbice R.

Canje R.

④ Crabwood Creek

Mount Roraima
⑩ ⑪

Kaieteur ⑲ Falls

Essequibo R.

Demerara R.

SURINAME

Rupununi R.

Lethem

BRAZIL

⑳
① 'River of the Savannahs'

Courentyne R.

N

BRAZIL

0 km   100   200   300

THE BAHAMAS

MEXICO

CUBA
JAMAICA
HAITI
DOM. REP.

BELIZE
HONDURAS

GUATEMALA
EL SALVADOR
NICARAGUA
COSTA RICA
PANAMA

COLOMBIA

VENEZUELA

GUYANA

Key:

∴ savannah

– · – inter-territorial boundary

INTRODUCTION

The Anglo-Guyanese poet, novelist, dramatist and essayist, **Wilson Harris** belongs to that group of pre-eminent twentieth-century writers whose works address the vulnerability of the age and identify new areas of imaginative resource in the culture. Singular in conception and scope, Harris's literary art is a highly individual fusion of hidden traditions of the imagination, native cosmogonies, alchemy, dreams, quantum physics; parables of man in the living landscapes; the aboriginal religions and cultures of Central and South America; the great Western tradition; fables of history and society; Jungian archetypes; hypotheses on time and space, and much else. Known in England chiefly for his novels and essays, Harris stands somewhat outside the frames of the English novel or the writings of the Commonwealth diaspora. Wilson Harris's first novel was *Palace of the Peacock* (1960) and his most recent at the time of writing is *Jonestown* (1996). The aim of this volume is to match Harris's career in the novel with his lectures, addresses and essays, from 1960 to the present day, and to make available, in a single comprehensive reader, something of his critical range.

Born in 1921 in New Amsterdam, Berbice County, in what was then the colony of British Guiana, South America, Harris's own blood-mix reflects that of the Guyanese nation: English, Hindu Indian, Afro-Caribbean and indigenous Amerindian ancestors all contribute to Harris's antecedents, so that in his very genes Wilson Harris embodies cross-cultural community. It is a Creole melding characteristic of the region.

At the age of thirteen Harris won a place at Queen's College, Georgetown, where he received a classical education. Up to two years before Harris entered the college ancient Greek was still taught, and when Harris matriculated in 1938, among his subjects a distinction in Latin. Perhaps because of Harris's affinity for the classical tradition, he was especially aware of a certain impasse where that tradition had been adapted to play a part in the development of a more recent literary art: 'All in all I was uneasy about the traditionalist novel.'[1]

---

1 Letter from author to editor, 18/11/97.

INTRODUCTION

The development of the novel, a literary art of the modern era, is heavily indebted to ancient Greek epic poetry and to the tragic drama of Greece then Rome. A convention such as the symmetry of time and place (the *tempus-locus* or the equation of catastrophe with a specific hinging moment in time) gives plot or a pact with symmetry. In Sophocles, for instance, Oedipus strikes an old man dead in a dispute at a crossroads. With that action, at that hinging moment, Oedipus fulfils a prophecy. The old man is his father. Oedipus enters fate: the murder determines him. By the time Oedipus discovers his mistake, the act is lodged in the past. There is symmetry between the act and the past in such a way that space itself is coerced, space becomes consecutive, and Oedipus's displacements in space, the succession of deterministic events. The succession of deterministic events gives plot to the drama.[2] Thus an art of dialogue, written in the heightened language of poetry to be enunciated and dramatized, was being drafted at the beginning of the 1600s, to equip the novel where masque, performance and enunciation had to be relocated from the stage of the theatre to the stage of the reader's imagination: the poetry, performance and masque of the classical drama were literally flattened to the printed page of the novel. Masque, performance and enunciation had meant that the classical drama could afford plot in a way in which the novel could not; for where no arrival into a new conception of language is attempted, where the novel is content to tell its story in a more or less entertaining fashion, the plot or pact with symmetry will obliterate dimensionality. Pacts with symmetry cause the poetry, performance and masques of drama to collapse in the printed page. Unless the novelist breaks the pact with symmetry, art and its inherent dimensionality disappear. Harris sensed that the conventional novel, especially as it came to be realized in the nineteenth century, did not altogether fit, that other resources were called for: 'This unease [about the traditionalist novel] became profound when I became a topographical and hydrographic surveyor and began my work in the interior [of Guyana].'[3]

Harris experienced the interior of Guyana as a river and land surveyor in the

---

2 The secularisation of European drama at the beginning of the Modern era took the nine Roman tragedies of Seneca (*d.* 65 A.D.) as their model. The Senecan tragedy, itself styled on the drama of classical Greece half a millennium earlier, were studied for their plot-structures. They contributed a convenient narrative frame for the Jacobean theatre, and, arguably, for the picaresque movement in the early English novel and its preoccupations with the rogue or rake's progress. By the nineteenth century, the novel promoted a belief in conventional sequence and finite determinations in moral, ethic, and religious stances: texts that claim a ubiquitous reality founded on a clearly-defined way of seeing men and women, living from birth to death in a solid material world; a permanent and, because invariant, lifeless enchantment with the adventures of the empirical ego. When Harris made a study of the imagination in the classical American novel [see Chapter 7: *The Schizophrenic Sea* (1983)] and examined the language of the conventional fiction and compared it to the moral intention of the author he found that the diction pointed one way and the moral institution another, that the two were discontinuous and riddled and undermined the conventional mould.

3 Letter from author to editor, 18/11/97.

1940s. The interior speaks through a music of silence, a language of silence. The interior is also a living organism, an organum of forest, rocks, rivers and cataracts. The experience of the interior brought home to Harris that the picture we hold of reality, and its reification in the conventional novel, were unacceptably static, and that by continuing to believe them, we are actually damaging the fabric of the culture in ways that threaten our own survival: 'I have expressed this unease in diverse and various ways through the fictions I have written. The life of the landscape/riverscape/skyscrape is pertinent to the reality of place. That life differs from human life but is of invaluable importance.'[4]

For Harris, living landscapes enact charismatic parables of Being that gives them kinship with our own conception of ourselves in the universe. They are a medium through which we participate in a theatre of consciousness. It was in the wake of his encounter with the interior that, from 1945, Harris began to contribute poems and pieces of journalism to the Guyanese–Caribbean literary magazine *Kyk-over-al*.[5] He published two volumes of verse: *Fetish* in 1951 and *From Eternity to Season* in 1954, revised in 1978. Until his move to London in the spring of 1959, Harris was known, among the small, self-possessed intelligentsia of Guyana's capital city, Georgetown, chiefly for his poetry and for his critical dispatches inspired by the solitude of the bush. Harris's mentor was the poet and critic A.J. Seymour, editor of *Kyk-over-al* and a leading intellectual in British Guiana between the 1940s and 1970s.

Harris's early books of poetry are declarations of serious intent. They also show a strict apprenticeship to the literary medium. At a surface level, for instance, it is possible to identify the technique of using personae from the *Cantos* of Ezra Pound, specifically in the speech-mask of Pound's Tiresias Theban through which Harris writes *From Eternity to Season*. Equally, Harris's poem series *The Spirit of the Fall* refers to the formal arrangements of T.S. Eliot in *Four Quartets*, and behind Eliot, Milton's *Paradise Lost*. Yet a close reading will show that these resemblances are contingent and that six years later, when Harris makes his début in the novel, the profound celebration in his novel is taking place not with the modernists but rather with one of the inspirations for literary modernism, Dante. For to write a new cosmogony, to reconceptualize the world in a singular yet comprehensive manner, surely brings Harris closest, in community to the author of the *Divine Comedy*. It also gives the clue as to how best to think about Harris's literary art and its rich and complex architecture. Let us begin by outlining some signal aspects of the writing.

4 Ibid. Not to be confused with naturalism, the coercion of social forces to nineteenth-century Darwinian sciences; such accounts attempting (in the deployment of character) the justifications of individual action. By contrast, the language of living landscapes are parables (comparisons) read into an extended family of man.
5 *Kyk-over-al*, named after *Kyk-over-al*, or 'Look over all'. Dutch island-fort on the Mazaruni–Cuyuni confluence and seat of Dutch Government in Essequibo county from 1621 until sacked by the English in 1662.

3

A comparative reading between the novels and the critical writing might match the source of Harris's exploration of inner time with Heidegger's *Ich-Zeit* or 'I-Time' (*Being and Time*, 1927); or the dream book phenomenology of certain novels with the technical expositions in analytical psychotherapy by C.G. Jung.[6] The circumstances in which those dream books came to the author ('by legacy') might further be compared with the fictional means of concealing intention employed by Kierkegaard, whose *Either/Or* (1843) is published by a pseudonymous 'editor', who tells how he came upon the papers by accident. Harris's reversal of historic destiny might seem to continue the unfinished liberation from systematics of Hegel's assertion that 'The history of the world is none other than the progress of the consciousness of freedom' (opening phrase of *Lectures on the Philosophy of History*, 1823–7).

Throughout these notes we find productive readings of Harris in the full flower of European thought. In the interior of Guyana, in the music of the living landscapes, Harris read deeply in this philosophical tradition, although when one comes to read him, one does not get the impression of literary indebtedness. Rather, astounding originality configures the writing. It is informed yet original and far-reaching in ways that constantly surpass expectation.

Consider, for instance, what might be seen to be Harris's exposition of Jung's therapeutic technique called Active Imagination. Active Imagination aims to re-imagine a fragment of fantasy or dream motif through creative means. One must stay with the actuality of the dream motif – its character, incidence, comparative meaning in life, comparative meaning in the dream – one puts these together and looks at how they make an intimate translation of one's own life. One must avoid focusing on what 'occurs to one' concerning the motif, but instead concentrate on how the motif functions in the dream itself. That act of re-imagining can take place through formal verbal interpretation, or through dance, painting, or even through the search and discovery of an ancient myth which seems to match one's own life-pattern over time. It is a process that can be seen to have been reinvented in the set-up of Harris's novel *The Four Banks of the River of Space* (1990):

> Anselm gave me his manuscript in December 1989 on the eve of his departure for Brazil to attend a conference on the fate of the South American rainforests. It was his plan after to embark on another expedition into the Macusi heartland. I did not expect to see him again.
>
> He gave me permission to edit his book of dreams and to add epigraphs.[7]

What Harris does in *The Four Banks of the River of Space* is not merely to

---

6 In particular C.G. Jung, Collected Works, Vols. V, VIII, IX:2, XII, XIII, XIV, XVI and XVIII, Routledge, Princeton-Bollingen.
7 *The Four Banks of the River of Space*, London, 1990, p.xi.

re-imagine the life of Anselm the individual; the intervention on Anselm's manuscript is one which, through the fabric of epigraphy, will re-imagine the entire art
of the novel. To 'add epigraphs' is equivalent to writing the novel. The word
epigraph comes from the ancient Greek *epi* ('upon') and *graphein*, ('to write'); it is
literally a 'writing above' or a superimposing of one text over another, so that two
texts of distinct provenance are meeting and re-reading themselves through one
another.

Then there is Harris's central preoccupation with the role and resources of
intuition. We might define intuitive resource at both conceptual and technical
levels. Conceptually it might involve the bringing of gestures from the future into
the actions of the present. It might also be the memory of the past one will
unwittingly store in the future. How is this possible? When Harris came to study
the anthropology of the Americas in a thorough way at the end of the 1960s, he
found that, through the intuitive resource, he had already anticipated much of
those uncanny findings in his first group of novels:

> 'I became aware of the bone-flute some years after I had written *The
> Guyana Quartet* . . . This led me to research the articles of Walter Roth, an
> Australian anthropologist, who travelled in British Guiana in 1909 for
> the American Bureau of Ethnology, Washington, DC. I had heard of
> Roth in the 1940s when I began my surveying expeditions into the
> primeval rainforests of Guyana but never read him until long after when
> I was fortunate in the late 1960s and the 1970s to have the opportunity
> for research in specialist libraries in Canada and the United States.'[8]

At the time Harris was writing his early fiction, therefore, confirmation of the
significance of the Carib bridge-bone-flute lay as yet several years in the future.
In this way Harris was bringing gestures from the future into the actions of the
present. And until Harris wrote the novels, the memory of the past had been
unwittingly stored in the future, for the memory of the bone-flute artefact had
disappeared from the creative consciousness of indigenous Amerindians even
before Walter Roth's reports at the beginning of the twentieth century. Thus,
until Harris recuperated the Carib flute from *vergessen*,[9] knowledge of the flute
was unwittingly stored in the future.

The poetic imagination will also discover intuitive clues in the author's own
text that enable him to redraft the manuscript at more compelling levels. Such
clues operate at the technical level of redrafting and revising the manuscript. By
redrafting through verbal clues, those verbal clues permit the author to see, not
merely with vision but *into* vision. The intuitive clue in the culture is the theme of
Part IV of this volume.

---

8 *Preface* to *The Guyana Quartet*, London, 1984, p.9.
9 Ge. The state of forgetting.

One other determinant in the aesthetic power of Harris's writing is the sense of unusual personal accomplishment it communicates – an unusual freedom from personal bias, agenda or ideology. This strikes one as allowing an inclusive vision of all our condition and constitutes, I feel, the creative well-spring of the whole enterprise.

In the spring of 1959, newly arrived in London, Harris put the 'Timehri' or 'mark of the hand' on fate and literary destiny. The manuscript for *Palace of the Peacock* was literally plucked from the pile of unsolicited manuscripts at Faber and published a few months later. When *Palace* came out in 1960, Harris was nearly forty years old. *Palace* had followed three discarded attempts at the novel. In his own words he had, 'travelled in the heartland of Guyana when, after discarding three novels, I struck what I knew at last was the right note with which to commence the [Guyana] Quartet'.[10]

All this was taking place in a literary London which at the time was largely unaware of the decisive role already being exerted by mainland Central and South America – her legacy, her circumstance – on the outstanding fiction of the second half of the twentieth century. By the time Harris arrived, London had already played host to what could be called the West Indian New Wave – the Caribbean literary renaissance at the end of the 1940s and the 1950s. Literary London published and created an international forum to West Indian writers at a time when there was not a single serious publisher in the Caribbean,[11] yet it

10 Preface to *The Guyana Quartet*, London, 1984, p.9.
11 V.S. Reid's *New Day* (1949) is considered a seminal work in the development of Caribbean fiction. The first Caribbean novel to use Creole as narrative medium it anticipates the region's literary renaissance of the 1950s: from Barbados, George Lamming's *In the Castle of My Skin* (1953), *The Emigrants* (1954), *Of Age and Innocence* (1959), *Season of Adventure* (1960); from Trinidad V.S. Naipaul's *The Mystic Masseur* (1957), *Miguel Street* (1959) and *A House for Mr. Biswas* (1961); also from Trinidad, S.D. Selvon's *A Brighter Sun* (1952), *The Lonely Londoners* (1956); from Jamaica, V.S. Reid's *The Leopard* (1958); and Michael Anthony's *The Year in San Fernando* (1965).

 That literary breakthrough was also being accomplished in other regions of the Commonwealth: in India, Nirad Chaudhuri's controversial *The Autobiography of an Unknown Indian* (1951); among many earlier major novels in Australia, Patrick White's *The Tree of Man* (1955); and in Africa, in particular, Amos Tutuola's *The Palm-Wine Drinkard* (1952), and *My Life in the Bush of Ghosts* (1954).

 The second wave from the Caribbean includes, from Belize, Zee Edgell's *Beka Lamb* (1982); from St. John's Antigua, Jamaica Kincaid's *Annie John* (1985). In these fictions the Caribbean man and woman are no longer direct provisions of the Colony but have become part of a self-sufficient, self-determining society.

 More recent fiction has also inevitably addressed the lives, in the UK, of second generation young adults of Afro-Caribbean, African and Asian parentage. In this sense, since the eighties and what is seen as the renascence of Black arts movements and the coming of a second generation of Black British voices, it is the performance arts that have perhaps been a more vital medium than the novel or verse. More than the solely written medium, it is the stage which seems to have underlined the swing away from what might be described as the sentimental racial awareness of Black bourgeois theatre, to the dramatic and activist set pieces of the performance poets Lynton Kwesi Johnson and Benjamin Zephaniah; the plays of Alfred Fagon, Biyi Bandele, Zindika, Trish Cook, Winsome Pollock; and the screenplays of Caryl Phillips.

would be misleading to view Harris as part of those movements. Harris's study of the fabric of the imagination sets his writing apart from the concerns of West Indian Caribbean writers. We must look for him elsewhere. Despite the sensational *éssor* of that first West Indian wave, Harris had cut his coat of different cloth. Experiments even more daring than those of the West Indian New Wave were being conducted on the South American continent, and in another language, and it is with this singular fact, rather than with the conventions of the West Indian novel, that Harris shares kinship. Quite independently, and without prior recourse to the Spanish novel being written on the Central and South American mainland at the time, Harris, in the English language, had separately and intuitively been inventing a fiction of reach and imaginative coherence.

It is worth emphasizing Harris's particular and intuitive kinship with the Central and South American literatures in Spanish, for it is a family resemblance germane to the attempts at classifying his fiction, attempts that too often align themselves with expediencies of race, skin, mother tongue and historical boundary lines. In 1960 Harris's *Palace of the Peacock* introduced a thoroughly new and original literature in English that was being written out of the simultaneous realities of the everyday and the mythos-epos,[12] where a diffuse and ungraspable present is rooted not, as is usual, in the past, but in paradoxically rehearsed futures. The Guatemalan–Mayan poet, novelist and diplomat, Miguel Angel Asturias (1899–1974) won the Nobel Prize in 1967 for writing just such works in Spanish. Barely a decade after Harris's first novel, the British literary world had already judged him to belong to such company.

> Here Harris has entered Latin American territory (Mexico), and he explores, simultaneously, its myths and everyday realities in something like the manner Asturias explored those of Guatemala.
>
> *Companions of the Day and Night*, though in prose, reads like a poem rather than a novel; it is an account of a dream translated into a language of power and great imaginative coherence; there is no rhetoric. It seems to me to be outstanding in fiction in the past 25 years: Asturias obtained the Nobel Prize for writing just such strange works. Harris is in such a class.
>
> Martin Seymour-Smith, in the *Financial Times*, 27 Feb 1975,
> reviewing Companions of the Day and Night.

In the decades since 1960 and the appearance of *Palace of the Peacock*, Harris's exceptional command of the questions underlying the culture and circumstance of the English language makes him one of the most gifted writers of the era and one of the outstanding literary innovators of the century.

---

12 The epic poem, novel or drama finding its principal resonance in mythology.

The essay and the novel

What is the role of the literary essay in the creative productions of the novelist? In addition to addressing the aesthetic of literature, the essay can also serve a crucial informing function for the individual work of fiction – a preliminary ground-plan to tease out explicit as well as hidden condition.

Thus I approached Wilson Harris in September 1996 with the idea of a single volume which would give fair representation of the critical activity that has been running parallel with his career as a novelist, that is to say, the period since 1960 and the appearance of *Palace of the Peacock*, his first novel. A provisional list was drafted by the author in November 1996 and developed with me over the period to the book's production. The resulting selection promotes a comparative reading between Harris's critical writings and his fiction and it is this which gives register to the present volume.

Four full-length collections predate the present volume. The most recent, *The Radical Imagination: Lectures and Talks* (1992), makes available seven essays written between 1989–1991. These address the net of associations formed between cultures producing literatures conversant with, but antecedent to, European models.[13] *The Womb of Space: The Cross-Cultural Imagination* (1983) is a book-length study of the American imagination.[14] *Explorations: A Selection of Talks and Articles 1966–1981* (1981) assembles fourteen essays from a fifteen-year period and has been a standard reader for Harris.[15] It includes the lecture series *History, Fable and Myth in the Caribbean and the Guianas* (1970, 1981, 1995);[16] and *Fossil and Psyche* (1974, 1981).[17] The six essays in the earliest volume *Tradition, the Writer and Society* (1967, 1973) contain formative ideas[18] which first appeared in articles Harris contributed between 1945 and 1959 to the magazine of Caribbean writing *Kyk-over-al*.[19]

Four or five developmental periods mark the essay collections, the first in the

---

13 *The Radical Imagination, Lectures and Talks*, English Department, University of Liege, 1992, 136 pp.

14 *The Womb of Space: The Cross-Cultural Imagination*, Greenwood Press, Westport USA, 1983, 147 pp.

15 *Explorations, A Selection of Talks and Articles 1966–1981* (Hena Maes-Jelinek ed., Dangaroo Press, Aarhus, 1981, 144 pp.

16 *History, Fable and Myth in the Caribbean and the Guianas*, first put out as a monograph by The National History and Arts Council of Guyana in 1970 (32 pp); revised for '*Explorations*', 1981 (23 pp.); and reprinted with introduction by Selwyn R. Cudjoe ed., Calaloux Publications, Wellesley, Mass., 1995, 50 pp.

17 *Fossil and Psyche* first appeared with The University of Texas Press, Austin, 1974, 12 pp., and was revised for '*Explorations*', 1981 (15 pp.).

18 *Tradition, the Writer and Society*, New Beacon Books, London, 1967; rpt. 1973, 75 pp. One might get a feel for formative ideas by glancing over the titles and the dates of the two essays which first appeared in *Kyk-over-al* magazine:

    1   Art and Criticism (1951)

    2   The Question of Form and Realism in the West Indian Artist (1952)

19 See above, n.5, p.3.

early to mid-1960s, when Harris was taking a position about his own novels in the Western canon. These deliberations produced the 1967 collection *Tradition, the Writer and Society*, in which Harris considers the future of the mainstream tradition and how its need to consolidate itself is both obsessive and likely to breach time and again its most cherished conventions. Paradoxically, Harris sees such a breach as a groping toward an alternative to convention – an alternative that offers a wider conception of possibilities and pulls the framework of fiction beyond the author's need for self-determination. For Harris, what makes realist fiction redundant is its fear of such a dynamic and its own inherent incapacity to accommodate it. The earliest essay in this selection, 'Tradition and the West Indian Novel' (see pp.140–51 in this volume), belongs to that period. It dates from 1964 when Harris had just completed his first group of novels that were later collected as *The Guyana Quartet* (1984). That essay, 'Tradition and the West Indian Novel' (Part III), engages the reader in all manner of ways; the clarity, the address, and not least in that it appears to anticipate in most provocative fashion concepts that were to become familiar in post-structural discourse at the start of the 1980s. These arguments bear on the effacing of narrative authority, the instability of signification, the positioning of theme in the figurative axes of language, and an attempt to disarticulate the monoliths of power. Later again, in the early 1990s, these concepts shared common ground in the new critical studies attempting to account for the literatures being produced by nations with a shared historical experience – literatures of distinction produced in the aftermath of independence from colonial rule in English, French, Arabic, Spanish, Portuguese and Dutch.

Where these theoretical stances are concerned, it could be noted in passing that Harris himself has no wish to be involved in the debates surrounding the methods or terms of the emancipatory, anti-imperialist project that is post-colonialism's broad agenda. As Stuart Murray has observed: 'Harris's refusal to engage with the orthodox postcolonial formulations of community, identity, citizenship, or sovereignty means he is also outside a number of neocolonial institutionalized instruments of control' (*Review of Contemporary Fiction*, Summer 1997, p.55). Harris's connection of life and art, his conception of the moral nature of literature, and his view of language as an enabling device toward a non-essential truth, places him outside standard post-structuralist theories of writing and outside the framework of a debate between postcolonialism and post-modernism, a debate with which he himself has little sympathy.

> The inevitability of the unknowable, the untranslatable, the ungraspable, underpins much of Harris's fiction – the pre-Columbian past that feeds the Guyanese present – and it is these ideas that produce a cleavage between his theories [. . .] and those emanating from poststructuralist and deconstructive practices.[20]

20 Stuart Murray, 'Postcoloniality. Modernity: Wilson Harris and Postcolonial Theory', *Review of Contemporary Fiction*, Summer 1997, pp.54–5.

While conscientiously we might make comparisons with these critical approaches and Harris's own theories, such stances are likely to be less productive than reading Harris the light of traditions of the imagination (literature, philosophy, anthropology, analytical psychology) that act as 'parallel texts' to his work. Thus the authors and books cited in my commentaries are also suggestions for further reading. They complement the study of Harris by extending a very real and direct kinship between the theatre of legend in South America and European authors and traditions. As a poet–novelist–philosopher, Harris's kinship with cross-cultural Europe has been paralleled with the German Jewish novelist–philosopher Martin Buber (1878–1965), whose conception of dialogical encounter[21] can be seen to be a meeting place of the West's imaginative traditions with the Hasidic tradition of parable: 'When we recognise man's finitude we must *at the same time* recognise his participation in infinity, not as two juxtaposed qualities but as the twofold nature of the processes in which alone man's existence becomes recognisable.'[22]

Buber's expression, '*at the same time*', might be compared to the simultaneous counterpoint that runs through Harris's conception of the parable of man that is to be found in the music of living landscapes, seascapes and skyscapes.[23] In the same study, *The Naked Design*, Hena Maes-Jelinek goes on to make co-extensions with the French philosopher–psychoanalytic scientist Gaston Bachelard (1884–1962), whose studies in 'taciturnity', 'reverie' and 'dream' indicate a marriage, of the arts and sciences compatible in conception to Harris's. As further reading I would add the writings of the French mythographer Paul Diel. *Le Symbolisme dans la mythologie grecque* (1966) echoes in uncanny fashion the uses to which Harris puts myth, as a revealer of inexactitudes in the conventionalized narrative. Diel's innovation is to discover that it can require a series of between five to eight distinct but related myths to treat a crucial theme, and that when one myth has exhausted itself and can go no further, the theme can be found to have been taken up and continued in a new myth. When we identify a group of myths with a shared theme, we begin to notice in inexactitudes in the conventionalized narrative of each particular episode. This forces us to revise our conception of narrative itself. As if by sudden insight, we arrive at an account more comprehensive than our prior appreciation of any one myth-episode.

New conceptions in myth, legend and folk-tale are powerful imaginative means by which the artist converts what historically, on the surface, has been uniform,

21 For a conception of the dialogical encounter, see Buber's *Ich and Du* (*I and Thou*) (1923).
22 Hena Maes-Jelinek, *The Naked Design: A Reading of 'Palace of the Peacock'*, Dangaroo Press, Aarhus, Denmark, 1976, p.12.
23 See 'The Music of Living Landscapes' (1996), pp.40–6 in this volume.

catastrophic experience into substantial creative genesis. I return to this in the Appendix ('El Dorado and the Grail Legend'). Additionally I would cite the interpretation of history Harris perhaps shares with the English historian Arnold Toynbee.

> In my search up to the present point, I have been experimenting with the play of soulless forces – *vis inertiae* and race and environment – and I have been thinking in the deterministic terms of cause-and-effect.[24] Now that these manoeuvres have ended, one after another, in my drawing blank, I am led to consider whether my successive failures may not point to some mistake in method.[25]

Toynbee's self-confessed 'mistake in method' bears on the potentially disenabling role played by unrecognized symmetries in a society's bid for self-determination.[26] 'I have been searching for the positive factor which, within the last five thousand years, has shaken part of Mankind out of the "integration of custom" into the "differentiation of civilisation".'[27]

That 'integration of custom' might be understood as the equating of character (singularity in physical appearance, shared history, political and moral philosophy, etc. – what Toynbee calls 'racialism') with the absolute stance of the nation-state: two societies, at opposite extremes in the spectrum of physical appearance, meet under unfortunate circumstances. They try to account for the stark differences in their relative fortunes and achievements. Neither one's language has ready-made terms to describe the encounter, so they lapse into a ready-made symmetry: the difference in human physique is equated with moral differences in the human psyche. These differences are used as a fixed measure, and both societies become victims of a fallacy built on symmetry – that of equating one characteristic with its justifying co-respondent. By contrast, Toynbee's 'differentiation of civilization' seems close to the play of arbitrating forces associated with what Harris calls 'an *asymmetry* within the infinity and genius of art.'[28]

On the cusp of the 1970s Harris began to discern a continuum of cross-cultural 'womb of space' that seemed to connect civilizations separated widely from one another in place and time. That connection seemed to be a certain fluid identity joining pre-Columbian antique art figures to the line, character and form

24 'So far, by the process of exhaustion, we have made one discovery: the cause of the genesis of civilisations is not simple but multiple: it is not an entity but a relation' (Arnold Toynbee, *A Study of History*, 13 *Challenge and Response*, abrgd., Oxford, OUP, 1972, p.97.

25 Ibid.

26 A bid for self-determination Harris has elsewhere called 'the exercise of individual sovereignty'.

27 Arnold Toynbee, *A Study of History*, p.97.

28 'The Schizophrenic Sea' (1983), pp.99–108 in this volume.

of decorative motifs in contexts (as separate as Tudor England, Zimbabwe, the modern United States) that would make influence impossible (see 'Profiles of Myth and the New World' (1996), pp.201–11 in this volume). Let us resist, for the instant, the compulsion to have fluid identity explained and to yield our minds instead to the potential bearing on the arts of fiction.

One obvious bearing of such cross-cultural resemblances is to give moral irony when societies alien to one another are juxtaposed in such a way as to cause us to reflect in the luxury of humour the rigidness of our own tribal and racial codes. 'There's a wonderful vase, a tall vase inscribed with histories of the world – I hope to come upon it in due course – in which she resides now playing that she rules the world from within the very objects that ruled her. It is her moral comedy, her version of moral irony' (*The Four Banks of the River of Space*, Faber and Faber, London, 1990, p.28).

It is a species of irony that Harris believes to be central to the achievement of the subjective imagination within a heterogenous context (see Chapter 10, 'Benito Cereno' (1983), pp.123–33).

At the start of the 1980s, curious to see what advances and experiments the arts of the imagination had been making in the English language outside England, Harris began a full-length study of the American literary imagination, *The Womb of Space: The Cross-Cultural Imagination* (1983). In a historical sense the initiative is close to that of D.H. Lawrence's *Studies in Classic American Literature* (1923). There are exactly sixty years between the two publications. What change in emphasis in the critical and creative response might we look for?

Lawrence was concerned with a rupture in the psyche between Old Europe and Young America. That was his axis. Lawrence lined up the defects, private hypocrisies but enviable resources of the New World literature; he was concerned with what our *attitude* should be to the upstart literature, and if, from our European viewpoint, our attitude should even matter. By contrast, Harris's study is an inside work. What Harris looks for is not attitude, but a telling medium through which to illuminate the classic American novel. He accepts the 'integration of custom' in which the American novel has been written, and is fascinated by how works of real distinction exert an unconscious attempt to free themselves from the rigid stances of the conventional nineteenth-century novel. In the classic American novel, Harris discovered a hidden text, one that possessed uncanny resemblances to the structures in carnival-masquerade. The hidden text in the classic American novel makes a twin with certain masked deities of the pre-Columbian Americas: Yurokon, Huracan, Kukulcan and Quetzalcoatl. These are masked gods, carnival gods that the present-day public festivals of carnival, masque and masquerade seek to recompose. Arts of fiction allow us to see through masks to the mask's true function, providing a kind of spectroscopy of the American imagination, and the texts uttered from behind such masks build uncanny bridges across time and race. The essays in Part II on Faulkner, Poe, Jean Toomer and Ralph Ellison date from this period.

As his book-length study of the American literary imagination was being completed, Harris started to write the *Carnival Trilogy* of novels (1985–90). By the time his fourth collection of essays appeared (*The Radical Imagination*, 1992), Harris was concluding *Resurrection at Sorrow Hill* (1993) a refiguration of his first novel, *Palace of the Peacock* (1960), and beginning what I consider to be the finest post-war novel in English, *Jonestown* (1996). With a single exception, the six essays in Part IV have been written since 1992.

This is the *collectus*. Let us attempt a useful reading. We began the heading by hypothesising the role of the literary essay in the creative productions of the novelist. We allowed that in addition to addressing the aesthetic of literature the essay will serve a crucial informing function to the individual work of fiction; a ground-plan to tease out explicit as well as the hidden. Harris has published twenty-one novels to date, and although this is a collection of his non-fiction, the links between his essays and his novels are sufficiently close to be reflected in the arrangement of this volume.

One of his fiction's most striking attributes is that it takes place in dislodged space. It is concerned with the recovery of dimensionalities that our received ideas, our conventional reckonings, flatten out or conventionalize. Now a fiction that proceeds in this way is akin to the language of dream, and I believe that Harris's entire body of fiction can be treated as a single continuous dream-book, whose text, just like a cycle of dreams over a number of years, is an inflection of thematic clusters and revisitations.[29] There are a number of persuasive reasons for approaching the novels in this manner.

First, a dream-book contains facts. They are facts because we cannot invent them; they do not answer our expectations. Our actual surroundings rarely furnish the dream material, nor do our most impressive experiences.

> We dream of our questions, our difficulties. There is a saying that the bridegroom never dreams of the bride. This is because he has her in reality; only later when there is trouble does he dream of her – and then she is generally the wife. We are quite unable to influence our dreams, and the actual surroundings do not necessarily furnish the dream material. Even when something really important or fascinating happens there is often not a trace of it in our dreams . . .
>
> Our dreams are most peculiarly independent of our consciousness and exceedingly valuable because they cannot cheat.[30]

---

29 A conception not so remote from the Australian Aboriginal Dreaming where man enters a family kinship with a living landscape. In the Aboriginal Dreaming, history is abolished. Tremendous people and the events surrounding them fall back into the landscape to become a prominent rock or tree or ground water. The man who is privileged enough to make the discovery of the place where history has 'fallen into the land' becomes that place's intimate descendant, and that 'land-fall' his intimate ancestor.

30 C.G. Jung, 'Lecture 1 (7 November 1928) in Dream Analysis', *Notes of the Seminars given in 1928–30*, William McGuire (ed.), *The Collected Works of C.G. Jung*, Routledge, 1984, pp.3–4.

We conclude that, unable to influence our dreams, unable to cheat with consciousness, the dream-book would contain facts-beyond-cause.[31]

The longer a culture stays in crisis, the more successfully it will hide its difficulties from the public domain. Thus the hypotheses that arise in a dream-book of the culture are imaginative responses to the condition of the age and can offer the artist a unique opportunity for working out a comprehensive reading of the character of the age. Prior to beginning his dream-book of novels, Harris found himself in a culture imaginatively at impasse. He began a dream-book of the culture because there seemed to be no other way of getting at the facts of crisis where those facts assert themselves in the language of dream:

> I feared to write in – and be written by – a demanding book that asserts itself in Dream and questions itself from time to time (even as I question the meaning of survival) as you will see as you read. One overcomes the fear of Dreams, I suspect, for I did not stop writing or being written into what I wrote . . .

(p.48 in this volume)

Dream comes from the Old English *dream* corresponding to Old Saxon *drom* meaning joy or music. This etymology will be of some consequence when we go over the material of the first essay in Part I. 'Joy' is from L. *gaudere*, to rejoice or give thanks; 'music' from a Greek root to do with the art of memory.[32] So the dream-book has to do with celebration through the art of memory. And because celebration can have to do with sound and noise and tumult and interval, with instruments of hearing and audition, the dream-book is also a composition in music and remembrancing; and just like a musical composition, no one part of the dream text will give a handy abridgement of the meaning. The statement of meaning is the whole text, the single continuous dream-book of novels that contains every contact between the artist and the world wherein the artist has been re-imagining the impact of that world.

So we take up the material, and try to work out the reading together. We avoid bringing to it the concepts and conditions we are familiar with. Instead we must say we do not know, but that here are some dreams, impartial facts, which might give information; then we allow ourselves to see through the dreamer's eyes, what kind of language does the dream use? What terminology? What kind of imaginative impact does the world make on him?

In the novel *Jonestown* (1996), Francisco Bone, the only survivor of latter-day

---

31 Cf. Schopenhauer's definition of 'the principle of sufficient reason' as that which 'authorises everywhere to search for the cause of *why*' (*The Fourfold Root of the Principle of Sufficient Reason*, 1813). Schopenhauer distinguishes between the notions of *reason* and *cause*, and it is in this sense that I make the figuration, 'facts-beyond-cause' as opposed to, 'facts beyond reason'.
32 Gr. *mnasthai* 'I am made to remember', mnemonic.

holocaust, inhabits Limbo Land. Francisco's attempts to construct a new conception of Time for himself, his 'trial at the bar of time', exposes him to the Storm of madness. A huntsman with his net finds Francisco and, paradoxically for a huntsman, cures Francisco's desire to enact extensions of the violence Francisco only just survived.

> 'Leap,' he said (in the gathering menace of the Storm), 'into my net and help me to hold the heart of the Predator at bay within rhythms of profoundest self-confessional, self-judgmental creativity. The leap into space I grant is dangerous. It is a kind of surrender to an unfathomable caring Presence that seems absent in a cruel age. It is the leap of the unfinished genesis of the Imagination that may bring to light unpredictable resources in an open universe that nets, in some paradoxical way, creature and creation. LEAP . . .'
>
> (p.75)

But Francisco is unable to leap. At least not now. Yet the intervention of the huntsman and his net brings about a change of heart. The fear and terror that make Francisco want to slay the Predator looses its grip. Francisco can now settle down on 'a Bag of memory leaves and pages' even though, 'The Predator knew of my lofty hiding place. He knew of my inner Dream-pillow or book.'[33]

Thus the dream-text is the written form of the dreamscape. In the dreamscape will be a number of promontories and I would point out three:

1   The so-called *Guyana Quartet* (*Palace of the Peacock*, *The Far Journey of Oudin*, *The Whole Armour*, *The Secret Ladder*), a homeland tetralogy written between 1960 and 1963 to unravel the masquerade of appearances that dog the conventional histories of colonialism;
2   A Carib diptych (*The Sleepers of Roraima*, *The Age of the Rainmakers*) published in 1970–71, which explores the vestiges of legend carried in indigenous peoples; and
3   The Lord Carnival trilogy (*Carnival*, *The Infinite Rehearsal*, *The Four Banks of the River of Space*) published between 1985 and 1990, which chronicles the way folk art embodied in Carnival can cause a slipping-off of the masks worn by a society.

These three groups, I feel, give shape to Harris's dream-book of novels, with his other works of fiction serving as breath-lines/breathing lines in a living dreamscape that releases circularities and revisitations in the dream-book of novels.[34]

---

33 *Jonestown*, London, 1996, pp.75–6.
34 The breath-lines/breathing-lines of the dreamscape being as vulnerable to smothering (a culture at imaginative impasse) as those of the living landscape.

Striking instances come to mind: the village of Sorrow Hill in *Resurrection at Sorrow Hill* (1993); the drowning/burial/resurrection portage in *Palace of the Peacock* (1960), which is revisited and relived in a perpetual uncertainty of its own demise.

Revisitation is part of the dream-book's inner structure. *Heartland* (1964), *The Eye of the Scarecrow* (1965) and *Companions of the Day and Night* (1975) all use post-scripts or epilogues. *The Eye of the Scarecrow* concludes with a 'POSTSCRIPT OF FAITH IN DARK ROOMS OF IDENTITY'; *Heartland* with, 'Zechariah Stevenson disappeared somewhere in the Guianan/Venezuelan/Brazilian jungles that lie between the headwaters of the Cuyuni and Potaro rivers. In the half-burnt down shell of the small resthouse . . . was found a bundle of scorched papers: when pieced together they grew into fragments of letters to one Maria, and three shattered poems' (p.93).

Companions of the Day and Night, meanwhile, edits and rewrites the papers and diaries in the 'Idiot Nameless Collection' that were scorched and burned in *Heartland* before being recovered by Black Marsden of *Black Marsden* (1972). The significance of the postscript–epilogue is that it alludes to a record of a vanished site finally understood, in *The Eye of the Scarecrow*, to be 'the foot-prints of the self-created self' (p.106).

Imaginative deposits[35] need not be just the private testament of the single individual, they can be the witness of several: 'the disjointed diary of the Forrestals (p.9)' in *The Waiting Room* (1967) holds written entries not just of a blind woman but also of her husband, of her previous lover, and those entries she co-authors with both men.

Other revisitations in the dream-book's inner structure are the journals of dream: the 'book of dreams' that is *The Four Banks of the River of Space*, the 'asylum book' that is *Resurrection at Sorrow Hill*, and the 'Dream-book' that is *Jonestown*. And orchestrating life in the dreamscape are Harris's guide-redemptors, his *conduors d'amour/conduors à mort* (conductors of love/conductors to death): Everyman Masters, the Virgilian facilitator in *Carnival* (1985), and Christopher D'eath, 'the spectre of Christ within Death', in *Resurrection at Sorrow Hill*.

If the Harris novel can be considered a dream-book of the culture, and the

> Commonsense engineers decided long ago in the eighteenth and nineteenth centuries that the cotton estates and the cane-farming estates, the sugar plantations, were to be laid out in rectangles and squares. As a consequence they smothered the breath-lines in a living landscape. And when the peasant rice farmer came into being he had to contend with disfigured cachments, in the coastal river systems, that would occasion excessive flood and droughts for him.
>
> (Wilson Harris, *Jonestown*, 1996, pp.171–2)

35 Collections of paintings, sculptures, dream papers, poems, translations that were either recorded on an unstable medium (paper, parchment, memory and recall) or had simply vanished and left nothing except hearsay to attest to their existence.

essays lay the ground-plan, we may suppose that the essay would do more than just work out plot or subject. If the essay promotes a reading forward and backward between the novel and its role as dream-book of the culture, we can suppose that the essay will provide the hunches, conjectures, hypotheses for the reality of the dream-book of the culture, the essay will do this chiefly by bringing into sharp focus our own background in received ideas and how these match or are contradicted by the phenomenology of the dream-book. If we suppose this to be the essay's prime function, then that would clarify the cross-match we desire between essay and fiction.

We began the heading with this aim. We outlined a chronology, and a period-icity. Now it is time to go over something of the genesis of modern Guyana, Harris's country of birth, for that country's unique circumstance in cultural community would offer Harris the literary artist an unprecedented opportunity. There exists a number of incontingencies in what at first glance would appear to be a straightforward model of history set out below. Hidden from direct apprehension are crucial items which remain recondite even to those acquainted with the region and its literature. The next heading will give a feel for these.

Guyana: geomythos and theatre of memory

By the beginning of the twentieth century the popular imagination was already aware of the tropical rainforests and mountains of the Guyana interior.[36] More serious were the anthropological accounts of the indigenous peoples prepared during the final quarter of the nineteenth century and the first quarter of the twentieth. Some are greatly illuminating in that they bring to light certain facts and exhibits that alert us to our own notions of the primitive and our own deterministic readings of history.[37]

---

36 The tall escarpments of the Mount Roraima plateau on the border with Venezuela and Brazil inspired Arthur Conan Doyle's science fiction *The Lost World* (1912), and Evelyn Waugh's travel book about South America, *Ninety-Two Days* (1934), gives a vivid resume of his passage over river and jungle.

37 Classical anthropological reports of the interior of the Guyana include E.F. im Thurn, *Among the Indians of Guiana*, Kegan Paul, Trench, London, 1883.

Walter Edmund Roth, *An Enquiry into the Animism and Folklore of the Guiana Indians*, 30th Annual Report of the Bureau of American Ethnology, 1908–9, Washington, DC, 1915, 109–453.

Walter Edmund Roth, *An Introductory Study of the Arts, Crafts and Customs of the Guiana Indians*, 38th Annual Report of the Bureau of American Ethnology, 1916–17.

Roth's aim was to produce documentation. He did not seek to engage in determinist discourse. For this reason his report is of considerable value to the contemporary reader. In contrast, Sir Everard im Thurn was curator of the museum in Georgetown and a man of some influence on the opinions and attitudes of the colony. For the contemporary reader im Thurn's book is prototype to the determinist attitudes that shape conventional appraisals of primitive peoples and by extension colonized races. I found the book – its premises, assumptions, world view – a lesson in human perspectives. A symphony of evasions that fails to engage honestly with its material and, in its own unassuming way, is deeply offensive.

Harris's encounters with Amerindian peoples began when he was a young man and started to survey the hydroelectric potential in the Guyana hinterland. There had been talk of new settlements for refugees in the wake of the Second World War, and hydroelectricity would have been a vital ingredient. If we are to follow the fiction of *The Four Banks of the River of Space*, Harris met the spirit of the Macusi god Canaima when surveying the Potaro River in 1945.[38] He encountered a group of Wapishanas in the Potaro–Kaieteur catchment in 1948.[39] He surveyed the Pomeroon River in 1950, and the Canje interior on and off between 1945 and 1955.[40] For Harris, the indigenous peoples and their habitat would make definitive ingress in his language and literary imagination, and some account of the region and the geophysical profile is therefore relevant.

Viewed from outer space, the region called the Guianas is a gatherer of vast river systems in an area comparable in size to western Europe. *Guiana* is an Amerindian word meaning 'land of many waters': interior rivers, coastal rivers, tributaries and the unexpected straight lines of coastal irrigation. Complex water systems originate in the steep, flat-topped mountains of the interior, descend through ferocious drops (cataracts, waterfalls) into savannah before sloping gradually to a coastal belt with the Atlantic.

Geologically, the Guianas originate in highlands in the north-central portion of South America and make a twin continental shield with the Atlantic; one stem flowing directly north, the other first south to the Amazon Basin then north-east to the sea. The shield is of old crystalline rock abundant in mineral deposits pushed into geophysical agglomerations of table-top elevations (2,500–3,000m), low hills (1,000m) and rolling uplands (300m). The Guianas extend from eastern Colombia, through the southern half of Venezuela and the Orinoco Basin, and into northern Brazil to the Rio Negro and the Amazon Delta. Positioned like a tongue on the lip of the Guianas are a French department (La Guiane Française), a Dutch overseas county (Surinam) and Harris's natal land, the Republic of Guyana.

The Republic is approximately the size of mainland Britain.[41] Ninety-five per cent of the population live on the river banks and a coastal strip. These broad bands are alluvial deposits – mud carried, then set down, by rivers. It is on these fluvial margins that agriculture is practised, for except on the inland plateaux and the coastal band, the land is thickly forested. Through that forest water flows in

---

38 *The Four Banks of the River of Space*, London, 1987, p.46.
39 *The Age of the Rainmakers*, London, 1971, p.61.
40 Preface to *The Guyana Quartet*, London, 1984, pp.9–10.
41 There is an ongoing quasi-military border dispute with Venezuela over the eastern basin of the Orinoco, over Mount Roraima, and over the upper course of the Cuyuni River, at any given period the territory claimed for Guyana being reckoned at between 215,000 and 235,000 square kilometres.

thick webbed lines. Peaks and plateaux rise from hundreds of miles inland and cast their rivers into the Atlantic. These high places are sometimes likened to spiritual sentinels of the region. Harris specifically develops their function as lookout, watchtower and symbolic face of a civilization in the Carib diptych of novels, *The Sleepers of Roraima* and *The Age of the Rainmakers*.

If the demographic community of Guyana takes its names from successive Dutch, French and English settlement, it is the Amerindian names that dominate the nomenclature of rocks, cataracts and tributary waterways. Their naming reflects the influence of Amerindian guides on early wandering Dutch traders ('*swervers*'); on official descriptions of the country made to encourage trade, such as Adriaan van Berkel's *Travels in South America between the Berbice and Essequibo Rivers* (1670–89); and on explorations and surveys of the then unknown interior, such as Charles Warton's *Wanderings in South America* (1825), Richard Schomburgk's *Travels in British Guiana* (1840–44); and lastly on inventories of the region's mineral wealth, such as Sir John Harrison's *Geology of the Gold Fields of British Guiana* (1908).[42] Thus the falls of the Kaieteur is a Macusi Indian word meaning 'thunderer',[43] the rocks and falls of Tumatumari, an anglicized root word meaning 'death' or 'sleep of song',[44] and 400 kilometres inland, Mount Roraima means 'seaward looking'.[45] These land fortresses and seaward arteries mark

42 Michael Swan, *The Literature on British Guiana*, Appendix E, in *British Guiana: Land of Six Peoples*, HM Stationery Office, London, 1957, pp.222–3.
43 Cf. A.J. Seymour, 'Name Poem' in *Selected Poems*, B.G. Lithographic Co. Ltd, 1965, p.22:

> Through all the years before the Indians came
> Rocks at Tumatumari kept their grace,
> And Tukeit, Amatuk, Waratuk
> Trained ear and eye for thundering Kaieteur.

On account of their height and head of water some of the falls possess hydroelectric potential. The Kaieteur has an unimpeded fall of 741 (222m) and is the highest in Guyana. Angel Falls at 3,281 (1,100m) in neighbouring Venezuela is the largest cascade in the Guianas and in the world.
44 Ibid., where *kept their grace* might be Seymour's metaphor for the grace granted in the sleep of the dead at Tumatumari. See also Wilson Harris, *The Music of Living Landscapes*, for amplification of the word Tumatumari: as 'womb of song', or 'sleep of song' (p.13) or 'sleeping yet singing rocks', and perhaps refigured in the novel *Jonestown* (1996) as 'the sleeping choir of the dead' (pp.40–6 in this volume).
45 Seymour, 'Name Poem':

> And there are mountain tops that take the sun
> Jostling shoulders with seaward-eyed Roraima
>
> These Amerindian names hold ancient sway
> Beyond the European fingers reaching.

Mount Roraima is the highest summit in the Guiana Highlands, its table-top massif (25 square miles) reaching 9,094 (2,730m) is a national park in the nook and angle of the Guyana–Brazil–Venezuela borders.

dramatic contrasts in the physical relief of the interior. Their violence, sudden-
ness and intransigence to human presence invite comparison with the uncanny
self that holds its face averted from human nature, and with an opening into
vision.

During the 1940s and 1950s, Harris's expeditions as a surveyor in the interior
took him to these geophysical sites known to be sacred to the indigenous Amerindians. Indigenous hunter–gather peoples surely used such sites as physical and
psychical lodestones in the circuits and migrations of the hunter–gatherer calendar. In attempting to make valid creations out of the lives lived in such calendars,
Harris is also attempting the partial recall of race – race, not as an isolated
branch of *Homo sapiens* but as peoples in the disseminated family of man. Receptive to circularities and reclamations, the novelist's art can embrace both the
hunter and the rescued, the gatherer and the gathered-in, and historic disappearance with perpetual re-entry into consciousness.

> I had no absolute model on which to base my Dream-book except that I
> sought to salvage unpredictable keys to tradition within the terrifying
> legacies of the past. I sought to be true to the broken communities, the
> apparently lost cultures from which I have sprung.
>
> (pp.49–50 in this volume)

As novels of the partial recall of race, *The Sleepers of Roraima* and *The Age of the
Rainmakers* are also gathering lenses to a startling and unique cultural programme:
how express the uncanny sense of continuance with peoples whom history
shows to have died out? How express an awareness of continuance that signals
itself as an overwhelming and terrifying presence felt by every sojourner in the
Guianas?

Both novels express the imminent disappearance of peoples from history; they
aim to make anew an essential imaginative fabric otherwise susceptible to obliter-
ation by histories of conquest. In *The Sleepers of Roraima*, the *Couvade* or 'sleeper of
the tribe' has 'some strange dream of history in which his grandfather's people
feared that they vanish from the face of the earth' (p.18); and in his Note to 'The
Laughter of the Wapishanas' in *The Age of the Rainmakers* Harris records a specific
encounter while surveying in the Kaieteuran Plateau in 1948.[46] He came upon a
group of Wapishanis who were reputed to be a 'laughter-loving' people. Harris
intuited that, as vestige of legend, the laughter of the Wapushani represented
caveat or *reservato mentalis* to their fatalistically inclined neighbours, the Macusis.
In this third story in the *Rainmaker*, Wapishana, the young tribe-girl, in search of
the colour and nature of laughter, climbs the drought-spiral (history), 'an ancient
staircase which at that moment looked as dry and brown and wooden as the
mourning leaf of the elder tree of laughter' (p.63). Later on, in 'Arawak

---

46 *The Age of the Rainmakers*, London, 1971, p.61.

Horizon', the fourth and final story in the volume, Harris adds new letters to the alphabet. He incorporates into the story-text a number of Arawak Indian hierographs. The effect of these is to rescue into the English language unfamiliar and unrecognizable words, semiotic remnants – in other words the partial recall of the vanishing race. The presence of the enlarged alphabet implies that 'there had been someone else to bear the prisoner [of history] company or to suggest that even long, long ago he knew I would come and thus he proffered me the core of his hospitality *in my absence* as I supped now with him *in his*' (p.91).

In these ways a race can sustain itself in the fable of history. Out of the resource of vanished civilization and a watershed/rainshed/bloodshed heartland, the artist can promote a gateway conception of the family of man in the Guianas.

Guyana, and the post-European contact pattern of history

The pattern of colonialism in the Americas embraces a number of well-worn interfaces:

1   Mutual discovery: a European nation-state encounters overseas indigenous peoples (fifteenth–seventeenth centuries);
2   First phase of commercial slavery: partial success in coercing these indigenous peoples into labour (early sixteenth century);
3   Second phase of commercial slavery: importing of African labour and setting-up of plantation infrastructure (seventeenth–nineteenth centuries); the contesting over territory by European nation-states (Portugal with Spain, England with Holland and France) leads to overall consolidation by a single European nation-state (early nineteenth century);
4   Abolition of commercial slavery: occasions of revolt (colony) and movements of social conscience (Europe) lead to gradual phasing-out of African trade in humans (after 1809), and the fall-out of former enslaved labour into agricultural or urban subsistence (after 1843);
5   Indentured labour: coercion of low-status Europeans (for Guyana, the Madeira Portuguese) and Asiatic low castes (southern India, China, Korea) into seven-year contracts of labour (mid–late nineteenth century);
6   Depreciation of single-crop economies and gradual collapse of financial base leads to a series of Commissioned Reports on future of colony: introduction of separate Constitution and universal adult suffrage accompany gradual withdrawal of nation-state from immediate sphere of influence (post-First World War);
7   Self-determination (Independence) and Commonwealth: sense of world community founded on a shared language and the culture-held-in-common of that language (since 1946).

It is a plausible model; one, seemingly, of self-evidence; one, in fact, with a high degree of persuasion; yet it is exceedingly misleading. This capacity to mislead is nowhere better illustrated than that it should have so unconditionally inculcated the very leaders who fought to bring independence to a colony. The enactments of charismatic leaders will tend to make explicit, in a way useful to study, the otherwise unexpressed ferment of a community. A leader whose vision of the future is too handicapped by a past which seems to revulse the individual's claim to dignity (and hence future distinction) becomes a victim of history. In succumbing to a pattern of history, he becomes immobilized, turned to stone, gorgonized by identifying too closely with unbearable fact. If, in the case of Guyana, independence was fought for and achieved with the same alternation of guilt and intolerance exercised in three previous centuries by the Dutch West India Company then by servants of the British Crown – if the liberators of the new nation became the new prime vectors of history's pattern – where look for a cure?

At Independence (26 May 1966), the population of Guyana approached 700,000. That figure peaked in 1980 at 800,000 before the growth-rate fell. Although accounting for less than one per cent of the population per annum, emigration has exerted since the late 1940s a potent psychological force in the economic life of the country. Guyanese who have become citizens of the USA, Canada and Britain now out-number by perhaps a third the official Guyana census. Their money supports relatives at home, allows materials and services to enter the country, and many who have made their lives in the northern hemisphere harbour dreams of retiring to Guyana. Thus it would not be surprising if, behind this contemporary dynamic, there should exist a number of controversial accounts of the discovery, ethnography, social history and potential resources of the country.

Guyana is known as the 'Land of Six Peoples': English, Portuguese, African, Hindu Indian, Chinese and Amerindian. That is its brand-mark, or in Harris's words its 'decoy of fate'.[47] Amerindinans are the indigenous peoples. They speak a number of surviving languages: Arawak, Atorai, Mapidian, Wapishana, Chiquena and Caribe. As hunters and migratory cultivators of the manioc or cassava root vegetable, Amerindians are part of a larger Central and South American community whose better-known families include the Olmec and Maya (Central American isthmus, Caribbean and circum-Caribbean), the Aztec (Mexico Valley) and Inca (Andes). Key specimens in Harris's human and historical laboratory, Amerindians have been the subjects of unfinished invasion, conquest and assimilation for over 3,000 years. They inhabited the mainland continent 3,000 years before Columbus and were invaded in successive waves by the originally island-dwelling Caribs, who give their name to the Caribbean region.

The French anthropologist Claude-Lévi Strauss (b.1908) first visited the Amazon Basin and the edge of the Guianas in 1935. There he found tribes

---

47 Preface to *The Guyana Quartet*, London, p.9.

numbering only seven or eight hundred individuals yet which displayed social hierarchies containing as many as two hundred separate levels of castes in the same tribe. He took photographs and began to study this perplexing combination of high social complexity and incongruously reduced numbers.

> Those about to browse through these photographs must be warned against [an] illusion: the belief that the Indians whom I show completely naked (although it often gets cold at night and in the early morning), sleeping on the ground under makeshift shelters of palm leaves and branches; who produce (and then rarely) only rudimentary pottery and, for textiles, weave nothing but small decorative items; who cultivate very small gardens between nomadic periods – that these Indians give us an accurate picture of primitive humanity. I myself have never believed this, and over the past twenty years evidence has accumulated to show that *the present picture does not reflect archaic conditions. The peoples of Central Brazil and elsewhere are remnants* – who have either sought refuge in the interior or been left stranded there – *of more advanced and more populous civilisations* whose indisputable vestiges are being exhumed and recorded at the mouth and along the whole course of the Amazon by archaeologists employing very up-to-date techniques [italics mine, AJMB].[48]

Two Spanish expeditions to the Amazon Basin are significant; one in 1541, the other exactly a century later. The first took place by accident – a lost detachment attempting to survive in unknown territory:

> the detachment set off [to look for food] on an unknown river later named the Amazon. After weeks of fruitless navigation that had cut them off from their base, the men, as a last resort, let themselves be carried downstream by the current. They eventually reached a region *where, for a distance of 3,000 kilometres, veritable cities appeared before their eyes.* According to the expedition's chronicler, Friar Gaspar de Carvajal, each city spread over several leagues along the banks of the river and comprised hundreds of houses of a dazzling whiteness (this notation recurs like a leitmotif, indicating that they were not simply huts). A very dense population lived here, apparently organised into many great chiefdoms, some allied, others hostile, judging from the fortifications adorned with monumental sculptures and the fortresses built on the heights. Well-maintained roads, planted with fruit trees, crossed cultivated fields. They went great distances to who knows what other inhabited centers. The raids the Spaniards made, at some cost to themselves, in order to survive

---

48 Claude Lévi-Strauss, 'Saudades do Brasil' [Notebooks on Brazil], *New York Review of Books*, 21 December, 1995, pp.19–20.

yielded, when successful, huge reserves of food, each sufficient to feed 'a troop of *one thousand men for a year* [italics mine, AJMB].'[49]

The second expedition, exactly a century later, continued Spain's systematic elimination of indigenous peoples and was prolonged into the eighteenth century by Portuguese *bandeirantes*, adventurers in the service of government agencies. The aim was to acquire large territories *limpiados*, that is, 'cleansed' (i.e. of all indigenous presence). In the 1641 expedition, according to one witness, the Indians were so numerous that an arrow shot at random in the air was sure to fall on somebody's head.

At the mouth of the Amazon is the island of Marajo, a quarter the size of mainland Britain. Marajo contains man-made artificial hills, each one covering several hectares erected both for sea and land defence.

> On the lower Amazon, remains have been unearthed of cities where, apparently, several tens of thousands of people once lived, as well as traces of unbaked bricks, substantial fortified constructions, and a network of roads leading to distant regions. Still discernible differences in types of abode suggest that these societies were strongly hierarchical. *Based on these data, it is estimated that the population of the Amazon basin was once seven or eight million* [italics mine, AJMB].[50]

By 1952 Lévi-Strauss had found the thesis for his seminal *Tristes Tropiques* (1955). He recognized as retrograde condition those remnants of a civilization – tribes that number a few hundred – which survived into this century.

> Only such a high population can explain the extreme complexity of the social organisation . . . It is inconceivable that such a social organisation would have been elaborated and applied by populations as small as those which survived into the . . . first half of our own [century].[51]

Lévi-Strauss's account does not fail to astonish and to astound. When compared to the general knowledge of the region and its indigenous history, one simply had no idea: *veritable cities for a distance of 3,000 kilometres; the population of the Amazon Basin was once seven or eight million; the present picture does not reflect archaic conditions; the peoples of Central Brazil and elsewhere are remnants.*

There are a number of crucial items to note here: as manifest in India's system of caste, complex social hierarchies are a feature of civilization-size populations. As can be observed among interns in modern war camps, even among decimated

49 Ibid.
50 Ibid., p.20.
51 Ibid.

peoples, among vestiges of a culture, memory of social order will tend to survive as an organizing currency. Survival over time appears to be a function of the strength of the founding civilization, not just of its social hierarchies, as Lévi-Strauss emphasizes, but also of less visible institutions. Such institutions or imaginative resources are the subject of Part III of this selection, specifically of 'History, Fable and Myth in the Caribbean and the Guianas'. Following two centuries of decline prior to 1930, and on account of acquiring important rights of occupation in inland reserves where they have their own education and development programmes, the Amerindian numbers in Guyana have since increased four-fold to 35–40,000 or about five per cent of the population.

Of the other five peoples of Guyana, nearly sixty per cent of the population is East Indian, and one-third is of African descent. Chinese account for two per cent of the population, while those of European provenance (Portugese, British) now number much less than one per cent. In the religious denominations, forty per cent are Christian, one-third East Indian Mohammedan (20%), Hindu (10%) and Madzassi (3%), and a tenth African Muslim. Indigenous religions are still practised. The high frequency of interbreeding means that systems of folk-belief distinct from one another propagate and spread. They creolize. The practices of folk-beliefs (African limbo, voodoo, obeah and Amerindian bush-baby, sorcery, masquerade and carnival) are rife, endemic and repressed. They hold a secret sway more compulsive than official religion and can be drafted as the real constitution of beliefs in the society.

Paradoxically, it is precisely among these superstitions, half-beliefs, old tales and folk medicines (beliefs, incidentally, that outrage the formed intelligence and riddle the very real and excellent primary school education) that there exists the possibility of a distinguished literary art for the country (see 'History, Fable and Myth in the Caribbean and Guianas'). This seemingly illiterate resource conceals hidden resources-of-depth that may empower the native writer and free him from a too exclusive assimilation to a colonial reading of the past.

English is the official language; Creole English (marked with Dutch, French, Hindu, African and Americanisms) is the vernacular. Hindi and Urdu are also spoken. Harris writes in *Carnival*, 'Mixed families were native to New Forest. The terms "black" or "white" or "coloured" were indeterminate and mutual in privileged or biased or acceptable tone. One saw what one dreaded or wished to see' (p.94). Cultural diversity is reflected in the racial composition of the different crews that populate Harris's *Guyana Quartet*. *The Secret Ladder*, for instance, begins with the Guyanese–English surveyor–engineer Russell Fenwick trying to keep together a team split not so much by renegade ill-discipline, but by sheer renegade incomprehension of each man for the culture of the other: Perez is a sly, indolent Portuguese, who, on account of his high-colour (fair skin), possesses social ascendancy over the others. Weng and Chiung are Chinese 'coolies' (Hindi and Telugu, *kuli*, day labourer) from a culture of supposedly inveterate gambling and drinking. Weng and Chiung would be descendants of indentured workers brought to the Americas from Korea and southern China in the nineteenth century to make up the shortfall in labour caused by the abolition of slave labour in 1834. Bryant, 'a thin-boned African', represents descent from slavehood, but along a gene-line that resisted miscegenation. Descendants of African slaves abandoned the plantations after emancipation in 1834 to become independent peasantry who survived on subsistence farming. Such communities re-adopted an African-style culture of small, rural, self-defined villages along the coast and river banks. By contrast there is Stoll, a pale-skinned mulatto or half-caste, who on account of his medium-fair skin is considered superior to blacks but inferior to whites. This intermediate, 'neither-fish-nor-fowl', 'not-any-tribe' 'in-between' condition creates an inner pressure to advance himself in the world. Stoll wants to become Fenwick's camp attendant. He wants to make something of himself. His circumstance is so reduced, however, that the best he can afford is Jordan, the crooked cook, to petition on his behalf. As a half-caste Stoll is at once severed from ancestral African roots and barred from society among the English. Van Brock is also a black, but one whose name recalls his ancestors' liasons with the Dutch plantation owners.

This social barometer is not explicitly stated in the novel. It is not, in fact, a concern of the novel. Where *The Secret Ladder* leads to is to a movement in scale. The land which the crew are to survey, putting gauges, measuring temperature, measuring depth of rainfall and so on, is inhabited by descendants of former escaped slaves whose leader is a Negro avatar named Poseidon. Poseidon is one hundred years old. He and his people distrust Fenwick and his crew. They do not accept that science will improve them. It is an extreme situation for both Poseidon and Fenwick. They are primed to experience in an acute way what the philosopher Heidegger termed *Dasein* (Being); they are about to find out a true relation of themselves.

> Fenwick has to talk with Poseidon and he notices the way that Poseidon's lips move is contrary to the things that Poseidon is supposed to be saying. In other words the physical appearance of Poseidon is one thing but the things that Poseidon is supposed to be saying come from a different age and a different generation . . . Under the extreme pressure of the situation, Bryant, the 'thin-boned African', and modern West Indian begins to side with Poseidon. He tells Fenwick: 'When Poseidon dies he is going to go back to Africa.' Now Bryant did not learn that in school or in university, what he learned in school was that such an idea was an illusion under which African slaves committed suicide. But you see, under the pressure of the extreme situation and siding with Poseidon he recovers the historical ideas of the slaves. He tells Fenwick that Poseidon was his grandfather: 'At least I feel that way towards him.' Fenwick is deeply disturbed, first of all by Poseidon and at what Poseidon is doing to Bryant.[52]

52 C.L.R. James, *Wilson Harris – A Philosophical Approach*, University of the West Indies, 1965, pp.12–14.

The crew is an active litmus of the threads and divisions at the heart of community in Guyana in the 1940s. The crew (minus the Hindu) is an accurate mirror of the template on which the now-independent nation was born. It is a template saturated with images of a terrifying past, images almost frozen with induration. Individuals locked in historical antagonisms at the heart of a society that will have to accept, eventually, the practice of more supple and fruitfulrelations.

What is the opening chapter in the dream-book of the culture; the clues that would cast a prognosticating and prospecting net forward into Harris's still-being-written book of dream? The adventuring, explorational boat crew in *Palace of the Peacock*, which recalls less the taming of the Guyana coastland and the establishment of agricultural infrastructure than the discovery of the interior. Donne is the owner of an estate in the interior; it is harvest time and he is hurrying back on the river. He intends to stop off at an Arawak village to recruit labour, but as he and his small crew paddle into the village waters they are astonished to see the entire village fleeing in canoes, refusing, as they paddle past and away, to look at Donne and his crew. Donne captures an old woman who has been abandoned in the exodus. He learns from her that the villagers recognized him and his crew as revenants from the dead and that they would not share their village with the dead. There had been a previous heroic crew just like Donne's who perished below a violent drop in the river (Sorrow Hill). Donne is furious. He determines to pursue the villagers and to get the labour he so desperately needs for his farm. He forces the woman into the boat and makes her take him to the place where he will find the villagers.

It would be misleading to suggest that the book's events are as clear-cut as this. We learn about these things from Donne's brother, a tutelary, nameless, twin who speaks as if from behind a veil. The crew appear to go up-river and to meet apotheosis by ascending, as opposed to descending, the waterfall. Their ascent of the cascade takes place not in an instant but, for a certain number of the crew, over several hours and days. The peacock's palace is none other than the stars of the southern night sky, whose scintillations seem especially brilliant and near. This is the palace the men enter. It is the imaginative equivalent of the array of the peacock's tail in its splendour, the *cauda pavonis* in which is displayed the rainbow the iridescent spectrum. The flesh of the peacock confers immortality on the eater, so the crew have names that recall perpetual history – an age of discovery that is both Elizabethan and Victorian. It is a recall-in-fiction that is partly remembrance of England's hard romance with the legend of El Dorado and the golden city (Mariella, the old Arawak guide, and Donne, punning on El Doradonne), partly recalling early explorers of the Guyana interior. Schomburg, the steersman, recalls Germanic descent, after the Schomburgk brothers, scientists and naturalists commissioned by the British and Prussian governments in the 1840s to explore the then unknown interior. Cameron perhaps recalls the Scottish priest Richard Cameron (1648–80) and the marked influence exercised by the Reformed Scottish Presbyterian Church in Guyanese Christian life. Da Silva is a generic name recalling a Portugese dynasty whose presence stretched from the Iberian Peninsula to the Canaries, the Ivory coast, the islands of the Indian Ocean to Goa on mainland India. Following the abolition of slavery in the 1840s, the Portugese of Madeira were originally shipped over and coerced into indentured work, but proved poor labourers. After 1848 the Portugese began to be replaced by East Indian indentured workers and, like the Chinese, the Portugese moved off the land and became city dwellers in the capital Georgetown (in the mouth of the Demerara River) and New Amsterdam (coastal river capital of Berbice County).

In peopling the *Guyana Quartet* with crews of mixed and intermingled racial origin Harris is making for our times a crucial anamnesis with the indigenous past: that of the Carib practice of taking wives from the tribes they conquered to engender a cross-culturalism in the new child who will embody both self and enemy.[53] Cross-culturalism, then, becomes an unfinished rehearsal in comprehensiveness. By teaching the male children to speak Carib and the females to speak Arawak, the Carib practice is an imaginative attempt to overcome cultural bias or partiality in their conception of themselves. If we continue our reading of *The Secret Ladder* (1963), we see how the leader of the surveying team manoeuvres himself into a cross-cultural space where he can experience a Heideggerian *Dasein* or 'being there'.

> They bring news to Fenwick that some of Poseidon's men have broken down the gauges that he has put up to measure rainfall and waterfall and so on. And two of Fenwick's assistants, they are foremen in charge, tell him: 'Now look at what these savages did. We should deal with them.' But Fenwick begins to experience the *Dasein*. He says, 'I do not think that what they did was in opposition to me.' Fenwick adds: "Yes, they may have broken the gauges, but I think that they were seeking to establish some sort of freedom which they think we threaten.' The foremen are eager to punish Poseidon's men. Fenwick says, 'No leave them alone. I think I will be able to work it out with them.' Fenwick, in other words, is experiencing the *Dasein*. He is 'living there', and the previous experience whereby he came from the Government with the instruments and a group to measure the land and do the things he thought of benefit to them, he has lost that completely, it was inauthentic.[54]

So we see the human signs, the actual, contemporary sense of Being; we see how the day-to-day level and the individual conjoin in the cross-cultural womb. But how exactly does that 'come and go' operate? How does time function in the 'womb of space'? What is time's mechanism?

53 I am grateful to Patricia Murray for helping me make this connection in her essay 'Creative Bridges: Some Aspects of Myth in "Couvade" and *The Four Banks of the River of Space*', *The Review of Contemporary Fiction*, Summer 1997, p.78.
54 C.L.R. James, *Wilson Harris – A Philosophical Approach*, p.13.

A great banquet was launched by the Doctor on the Day of the Wedding. It taxes me now to remember the places where everyone sat, even though I sailed from the future into the Banquet, sailed with the Memory of the past that one stores in the future. Sailed with the architectures of the future back into the past. It was necessary to extend the dining-room in which Jones and Deacon and I had eaten our last meal together, in Jonestown, on the eve of the holocaust November 1978, into Port Mourant 1954 (p.196).

'It was necessary to **extend** *the dining-room in which Jones and Deacon and I had eaten our last meal together, in Jonestown, on the eve of the holocaust November 1978, into Port Mourant 1954.'* So we see how a particular attitude in consciousness, a particular state of awareness, a particular *éveille*, creates envelopes between an unapprehended past and a reappraised future. This is what one does in the womb of space. One pre-incarnates, one post-incarnates, one prolongs the self in the fable of history.

Crisis and the individual talent

Tradition in art fosters a certain permanence of outlook. If the individual is to develop a sense of tradition, there needs to exist a certain accumulation of works of distinction. Societies that subordinate their creative *élan* to strategies of denial or indifference unwittingly enter a prolonged rite of self-decimation – a practice touched on with admirable succinctness in *The Four Banks of the River of Space*:

> Anselm gave me his manuscript in December 1989 on the eve of his departure for Brazil to attend a conference on the fate of the South American rainforests. It was his plan after to embark on another expedition into the Macusi heartland. I did not expect to see him again.
>
> He gave me permission to edit his book of dreams and to add epigraphs. Like myself he is Guyanese by birth (born in Georgetown in 1912) and knows the country well. I have made a number of inquiries but these have elicited no information whatsoever about the family background to which he refers in his book nor of his work in British Guiana as an engineer, sculptor, painter, architect, composer. It is as if he never existed.[55]

It would be no exaggeration to say that, unlike their Hispanic counterparts in Central America, Peru, Chile or Argentina, the literary artists of the English-speaking Caribbean have no recognized status in the community. It is the politicians – among them the recipients of national scholarships, those educated to

55 *The Four Banks of the River of Space*, pp.xi–xii.

doctoral level in England, and others writing notable studies of political history – who mobilize public opinion and command literacy. Constant inculcation by the public sphere, the unremitting reduction of one's acts and choices into questions of policy, puts an imaginative frame around the individual. In practice, in an imaginative capacity, such frames are illiterate ones, and the concept of a literate imagination would be enigma to many. Without the blocks and checks to individual action exercised in the larger democracies, the abuse of trust in political office in countries such as Guyana can be endemic.

The literate imagination is a condition Harris addresses in the essays in Part II. Where it is in abeyance many of the accomplishments that produce an integrated society – the broad-based practice of arts, humanities, artisanry – are entirely absent. This has little to do with economic development or insufficient formal education; it is rather an attitude, a Philistinism taken up and worn like an inverse order of merit that has been one of the unanticipated legacies of independence.

I noted earlier how the liberators of a nation can fall victim to a disempowering pattern of history. To reject accomplishment because it shows the face of the colonial past is the most frequent intervention. What concerns us here is the legacy of the English language and how unconditional acts of rejection endanger it.

A mother tongue coerces its speakers into near insoluble kinships – of education, world view and, inevitably, of culture. Since the dissolution of empire, it is the English tongue, as opposed to English rule, that has shaped the peoples of the Commonwealth into shared destiny. Because many people in the Commonwealth speak the same language and have a similar education, they hold, in addition to their own domestic traditions, a culture that is shared with 1.5 billion others. There is shared familiarity with the same books, music, poetry, world view. What is the role of individual groups in such a continuum? 'The tough aesthetic of the New World neither explains nor forgives history. It refuses to recognise it as a culpable force.'[56]

Neither the Nobel laureate Derek Walcott (b. 1930), who wrote the above, nor Harris suggest that absolute escape from historic burden is either possible or desirable. Neither seek to refute or reject history – both recognize that by openly fighting a tradition you serve to perpetuate it. What Harris does instead is to visualize that the 'need to stagger the burden of memory, replete with guilt, is essential to the creation of a new age'.[57]

Harris's innovations in the novel (the attention to whole areas of experience unacknowledged by the conventional novel) are extraordinary solutions to coercive historic pattern, and, by extension, to narrative convention:

---

56 Derek Walcott, 'The Muse of History' in *The Arnold Anthology of Post-Colonial Literatures in English*, John Thieme (ed.), Arnold, London, 1996. First published by Anchor/Doubleday, NY, 1974 in Orde Coombs (ed.), *Is Massa Day Dead?*

57 Wilson Harris, 'Profiles of Myth and the New World', W. Zach and K.L. Goodwin (eds), *Nationalism vs. Internationalism, (Inter)national Dimensions of Literatures in English*, Stauffenburg Verlag, Tübingen, 1996, p.83.

for the method by which we are taught the past – the progress from motive to event – is the same by which we read narrative fiction; therefore to re-map human experience, to renew a grasp of the human psyche at once phenomenal and cultural, we must dismantle the narrative convention and its tie-in with the fatal realisms of society.[58]

Guyana, as part of the South American context, is a vivid medium of divergences from expectation. It confounds the expectations of the traditional novel: the static beliefs, the conventional sequence, the finite nature.[59]

Where cultures encounter one another, as they do in South America, they recompose themselves into what can be thought of as a body of civilization in which come alive ramifications that can never be absolutely seized but which register as an immense and subtle transfer of masks. Harris's *essais* or 'trials of the imagination in masks' will outline the new burdens upon us as we apprehend new parables of man.

The essays

The nineteen lectures, talks, addresses and essays in this volume present unusual and valuable hypothesis in a number of areas: the archetypal fiction (Part I), the concept of the cross-cultural community (Part II), the particular sensibility of the native Guianas (Part III), and the function of the arts of the imagination in renewing the practice of fiction (Parts III and IV).[60]

---

58 Ibid., p.79. *But what influence can staggered memory and staggered guilt exercise on the fatal realisms of society?* If the cross-cultural picture of ourselves dates back, in the novel, to the late 1940s and the fictions first written in the South American continent in Spanish of authors such as Angel Asturias and Lezaza Lima, and later independently by Harris in English, and if the cross-cultural conception of ourselves could have been elaborated as early as the traditional novel of the nineteenth century, then the delay is already a staggering of memory and guilt across centuries.

59 With the exception of Belize and, in part, Argentina, the Republic of Guyana is the only English-speaking territory in mainland South America. Elsewhere Spanish and its Creoles is the dominant language, with Portuguese in Brazil. (French and Dutch Guiana, on mainland South America, where French and Dutch are official languages, are not nations in their own right but overseas provinces of France and Holland. We noted that Harris's books are distinct from the literatures belonging to the Caribbean isles and divergent from the novel in England. This leads us to ask ourselves how best to classify a writer: by language, nationality, country of birth, or by affinities with particular traditions? In a wholesome assessment, what is the relative weighing of each one? Harris is possibly most usefully viewed not so much part of national movements but as a landmark innovator in literary form who mediates between a number of imaginative traditions; innovation coming about by the immense historical burden sustained in the novel and the essay.

60 Five essays appeared in previous collections: 'Tradition and the West Indian Novel' in *Tradition, the Writer and Society* (1967, 1973); 'History, Fable and Myth in the Caribbean and the Guianas' in *Explorations, A Selection of Talks and Articles 1966–1981* (1981), 'Reflections on *Intruder in the Dust* in a Cross-cultural Complex', 'The Schizophrenic Sea', and 'Concentric Horizons' in *The Womb of Space: The Cross-Cultural Imagination* (1983).

I allow these themes to give the volume its particular inflection. They capture Harris's inflections and modulations, enables the rapid placing of themes and trends, facilitate the marking of imaginative bridges to different areas of his novels, and impart a sense of cohesion to the creative topography. A summary of motifs, conceptual difficulties and elucidations appears in the prefaces to each section, each one promoting a single, arresting exposition of the essays that follow.

Part I

Essays No. 1–4 relate to time and event in literary composition whilst giving a thematic survey of the territory. They have in mind both readers studying Harris for the first time and those who are already familiar with his work. 'The Music of Living Landscapes' (1996) is a biographical account of the artist and the imaginative life; the integration, in the creative life, of South America, the author's continent of birth, and his home of forty years, England. 'Letter from Francisco Bone to W.H.' an extract from the novel *Jonestown* (1996), gives lucid summary of the cross-cultural spectrum in the Americas. 'New Preface to *Palace of the Peacock*' (1998) expands on the preceding essay. It identifies the cross-cultural spectrum in the Americas with the Carib bone-flute and the latter's role as architecture or organizing principle in Harris's dream-book of the culture. 'Merlin and Parsifal: Adversarial Twins' (1997) locates in a European context the twinship structures that riddle the imaginative productions of the Central and Southern America.

Part II

Essays No. 5–10 are studies in the American literary imagination. The focus is the conventional novel's capacity for concealing premises alive in the work but reluctant to be raised to consciousness. Harris unravels the way these premises conceal themselves in curious ironies at the heart of the text, and uncovers new critical perspectives on a rich seam of fiction. 'Literacy and the Imagination – a Talk' (1989) presents the concept of the literate, as opposed to the illiterate, imagination; how, in a world that preaches the uniformity of the individual, one might practice the imagination as one would practice an art. 'Reflections on *Intruder in the Dust*' (1983), 'The Schizophrenic Sea' (1983), and 'Concentric Horizons' (1983) stand together; they show how white writers and black writers in the United States serve as uncanny stepping-stones to one another as the conventional novel first undermines itself and then forces on its practitioners the recognition of the need for more comprehensive stances. This essay-trio covers four authors and a range of works over a hundred-year period – Poe (1838), Toomer (1923), Faulkner (1949) and Ellison (1952) – and its extended treatment led me to place it before the earlier essay on Melville, 'Benito Cereno' (1975). 'Jean Rhys' "Tree of Life"' (1985) identifies a subtle imaginative unity in that author that might in fact resolve the dispossessed individual and the dispossessed culture. 'Benito Cereno' prepares the ground of concepts and connections that would structure Harris's later full-length study of the American imagination, *The Womb of Space: The Cross-Cultural Imagination* (1983), and which opens with the essay-trio on Faulkner, Poe, Toomer and Ellison.

Part III

Essays No. 11–13 identify the native, imaginative resources of rainmaking vestiges, limbo, vodun (voodoo), the Carib bush-baby, masquerade and carnival as hidden resources-of-depth to empower the native writer of the future. The essays in this group speak of the intuitive origins of the Caribbean literary imagination, the different kinds of society embraced in commonwealth and their consequence on the literatures now being written. 'Tradition and the West Indian Novel' (1964) first looks at the false alignment between the post-war West Indian novel and the traditionalist nineteenth-century narrative then offers crucial reformulations for subsequent writing. 'History, Fable and Myth in the Caribbean and Guianas' (1970) is a three-lecture series reproduced here in its 1995 revision. It begins with an important review of historiographers of the English Caribbean basin, whose well-intentioned accounts nevertheless prolong a legacy of distortion. The lecture series then continues by way of an outline of the 'native host consciousness' of the Guianas and the search for viable and sustainable languages of self-reclamation. 'Quetzalcoatl and the Smoking Mirror: Reflections on Originality and Tradition' (1994) deepens, through the phenomenology of masque and masquerade, the intuitive resources discovered in the preceding essay.

Part IV

Essays No. 14–19 reflect on the resources of depth in the arts of the imagination and point-up the broad spectrum of opportunities available to the writer for revisioning himself in the culture. 'Profiles of Myth and the New World' (1996) concerns pre-Columbian traditions of fluid identity. New World artefacts bear striking resemblances to civilizations remote in time and space from Central and South America; but how can one explain this? Harris examines five such artefacts (a figurine, a sculpture, a carving, a massive stone head) and discerns a potential bearing on the art of fiction. 'In the Name of Liberty' (1990) can be read as supplement to 'Literacy and the Imagination – a Talk'. It cites again the findings of Frances Yates, a scholar of the Renaissance (*The Art of Memory*, 1966). The argument deals with arts of 'visualization in depth' that can rescue a society from prematurely framing itself inside codes and dogmas that will gradually exert a stranglehold on its viability. 'Aubrey Williams' (1966) discusses the painter, also a fellow of the Royal Astronomical Society – yet who was virtually unknown in his native Guyana. This short address reflects on how the rhythms of tone and colour in Williams's canvases are alive with Amerindian symbols that seem to express movements in time and sensibility. 'Apprenticeship to the Furies' (1996) traces the parables (the muses) and passions (the furies) visualizable in the vessel of the human body and actualized in the act of creativity. 'Creoleness, the Crossroads of a Civilization?' (1998) has epochal ramifications. Beginning with Harris's own childhood experience in the mixed-blood society of Guyana, it weighs down on the empirical tradition that admits solely to data received through the five senses. 'The Unfinished Genesis of the Imagination' (1992) completes the selection. If one conceives of the poetic imagination as a living landscape or parable of being, then its structures might include the abyss or breach in the partial model of tradition. It might conceal motifs crucial to our survival and yet which go undiscovered; it might also present itself in non-continuous imageries that produce what can be termed a paradox of wholeness.

In conclusion, we might ask how does one work with the dream-book? If we read these essays as Harris's hypotheses for writing the dream-book of the culture, represented by the whole sequence of his novels, then their greatest value lies in their divergence from a common background of literary conventions and shared assumptions about the nature of the world and the degrees of evidential support.

A.J.M. Bundy
University of North London
August, 1998

Part I

THE ARCHETYPAL FICTION

PREFACE: THE ARCHETYPAL FICTION[1]

Harris's novels set out to establish a new dialogue with reality in all its guises (p.43). It is a reality one could call archetype. And what is archetype? We spoke, in the Introduction, of circularities and revisitations in the territory of Harris's novels. Circularity and archetype and intimately related. The one corresponds the other.[2]

1 Harris has defined the art of *fiction* as accepting 'the enigma of self-proportion' *The Waiting Room*, London, 1967, p.9. For a definition of the archetype, see n.2 below.
2 The physical shape of ideas (circularity, roundness) is not itself the archetype but rather a found means that corresponds the archetype.

> The thinking in the Psalms and of the prophets is 'circular. Even the Apocalypse consists of spiral images . . . One of the main characteristics of Gnostic thinking is circularity.' . . . Dogma [doctrine or belief] is 'circular' . . . round in the sense of a living reality . . . [Koepgen in *Gnosis des Christentums*] calls attention to the 'fact of not knowing and not recognising which lies at the core of the dogma itself' [p.51]. This remark indicates the reason or one of the reasons for the 'roundness': dogmas are approxim*ative* concepts for a fact which exists yet cannot be described, and can only be approached by circumambulation. At the same time, these facts are 'spheres' of indeterminable extent, since they represent *principles*. Psychologically they correspond to archetypes. Overlapping and interpenetration are an essential part of their nature.
> C.G. Jung, III. *The Personification of the Opposites*, para. 123, note 54, in *CW* XIV, *Mysterium Coniunctionis*, trans. R.F.C. Hull, Routledge, 1963, pp.102n–103n.

As the shape of the idea 'archetype', the 'round' has all parts of its surface equidistant from the centre. The rounded life is one in which all activities carry equal weight. The centre is the origin or principle (L. *principalis*, first, chief, original). In the archetypal fiction that principle or origin usually resists direct perception, so that the roundness or surface-experience exhibits qualities of indeterminacy. Indeterminate both in the sense of having an unlimited number of solutions (L. *in* + *determinabilis*, not finite) and in the sense of uncertainty of size or duration. When the 'round' is an object it assumes the proportions of a sphere. As experience, that sphere has 'indeterminate extent', i.e. we do not know the exact radian or distance from origin or, alternatively, the time at which the sphere of experience will converge. When sung, as in a canon, the round is taken up sequentially by a different voice. Thus, in the archetypal fiction, the given round is subject in each new section to revisions; a new voice, a striking approach, a variant in circumstance. *Roundness* then is characteristic of the archetypal fiction. *Circularity* means that the fiction approaches its end by indirect means, by

Harris has identified in the continent of South America a self-regulatory human laboratory in which startling divergences from traditionalist expectations have taken place. The history, languages and literature of that continent function as the proof of an unusual theorem which revises the pattern of received histories. The legacy of ancient Americas operates as if, 'all the races of the earth should have travelled there in order to become models for their craftsmen and artists' ('Profiles of Myth and the New World', p.203).

In a first instance, a humane laboratory will revise patterns such as the model of history outlined in the Introduction. It revises them via displaced transparencies that seed in other cultures and come, as it were, to the Americas for clarification. When viewed through the spectroscope of the Americas such transparencies fall back into place and can be fruitfully read. This gives rise to what Harris terms the cross-cultural phenomenon: the self-recognition of one civilization in the culture-bed of the other ('New Preface to *Palace of the Peacock*'). The cross-cultural is to be distinguished from the multi-cultural, the cosmopolitan, which is a forum created out of mutual commercial interests and in which different cultures can operate at the same point in time.

circumambulation, within an indeterminate sphere of experience. *Overlapping and interpenetration* are an essential part of its nature, so that in 'Letter from Francisco Bone to W.H.' (see pp.47–52 in this volume), archetype is realized as

> overlapping layers and environments and theatres of legend and history [that one might associate with Jonestown]

A further ramification of archetype is that Harris's words often take their chief meaning from their strict etymology: *Associate with Jonestown*, for instance, not conveying the usual sense of 'things which make one think of Jonestown' but is the Latin *ad + socius* allied to; literally 'things allied and alloyed with Jonestown'. In this sense, Jonestown stands for a new contract with Being, an independent entity in its own right as opposed to an arbitrary collection of alike-seeming thoughts and inspirations. It is a specificity that gives the archetype its particular resonance and implication to promote unique composition in the body of fiction.

Yet the hypotheses of the archetypal fiction are approxim*ative* concepts. Approximative because they issue from chronic states. States that come about from *the fact of not knowing and a not recognising*: Harris's *overlapping layers and environments and theatres of legend and history*. One associates such layers with discontinuities in our experience of Being; moments of terminus and the fall from the fixed stars (disaster); trauma and disappearance, but also redemptive movements from the future and reversal of the past. 'Archetypal dreams employ symbols of brokenness to depict the shedding of habit.' ('The Music of Living Landscapes'). Breakage or fragmentation from previous habit enables the dream to rewrite itself into new structures and, as I noted in the Introduction, also to write a new structure into the author.

Moments of terminus are also ruptures in the fabric of time. Ruptures in the fabric of time release or secrete the composite epic. The epic is composite because pieces of different time (the past, present, relived future) come together and make a bridge through the rupture in time. One can interpret composite epic as a Masquerade or Carnival or Jamboree or All Hallows Feast in which long-vanished texts re-emerge and re-present themselves in 'The language of the heartland, relying as it did upon a curious jigsaw of intangible resources, set in variable perspective' (*Heartland*, 1964, p.88).

The Conquistadors come to the Caribbean and show their faces to the Carib. They show the faces of fear, hatred, greed and war. The Carib look at the Conquistadors and see, as if for the first time, the masque of conquest they themselves have been performing around the Caribbean for two thousand years. To Harris, it was bitter self-knowledge, as much as inferior military technology, which defeated then extinguished the Carib.

The second instance is the overlap of the literary medium with the nature of the enquiry. The central fact of the archetype is that, as cultural expression, the archetype is neither known nor recognized until it is in some sense fulfilled; we become aware of the archetype's fullness only in retrospect, in the waning of events. Thus the archetypal novel addresses facts which exist yet which resist direct apprehension. In this way the archetype is a species of inductive knowledge. An unobserved matter of fact not subject to causal reasoning but which, once discovered, is taken for self evident. As the prime imaginative source for literary fiction, the archetype puts a burden of conscience on the artist; it acts as if it is inviting the artist to address those diffuse areas of consciousness that seem to stand outside the world of sense-perception. The artist is obliged to create a 'new conceptual language' with which to transpose *nonsensational* realities (see 'Merlin and Parsifal: Adversarial Twins', p.61). A literary medium that deals with these things proceeds, as it were, by posing new riddles.

Harris uses certain words in a specialized sense. In 'The Music of Living Landscapes', I would think of *music* as the medium of memory, the thing with which we are mused or made into by memory (Gr. *mnasthai*, 'I am made to remember, mnemonic'); I would interpret *Lazarus* as figuration for the tree of life. By abjecting nature we disease the tree of life; the *anatomy of Nemesis*, the course or diagnosis of disease. Technology, as a *lux moderna*, a modern insight, a new epochal attitude to problem-solving, a technology that kills the tree of life will return as living branches in the newly risen tree. Each new-sprung branch lives by the indulgence of a newer and future technology. In this essay, past acts of violence cause the subsequent generation to live provisionally, fearfully, in a way that will encourage new atrocity. Thus the *technology of resurrection* is both the imaginative means at our disposal for overcoming bias and fear, as well as the means for making living contracts of Being with the past.

1

THE MUSIC OF LIVING LANDSCAPES

Unabridged version of typescript submitted to BBC Radio 4. An edited version was broadcast 12 November 1996. Sound effects, flute variations were by Keith Waithe.

Perhaps I should tell you that I studied land surveying and astronomy as a young man. That was really the launching pad for expeditions into the deep, forested rainforests of Guyana, so that I became intimately and profoundly involved with the landscapes, and riverscapes, of Guyana.

As a surveyor one is involved in mathematical disciplines, and astronomy, and one has, or I have, the sensation that the part of the cosmos in which we live, and the rainforests, are the lungs of the globe. The lungs of the globe breathe on the stars.

It seems to me that, for a long time, landscapes and riverscapes have been perceived as passive, as furniture, as areas to be manipulated; whereas, I sensed, over the years, as a surveyor, that the landscape possessed resonance. The landscape possessed a life, because, the landscape, for me, is like an open book, and the alphabet with which one worked was all around me. But it takes some time to really grasp what this alphabet is, and what the book of the living landscape is.

Let me begin my address by asking –

Is there a language akin to music threaded into space and time which is prior to human discourse?

Such a question is implicitly imprinted in legends of Guyanese and South American landscapes, preternatural voices in rivers, rapids, giant waterfalls, rock, tree.

A fish leaps close to where I stand on a riverbank, in the great dark of the South American rainforest night, and look up at the stars.

Theatre of memory! I hear that leap or voice of rippling water all over again across the years as if it's happening *now*, this very moment, within the Thames of London beside which I have often strolled since arriving in England.

And one meditates here by the Thames – as one meditated there not far from the Amazon or the Orinoco – upon the fate of the earth and its species.

Outer space is steeped in dangers and in environments hostile to life. Yet, it is said, the human animal is a child of the stars.

That child must carry, surely, an instinct for creation. Not only an instinct for the fury of creation, the fiery birth of constellations, but an instinct for immensity and silence, the music of silence within contrasting tone and light and shadow as they combine to ignite in oneself a reverie of pulse and heart and mind.

Inner ear and inner eye are linked to eloquent silences in the leap or pulse of light in shadow, shadow light, as if the fish in remembered rivers fly through an ocean of space and witness by enchantment, it seems, to the *miracle* of living skyscapes, oceanscapes, riverscapes wherever these happen to be, on Earth, or at the edge of distant galaxies.

I was born in South America and I left British Guyana for the United Kingdom at the age of thirty-eight.

Guyana is a remarkable wilderness. It has known Spanish settlers, then French and Dutch rule but became a British colony in the early nineteenth century.

Its population is less than a million but encompasses peoples from every corner of the globe, Africa, India, China, Portugal.

In area it is virtually as large as the United Kingdom and one sees graphically, I think, on a map the two oceans, so to speak, that flank the narrow strip of coastland along which the greater body of the population live and sound their drums of India and Africa. One flanking ocean – with its subdued, perennial roar against sea-wall and sea-defences – is the Atlantic, the other is green and tall, unlit by the surf of electricity on rainforested wave upon wave of wind-blown savannahs running into Brazil and Venezuela.

There are Amerindian legends which tell of sleeping yet, on occasion, singing rocks that witness to the traffic of history, the traffic of expeditions in search of El Dorado that Sir Walter Raleigh would have contemplated when he voyaged up the Orinoco before he lost his head in the Tower of London. The rocks sing an unwritten opera of El Doradonne adventurers.

Amerindians such as the Macusis, the Wapishanas, the Arawaks – whom Raleigh would have encountered – are still to be found in Guyana and South America. They have suffered – since Columbus's and Raleigh's day – decimations and the continuous depletion of their numbers at the hand of Europe across the centuries.

They were close to extinction at the beginning of this century but have survived in small numbers against all the odds.

I came upon them frequently – indeed they were sometimes members of my crew – in landsurveying expeditions into the heartland of Guyana and was drawn to their still demeanour and mobile poise as huntsmen and fishermen.

Through them I learnt of the parable of the music of the fish in a rippling stream. They baited their fisherman's hook with a rainbow feather from a macaw or a parrot and with a twist of the wrist – as if they addressed an invisible orchestra – made it dart in the stream towards the leaping fish.

Feather from a wing and eager fish were united, it seemed, into an orchestra of species and a sacrament of subsistence they (these ancient peoples) had long cultivated since their ancestors emigrated twelve thousand years ago from Asia across the Bering Straits into the continent we now call America.

Emigration – in distant ages as in modern times – is the nerve of spiritual enterprise in all communities; it is driven by private necessity as well as economic and historical impulse, by hope, desire, promise and innermost vocation.

I emigrated to the United Kingdom in the late 1950s and lived with my wife Margaret in Addison Road, close to Holland Park, a stone's throw from Kensington Gardens.

It wasn't long before I resumed the orchestration of elements in fiction – which I had begun in the landscapes of South America – with the novel *Palace of the Peacock*. This was the first volume in a related series to be entitled *The Guyana Quartet* upon which I worked in the early 1960s.

I had few friends in England, none of influence, and at such times when the future is grave and uncertain and one is a stranger in a great city one is visited by archetypal and troubling dreams.

Archetypal dreams employ symbols of brokenness to depict the shedding of habit. A naked jar sings in a hollow body, sings to be restored, re-filled with the blood of the imagination. The jar sleeps yet sings.

The jar is adorned with many elusive faces. It is inscribed with the head and the body of a boatman in a South American river. The boatman contends with mysterious currents. The paddle with which he strokes the rapids is seized by a streaming hand arising from the bowels of the earth . . .

An orchestra reawakens in my mind instinctive with a surge of terrifying music in the voyaging boatmen in *Palace of the Peacock* and I turn a page in the book and write –

> The boat shuddered in an anxious grip and in a living streaming hand that issued from the bowels of earth. We stood on the threshold of a precarious standstill. The outboard engine and the propeller still revolved and flashed with mental *silent* horror now that its roar had been drowned in other wilder unnatural voices whose violent din rose from beneath our feet in the waters.
>
> (*Palace of the Peacock*, 1960, p.21)

The *silenced* roar of the engine filled the boatman with dread. The engine was strangely alive in the void of his senses, void because in the heart of danger he could *see* its activity but no longer *hear* its voice as it assisted him and his crew as they paddled against the torrent . . .

But surely there is more to silence than a void in civilization? Is there not an inner music to silence, an inner attunement of ear and eye to sounding waters and painted skies, painted earth?

I took a night job for a few months in the winter/spring of 1960 in a North London factory.

On leaving the workplace early mornings I took away the hoarse call of the wheels of industry and the clamour and the grind of sliced metal as dawn broke like a white-feathered bird in the early spring blossom of a horsechestnut tree at the gate through which the factory workers streamed to kick-start a motor bike or take a bus or drive a car. Layer upon layer of noise drowning noise.

Even as I moved through the gate in the stream of workers I knew the rain-forests in Brazil and Guyana were under threat, erosion of soils was occurring in the United States and around the globe, weather patterns were changing . . .

Nature is not passive. Nature erupts into orchestras of Nemesis.

Yet it *knows* our peril for we are in nature, of nature's chorus in response to hurricane or waterfall. Nature arouses us to speculate on orchestrations of inner eye and inner ear beyond every void of the senses, beyond every grave of the senses . . .

I left the factory in the Spring of 1960 imbued with a sensation of profound necessity in the life of the imagination to visualize links between technology and living landscapes in continuously new ways that took nothing for granted in an increasingly violent and materialistic world.

The haunting and necessary proportions of a new dialogue with reality in all its guises of recovered and revisionary tradition drew me into an anatomy or shared body everywhere in all things and species that give colour and numinosity to space . . . Lazarus emerges in the first volume of a *Carnival Trilogy* which I wrote in the 1980s.

Inner ear and inner eye are his resurrected anatomy attuned to the music of painted silence in pulse and heart and mind arisen from the grave of the world.

He travels one winter day from his workplace on a bus that stops to pick up passengers close to a fence at Kensington Gardens.

He sees a carpet of burnt autumn leaves across the fence. A veil descends from a cloud in the sky shaped like a pinnacle of flood. The veil breaks into smoke and mist and runs into a hollow depression within the painted silence of the leaves that are eloquent with the immensity of changing seasons, contrasting tone and texture. Inner ear and inner eye weep for all things like the dew of rain. Lazarus is aroused to the beat of cosmic love as he contemplates the trampled leaves in the passage from *Carnival* I shall now read.

> In the winter light that seemed to echo with intimate yet faraway vistas . . . Lazarus felt the imprint of black fire, black tone, numinous wonderful shadow . . . Yes, mind, heart, shadow . . . was the mind of Lazarus in attunement to ivories of sensation, russets, and other alphabets of the elements within every hollow epitaph of memory, every hollow grave.
>
> Winter lapsed into the carpet of autumn leaves under the bole of a tree that the bus was passing The trampled leaves appeared to smoke with an arousal of spirit, trampled greenness, trampled yellow paint, in the hollow depression of time and place from which one arises to discourse with silent music within the roar of a great city.
>
> *The Carnival Trilogy* (1993), pp.140–41

PAUSE. MUSIC THAT DIES YET SEEMS TO ECHO ENDLESSLY IN RISEN CONSCIOUSNESS AS IN THE LAST SOUNDS IN GUSTAV MAHLER'S NINTH SYMPHONY.

Lazarus may have arisen in the early 1980s in *Carnival* but alas the grave of history continues to yawn wide even as I speak now in the year of Our Lord 1996.

The savage exploitation of rainforests continues in South America. Trees are felled like dumb creatures. River catchments are impoverished. The muse of nature within the consciousness of peoples is threatened. A deadly cyanide overspill seeped into the great Essequebo River of Guyana in 1995. The grave is deep despite every carpet of leaves that Lazarus paints with music.

When I speak of *silent music* – in the short passage that I read from *Carnival* – I am intent on repudiating a dumbness or passivity with which we subconsciously or unconsciously robe the living world. Living landscapes have their own pulse and arterial topography and sinew which differ from ours but are as real – however far-flung in variable form and content – as the human animal's. I am intent on implying that the vibrancy or pathos in the veined tapestry of a broken leaf addresses arisen consciousness through linked eye and ear in a shared anatomy that has its roots in all creatures and in everything.

Consciousness of self in others, consciousness of diversity that breaks the mould of prejudice, remains a mystery to science.

In mystery lie orchestrations of comedy that fuel the imagination to release itself from one-sided dogma whether in science or in religion. Astronomers have sought to fathom the age of the universe only to stumble in a comedy of space in which subordinate parts within the universe seem older than the parent universe itself. One awakens at times to one's frailty in the cradle of the mind in particles that settle on one's brow or hand or skin, sailing particles from distant mountains and valleys that seek their mysterious parentage in all substance or in the alchemy of sound in a rainbow.

Such, I believe, is the implicit orchestra, of living landscapes when consciousness sings through variegated fabrics and alternations of mood, consonance as well as dissonance, unfathomable age and youth, unfathomable kinships.

In an age of crisis the marriage of consonance and dissonance – transmuted into unpredictable and original art that challenges the hubris of one-sided tradition – is an important factor, I think, in the re-sensitizing of technology to the life of the planet.

The taming of the wilderness has always been an uneasy programme, however desperately pursued, in the body of civilizations.

When I come upon a felled tree in a park in England it sometimes shapes itself in my inner eye as the epitaph of a murdered forest in Brazil, or Guyana, or Venezuela.

I seek – as if imbued by Lazarus's mind in my mind, Lazarus's dream of cosmic love – to re-clothe that tree with the music of consciousness, with rustling, whispering branches in the foliage it has lost.

I picture the tools that felled the tree as newsprung branches themselves within a parable of creation which gives breath to iron or wood or rock. Adam was moulded, it is said, from clay. Thus the technology that killed the tree arrives or returns as living branches in the risen tree itself.

Each newsprung branch – whether wood, or iron or stone – sees itself now as susceptible to a more deadly invention or tool than it had been when it felled the kinship, resurrected tree, parent or child, to which it has returned. The risen tree, in my consciousness, veils flesh-and-blood into itself within a revisionary dynamic of creation and re-creation. Even as the technology of clay was moulded in genesis into Adam's pulse, Adam's breath.

Cities have come to nestle in branches of clay or stone in valleys or mountains. They too may be re-visited with an inner eye to see how vulnerable they are. Their hope is born of the life of imagination's tree in which sculptor and painter and architect and carpenter and mystic sensitize and re-sensitize themselves to rhythms and pulses orchestrated through being and apparent non-being.

In such a re-visionary muse, or music of consciousness, the tree suspends itself, promotes itself by degrees, within theatres of crisis that might be seen or read or gleaned through a variety of perspectives . . .

The sleeping yet singing rocks of ancient Amerindian legend grow in that tree . . .

I hear them as I stand in the open parkland in Kensington Gardens half-a-mile or more from the orchestra of the traffic arriving at, or coming from, Marble Arch . . .

Where is Marble Arch? In this instant I am uncertain for I am drawn back in memory across decades to the Tumatumari falls in the Potaro River of Guyana not far from the place called Omai where the cyanide spill from industrial workings entered the great Essequebo River in 1995.

Tumatumari is an Anglicized word drawn from an Amerindian root text and it has been translated in different ways to mean 'womb of song' or 'sleep of song' or 'sleeping yet singing rocks' in a Dream time, Dream space.

I visited Tumatumari in the mid-1940s to investigate hydro-electric potential in the vicinity of the falls.

I lay in my hammock at nights listening to the falls: hoofs of horses were running in the night as the rapids drove upon, slid over, pounded on rock: the high heels of invisible women clicked on a pavement and approached from the chasm of the river: there was the sudden grind of gears, there was motorized traffic: there was the back-firing of a car at Marble Arch . . .

The wind changes over Tumatumari as it changes over Bayswater Road and in the orchestra of memory and place which tunes into distant rain in a forest. So far away it sounds like the stealthy, drizzling approach of fire or a flute-playing ghost in the elements, a violin fashioned from sudden, scarcely visible lightning or metallic storm.

The rocks perform a tidal function in the scaffolding of the traffic of rivers. A fantastic balance between conservation and discharge of resources is achieved in the sculpture and placement of the rocks.

In my years of surveying rivers I was drawn into the sensation that sleeping and singing rocks are also dancers (stationary as they seem) even as trees and plants are known to walk under the close scrutiny of science.

The phenomenon of apparently immobile rocks which play a tidal role in non-tidal rivers is a miracle of evolution. Non-tidal rivers run ceaselessly downwards from their headwaters or sources in a distant watershed. They lie above the reach of the ocean tides which cannot therefore exercise a check upon their volumetric decline and discharge. They would become a huge empty ditch or trench were it not for the sculpture and placement of living rocks – their shape, wave-sculpture, escalation, placement in the fury of the rapids – within great river systems. They dance an inner, staggered, relay dance subsisting on the volumetric ball of the river that they bounce from hand to foot in their guardianship of resources, in their cultivation of the mystery of freedom and passage through diverse channel. They run and dance without appearing to do so even as the tree of life carpets the ground yet rises and walks in the limbs of Lazarus.

The body of the dancer in a living landscape is the technology of music.

The body of labour in living vocation resides in the technology of the resurrection.

Consciousness attunes itself to living landscapes within the dance of a seed in the soil . . . From such a seed great cities grow and their echoing tracery is in the fall of a feather from the wing of a bird.

In that feather is the technology of space fused with the murmur of threatened species that still arise and address us . . .

2

LETTER FROM FRANCISCO BONE
TO W.H.

Trinity Street
New Amsterdam

Dateless Day

Dear W.H.,

I have learnt of your sympathies for voyagers of the Imagination and trust therefore that you will undertake the task of editing the enclosed manuscript or book.

I am the only survivor of the 'tragedy of Jonestown', which occurred – as many people know – in late November 1978 in a remote forest in Guyana.

The Longman *Chronicle of America* tells of the 'tragedy of Jonestown' and of the scene of 'indescribable horror' which met the eyes of reporters from every corner of the globe when they arrived in stricken Jonestown after the self-inflicted holocaust engineered by a charismatic cult leader, the Reverend Jim Jones.

In my archetypal fiction I call Jim Jones Jonah Jones. All of the characters appearing in the book are fictional and archetypal. In this way I have sought to explore overlapping layers and environments and theatres of legend and history that one may associate with Jonestown.

Not all drank Coca-Cola laced with cyanide. Some were shot like cattle. Men, women and children.

Francisco Bone is a disguised name that I employ for myself. I suffered the most severe and disabling trauma on the Day of the Dead (as I see and continue to see in my mind's eye the bodies in a Clearing or town centre in Jonestown on November 18). The shock was so great – I blamed myself for not taking risks to avert the holocaust – that though I was wounded a numbness concealed for some time the physical injury that I suffered. The consequences of such 'numbness' occupy different proportions of the Dream-book.

When I escaped I dreamt I was dead and gained some comfort from rhymes of self-mockery, from handsome skeletons, all of which helped to promote the theme of Carnival Lord Death in the Book when eventually I began to write it. One such self-mocking poem – which I came upon when I arrived in New

47

Amsterdam before I had started writing – is the first epigraph that I use. That poem helped me to offset the hell of Memory theatre for a while and to join strolling players on a village Amsterdam green. I relished the Jest that I associated with eighteenth-century Dutch plantation owners who superimposed structures and promenades upon the bank of the Berbice River in the vicinity of New Amsterdam. When I arrived in 1985 to write my Dream-book I strolled on a promenade called *village Amsterdam green* that ran from the township to a mental hospital. Patients and townsfolk tended to stroll arm-in-arm dressed in masks of Bone at Carnival time. I sought a pleasant hole to simulate the grave into which I should have fallen on the Day of the Dead. Why me? Why did I survive? It was this thought that drove me to write . . . Questions as much as thought! No easy answers.

I feared to write in – and be written by – a demanding book that asserts itself in Dream and questions itself from time to time (even as I question the meaning of survival) as you will see as you read. One overcomes the fear of Dreams, I suspect, for I did not stop writing or being written into what I wrote . . .

I was obsessed – let me confess – by cities and settlements in the Central and South Americas that are an enigma to many scholars. I dreamt of their abandonment, their bird-masks, their animal-masks . . . Did their inhabitants rebel against the priests, did obscure holocausts occur, civil strife, famine, plague? Was Jonestown the latest manifestation of the breakdown of populations within the hidden flexibilities and inflexibilities of pre-Colombian civilizations? The Maya were certainly one of the great civilizations of ancient America and the fate of their cities – such as Palenque, Chichén Itzá, Tikal, Bonampak – has left unanswered questions. Teotihuacan in Mexico raises similar enigmas. The unsolved disappearance of the Caribs in British Guiana is another riddle of precipitate breakdown. And there are many others. The amazing story of the Arekuna Indian Awakaipu is well documented in Georgetown in the 1840s. Awakaipu persuaded representatives from many Indian peoples to offer themselves as a sacrifice at the foot of Mount Roraima in order to recover an 'enchanted kingdom'.

The Maya were torn by the notion of eternity's closure of time and another shape to time, blending pasts and futures to unlock closure or pact or plot.

The weight of charismatic eternity and a capacity to unlock closure became real and profoundly pertinent to me and to my age . . .

I drifted into what seemed an abnormal lucidity upon chasms of time. The price one pays for such voyages is far-reaching. One becomes, it seems, a vessel of composite epic, imbued with many voices, one is a multitude. That multitude is housed paradoxically in the diminutive surviving entity of community and self that one is.

All this emerges at its own pace in the Dream-book but the preliminary capsule that this letter is shows how vulnerable I still am some sixteen years after the Day of the Dead. The fabric of the modern world has worsened, it seems to me, in that span of time. The torments of materialism have increased . . .

It is essential to create a jigsaw in which 'pasts' and 'presents' and likely or unlikely 'futures' are the pieces that multitudes in the self employ in order to bridge chasms in historical memory.

To sail back into the past is to come upon 'pasts' that are 'futures' to previous 'pasts' which are 'futures' in themselves to prior 'pasts' *ad infinitum*. There is no absolute beginning, for each 'beginning' comes after an unwritten past that awaits a new language. What lies behind us is linked incalculably to what lies ahead of us in that the future is a sliding scale backwards into the unfathomable past within the Virgin womb of time . . .

The future brings terrifying challenges but it also brings foetal shapes, tender and young possibilities that enliven us to scan gestating resources in the womb of tradition that we have bypassed or overlooked or eclipsed . . .

As the severity of trauma began to break by degrees uncanny correspondences seemed to loom as I voyaged between Maya twinships of pasts and futures and the Mathematics of Chaos.

Chaos is misconceived as an anarchic phenomenon. Whereas it may be visualized as portraying an 'open' universe. Continuities running out of the mystery of the past into the unknown future yield proportions of originality, proportions of the 'genuinely new' . . .

Composite epic is rooted in the lucidity that fractions or fictional numbers, fictional multitudes, bring. The walls of ruined schools and houses and temples and hospitals and theatres are full with presences and voices though apparently void and empty. Such is the mystery of Chaos. The weight of Chaos is sometimes apparitional, sometimes concrete. Such mathematics enhance an intact mystery in time. Because it is intact yet beyond seizure it acts upon us in apparitional Old Gods or Prisoners (dogma, ideology) locked into the gaols of the past; acts again in dismemberments of such Prisoners who walk on water or in space beyond fixtures or unities of place.

'Unity of place' is a dogma or an ideology in some quarters. But my apprenticeship to the furies acquaints me with a different topography or map of the Imagination that breaches the human-centred cosmos that we have enshrined. There are extra-human faculties and voices that bring contours into play to lift place into both familiar and unfamiliar dimensions which fall outside of presumed norms or absolute models of fact and fiction.

The trauma that I suffered in Jonestown may have imprisoned me absolutely in a plot of fate. But thank God! it aroused me instead to contemplate a hidden mathematics within the body of language . . . Language is deeper than 'frames', it transgresses against the frames that would make us prisoners of eternity in the name of one creed or dogma or ideology.

Maya 'twinships' between the buried past and the unknown future – which are regarded as bewildering to the Western mind – seemed of burning and invaluable moment to me in their bearing on factors of originality and living time. I had no absolute model on which to base my Dream-book except that I sought to salvage unpredictable keys to tradition within the terrifying legacies of

49

the past. I sought to be true to the broken communities, the apparently lost cultures from which I have sprung . . .

A word about New Amsterdam before I close this letter. I wandered for some seven years – sometimes in states of partial but acute amnesia – before I arrived there and began writing the Dream-book. I dreamt I was translating from a fragmented text or texts that already existed . . .

New Amsterdam is one of the oldest towns on the Guyana coastlands. It is a relic of the Dutch empire of the eighteenth century and was absorbed into British Guiana in the early nineteenth century. Its crumbling walls and roads witness to the erosion of townships and settlements and villages along the coastlands that stand as memorials to Spanish, French, Dutch, British colonization across the centuries.

Over the past half-century the population of Guyana has fallen from a million souls, it is said, to three-quarters of a million within a country almost as large as the United Kingdom.

This decline, which is due in large part to emigration, energizes the imagination into an apprehension of earlier peoples, Aboriginal ghosts whose presence is visible still in their nomadic living descendants.

Thus the mixed peoples of African or Indian or European or Chinese descent who live in modern Guyana today are related to the Aboriginal ghosts of the past of whom I spoke a moment ago: if not by strict, biological kinship then by ties to the spectre of erosion of community and place which haunts the Central and South Americas.

This over-arching Ghost throws some light on the play of 'extinction' within my Dream-book . . . I was driven in my flight from Jonestown to reflect on myself as an 'extinct' creature. I dreamt I had been robbed of my native roots and heritage. I suffered from a void of memory. I belonged to peoples of the Void . . . *But there was a catch, a shock of breath, in this sensation* . . . The *shock* of the 'peopling of the Void', the animals of the Void, the creatures of the Void, became so extraordinary that 'extinction' imbued me with breath-lines and responsibilities I would not otherwise have encompassed. I became an original apparition in my wanderings within over-arching Ghost in coming abreast of extremities of loss, in visualizing my own 'nothingness' as intangible 'somethingness'. Memory theatre was born in such theatres of humility. 'Extinction' attired itself in many parts – as an actor may learn to play staggered roles and numinosities – it grew into bodily extensions, masks, limbs, prompted and sculpted by the comedy of ghosts within active traditions. A train of disturbing rehearsals and heart-searching conscience came into play . . .

Yet I was reminded that I lived in a world threatened by an explosion of numbers, *not* by declining populations. But this deepened, if anything, my inner experience of place and time. Without Memory theatre – and the art of self-rehearsed 'extinctions' in a series of stages upon which one retraces one's steps into a labyrinth of deprivations and apparent losses – the 'peopling of the Void' in all its extremities of *explosion* and *implosion* will not embody heart-searching conscience, heart-searching caveat, but will cement predatory blockages, predatory coherence.

Keys to the Void of civilization are realized not by escapism from dire inherit-ances, not by political glosses upon endemic tragedy, but by immersion in the terrifying legacies of the past and the wholly unexpected insights into shared fates and freedoms such legacies may offer. In the death of politics (however ritually or conventionally preserved in the panoply of the state) may gestate a seed of re-visionary, epic theatre rooted in complex changes in human and animal nature . . .

The mystery of the Virgin-archetype in the 'peopling of the Void' implies a form virtually beyond comprehension, a form shorn of violence in its intercourse with reality, but – as with all archetypes – it comes to us in its brokenness to activate nevertheless, it seems to me, a reach of the Imagination beyond all cults, or closures, or frames . . .

I suddenly realize that I should not close this letter without a comment on variations in the spelling of 'Guyana' or 'Guyanas' or 'Guianas' . . .

I appeal to your tolerance, W.H. – when you edit my Dream-book – to accept these deviations or distortions as meaningful in the context of partial amnesia and confusions that I endured in the great forest.

My fluctuations of memory, in my wanderings for seven years in the wake of the 'tragedy of Jonestown', are rooted as well, I am sure, in the amnesiac fate that haunts the South and Central and North Americas across many generations overshadowed by implicit Conquest.

Hidden textualities of pre-Colombian and post-Columbian place are hinted at in the word 'Guiana' which British colonizers framed, for political convenience, when they came into possession of the Colony in the early nineteenth century.

'Guiana' springs from a variable Amerindian root-text which means 'land of waters'. It is as if one becomes aware of fragmented page after page in a volume or book long suppressed or hidden. How apparitional is 'British Guiana' or 'French Guiana' or 'Dutch Guiana'? How concrete are 'Guyanas' in vowel or innermost anatomy of flexible texts extending backwards into pre-Colombian age?

'British Guiana' became 'Guyana' in 1966. A link was implied with an older frame one may perceive in Spanish maps of the region encompassing the 'Guianas' and Venezuela and North Brazil. Cross-culturalities running through 'Guianas' and 'Guyanas' are invoked, it would seem, in the Dream-body of history, and in implications of the indebtedness of one convention to another through layers of space and time.

It may seem inevitable or convenient to submit to one frame or name but, in so doing, cultures begin to imprison themselves, involuntarily perhaps, in conquista-dorial formula that kills alternatives, kills memory. Not only were Africans who came through the Middle Passage deprived of their names by slave-masters but in the twentieth century Arawaks and Macusis and Warraus and others have begun to adopt English or Portuguese or French or Spanish names and to suppress their native place names or animal names . . . There may be no harm in such adoption provided an inner/outer masquerade or Carnival lives in the imagination and is susceptible to many worlds, to parallel universes of sensibility, in Memory theatre. And what is Memory theatre but an acceptance of amnesiac fate that diminutive survivors begin to unravel . . .?

Long-vanished texts secrete themselves everywhere in Aboriginal, fragmented theatres of place, in living (sometimes mutilated) landscapes, riverscapes, sky-scapes, apparitional at one level, concrete at another . . .

Elusive El Dorado (City of Gold? City of God?), whose masthead is consumed and refashioned on sacrificial altars in every century around the globe, may have a buried harbour in that compass or 'land of waters'.

Adieu my friend.

Francisco Bone

3

NEW PREFACE TO
PALACE OF THE PEACOCK

This is my second Note or short preface to *Palace of the Peacock*. My first was actually an amendment in 1988 to a *Note on the Genesis of the Guyana Quartet*, when the four novels constituting the Quartet (of which *Palace* is the first) were collected and issued in one volume in 1985.

Kenneth Ramchand, the Caribbean scholar, wrote an introductory piece to the first paperback edition of *Palace* in 1968.

It is useful now, I think, as the 1990s draw to a close, to bring into some relief certain features in *Palace* which respond to a creative ferment that has been happening in the Americas since 1960 when the novel first appeared.

That ferment is curiously relevant, I find, to the body of fiction I have written through *The Guyana Quartet* and succeeding novels up to the latest, *Jonestown*.

Critics now see *Palace* within a context of 'magical realist' fiction and therefore relevant, across the years, to an innovative tradition that has become fashionable, though scarcely articulated or considered in 1960.

Of note also is a new emphasis on variants of 'music' in prose and poetry. It is arguable that this is nothing new (when one reflects, for instance, on the Harlem renaissance earlier in this century) but the innovative daring of distinguished black American poets – who are the recipients of notable prizes – became sharper within the present decade and in the 1980s.

In tandem with all this is a remarkable and phenomenal upsurge of interest in pre-Columbian cultures, arts, civilizations, and the parallel resources these offer to visualizations of architectures of tradition long vanished or eclipsed.

Much more could be said of this ferment, and the field of consciousness it embraces, but I shall restrict this Note to the particular variant of 'music' (possibly original) in *Palace*.

I speak of music – the 'spirit-bone' of the Caribs which may be associated with South American rivers – in the prefatory Note I wrote to the Quartet in the mid-1980s but I am better placed now to outline the specificity inherent to such rhythm. The seed of the Carib bone-flute constitutes an evolving tone which is pertinent to the entire body of fiction I have written. There is no straightforward metaphor that mirrors this evolution but in my mind it corresponds to a paradoxical veil or density in the ancient 'bone-spirit' which falls upon invisibles in space and makes them visible. I shall give an illustration of this shortly.

But first it is necessary to outline, as succinctly as I can, the archetypal ground and numinosity of tradition infusing, so to speak, the bone-spirit or bone-flute. The latter is the uncanny termination of a bridge of rhythm arcing or curving from pre-Columbian Mexico into the pre-Columbian and post-Columbian Guianas in South America. At the ancient Mexican origin or genesis of the bridge is the apparition of Quetzalcoatl (quetzal, the heavenly bird, coatl, the wise serpent). The bird-wing of the bridge flies in space, half-seen within the rhythms of space, partially unseen. The scale of the serpent orchestrates minutiae of soil and rain which fill crevices in the body of the earth, river beds, caves, oceans. The serpent is tidal, it is oceanic, it is terrestrial.

Further along the bridge looms Kukulcan, the obscure ancestor of migrating species. He is also an androgynous incorporation of the womb. Man is born of woman and, in shamanic legend, woman of man.

Next arises Huracan or Hurrican who shakes the bridge to its foundations and demolishes worlds. Hurrican subsides into the bone-flute of Yurokon, the eternal child. Yurokon is the termination of the history or story-line of the bridge in the Guianas.

Yurokon's mother is sometimes identified with muses or furies who have suffered abuse at the hand of the Caribs.

Yurokon is Quetzalcoatl's cousin. His Guianese parents are the doomed Caribs. His veil arises from a cauldron in which the Caribs cook a morsel of flesh stripped from the bone of the conquistador or invader. Yurokon therefore coincides with the Spanish and European conquest of the Central and South Americas. The ritual consumption of a morsel of flesh plucked from the enemy plants knowledge of the invader's plans and intentions. The Caribs were doomed though they fought fiercely. Thus Yurokon is the birth of bitter self-knowledge and extremity. The evil of conquest in the invader smarts and exacerbates a sensation of mutual horror in the Carib spirit which entertains an identical lust for triumphal victory.

The accent upon a terminal moment in the history of an age, in the bone-spirit, creates a cloak of uncertainties about the consequences of change; and the need to transgress certain frames becomes a native universal theme or implicit legacy. This is the music of time within clustering imageries upon the bone-flute.

Donne dies many deaths in *Palace of the Peacock*. He *relives* the terminal moment of history in the uncertainty of his own demise as portrayed and re-enacted by his nameless twin brother who dreams him back to life. Life becomes a relived, terminal, but paradoxically regained threshold into rhythmic space or nuclear turning point between times past, present and future. Such is the trial and rebirth of community encompassing intimate strangers, in the Dream of space time, intimate re-visionary invader, intimate re-visionary invaded, native host, twin-ships, twin-bridges, lost cities that vanish to reappear within the elements, muses, furies.

I must confess I have been haunted since childhood in British Guiana, South America, where I was born, by vanished cultures and places and kingdoms. One such legendary kingdom was ancient El Dorado. No one to my knowledge has seen El Dorado. It seems to move and transplant itself within the great rain forests that lie between the Amazon and the Orinoco. Sir Walter Ralegh failed to find it in his last voyage into the Orinoco in the early seventeenth century. As a consequence he lost his head in the Tower when he returned to London.

When one visualizes Ralegh against the backcloth of bone-spirit bridge his death is another echoing passage into relived termini (which Donne endures) and re-visionary cross-cultural medium between the Americas and Europe.

The story-line of his narrow expedition is fractured into the prism of far-flung voyages . . .

My own expeditions as a land and hydrographic surveyor in the 1940s and 50s led me to intuit rhythms to riverscapes, landscapes, skyscapes which exposed an apparition and magical palace within changed and changing bridges of time.

El Dorado possesses its archetypal equation between place and placelessness, in orchestrated elements, wind, fire, earth, water. Such orchestration implies the arousal of hidden worlds, the Word of creations in the bone or skeleton of cities to be relived again within architectures of time. El Dorado is fabulous but it is not only a legend of relived memory and the City of God one seeks everywhere. It is a grave and blood-stained canvas of greed for gold and territory across centuries.

At the very outset of *Palace of the Peacock*, Donne is envisioned – in the tradition I have sought to outline – as dying more than one death, experiencing more than one terminal moment in history. Did he die on the gallows? Was he shot by the fury Mariella (the woman he abused)? Later it is suggested he was drowned. Three deaths at the hand of muses or furies of place and time revisited by his nameless twin brother who dreams him back to life . . .

Here is the passage at the outset of *Palace* to which I allude:

> A horseman appeared on the road coming at a breakneck stride. A shot rang out suddenly, near and yet far as if the wind had been stretched and torn and had started coiling and running in an instant. The horseman stiffened with a devil's smile, and the horse reared, grinning fiendishly and snapping at the reins. The horseman gave a bow to heaven like a hanging man to his executioner, and rolled from his saddle on to the ground.
>
> The shot had pulled me up and stifled my own heart in heaven . . .
>
> I dreamt I awoke with one dead seeing eye and one living closed eye . . .
>
> Mariella had killed him . . .
>
> (*Palace of the Peacock*, 1988, pp. 19–21)

The nameless, dreaming twin brother 'I' rides towards El Dorado and re-enacts in himself a theatre of revenge inflicted on the Eldora*Donne* fugitive of time his brother has become across the aroused or awakening centuries. For his brother, the conquistador, is now native – in an evolution of the unfinished genesis of the Imagination – to the soil of Old/New worlds. Donne's ghost and that soil are becoming visible again within the gaps and holes and hiatuses of recorded histories.

Such visibility is made possible by the density or rhythmic veil of 'wind . . . stretched and torn . . . coiling and running in an instant'. Not only that. The 'invisible' wind is outlined into a luminous tension between implicit rope or noose and 'stiffened' bullet.

It is not my intention to say much more in this brief Note. Except a word about muses of time and place. Even as Donne embodies a plurality of voyagers, a plurality of living deaths, so Mariella (whom he abuses) embodies a plurality of women. These are made visible as terror-making faculties and the regenerative womb of time when the skeletal fabric and artifice of history's masquerade acquire luminous density in the music of living landscapes.

There is the ancient Arawak woman whom Donne and his crew seize and conscript into a guide.

> Tiny embroideries resembling the handwork on the Arawak woman's kerchief and the wrinkles on her brow turned to incredible and fast soundless breakers of foam . . .
>
> The crew were filled with the brightest-seeming clarity of tragedy, as cloudless as imperfectly true as their self-surrender to the hardship of the folk they followed and pursued: the cloudy scale of incestuous cruelty and self-oppression tumbled from their eye . . . Their ears were unstopped at last . . .
>
> (*Palace of the Peacock*, pp.62–4)

Finally with respect to Mariella's embodiment of women and a womb of potentialities beyond every frame of abuse comes a revelation of the 'bone-spirit' in the woman dressed in nothing but her hair.

Such artifice rooted in nature is peculiarly subtle in its orchestration of elements. There is rhythmic linkage between ear and eye foreshadowed in the ancient Arawak woman and Donne's crew. In pre-Columbian legend 'ear' and 'eye' and 'head' could assume different personalities to be combined and recombined into a music of the senses. My intuitive interpretation of such recombinations is that a hidden capacity slumbers in nature and everywhere to address a labyrinth of healing in a conflict-ridden age. Within such a labyrinth, adversarial twins – not necessarily connected by blood or race – become psychically supportive one of the other in trials of the Imagination.

In those trials a 'material nexus binding the spirit of the universe' gives way to a 'threadbare garment' envisioned by ear and eye: as though ear sees, eye listens, within a medium of visionary music.

Such artifice – if artifice it is – brings a pregnant apparition into the silences of space that have neither a beginning nor an ending.

The woman was dressed in a long sweeping garment belonging to a far and distant age. She wore it so absent-mindedly and naturally, however, that one could not help being a little puzzled by it. The truth was it was threadbare. One felt that a false move from her would bring it tumbling to the ground. When she walked, however, it still remained on her back as if it was made of the lightest shrug of her shoulders – all threads of light and fabric from the thinnest strongest source of all beginning and undying end.

(Palace of the Peacock, p.106)

4

MERLIN AND PARSIFAL
Adversarial Twins

At this time in the life of our civilization it seems to me vital and essential to explore the hidden rapport which may exist between adversarial cultures. We need to draw, I would think, upon the diverse resources of our entire humanity if we are to cope with – and begin possibly to transform – a formidable *malaise* in the cross-cultural body of civilization.

When I was a young man, surveying in the rainforests of British Guiana on the South American continent, it was confidently asserted by the authorities that malaria would be defeated within my lifetime. Malaria is returning with a vengeance in many areas of the globe even as I now speak. The mosquito – the carrier of the malaria bacterium – is seen now as a pest to be exterminated despite the complex network of association in nature that will be damaged. One leaps from the extermination of pests into an intricate web of consequences we scarcely understand within the arterial topography of the human species and of natures in all their paradoxes and variables.

That web of paradox and variable engages us with complex landscapes, riverscapes, skyscapes, oceanscapes which have been altered across the centuries in the name of conquest and progress.

I often speak of living landscapes but it is vitally necessary to remember that civilization has created a variety of man-made environments and landscapes within the topography of regions and islands and continents and seas and that a price has to be paid by every generation. We may live longer but we may be subject to peculiar contagion and spiritual torpor or illiteracies of the imagination.

We have changed the courses of rivers, we have altered the lie of the land, we have built settlements in river catchments, we have dismembered cultures, the culture of grasses and forests as much as of human tribes and animal species. We clothe ourselves in a technocratic and utilitarian realism when we engage a robot to sow seed or pick fruit.

Every alteration in the fabric of a living landscape is akin to a man-made garment society wears. Society clothes itself in man-made caves, towering fabricated hillsides or skyscrapers, underwater mechanical crocodiles, bird-rockets, agile, engineered dinosaurs and tanks.

It is fascinating therefore to address the ancient legend of Merlin and Parsifal which C.G. Jung claims is pertinent to our age. Merlin's cry, Jung claims, is still not understood. In the Merlin/Parsifal legend a far-flung theatre slumbers which bears on a hidden self-confessional, self-judgemental rapport between all cultures. It is the nature of that rapport, how it may be visualized, how it may speak to us in complex texts, which haunts the imagination. *Merlin's cry!* For centuries our planet has been the scene of wars and feuds which exacerbate grievously the perils to which all species (fauna and flora) are subject.

Let us remember that Merlin, the great magician of the Arthurian Round Table, was trapped in a tree or a cave. He symbolizes in tradition a network of association involving forests and caves which became his prisonhouse. He felt himself betrayed not only by his female apprentice and lover presumably but by the very dragon of knowledge he courted and exploited. Parsifal, his adversarial twin, who benefited enormously at times from his wisdom, remained apparently superior to nature in advancing technologies. Parsifal nevertheless was also a prisoner: the prisoner of inflexible sovereignty, sovereign institution (or bastion against the evolution of a wider and deeper community), sovereign ego, in which he more or less successfully manipulated the banner of Christ to endow every crusade on which he embarked.

Both Merlin and Parsifal are prisoners, I would venture to say, but Parsifal has long arrogated on to himself the banner of justified conquest in the realism of war, trade, money and privilege.

The language of Parsifalian ideology is now, one would think, part and parcel of the formerly colonized globe. Everyone writes and thinks in virtually the same fashion or mode. But fashion is still subject to unease and eruptive lament arising from the subconscious and unconscious in the trapped or imprisoned magic of Merlin. C.G. Jung speaks of that eruptive lament as *the cry of Merlin.* It is left therefore to Merlin (however apparently incomprehensible his cry) to imply a creative breach in the seemingly invincible core-bias of communication which Parsifal has framed and enshrined. Jung ventures to say that a 'new conceptual language' is needed to breach that core-bias if a deeper hidden rapport is to come into play between Parsifal (and all that Parsifal entails as a vessel of sovereign power) and apparently trapped Merlin (and all that Merlin entails as a vessel of shamanic lore and a visionary, stranger, self-confessional, self-judgemental orbit slumbering in the iron-clad but deceptive logic of ruthless materialism . . .). But alas – if I read Jung aright – he had grave misgivings as to whether such a psychophysical, self-corrective medium of communication is likely to be achieved in our age however necessary this is. I understand his misgivings but it is my view that the breakthrough needed can be demonstrated within the body of intuitive experience. I shall return to this matter in a moment or two.

There is no doubt that Jung was torn by the issue and I was deeply stirred when I came upon an anecdote associated with the Tower at Bollingen.

The mason brought Jung what appeared to be the wrong cornerstone for the Tower. Jung tells of his encounter with the mason. I quote:

> When the stone was finished, I looked at it again, wondering about it and asking myself what lay behind my impulse to carve it. The stone stands outside the Tower, and is like an explanation of it. It is a manifestation of the occupant, but one which remains incomprehensible to others. Do you know what I wanted to chisel in the back of the stone? *Le Cri de Merlin.*[1]

Stanley Romaine Hopper, an American scholar, alludes to T.S. Eliot's *Ash Wednesday* in an essay he wrote some years ago and to a line in the poem which runs *And let my cry come unto Thee.*

Hopper is of the view that this cry in *Ash Wednesday* 'is not unrelated to that of Merlin in Jung's surprising anecdote. Jung dedicated his Tower at Bollingen in 1950. His "stone" had been ordered to serve as a cornerstone, but when delivered, it was a square block rather than a triangular stone. The mason would have rejected it, but Jung exclaimed "No, that is my stone. I must have it" '.[2]

It is of interest to note that the stone was placed on the *outside* of the Tower as if it witnessed, I would think, to a re-visionary dynamic in space and time to which the 'finished' Tower remains susceptible. The 'finished' Tower then is implicitly 'unfinished' and achieves an echo or living voice in Merlin's cry.

In the degree that the Tower symbolizes civilization then civilization is susceptible to echoes of the chasm between Merlin and Parsifal.

Hopper tells us that on one side of the outcast stone Jung carved the verse of the alchemist Arnaldus de Villanova, who died in 1313.

> Here stands the mean, uncomely stone
> 'Tis very cheap in price!
> The more it is despised by fools,
> The more loved by the wise.

> Jung's theme [Hopper explains in his essay] is that Merlin represents an attempt by the medieval unconscious to create a parallel figure to Parsifal. He regards Parsifal as a Christian hero, and Merlin as his 'dark brother'. Merlin, the anti-type to Parsifal, was the son of the devil and a pure virgin; but the twelfth century's categories for thought provided no means whereby Merlin's depth significance could be grasped in this way. Hence Merlin ended 'in exile' and his cry still sounded in the forest after his presence had vanished to be seen no more. 'This cry that no one could understand,' argues Jung, 'implies that he lived on in unredeemed form. His story is not yet finished. And he still walks abroad.'
>
> 'But if Merlin still walks abroad, it may well be in forms so strange and unexpected that we can scarcely recognise him.'[3]

At the end of his essay Hopper quotes a German text which identifies Merlin with tree and forest and bloom: a device instinctive to the soil and the land.

Merlin becomes 'the white-thorn hedge [which] blossoms imperishably'.[4] Even so the cry remains and is still being heard.

This brings me back to the 'new conceptual language'[5] of which Jung spoke. He writes of this in his essays on synchronicity where a cosmic/psychic or 'psychophysical narrative' is addressed which – if I understand him aright – would bear on trials of the imagination involved in the re-birth of a genuine cross-cultural age within the body of civilization. In such a medium a hidden rapport between cultures, sovereign ego and foreign self, reaching into the depths of nature, would begin to constellate itself in clusters of imageries and motifs which tend to be flattened out within conventional narrative.

Such clusters, I believe, carry the burden of Jung's cosmic/psychic medium to transform our understanding of the abode or house of passion and self-responsibility we inhabit. The concept of sovereignty as an absolute premise would give way to a redemptive faculty in the body of cross-cultural humanity.

Curiously enough Jung seems to recoil from the possibility of such radical spirit that he himself entertained. He felt that such a medium, however desirable, needed to be 'mediated by sense organs' and he was uncertain that this mediation could be achieved in language or Word.

Do we not see here – in Jung's recoil – one of the curious paradoxes in European genius? Jung is not the first great European thinker to bring tradition upon a frontier that is never crossed into the creation of a new community requiring a re-visionary dynamic in the language of the imagination.

Far be it from me to point to the present debate on a new European community and a capacity to unveil a hidden rapport between diverse European cultures. But that debate – and the recoil from Europe by sophisticated and learned men and women (who have been educated in the best universities in the land) – is food for thought!

I am sure that the mediation by sense organs (which Jung requires as indispensable to the new medium of the imagination he addresses) is achievable in fiction as a threshold into altering the Parsifalian core-bias in civilization.

Jung has not reflected as far as I am aware on how the 'sense organs' are fictionally, dialectically and numinously clothed and re-dressed within a self-judgemental, self-confessional art.

Self-confessional, self-judgemental art is perhaps as close as we may come to a *fiction* of absolute knowledge which is redemptive in its insights into the interconnectedness of all species and beings and things. Here resides a key to the deepest intuition of multi-faceted Incarnation involving all creatures and creations in a complex evolution embracing elusive Spirit through which we share agony and ecstasy. Indeed this is the uncertain organ, but I think enormously real heart of synchronicity, which brings its *fiction of absolute knowledge, steeped in shared agony and ecstasy*, into mind and memory.

Ancient vestiges of synchronicity reside in the 'lamb of God', in the 'dove of peace', in the 'wisdom of the serpent'.

Such linkages of the creaturely lamb and the divine, of emotion/passion/

wisdom/peace and the dove or serpent, are a-causal. They breach the logic of cause-and-effect realism. Their interweaving implicitly raises a reality that cannot be glossed by appeals to poetic ornament or picturesque metaphor. The hinge of their expression implies an architecture of the imagination fuelled by 'a new conceptual language' in which the 'sense-organs' of creature-in-creation elicit a *quality* of voice and expression unlike conventional, one-track progressive realism.

Once we accept that primordial landscapes/riverscapes/skyscapes/ocean-scapes have been manipulated and altered, that man-made excavations into primordial fabric are structured, and that these seem identical even as the road or pavement underfoot seems part and parcel of the soil or earth through which it runs, then we may become attentive to a *quality* of the Word that touches a core-organ in ourselves which breaches the core-bias by which we are conditioned within a progressive and uniform realism.

True, once again, core-organ and core-bias are synchronous and a-causally linked. The heart of such synchronicity resides in Merlin's cry – *let my cry come unto Thee*, the cry of any trapped beast or slaughtered creature under the wheels of progress. The *quality* of the voice *in ourselves* is elusive, it cannot be seized, but its enormous truth seems to me the very essence of dialectic and numinous art, the essence of living diversity which tends in a progressive age to be flattened.

To breach the uniform pavement that we tread on earth which has its extrapolation into space (when we fly in an aeroplane as though the sky were a flattened field which had dispensed with primordial verticality and horizontality except in moments of crisis or precipitous descent) *is to arouse in such a breach* a density of perception that gives reality to interwoven primordial and man-made worlds. Such density releases a cluster of imageries that have come close to erasure in the surfaces and the pavement of conventional communication.

The flattening of space defies Einsteinian curvature or quantum expansion but reflects the triumph of a populist and mechanical vocabulary of progress. Travel around the so-called village of the globe is made easy, swift and accommodating. Yet there lingers an unspoken apprehension of an incalculable price to be paid in pollution, in the extinction of species, and in other elemental implosive cycles which leave their shadow upon the psyche of nature.

Could one trace Merlin's incomprehensible cry in such unspoken apprehension? Self-responsibility for mechanical progress – when it becomes numinously genuine – implies of necessity an art in which the language of the imagination visualizes 'space' differently from a purely logical field or tamed universe or adjunct of sovereign species . . .

The paradoxes of 'absolute knowledge' are instructive. A tamed universe – from which all secrets are wrested – gained by technology implies 'absolute knowledge'. The *fiction* of absolute knowledge punctures the hubris of technology and sets up a *quality* or voice half-infused with ecstasy but equally with unfathomable lament for the fate of all species and fossils and witnesses to the mystery of creation.

I shall read a passage from my Mexican novel *Companions of the Day and Night*, which offers perhaps a quick illustration of clustering imageries that bear on the quality of self-confessional, self-judgemental lament and ecstasy.

Let me say first however that when I wrote *Companions* I did not have Merlin in mind. Nevertheless the Fool or Idiot or Shaman who appears in *Companions* is a strange and unpredictable form – I am inclined to say with hindsight – of Merlin.

The wood or log in which the Fool sails sensitizes the rhythm of sense-organs trapped in a forest but voyaging out to be redeemed and to redeem Parsifal.

Those organs create a distinction between a primordial landscape and the shaping of man-made hollows with which the Fool or shaman clothes or dresses his voyaging body and its organs in a sailing tree or carven ship.

Merlin's voyage re-traces Parsifal's conquests in a self-confessional, self-judgemental light.

Let me read a few lines from the passage in *Companions of the Day and Night* to which I alluded a moment or two ago:

> The Fool secured a room in a lodging house, fell into bed, sun-drenched sleep, dreamed he was a man floating on a log. Then he became the log.
>
> A log may drift back into the past, preparations for a journey, shores of the past . . .
>
> It was autumn, the Idiot dreamt, an autumn spent hollowing a canvas of space, hollowing oceans on which to sail, hollowing sky within which to fly to Mexico; hollowing evolutions of murder and sacrifice through which to carve a queen of beauty and sorrow in the edges of copper, gold and scarlet leaves carpeting the ground.[6]

You do see, I am sure, how the 'hollowing of space' corresponds to man-made structures and environments in synchronistic parallels with primordial elements. The Fool flies to Mexico within the man-made 'hollowing' of the sky. He wears the hollow sky as a garment on his back. Implicitly he wears the hollow land as flesh to be consumed, the animals upon it, the chemicalization of the soil, and in hollowing sea and land and sky inevitably species die at his hand to give way to a man-made world, man-made progress.

You may rightly say progress is desirable. That may be true but rarely do we – in conventional narrative – imply the pressures on the sense organs and their conversion to numinous conscience as they participate in murder and sacrifice. 'Sacrifice' – in shamanic lore – implies a sacramental awareness of the species we destroy or consume in the name of progress. 'Murder' is a stark confrontation with the 'queen of beauty and sorrow' whose flesh is in the birds of the air, the fish in the sea, the fox in its hole, the deer on the hill, the butterfly energized by the sun.

All these creatures are the flesh of the Fool's autumn bride (or queen of beauty and sorrow) as he hollows or cuts or carves his way around the globe. It is the *quality* of the voice – *strangeness* as well – which makes real such a wedding of faculties. That voice arouses a profound echo of music in bridal flesh to gauge rhythms of anguish in raped species. Music in fiction, in my estimation, reaches through and beyond poetic ornament or metaphor into a real engagement with unfathomable coherency in the body of an entire creation.

Let me read another paragraph from the same passage.

> 'The art of murder', the Idiot said to the angel in his bed, 'is the art of love of heaven too through winged premises. Have I not buried you in the sky as I secreted you in the sea? A tree may fly with a leaf and flash its skin, secrete its animal, secrete its darknesses. All these prospects and more add up to executions and menaces buried in wings of time, wings of space.'[7]

That passage with its cluster of imageries sustains I would say a rhythmic harmony (and addiction to the magic of intercourse secreted everywhere) in the fabric of evolution: love of heaven is a quest for instrumentalities in a conquest of the heights and the depths. Those instrumentalities are bred from intercourse with the imagined, flying animal in the skin of a tree or flesh of a leaf.

Such echoing concordance addresses all borderlines between sacrifice (or sacrament) and execution. An illumination of the menaces to which all nature is susceptible offers an invaluable gauge into humanity's debt to voiceless and voiced creatures.

Love's ecstasy and uncanny lament is its precarious but real bridge between the pitiful and the pitiless. The forces that divide love from conquest cannot be taken for granted. They interweave in unpredictable and startling ways.

A few concluding remarks.

Absolute knowledge is treasured as the literal goal of science. What is the goal of art? Profoundest self-confession, self-judgement is the supreme goal of art. For absolute knowledge – if it is attainable – may well be a deception if it were nothing more than a technicality that irons out, smooths out, erases all differences in favour of a universal formula. Everything would be flattened out presumably in the simplicity of a triumphant code.

Self-judgement, on the other hand, in the density of art, implies the price humanity and the animal kingdom pay to perceive themselves within inter-changeable roles of bride and bridegroom, priest of God and sacrificial victim, and indeed scientist and artist in the alchemy of *unfinished* knowledge, unfinished genesis of the Imagination.

The voice or cry or lament, joy and pain, in every trapped/released creature, is the mystery of self-knowledge.

Is it not possible and likely that the simplicity of an absolute theory articulated through astronomy, for instance, in an *expanding* universe is itself but the mathe-matical and tenuous surface of a hidden dimension suffused by a re-visionary dynamic to re-shape itself, primordial self interfused with man-made logic?

Scientists are fallible. They are men and women like ourselves. Their fallibility is masked by objective criteria. Such fallibility is the domain of art. All theories are ultimately masks for hidden diversities. The intricacy of those masks is therefore a revelation of intangible and tangible bodies orchestrated, let us say, in terrestrial and cosmic theatre in which we invent plays within another primordial theatre. Such invention, such primordiality, may require – indeed does require – a new accent or 'new conceptual language', as Jung puts it, at varying stages of civilization . . .

One final word.

The phrase *live fossil nursery of language* appears in my recent fiction *Jonestown*.

'Live' refers to a living language, 'fossil' bears on the great age of the language. 'Live' and 'fossil' therefore seem antagonistic in that the living language is susceptible to new roots interwoven with old, fossil roots. That interweaving seems to reflect a tension and rivalry of forms. But 'nursery' implies trials of the imagination in which 'old' and 'new' become *psychically* supportive one of the other in the music of the senses.

This may be borne out, I feel, by 'shadow of music' (*Jonestown*, p.108). The passage I have in mind runs as follows:

> One is possessed by shock when one flees from the dead and discovers a measure of disguise they possess in instruments and furniture that one had long ignored as passive features of nothingness. That shock is implicit in the shadow of music upon frontiers of being and non-being that begin to levitate and change places.

Here, it seems to me, we rely on the mystery of art which is *not* susceptible to a formula or a code but which allies itself to absolute knowledge beyond a vulnerable humanity seeking it nevertheless ceaselessly.

Shadow of music is real for it brings what is virtually unseen but not unhearable or unseeable, even as sheer quantity and number lose their claustrophobic tyranny or progression backwards into the nothingness of the past, forwards into multiplications of meaninglessness in the future.

The loss of absolute quantity in the nothingness of the past or in multiplications of meaninglessness in the future is a failure to encompass numbers in material exactitude. But the shadow that flows through such a loss or failure transforms itself into music or rhythm which seems to take us beyond the grasp of words. And yet it brings most closely to attention the scope of language to find a Presence out of partial liberation combining and re-combining into trial and metamorphosis. Nothing is taken for granted, nothing is final, in the pursuit of a Presence that lives through apparent negatives, it seems, which harbour 'levitation and change', or transfigured things, in the vulnerable, awakening consciousness of humanity.

Notes

1 *Anagogic Qualities of Literature*, Pennsylvania State University Press, 1971, p.9, Epigraph (C.G. Jung) *Le Cri de Merlin* to essay by Stanley Romaine Hopper.
2 Ibid., p.10.
3 Ibid., pp.10–11.
4 Ibid., p.33.
5 C.G. Jung (*The Collected Works*, vol. 8), Routledge & Kegan Paul, 1987, p. 512, Synchronicity and the need for a 'new conceptual language'. See also Pierre François's essay on 'Companions of the Day and Night' in *The Contact and the Culmination*, University of Liège 1997, p.241.
6 *Companions of the Day and Night*, Wilson Harris (Faber and Faber, 1975), p.34.
7 Ibid., p.35.

Part II

CROSS-CULTURAL COMMUNITY AND THE WOMB OF SPACE

PREFACE: CROSS-CULTURAL COMMUNITY AND THE WOMB OF SPACE

The landowners in the Southern States ('Reflections on *Intruder in the Dust*, in a Cross-cultural Complex'), and the whalers at Nantucket Isle ('The Schizophrenic Sea') hold views of the world which claim to be universally valid but which must actually coerce to their aid alien cultures and alien elements buried at the heart of their own world (if they are to substantiate their claims). Harris looks to classic American literature and sees an earlier paradigm from which could have been predicated the cross-cultural picture of ourselves.

Patterns of claustrophobia shape William Faulkner's *Intruder in the Dust*: '*breathlessness, immobilisation* and *suffocation* ... secrete[s] a precipice of emotion down which the young Charles Mallison falls.'[1]

Fall followed by restitution make a sine wave with consciousness. Fall and restitution riddle consciousness: 'descent defines ascent of new birth, new awareness, and vice versa. Both are native extremes to each other [as] unconsciousness [is] to the precarious and stretched limits of consciousness.'[2]

The abruptness with which *numinous dualities* (fall/restitution, pride/humility, individual conscience/institutional bias) slip into and out of one another, serves to undermine the model of stasis on which Faulkner builds convention. It shows such models to be, 'partial conceptions within a riddle of unfathomable being'.[3]

Charles Mallison falls 'into the grave of the creek'. Black Lucas Beauchamps enters the fiction like an *envoi morts*, a voodoo 'sent dead' who observes Charles's fall, but stands back. That standing-back outrages convention: 'Who was black Lucas, [Charles] wondered in confusion, to behave as if he were white, pitiless and proud?'[4]

1 'Reflections on *Intruder in the Dust*', p.92 in this volume.
2 Ibid.
3 Ibid.
4 Ibid.

69

Charles makes a fateful identification with Lucas. Charles emerges from the creek bound to Lucas 'by resentment and awe'. Charles enters a precipice of emotion that approximates the structure of *hungan*, the voodoo sorcery of hate and vengeance. An immaterial bond or unconscious alliance grows between the boy and the black man. A complex bridge or projection between one culture to another, 'that helps us read the action of *an insensible community* in new dark lights'.[5] *An insensible community*, 'constructed out of curious subjective shapes *indistinguishable* at times from their environment, paper, wood, stone'.[6]

In what way *indistinguishable*? Vinson Gowrie's grave is opened in order to establish whether the bullet that killed Gowrie did indeed come from Lucas's gun: 'That opened grave is prime corollary to young Mallison's physical/psychical fall and is fraught with unsuspected self-discovery'.[7] Viewed through the lens of alien voodoo culture, that exhumation also makes of Gowrie an *expédition [des] morts*, something 'freed from the feet' of the dead. The return from the opened grave is a voodoo instrument of vengeance. Vinson Gowrie's return from the open grave unconsciously converts the Gowries from a respectable family into a voodoo instrument of vengeance. Unconsciously it converts the Gowries into a clan whose number includes revenants and the footloose-and-freed dead. Viewed through the lens of alien voodoo culture, the appeal to justice subverts the frame of convention, for justice's chief exhibit is unwittingly also a voodoo accessory of vengeance. Such narratives, therefore, effectively sabotage conventional institutions. That sabotage of moral intention is the undiscerned irony in Faulkner. The story, its incongruities and discontinuities, is written one way while the moral intention tries to point another. It is precisely the sabotage of intention that brings one to the complex bridge or mesh of one culture with another and enables one, through one's art and science, to intervene on the acts of an insensible community.

Pride and superiority are commodities of tradition reserved for Faulkner's whites. When black Lucas enacts the same imperative, when Lucas attires himself in the vestments of authority, he outrages an institution complacent with its own sense of even-handedness. Harris proceeds by imaginative transposition. In 'The Schizophrenic Sea', Harris reimagines Lucas put back in time one hundred years and pre-incarnated as Seymour, the authoritarian black mutineer on board the *Grampus* – carnival ship of Edgar Allan Poe's *Arthur Gordon Pym*. Now this is a technique Harris had developed eight years previously in *Benito Cereno*, a study of a story from Melville's *Piazza Tales* (1856). Harris displaces himself to the heart of the text.

I have attempted in my critical analysis of 'Benito Cereno' to become an

---

5 Ibid.
6 *The Eye of the Scarecrow*, London, 1965, p.107.
7 'Reflections on *Intruder in the Dust*', p.95.

actor playing a part, to act, as it were, in some degree, the role of Captain Delano. This is an idea which I find helpful in immersing one-self in imaginative fictions – to take a character or group of characters as black-comic parts one could oneself play . . .[8]

If I, the reader, become an actor playing a part, I can consult the depth of my own experience as the measure of a particular climate in the work. When, for instance, I assume the role of Seymour in Poe's *Arthur Gordon Pym of Nantucket*, I find in the role of Seymour a number of *revealing inexactitudes* when I compare that role with my own sense of scale: 'Seymour reflects an authoritarian conviction in the nineteenth century, a pitiless capacity to inflict injury upon oppressor and oppressed who stand in his way.'[9]

For Harris, myth is the narrative of a numinous or revealing inexactitude. By sounding myth we also sound ourselves. Poe, the author, identifies Seymour, character of fiction, with tyranny and authority. Poe makes Seymour *symmetrical* with tyranny and authority. Under Poe's pen Seymour is written as a *quantity* equal in measure to tyranny.

For Harris, Poe suffers from the fallacy of symmetry, an equating of character and absolute stance that Harris calls doomed symmetry. Harris imagines another kind of measure more fundamental to the arts of the imagination.

> The play of arbitrating forces should be associated with an *asymmetry* within the infinity and genius of art. This does not in any way imply that symmetries are false but it demonstrates that orders of symmetry may *appear* universal – may seek to pre-empt infinity – though they may actually be no more than useful, sometimes brilliant, extensions and inversions of a binding prejudice and locality [my italics, AJMB].[10]

So symmetry acts as a hubris or false pride that tries to stand in for the universal. It claims title to universality before the individual can bid. Symmetry becomes institutionalized and masquerades as the universal. It *pre-empts*. Injustice is one such *locus of hubris*; mental pain, another; the charisma of skin colour and racial character yet another. For Harris, each such locus expresses ultimatum. Symmetry creates universal camps in which the innocents suffer, and Harris wonders if innocents suffer not so much from tragedy and fate but from the lust for symmetry that drives the powerful.

Carriers of symmetry (*surrogates* for the insensible community) unwittingly speak from behind masks of twinship. The surrogate is also a creative womb. He is a hollowing-out. He must make room in himself for a partial exchange of

---

8 *Benito Cereno*, 1975, pp.128–9 in this volume.
9 'The Schizophrenic Sea', 1983, p.100 in this volume.
10 Ibid., p.107.

character with his twin. Pym defeats the mutineers by masquerading as 'the galvanised corpse of a dead seaman'.[11] This is a composite corpse, *matière morte/ matière ambulante*, like a Frankenstein jolted by electric shocks into un-death. In the essay, this *revenant* stands for the temporary resuscitation of the crew and its former, but now decayed, convention of order and discipline. Seymour and the mutineers are struck down by their symmetry with discipline. They are disarmed by the spectre of what they have destroyed.

Pym's revenge takes the form of *carnival*, literally, a lightening of the flesh: cannibalism. Although food and drink and stores are to become available from the salvaged ship, Pym and his crew eat the sole survivor of the mutineer crew: 'Cannibalism is foreshadowed by ... devouring insight (Seymour) into a dying age (slavery) whose fate leaves every survivor a metaphysical orphan [L. *orbus*, bereft], metaphysical blood to be consumed and re-born.[12]

Now there seems to be a certain ambiguity in the procedure. Ambiguity of terms versus ambiguity of method. On the one hand, Harris calls for an open imaginative art founded on *asymmetry*; the not-aligning with one-faceted stances. Yet, on the other hand, in expressing that asymmetry, Harris writes in strategic oppositions, binary fusions, pairs of symmetries:

(a) 'the Blessed Fury'[13]
(b) 'the broken archetype'[14]
(c) 'slow-motion lightning'[15]
(d) 'ontic tautology'[16]

Such pairs of symmetries are not confined to concepts but extend to the inherent condition of those who people Harris's fictions:

> the inmates are both dead and alive, ordinary men yet dual personalities, who in their schizophrenic dividedness impersonate famous historical figures like Montezuma, Leonardo, or Socrates. They harbour the tension between destruction and survival, annihilation and the pull toward resurrection, between despair and faith, the crucial choice men face in the 'Age of Sorrows,' miniaturised in their asylum.[17]

In the schizophrenic, in the mind divided against itself, the fragmented masks of

---

11 Ibid.
12 Ibid.
13 'Apprenticeship to the Furies', p.234 in this volume.
14 Ibid.
15 'The Unfinished Genesis of the Imagination', p.259 in this volume.
16 Ibid., p.249.
17 Hena Maes-Jelinek, 'Charting the Uncapturable in Wilson Harris's Writing', *Review of Contemporary Fiction*, Summer 1997, p.92.

personality are dualities, trinities, *tetrameria* and *quintameria* in the composite body of tragedy. But the monolithic masks in which we attire history, with its 'blanket of value-codes whose edge is the nightmare of the sacred',[18] can also induce a 'schizophrenic dividedness' in the sensible individual. When we take hold of the rags and strips and pieces of such a mask we are holding up fragments of sacred things in which to reclothe ourselves, the world, the imagination. Yet each fragment is in itself a symmetry, a one-faceted stance; and a language that proceeds by dualisms, by *bina*, by pairs of symmetries, would seem to perpetuate symmetry in the world. How does juxtaposing two symmetries create an *a*symmetry? What is the philosophic basis for Harris's procedure?

It is a basis whose best amplification is to be found in alchemy, an imaginative–philosophic treatment of consciousness. In alchemy, the known self occupies an intermediate position between chaos and creation, like the soul placed between two symmetries. In this way pairs of opposites create the phenomenology of a paradoxical self, man's totality. And the coming together of pairs of opposites creates a new conjunction whose character is neither the one known thing nor the other, *but a third unassimilable or in-between thing.*

> The factors which come together in the *coniunctio* are conceived as opposites, either confronting one another in enmity or attracting one another in love. To begin with they form a dualism; for instance the opposites are *humidium* (moist)/ *siccum* (dry), *frigidum* (cold)/ *calidum* (warm) . . . *coelum* (heaven)/ *terra* (earth), *spiritus-anima* (spirit-soul)/ *corpus* (body) . . . *manifestum* (open)/ *occultum* (occult; also *celatum*, hidden), *vivum* (living)/ *mortuum* (dead, inert) . . . [The English alchemist Sir George Ripley (1415–90), Canon of Bridlington] says: 'The coniunctio is the uniting of separated qualities or an equalling of principles.'[19]

The coming together of pairs of opposites produces a third unassimilable thing,[20] a new vessel and organ capable of assimilating adversarial regimes.

Summary

Twinship can be defined as the unrealized synchrony between two or more cultures which, at first sight, seem remote in time and circumstance. Dominant cultures tend to align themselves with symmetries that close down the arts of the imagination, but these attempts at unjust closure come back to haunt later artists. In this light, Harris examines two black writers, Jean Toomer and Ralph

---

18 'The Schizophrenic Sea'.

19 C.G. Jung, *Mysterium Coniunctionis*, *CW*, Vol. 14, trans. R.F.C. Hull, Routledge, 1963, 1970, 1989, p.3.

20 What Jung terms, psychologically, a *tertium non datur*, a third thing not given.

Ellison. Toomer was part of the Harlem artistic renaissance of the 1920s. Ellison published *Invisible Man* (1952) two years after Faulkner received the Nobel Prize for Literature. Harris's 'Concentric Horizons' (1983) discovers a stepping-stone function of Jean Toomer's *Cane* (1923) and how it supports intuitive structures that reach from the sensibility of Melville in *Benito Cereno* (1856) in the mid-nineteenth century to the kind of sensibility that was to besiege Ralph Ellison and his important novel of race in the mid-twentieth century.

I began by noting that the cross-cultural picture of ourselves could have been predicated from the discontinuities that exist in the classical novel.[21] We noted that writers of imaginative capacity were unsighted – unaware of the synchronicities with alien cultures their own narratives sought to consume – or that such writers saw but simply refused to countenance the fact that the complacent frames embodied in the traditional novel were undone by their own conceptions of fiction.

A note on the word *carnival*, used with a number of variant inflections in 'The Schizophrenic Sea'. *Carnival* is from the L. *carnis* + *levare*, to lighten (alleviate) flesh. The sub-title of 'The Schizophrenic Sea' is 'Carnival Twinships'. We have already defined twinships as a special kind of synchrony between alien cultures which creates the cross-cultural space. 'Carnival twinships' might be defined as masque or occult procession in which invisible dynamic forces are given a living face, enacting, for a for a brief time, a visible drama; 'carnival age' as an age of disguises that make a scaffold for history; 'carnival tragedy' as the fundamental face of humanity before catastrophe causes the shedding of dignity; and 'carnival block' as an insensibility causing repeated breakdown in social order. Examples of unilateralism, what Harris calls 'symmetry', can be thought of as a mask that fixes a particular insensibility. The 'carnival visage of pigmentation' means to lighten the flesh or to de-pigment.

21 'Quite recently, someone lent me *A Brief History of Time* by Stephen Hawking. He mentions in this study "Our modern picture of the universe dates back to only 1924 [Rutherford's model of the atom]" . . . and reiterates this on several occasions such as that "this behaviour of the universe could have been predicted from Newton . . . yet so strong was the belief in a static universe that it persisted into the early 20th century . . ." ' Letter from author to the editor, 18 Nov 1997.

5

LITERACY AND THE IMAGINATION – A TALK

I responded immediately to Alistair Hennessy's suggestion that I should take up the topic that I sought to outline at the Commonwealth Institute in October 1986, and that topic had to do with literacy and illiteracy. It seems to me that this is a matter which must engage the imagination of writers. In pondering upon this issue I felt that there were certain new implications, new emphases that I could bring into play which I did not actually discuss at the Commonwealth Institute, so what I propose to do is to keep to the main outline that I pursued there, but to bring into play some extra considerations.

Let me start by quoting the report from the *Times Higher Education Supplement* which I actually read at the conference. This appeared, I think, early in October and it's called 'A sign of the illiterate times in the United States':

> Virtually every young American adult can sign his or her name and nearly 95% can read at the level normally expected of eight-year olds. This places America at the head of the world's literacy league table

the report says, and then goes on to say that that is the good news. But there is also some bad news. The National Assessment of Educational Progress which produced the report, after testing 3,600 adults between the ages of 21 and 25, found that although almost 95 per cent could read a simple newspaper article, fewer than 40 per cent understood it. Just 20 per cent could use a bus timetable to get from one place to another. Only 38 per cent could work out the cost of a meal by reading the menu. And 43 per cent had trouble following directions on a map. When asked to interpret a four-line poem by Emily Dickinson, fewer than 10 per cent could do so. The report which cost $2,000,000 predicts that the illiteracy rate will continue to rise during the next decade unless action is taken to help the growing minority population. Among blacks who took part in the survey, just ten per cent could understand a newspaper article, two per cent could interpret a bus schedule, and even fewer were able to utilize unit pricing in a supermarket. Hispanics did a little better but still scored lower than whites.

It does seem to me that when one dwells on the alarming proportions of illiteracy one could either approach it as a technical problem – a matter of teaching people to read and write in a mechanical way, or one could look much more deeply into the very sources of tradition, the very sources of the imagination. It seems to me that an imaginative writer cannot turn away from matters which have such a bearing on democracy, because all of this is bad news for democracy. This is something I have thought about for a long time, in fact it has haunted me in various ways. Some of you who have read *The Far Journey of Oudin* may remember that Beti, the Indian woman, is illiterate – and I shall return to that later in this talk. But it occurs to me that a solution to such a problem (though of course there is no absolute solution to matters of this kind) is a complex one for which one has to look very, very deeply into the resources of one's civilization. And I tend to think that one has to ask oneself questions about the nature of tradition. There is an enigma to tradition. For example, scholars declare that if we were to attempt to chart four cornerstones in Western literature, we would look to the work of Shakespeare, Dante, Goethe and Homer. Now that seems (on the face of it) a straightforward proposition. But then we turn to what Frances Yates has to say and we discover that the traditions which informed Dante and Shakespeare have virtually disappeared. Frances Yates has made an innovative and a remarkable attempt in her book *The Art of Memory* to salvage some element of the traditions which have been lost. But basically, the cross-cultural roots which may lie in Shakespeare or in Dante have apparently vanished.

So there is a considerable deprivation which haunts our civilization. But then, in parallel with that, let us look at the pre-Columbian world. What do we really know of the pre-Columbian world? We know very little. Most people who comment on the sculptures of the pre-Columbian world tend to look at them with some degree of awe, but to find them peculiar, very peculiar indeed because they diverge from what they assume sculpture to be and we know (it is my surmise anyway) that those sculptures, even in their terrifying proportions, are not to be judged as realistic sculptures. Very often if one probes deeply enough one would find that there is some kind of subtle, profound ecstasy which is associated with those terrifying masks. I attempted to bring this into play in *The Secret Ladder* when the woman Catalena lies on the ground in desperate plight. She fears the rapists who are hovering over her and at that moment she is addressed by a sensation of an enormous presence that appears to hover over her and offers her relief – offers to pull her out of her predicament. But then, when she focuses her eyes to discern who or what this presence is, what does she see? She sees two of her enemies. Two of her dreadful enemies. She is in fact saved – I won't go into the complications of the narrative. She does escape, but what is striking, is that her escape, that moment of ecstasy in which she felt that she was about to be lifted out of a nightmare – that moment of ecstasy was interwoven with the faces of her enemies and the faces of her enemies looked like masks of terror. Therefore when one looks at some of these terrifying masks which one associates, for example, with pre-Columbian America, and I would suggest with areas of African sculpture, at first sight one may think that they are terrifying in a realistic

76

sense without understanding that there may be another kind of moment threaded into that terror, and that there is some kind of balance between sacrament and terror and this is something we do not understand because, it seems to me, we have lost the capacity (or virtually lost the capacity) to understand it in realistic terms. We may have to alter the criteria which we bring to bear on certain matters. When one becomes aware of these deprivations, it does seem to me that those losses have consolidated themselves into a kind of uniform function, the sort of uniform narrative which we tend to read. We tend to read the world in a uniform kind of way, a uniform kind of narrative, a uniform kind of frame. That kind of thing may very well be one of the consequences, one of the deprivations we endure in the light of the traditions which we have apparently lost.

Now it does seem to me that within the compass of such uniformity, such uniform function, one may say that common or garden illiteracy (the kind of illiteracy which the *Times Higher Education Supplement* reports upon), that that kind of illiteracy is mirrored within illiteracies of the imagination at every level of society. Now illiteracy of the imagination is another matter. There are many levels of society in which it appears that people are quite competent – they read within a uniform kind of frame. But their imaginations may be illiterate. Let me give you two quick illustrations on this matter of uniform function. When I travelled into the interior of the Guyanas I led surveying and engineering missions. The crews that I took with me, most of them, were excellent in terms of what they could do, but very few could write beyond signing the pay sheet. They might have been able to read a paragraph in a newspaper, or to read a newspaper in a crude kind of way. Those men were described on the pay sheet as boatmen, bushmen, chainmen, woodmen; described within a uniform function – they operated within a rigid function and they were excellent within that function. The bushman may be someone (he may be a hunter or whatever) who does his job extremely well, but he has grown oblivious of all sorts of subtleties and vague outlines within the bush itself. In order to exercise that block function of hunting and slaying, he has to eclipse a great deal. Their fathers operated like that, their grandparents operated like that – they were locked within a kind of block function. In other words, the world they saw was a world which was stable. Now that's curious – not unstable, but stable. So much is said about stable societies – we want stable societies. But what do we mean by stable societies? If by stable societies we mean we want people who are locked within block functions, uniform functions, then what does that society serve? What purpose does it serve? Perhaps a little bit of instability in such a context might have creative consequences. Unfortunately we have seen violence erupt out of block societies. We have seen dreadful things happen, and therefore we know that sometimes societies run amok and it becomes necessary to probe much more deeply into the kind of world we inhabit.

Now what I have outlined to you is a group of people who could be described in the way this article describes illiterates. A point to note is that they felt that, operating as they did, performing their function as they did, it was unnecessary for them to extend themselves in any way. In fact they felt a degree of uneasiness about extending themselves outside of that kind of function. They had accepted themselves within a certain kind of hierarchy, a certain kind of function. And to extend themselves beyond this was a matter which aroused uneasiness, and one sensed therefore that if they were to break that kind of frame something had to happen within themselves which would allow them to conceive of themselves as agents within a world which needed to be revised fundamentally in many of its aspects.

Let's now take another aspect of this matter and lift it away from sheer illiteracy to illiteracy of the imagination. We have heard recently that President Reagan is the best communicator of any President in the history of the United States. His statements are very clear and yet it does not take us long to recognise the psychological fallacies which run through his so-called clarity. Psychological fallacies (I am borrowing the term which William James used in his writings and which Ehrenzweig took up again when he came to examine the deficienty of *gestalt*. Actually William James's term was the 'psychologist's fallacy'). We have that kind of clarity – what I would call false clarity. There are many kinds of statements which are made apparently for the benefit of masses of people. Reagan is supposed to be immensely popular. He communicates with this kind of clarity embodied in the William Jamesian 'psychological fallacy'. So many things are eclipsed, so many things are lost sight of, and masses of people respond because the way he communicates allows him to operate within a certain sort of frame which seems to simplify everything and to make it easy, so that there is no difficulty in comprehending what is being said. But we are up against this matter of false clarity. In fact, in the Western democracies today they tend to define it sometimes as dis-information. What is tragic is that this cult of dis-information, which has to do with what is called realism, pervades many democratic societies. In a sense I suppose they feel that the masses of people to whom they speak, the masses of people they address, have to be treated in that way. But we see, running alongside this kind of false clarity, the tragedies which are occurring in the so-called Third World. The rise of authoritarianism, the rigged elections, the psychological fallacies which are being perpetrated, the false clarities which are being perpetrated.

And one comes up against something which I think addressed the imagination of Herman Melville when he wrote *The Confidence Man* – his most desperate novel. But before that, we have a novel like *Bartleby*. Bartleby gradually relinquishes all communication with the society in which he lives. He is given various functions to perform and he steps away from them into a field of the unconscious. *Bartleby* is one of the Melville's major short novels in which he expresses a profound dissatisfaction with the vocabulary of his age. He comes to a certain frontier and he creates this figure of Bartleby and you find that he is addressing a deep-seated problem, the problem of deprivations, the problem of tradition. How, in fact, to say certain things which he finds himself unable to say. And in order to express this profound dissatisfaction with the vocabulary of his age he has an extreme character. Bartleby, who gradually sinks into the field of unconsciousness.

But we find it again in *Benito Cereno*, one of the strangest novels of the 19th century, totally neglected by the critics of the day. It is interesting to note this brief quotation from that novel: 'Here was evinced the climax of that icy policy transforming the man into a block, or rather into a loaded cannon.' We have a character locked into a block function, unable to do anything else but exercise that function, wherever it led him. No wonder we live in a world of such fanaticism. If we have cultures which are locked into certain functions, which read the world only in one way, then fanaticism grows out of that, terror grows out of that – a total refusal, a total difficulty to read the world in any other way, to make any other kind of adjustment. That's one of the things that tormented Melville.

But we find it also with Ralph Ellison, the black American novelist. I say 'black' American novelist. (Why should I say black? I should have said that Melville was a 'white' American novelist. So here am I falling into the same trap. Nowadays they speak of female novelists but I never hear them speak of male novelists. It's an insidious thing, the way things have to be placed within a frame, within a function. It's so insidious that we all inevitably fall into it because we think if we don't someone may wonder, for example, who Ellison is. They may think that Ellison is a white man – or something like that. It's all so absurd.) But Ellison, anyway, was also aware of the vocabulary of his age, and that that vocabulary needed to be transformed at many levels, in many curious ways. In a critical chapter from my book *The Womb of Space*, in which I speak of Ellison, this is just a brief quotation. I say:

> The narrative [of *Invisible Man*] seeks to unsettle the shape of territorial imperatives. Light is dark ground, gold is false ground, declarations of virtue or rightness may prove to be propaganda and the ground of lies.

You may remember Ellison's statement – 'Broadway is the darkest place on earth.'

Now Claude Simon is arguably the finest living French novelist. Here is a brief quotation from his novel, *Flanders Road*: 'A progression at the heart of which one remains frozen, insensible to others.' Simon wrestles with this block function, this uniform thing. He wrestles with it to the point of desperation. Eventually, the character, the main protagonist, commits suicide. But how does he commit suicide? By riding into the front ranks with the army, exposing himself to a bullet! He therefore becomes a hero. He decides that the best way to commit suicide is to place himself within the block function of his age so that no one would know what his true motives are. No one would guess what is haunting him, what is pushing him, because within the block function he is sanctified. In other words, Claude Simon, fantastic writer as he is, pulls away from the ultimate challenge. He wants to consign his protagonist to some ground of absolute purity and he can only do this by visualizing the bayonet that enters the protagonist's skull as of virgin purity. The bayonet is of virgin steel, it's absolutely pure. So there again we get the block function. Absolutely pure virgin steel that enters his forehead and creates a kind of cyclopean wound – a third eye. That raises some other issues which we haven't the time to explore. But there he suddenly shifts into a kind of unconscious ground with the cyclopean envelope and therefore a question mark comes at the end of his novel. Are there not other resources which the novelist could have explored?

Now I think all these matters bear on illiteracy. They bear not only on com-mon or garden illiteracy, but also on the illiteracy of the imagination. As an imaginative writer I work with narrative which I revise by scanning each draft carefully and looking for clues which lodge themselves in the draft, clues that may appear to have been planted by another hand. It is as if when one writes, one puts things into the draft which one was not conscious of placing there, and then when one comes back and scans the draft closely, suddenly one is aware of these clues. They become important and one revises through these, concentrating very closely on the ramifications of that image. The unconscious mind has come up, has addressed the conscious mind, and the ramifications of that dialogue become of immense importance. One pursues that with all the concentration at one's command, so that as one goes on, one may come upon another clue which may in fact cause one to look back at what one has done previously and to make certain changes. So the whole thing then becomes susceptible to this kind of complex strategy.

Now at the Commonwealth Institute I gave a concrete example of how this works with *Carnival*, by looking at an epigraph which I placed in this novel, after I had completed the novel. It was an epigraph which related to an ancient myth of which I knew nothing, and the curious thing is that the strategy that was coming through the novel was validated or proven by that ancient myth. I shall return to this matter a little later. What I'm saying is that a writer may proceed and may find that meanings begin to emerge, a certain logic begins to emerge, which he has not imposed on the narrative, and that logic eventually is proven or validated. He discovers (he may also never discover it) that there are myths, ancient myths, which lie like fossils in the ancient past, that come alive within his own work so that the substance of tradition, which we apparently have forgotten, begins to re-enact itself, to come through the imaginative tradition.

Before I give you that concrete example from *Carnival*, let me say something about Beti, the Indian woman in *The Far Journey of Oudin* to whom I referred earlier. Beti is an illiterate woman and the problem was how to visualize the ways in which she begins to break the kind of uniform tradition in which she is held by her family. She lived on the Guyana coastlands, her family saw her as someone who functioned in a certain way. It was not important for her to learn to read or write, in fact, if she did so it was a kind of heresy. What was important was that eventually she would marry, some sort of dowry, some sort of exchange to do with a dowry would take place. That was her place in that society. Now those men – her uncles and her close family – had committed a crime in that they had

80

killed the heir. The heir to the property was an outsider – a half-brother or something like that. Now one hears such rumours on the Guyana coast. There is a kind of density of conspiratorial time. These rumours have a very peculiar way of turning around, changing, reshaping themselves within such densities of conspiratorial time, and when I came to *The Far Journey of Oudin*, a peculiar clue appeared in it which may be described as a crucial rehearsal (in fact that is the phrase which appeared). At the time I was not in a position to evaluate it properly. It struck me as having immense importance – in fact over the years this matter of the crucial rehearsal has become very important. The new novel I have written which is called *The Infinite Rehearsal* implies that there is no final performance – a civilization never arrives at a final performance – the final performance is itself a privileged rehearsal. Now in the case of Beti, the illiterate woman, one had to find some way, intuitively, of breaking the uniform block function or ritual family obsession that imprisoned her. She is rescued by Oudin who is the double of the murdered half-brother. She is rescued by the double who figures in a very peculiar way. He does not figure in the sense in which doubles are used in European literature. In European literature doubles tend to be sinister, but the double, as I found myself moving into it, had to do with this theme of rehearsal. What do we find? Oudin abducts Beti, takes her away from her family and flees across the landscape into the forest and is pursued by Mohammed and the others. But every step that he takes seems to me a curious rehearsal in which he is once more involved in the things that happened to his double, the murdered heir. We come to various positions in the novel in which it is as if in taking on the burden of the double, in rehearsing what occurred earlier on, he is open to very strange situations, perceptions, insights.

First of all, even though he is rescuing Beti (and this would appear to be a good thing), one has to remember that he once worked for the very people whom he is seeking to outwit. He worked as someone who helped his employer to steal, who did other nefarious things, and he carries within himself some aspects of the cruel employer. So his rehearsal requires of him a shift of emphasis in which he has to judge himself, he has to become profoundly aware of his own position as someone who worked for the employer against whom he is rebelling. In other words, his protest against the employer is not merely a protest, his rebellion is not merely a rebellion, he has to go much deeper into the soil, the things that conscripted his employer – he has to do much more than run away from his employer. He has to break the spell, the charisma, the enchantment which ruled his employer and the society to which his employer belongs. He has to break a certain kind of mould. He has to do more than protest against the society. He has to understand the society deeply enough to appreciate the kinds of psychological fallacies which have gripped those against whom he rebels. All this he has to take with him, and in fact he is unable to do it by himself. The illiterate woman comes in and plays a crucial role because at a certain stage in this re-enactment of the past, she is suddenly aware of his acute helplessness. Here is a man who pulls her out of a prison, takes her away like a romantic lover and then suddenly she discovers that he carries ingredients of the past with him, that he carries an acute helplessness with him, and it is at this moment that something in her breaks, some kind of stimulus happens which allows her to break the mould and then she *reads* him, as if she is *creating* a fiction. *So we have this peculiar position in which she creates him as a fiction and he creates her as a fiction.* And we find then that the uniform text is broken.

It would take too long to give actual quotations from the novel, but the uniform text is broken and other texts come into play which have been hidden away, lost away, for centuries if you like, and as these come into play, suddenly Beti realizes that she is now in a position for the first time to *read* the world, to *write* something within herself, *through* herself. There is a stimulus in her, it's not just a mechanical proposition any longer. This question of breaking our illiteracy is not just a mechanical proposition. Nor is it a protest – she is not doing this simply to gain a certificate at high school, a certificate at university. She is not doing it simply as a protest against her society to say 'look, I can do this as well as you' or 'I can strike you in the eye' or 'I can do this or that.' Something has happened to her which is so crucial that she now has confidence in guide-lines and guide (Oudin, the rescuer, turns into a guide born of unconscious reserves and resources that she senses for the first time). It is a small step, in a way, in terms of the novel, but it is also a major step because for the first time she is able to sense that the person who rescues her brings with him the seeds of the past, the seeds of a certain kind of property function, a certain kind of family function. All these seeds come with him, so that suddenly he is reduced and helpless, he's like a dead man at a certain stage whom she has to carry, whom she has to sustain, even as she *reads* him, *writes* him into herself in a new way. So she *reads* this peculiar thing to do with doubles and she is susceptible to him, she is open to him in a new way. A certain kind of stimulus comes into play that opens out. It's as if there is no author. The novel ceases to have an author. It ceases to have an authoritarian code built into absolute functions and realisms. Now I happen to know that some post-modernists would claim that they too advance this notion that the author can be erased from the text. At a certain level I agree with this, but at another level I diverge from it profoundly because in my case, what I am saying is that when the author ceases to be the kind of realistic author which one usually looks for, what one is breaking is the authoritarian model, the author becomes himself a fiction created by his own characters, the authoritarian model is broken and in breaking it, one has become susceptible to a tradition which one has apparently lost.

I remember one of the things Frances Yates says about Shakespeare. She points out that in terms of the Shakespearian theatre as it was understood (the little that she has been able to discern), the actors on the stage could relate to images which were in the theatre and those images spoke to them so eloquently that the lines they uttered were not only verbal lines, but they were also charged with images which had many layers of meanings in them. This is precisely what is happening to Beti when she suddenly discovers that the man who has rescued her comes out of the past – he has an authoritarian element in him. He also has the element of the rescuer and the unpredictable reality of a guide. He is caught between these functions, he is so squeezed by them that he appears to die, to collapse, and at that moment she sees through his helplessness into the soil of tradition and she is able to sustain him, she is able to read him, she is able to create a fiction even as he creates a fiction so that the author seems to disappear in the sense that the text comes alive, comes profoundly alive as if the true source of the text *is* tradition. The tradition is such that it makes the author, it makes the characters. The characters create the writer as well. The writer then breaks the mould of authoritarian author controlling, governing, rigging the sentiments of a constituency of realism. Rather he or she is susceptible to an unpredictable movement of consciousness-in-unconsciousness. It is a question of utter obedience to intuitive clues, a question of vital concentration, a question of response to a balance of forces, apparently eclipsed voices and cultures one has been brainwashed to ignore.

Now this is not a new thing, the ancient Greeks understood it when their sculptures apparently came alive – Pygmalion and Galatea. As Pygmalion sculpted, suddenly he saw things which were planted in the sculpture which he had not seen before. He revised around those and it came alive. The ancient Arawaks with the strange shaman who sculpted the cherry tree and created out of it a retinue, a family; it's the same principle – that you work on something and that material comes alive because things are coming up out of the soil, out of the world's unconscious – those clues come into the work one is doing, they address one so profoundly, sharply, intimately, that the work comes alive and then one, in a sense, disappears because one is created by the things one creates. One may have to go further than the notion (the Nietzschean notion) that God is dead. It is not that God is dead but that God may have ceased to be the kind of absolute author of events which one assumed Him to be (or Her to be – the feminists would say that God is as much feminine as masculine – why not?). The point is that the death of God may in fact bring about, paradoxically, a replay of forces that may revive the drive and dynamism of creation so that the Creator is there within some complex, thrusting, marvellous tradition in which authoritarian codes are transferred into living substance, living text *through* and beyond the absolute functions which have led to the kind of despair we have seen in Herman Melville, the kind of despair we have seen in Ralph Ellison, the kind of despair we have seen in Claude Simon. All of those writers are reacting against the deprivations which have come down to them over centuries.

Perhaps I could give you an example by looking at the very first paragraph in the Guyana Quartet, in *Palace*. I'll read that and look at it again. Now this novel was written after three or four novels had been discarded. Some of the clues that come into this novel had already begun to appear in the last novel which I discarded. I found the force of those clues so strange that I could begin to revise through them. Thus it is as if I disappeared and the text came alive. Now it is my judgement that the imaginative arts, the roots of tradition, may lie in a complex dialogue. The democracies we have we need to understand in depth to renovate, to make vital. Fascism is a tragedy. So the ways in which we can break the obsessional codes which threaten our society are of immense importance. These matters should engage the creative imagination. If we understand that we may then begin to tackle questions to do with literacy, not just literacy in the common-or-garden sense – literacy of the imagination. Otherwise we merely fool ourselves. Lots of people may be able to write and read competently, but if they are locked within block functions, either they submit (within a hierarchical model) or they rebel, violently, they burn property, they do terrible things, they protest against the society without a grain of understanding that they carry within themselves the very seeds of disaster against which they protest. Unless they can understand that, complex, inner revision, complex, outer dialogue, is lost.

Now, take that opening passage from *Palace*; it runs: 'A horseman appeared on the road coming at a breakneck stride.' 'Breakneck' was a word that had been considered within a series of drafts, placed there to imply not only that we are coming to a position in which we wonder whether the horseman is going to be hanged, but also it is the first kind of fissure in the authoritarian fixture, the conquistadorial horseman – we begin to slice into it. 'A shot rang out suddenly, near and yet far, as if the wind had been stretched and torn and had started coiling and running in an instant.' Now we don't know really how Donne, the conquistadorial horseman, died. He may have been hanged, he may have been shot, he may have drowned with the rest of the crew. Those uncertainties exist. But curiously enough, when we put 'a shot rang out suddenly, near and yet far, as if the wind had been stretched and torn and had started coiling and running', we have a line – a line running into the past, through the present, and implicitly into the future. Now that is a line which one cannot take for granted. There is no complacent position to that line, because if we don't know whether the horseman was hanged, or shot, or whether he went under with the rest of the crew, it means that our expectations are overturned and broken at certain stages in the narrative. We have to expect that because the line that is running through is a line that one has to chart in terms of the overturning of fixtures. It is not a line that one can complacently seize upon. It is a line that runs so deeply into the resources of the tradition which has apparently vanished that it cannot give itself to us in some sort of complacent way and, as a consequence, there are times when we seem to lose the line as if it has broken, as if it has been severed. And yet it has not been severed, and therefore we have to see how, with the breaking of one thing, we allow ourselves to look much more deeply into our resources. And therefore we have 'A shot rang out suddenly near and yet far' etc. What is true is that a wound has been administered. Donne has died, and that wound is a wound which addresses us all because we have also been implicated in that wound. That wound becomes a way of rediscovering ourselves, rediscovering what we carried, what we have to address, the way we have to judge ourselves, the way we have to go forward.

The horseman stiffened with a devil's smile and the horse reared, grinning fiendishly and snapping at the reins. The horseman gave a bow to

84

heaven like a hanging man to his executioner and rolled from his saddle onto the ground.

So we see the line coming through the horseman, through his stiffening, and now, suddenly 'the shot had pulled me up and stifled my own heart in heaven.' Suddenly the dreamer is implicated in that line. He becomes the horseman, the dead man lying on the ground. So the dreamer now approaches *himself* as the dead man lying on the ground and thus the dreamer becomes a fiction – the psyche of conquest yields, however monolithic its establishment in the history books.

> His hair lay on his forehead. Someone was watching us from the trees and bushes that clustered the side of the road. Watching me as I bent down and looked at the man whose open eyes stared at the sky through his long, hanging hair. The sun blinded and ruled my living sight but the dead man's eye remained open and obstinate and clear. I dreamt I awoke with one dead seeing eye and one living closed eye.

Now we see here another aspect of this rehearsal, this infinite rehearsal, because one is rehearsing the various ways in which the horseman may have died. We come to the wound, the central wound which has been administered. But instead of leaving it there, instead of polarizing the horseman and saying here is the conquistadorial horseman, he is the one who persecuted all these people in the savannah, and on the other side are the people he persecuted – instead of polarizing them, we begin to rehearse the position in such a way that one descends into the horseman, one becomes the horseman, and in becoming the horseman one is then in a better position to judge how close one may come to simply repeating the tragedies of the past. It is very easy for a society to overturn an oppressor, but it is equally easy for those who overturned the oppressor to become the oppressor in turn. If one polarizes the world dreadfully, the oppressor and the oppressed, then one is no longer in a position to understand who the oppressor is, how he relates to one, who the oppressed are, how the oppressed relate to one. To understand that, one has to rehearse the implications. The very uncertainties that lie behind South American history ·may become a pregnant resource. There are many cultures in South America, Central America which have disappeared; we do not know why or how; we do not know how those cultures came into being. We look at an ancient city state like Teotihuacán in Mexico. We do not know why those people fled that city. The very name Teotihuacán was given by the Aztecs – 'the place where the gods were made'. So the Aztecs who were apparently so close to Teotihuacán in chronological time do not know Teotihuacán's original name! They do not know why the city – (one of the most important open city complexes of the ancient world) was abandoned by its inhabitants. Such enigma is native to South and Central America. Such uncertainties become a complex source for rehearsal in which the 'I' narrator descends into the horseman, into the conquistador. The whole thing is rehearsed so that a kind of line comes through. It's not an evasion because it does not evade the wounds which have been inflicted on the society – it's not an evasion – but yet a line comes through that seems to go deep into the past. For example, when one reads 'I dreamt I awoke with one dead, seeing eye' (the eye of realism) 'and one living, closed eye'. What is the living, closed eye? The living, closed eye is a threshold into tradition, lost traditions – it's living, but it's closed. As much as to say that the traditions which nourished Shakespeare or Dante or Homer – the cross-cultural traditions which nourished those writers and which bore upon the great pre-Columbian sculptors – whose traditions are alive, and buried within ourselves, within the world's unconscious. The living, closed eye therefore *is* a verbal construct, but it is something sculpted as well. In the beginning was the Word, in the beginning was the language of sculpture, in the beginning was the intuitive/inner voice of the mask, in the beginning was the painted cosmos and its orchestra of light and darkness. How does one sense the tapestry of these relations? The 'I' narrator becomes susceptible to a body of fiction he creates and by which he is created within a multi-textured, multi-varied dialogue encompassing the music or tonality of darkness and light, the utterance of pregnant mask and sculpture – all threaded into the fabric of many presences, known and unknown, sometimes *there* or *here* but apparently unknowable (however eloquent, however active). The story is told by the 'I' narrator and you can see that there are many texts. Who are the people watching at the side of the road? That's a story in itself which we do not know, perhaps will never know. Who were the others? There are all these different texts. There is no uniform text but there are different texts playing against each other, as much as to say that if you were to have a profound, creative democracy, you must have various texts playing against each other in such a manner that the tradition comes alive so marvellously that one begins to break the apparition of tyranny, the habit of conquest.

It is of interest to note (and *Palace of the Peacock* appeared in 1960, *Oudin* in 1961 – I don't know who were the post-modernists at that time) that the 'I' narrator disappears in the novel at a certain stage, just goes under and disappears (*but returns within a new community*), and I see that the post-modernists are claiming that the author disappears, the author vanishes. The way I diverge from the post-modernists – I must insist on this – is that the post-modernists have discarded depth, they have discarded the unconscious, thus all they are involved in is a game, a kind of game, whereas what I am saying is not just a game. I am convinced that there is a tradition in depth *which returns, which nourishes us even though it appears to have vanished*, and that it creates a fiction in the ways in which the creative imagination comes into dialogue with clues of revisionary moment. The spectral burden of vanishing and re-appearing is at the heart of the writer's task.

Finally, a personal comment on ways in which this matter of revision operates and how a work may be validated. There are two epigraphs in *Carnival*, one is from Dante, which I won't read, but that is deliberately chosen. The other from Norman O. Brown's *Love's Body* was not deliberately chosen – that was an epigraph which I stumbled upon when I had completed the novel. Norman O. Brown's *Love's Body* is an encyclopaedic work in which appears a variety of myths, legends, etc. The particular epigraph from *Love's Body* appearing in *Carnival* is drawn from one of these myths. I had not heard of it before. May I quote the first sentence in that epigraph: 'The wanderings of the soul after death are pre-natal adventures, a journey by water in a ship which is itself a goddess to the gates of rebirth.' It's a very peculiar combination of imagery and idea, and yet you will find, if you read the novel closely, that that myth, that apparition, appears in the novel, *not in a static way*. It is as if the outlines are there, they are visible but they have evolved within the unconscious; there are new complications and edges, there are new elements. It's as if when one comes into half-consciousness, half-conscious dialogue with the deep-seated past, one needs the past but the past needs one. The past remains locked away unless it can be re-visualized, taken up at another level, rehearsed profoundly at another level to release new implications, a new kind of thrust.

Now, let me take you through this very quickly, it's one of the strands in the novel. The thread of New World's carnival *subversive* (*not* escapist) strategy revisits dimensions of allegory. *Subversive* in that the museum configuration associated with allegory, is overturned. New World subversive carnival may become an invaluable asset in the creation of a vital, modern allegory. Here is the young boy who runs up to the house in a state of anguish:

> His trapped, sobbing breath had ceased and he moved gingerly towards his parents' room. The door was very slightly ajar. He was about to rap or push when he glimpsed something through the slit of space. It was his mother's tears that he saw, tears that masked her and suddenly made her into the mother of a god in the play of carnival. She was sitting at a mirror and her tears were reflected in the glass.
>
> (*Carnival*, p.26)

So we have the mother of a god in the play of carnival. Mother of a god implies a *goddess*. The *ship* which is itself a *goddess* is still to disclose itself. Note the dimensions of allegory. The young boy is Everyman Masters, Jonathan Weyl's Dantesque guide. Masters returns from the dead and unveils his youth to Weyl, his flight from the seashore into his parents' house. (There are other important guides in *Carnival* but I shall not touch on these. I mention them only to endorse my feeling about the conjunction of carnival and revitalized allegory.) May I continue with the quotation I read a moment ago and its allusion to a goddess in the play of carnival.

> She did not turn. He did not disclose he was there. He felt nevertheless that she knew; he felt as she touched her glass breasts in the mirror that

she knew he was inside her, halfway between a wall of glass and a cavity of flesh, that she knew he was looking through her into a kind of fire that mingled with her tears.

(p.27)

Note the clues through which to visualize a backward and forward play of imageries – *in the glass* (she is at the mirror), 'glass breasts', 'womb of glass and flesh' (this bears on the ship in the storm that comes later in *Carnival*). Young Masters sees himself in her, he sees himself reflected in her as an endangered foetus . . .

There is the pre-natal text, the pre-natal adventure, in the epigraph from Love's Body. (And remember Masters is the dead man who has returned to address Weyl, to guide his friend.) Note the correspondence with the epigraph 'the wanderings of the soul after death'.

Two other quotations bring us into the realm of 'the ship which is itself a goddess'.

Queen Jennifer [that's his mother, the Carnival Queen] stepped out of a shower, out of a waterfall, out of an ocean, into the bedroom. I was lying half asleep, half awake on her bed. *She handcuffed me to her body as to the mast of a ship.*

(p.95)

So there you have your 'ship which is a goddess' – *she handcuffed me to her body as to the mast of a ship.* And, finally, we have the passage when Masters and Weyl leave South America:

The storm hit the vessel at last. The glass sides of the ship, darkened and it was as if I saw it now, I saw the sea in Masters' eyes. The sea was black and white fire ran along the ridges and valleys of space. I held to my dream-support for bleak life and yet this was my leap into purgatory all over again – purgation through the terror of beauty.

(p.91)

So we see the glass sides of a ship (the womb of the ship) which reminds you of the glass woman – half glass, half flesh. You see elements of that epigraph as one of the strands in the novel. We see the elements there as you read the novel backwards and forwards, a *novel which is revised through intuitive clues that came up out the unconscious into the drafts.* One revises through them and finds oneself engaged in a strategy *that is validated or proven by an ancient myth.*

No need to explore further the intuitive strategy at which we have been looking. Indeed we have done so in order to attempt an illumination of paradoxes of creativity that bear, I believe, on the so-called Third World where legacies of conquest have marginalized and eclipsed many cultures. Needless to say perhaps

I am particularly concerned with the Caribbean, the Guyanas, and the Central Americas where a cross-cultural medium of traditions may be discerned.

Many of the moral precepts associated with allegory have possessed ascendancy there even as the form of allegory – allegory as creative vehicle – became moribund. We have looked at the deficiencies of pure realism in this informal talk. Within that context it is arguable that the revitalization of allegory – the profound illumination and reality of inner guides and guidelines – may well be acutely pertinent to apparently marginal societies.

Implicit in all this is the notion that a truly creative alchemical response to crisis and conflict and deprivation – a response that engages with formidable myth – may well come from the other side of a centralized or dominant civilization, from extremities, from apparently irrelevant imaginations and resources. The complacencies of centralized, ruling powers – where language tends sometimes to become a tool for hypocrisies and false clarities – begin to wear thin at the deep margins of being within a multi-levelled quest for the natures of value and spirit. That quest becomes more and more imperative within endangered environments and species and communities.

Inner confidence, inner hope, may gain unpredictable momentum at the edges of capacity, *through* fissures of capacity in which the scope and the potentials of buried traditions re-vision themselves.

6

REFLECTIONS ON *INTRUDER IN THE DUST* IN A CROSS-CULTURAL COMPLEX

The Fall

Intruder in the Dust is a comedy of psyche and the implications that reside in such a theme (or combination of themes) tend to be overlooked by critics who indict the novel for its 'provincialism' or 'rhetoric'.

It is true that a case can be made against the novel for hardened convention that is akin to provincial stasis, but once we begin to see the action of dark comedy within the narrative, a strange light, I find, arises through which 'provincialism' relinquishes its powers and a body of harlequin features – rooted in many cultures – comes into play and points to a universe of unsuspected diversity, correspondence and potential.

Likewise what seems unnatural rhetoric at first sight in the narrative acquires a capacity to illuminate patterns of claustrophobia which reveal themselves first as buried premises, then almost simultaneously as heightened premises that are reluctant to come forward or upward as if they resist the excavation of imagination that acts upon them in the soil of place, as if they are conscious of being unreal in being raised from a state of long eclipse into the bewildering lights and pressures of consciousness.

It is necessary to note the curious anthropomorphism at work in the novel. The writer appears to create the premises he depicts but is also created, so to speak, by them. His premises are *alive*, they are reluctant to be raised to consciousness. This comedy of thrust and counter-thrust between the writer who makes a world of peculiar sensations and is also *made*, in some degree, by the world he makes (as if the world he makes is truly alive in its own right) is the substance of rhetoric Faulkner employs. This thrust – and intuitive return thrust – with its wealth of perspective, tends to be blocked and flattened, in some parts of the novel and as the novel draws to a close, by a prickly regionalism or fortress homogeneity, exercised by Faulkner's hierarchy of intentions. This imposes a barren philosophical climax that gives some weight to the charges that have been levelled against the work.

It is only proper and fair to summarize those charges by quoting an actual

90

passage, representative of adverse critical opinion, from Edmond L. Volpe's study of William Faulkner.

> [This] is his most provincial novel. His analysis of the Southern con-
> sciousness illuminates the complex psychological and social forces that
> make the intelligent white Southerner a unique phenomenon of the
> twentieth century. But because Faulkner treats his subject as a special
> problem – everyone not born a white Southerner is an Outlander – the
> significance and value of his book as art is minimal. Of even more
> importance, perhaps, in accounting for the failure of the novel as a work
> of art is Faulkner's assumption of the role of spokesman for the South.
> He sacrifices his art to social analysis and preaching. The result is a
> propaganda novel. The melodramatic plot in which two boys – a Negro
> and a white – and an old woman open a grave to prove that the Negro,
> Lucas Beauchamp, about to be lynched for the murder of a white man,
> is innocent, is too slight a story to maintain the weight of rhetoric
> Faulkner heaps upon it.[1]

The tasks of a critic are manifold and difficult, especially when it becomes necessary to descend with the creative imagination into half-excavated, half-reluctant, living strata of place that lie under reinforcements of habit or conven-tion or fortress institution that may parade itself as moral imperative. But it is clear that Volpe makes no effort to grasp the irrational coherence – the capacity for fictions within fictions, truths within truths all 'writing' each other in being 'written' by each other, that breaches conventional logic and gives the novel its complicated power and focus. Thus, in my judgement, he is drawn into an aston-ishing under-estimation of a complex and demanding art in which the emphasis shifts from ruling ego to intuitive layers of self or selves, and a transformed mosaic of community comes into play. That transformation lapses into misgiving, retreat, hollow moralizing and hollow spokesmanship for the South at stages of Faulkner's narrative, but its significance is nevertheless profound and far-reaching.

When I say 'intuitive' layers of self, in contradistinction to 'ruling' ego, I mean a darkened psychic concentration that so pools itself it becomes an interior mirror reflecting outer activity. It loses the biased rituals of material property in favour of kinship with images that cease to be passive or submerged; instead each image is an apparent catalyst of discovery, it acts upon the falling or ascending weight of a subtle imagination immersed in what it appears to describe.

Each image, therefore, confesses to textures which make paradoxically real a universe ceaselessly subject to qualities of alteration within creator and created, a universe that can never be taken for granted as dead matter; objective status is eternally flawed, eternally aware of breached limits, eternally susceptible there-fore to an organ of wholeness that is never achieved (or identified permanently in nature or in psyche) but is paradoxically there nevertheless at the heart of a creation in which pressures of dialogue, spheres of duality, exist between creator and created. Both are, in a context of human frailty and imagination, partial conceptions within a riddle of unfathomable being or timeless moment.

This issue will emerge in a variety of ways within the womb of space and labyrinth we pursue. Its occurrence in *Intruder in the Dust* thrusts the reader, at times without warning as if to invite a 'lived' and 'living' experience of suppressed, still momentous, dialogue, into the peculiar *breathlessness, immobilization* and *suffocation* that accompany claustrophobia – a claustrophobia that looms early in the novel, and secretes a precipice of emotion down which young Charles Mallison falls, to play a crucial, nervous role in coming abreast of the rising premises of otherness within an excavation of psyche and place.

The psychical consequences of that fall are threaded into himself, into his companion Aleck Sander and indeed into the entire cast of the novel, by degrees of implication and casualty woven into the texture of the narrative. In the first place, the formidable narcissistic core of the society Faulkner immerses us in seems phenomenally bruised in young Mallison's fall. This multiple bruise – inner and outer – that unites him to others is a tribute to his youth, his capacity for fantasy, and to the irrational and intensely human awareness built into the crevices of childhood, of layers of imagination he shares with the entire community, however hidden such layers are by the carapace of institution or complacent habit.

The shock inflicted on complacent institution by the consequences of the fall is, in substantial part, a clue to Faulkner's irony (unconscious irony, I would think) in wedding falling/rising place to the riddle of consciousness. The precipitous fall is an uplift in terrain, an uplift of figures who loom into him with such astonishing exaggeration of contour and paradoxical exactitude that he can no longer remain blind to them as in the past. One exaggerated contour is as much part of the illusion and blow of exactitude within the opening eye; descent defines ascent of new birth, new awareness, and vice versa. Both are native extremes to each other, unconsciousness to the precarious and stretched limits of consciousness. And therein lies the spirit of the paradoxical museum of the world embodied in stasis that becomes unpredictably active; the fossil of age begins to live in persons who seem to wear their very skins like close-fitting yet interchangeable costumes of vertical destiny and abrupt sensation, mirrored features, one in the other, black in white.

The abruptness with which they slide into and out of unconscious habit is a revelation of the vertigo of exactitude, illusory exactitude, humour of exactitude, and this undermining of stasis – a stasis which parades as the exact truth of tradition – leads to built-in evolutions, long eclipsed or forgotten, that exist within the most hardened property or consensus of fate.

In that disclosure of eclipsed evolutions lies the dawn, the thread of dawn, woven into potential heterogeneity, and arching through European, African and pre-Columbian hidden antecedents to which Faulkner refers – 'the whole sum of their ancestral horror and scorn and fear of Indian and Chinese and Mexican and Carib and Jew . . .' in the psyche of place.[2] It is a darkened illumination or obscure light, as much a source of dread as of hope, and this fittingly becomes a symbol in itself of overshadowed or diminished poetry that lurks in the novel, and gives to the prose an awkwardness at times, an awkward and pregnant illumination of consciousness that seems oddly right in drawing one into the consequences of Charles Mallison's fall and its extensions into the entire community, the living and the dead.

> It was cold that morning . . . and the standing water . . . was skimmed with ice . . . scintillant like fairy glass and from the first farmyard they passed . . . came the windless tang of woodsmoke and they could see the black iron pots already steaming while women in the sun-bonnets still of summer or men's old felt hats and long men's overcoats stoked wood under them and the men with crokersack aprons tied with wire over their overalls whetted knives . . . by nightfall the whole land would be hung with their *spectral intact tallow coloured empty carcasses immobilised by the heels in frantic running full tilt at the centre of the earth.*
> . . . Aleck Sander and Edmonds' boy with tapsticks and he with the gun . . . went down through the park to the creek where Edmonds' boy knew the footlog was and he didn't know how it happened, something a girl might have been . . . excused for doing but nobody else, half-way over the footlog . . . when *all of a sudden the known familiar sunny winter earth was upside down and flat on his face and still holding the gun he was rushing not away from the earth but away from the bright sky* [italics mine, WH].[3]

Mallison falls into the creek. A sense of bulk and protuberance, the trade of slaughterhouse in farmyard and factory he has passed on his way to the creek, casts its shadow over him like a pregnant design, an exaggerated contour, illusory exactitude, yet his reflection on 'a girl [who] might have been excused' sustains something of the smothered graces of the half-drowned, shot rabbit he has himself become. They were on their way to hunt and kill rabbits but young Mallison himself falls into the 'grave of the creek'.

Aleck Sander thrusts a pole into the creek but it is the iron-faced black commanding Lucas Beauchamp – proud and pitiless as the white farmers on the land – who looms out of nowhere, it seems, and takes charge of the operation: 'and he could remember still, the breaking ice . . . *his clothes like soft cold lead which he didn't move in* . . . he saw two feet in gum boots . . . the legs; the overalls . . . *a Negro man with an axe on his shoulder* . . . Lucas Beauchamp . . . watching him without pity [or] commiseration . . . not even surprise: just watching him [italics mine, WH].'[4]

In that passage, as in the previous quotation, the sense of exaggerated contour and paradoxical exactitude addresses us, but above all one begins to perceive, I would suggest, an intuitive threshold into *expédition* or *l'envoi morts* within broad daylight theatrical narrative.

It seems that Faulkner was not consciously aware of such a threshold or how strangely his imagination had been pulled into coincidence with black theatre of psyche, the *expédition* or *l'envoi morts* that a notable scholar Alfred Métraux defines in his work on *Voodoo in Haiti* (London 1972).

Had he seen it – had the life of heterogeneity, in unconscious or intuitive dialogue with his creativity, come home to him – he would have been driven, I think, to revise the one-sided moral conclusions built into the closing premises of the novel.

Métraux writes, 'The most fearful practice in the black arts – the one which the ordinary people are always talking about – is the sending of the dead (*l'envoi morts* or *expédition*) . . . The laying on of the spell is always attended by fatal results unless it is diagnosed in time and a capable *hungan* succeeds in making the dead let go.'

That the corpse of Vinson Gowrie may be interpreted as institutionalized spectre of prejudice 'sent against' Lucas Beauchamp enriches the depth-potential of *Intruder in the Dust* and suggests an activity of image beyond given verbal convention into non-verbal arts of the imagination in the womb of cultural space as though an *unstructured* force arbitrates or mediates between articulate or verbal signs and silent or eclipsed voices of nemesis in folk religions whose masks or sculptures subsist upon implicit metaphors of death-in-life, life-in-death.

The force of that intuitive threshold cannot be but marked and peculiar – in its hidden seismic pressure – on the prose style of *Intruder in the Dust*. It is bright yet dark upheaval, day yet night. The precipice of emotion down which Charles falls is in the nature of a dream or a suspended contour of night in broad daylight, 'soft cold lead [in] which he didn't move' yet 'carcasses immobilized . . . full tilt at the centre of the earth'.

That contour of dream triggers both human rabbit and pregnant execution within the womb of space. The trigger lodges itself in the looming presence of Lucas Beauchamp standing above the 'grave of the creek' with an axe on his shoulder. The pitiless gaze he directs upon hapless rabbit or victim of the hunt in metaphoric senses differs little from the severe detachment he is to evince not long afterwards in the novel, when he stands not with an axe but with a gun in his hand over the dead body of Vinson Gowrie, and finds himself as a consequence not only accused of murder but threatened by an outraged community, outraged convention, for his insolence to and disregard of enshrined patterns of behaviour.

He has aroused the fire of institutional bias, the sorcery of hate enshrined in institutional 'corpse', sacred vengeance or 'sent dead' in Voodoo vocabulary. The two scenes are linked together, the scene at the creek and the scene over the sacred body of a dead Gowrie from Beat Four where the Gowrie clan rules, to symbolize territorial imperative or regime.

Young Mallison's fall in broad daylight winter morning theatre possesses another hidden underside or premise that comes to light in the nightsky, so to speak, of a culture, in constellations hidden by the deed of the sun. That thread embodies the mantle of the *hungan* that is to fall upon young Charles Mallison,

Aleck Sander and elderly Miss Habersham (whose relationship to Lucas's family we shall discuss later).

Charles knew, when Beauchamp was accused of shooting Vinson Gowrie in cold blood, that he too would have subscribed to that view which rested on daylight appearance – on the gun in Lucas's hand as he stood over the body of the murdered man, as he had stood before with an axe on his shoulder over a mesmerised creature in a creek – but Charles had been changed by his fall into the theatre of a grave like one masked, as in a dream, by his own slain pride, slain habit. He had felt himself bound to Lucas then by resentment and awe as he emerged from the creek. He had been confused by the other's pitiless gaze, by the uncompromising spirit in which he had been shepherded into Lucas's house, tended and fed there.

Who was black Lucas, he had wondered in confusion, to behave as if he were white, pitiless and proud? We shall return to the ground of Lucas's hospitality later; I mention it now to endorse young Mallison's double sensation of receiving a blow, woven into his fall, that dismantled Southern racial protocol or privilege, and of being engulfed by a wholly intuitive constellation, a seismic and unconscious dimension, the nightsky of a culture that invokes the spectre of dead Gowrie as nightmare protuberance, pregnant hate, 'sent dead' against the living to draw blood.

Thus begins a rare pressure of mental imagery within the contours of factual deed, a subtle fable of mental exactitude, therapeutic dimension: rare pressure because it is an alliance or link, an immaterial bond, that begins to grow between black Lucas and the youth Charles Mallison from the day Charles experiences the vertigo of stasis. It embodies the art of the *hungan* to unravel the sorcery of hate.

It is the life of complex projection from culture to culture that helps us to read the action of an insensible community in new dark lights. Culture is deed, instantaneous bright deed, as well as active reflection in the depths of otherness. The nature of that reflection is sometimes akin to darkness, sometimes akin to the nightsky, the dark night which alone mirrors constellations and stars invisible in day.

The opening of Vinson Gowrie's grave in sacred Beat Four territory by Charles, Aleck and old Miss Habersham lies at the heart of *Intruder in the Dust*, to establish that the bullet that killed Gowrie did not come from Lucas's gun. That opened grave is prime corollary to young Mallison's physical/psychical fall and is fraught with unsuspected self-discovery that ignites a trajectory which affects the entire community, and discloses internal corruption and treachery within the dignified *persona* of the Gowrie clan. The very spectre of involuntary Voodoo vengeance, sent against an alleged murderer, proves itself in that theatre of a grave as less a matter of inflamed desire for justice by outraged propriety (harsh and sinister rocket from a fortress of strength) and more a symptom of internal disease within hoary tradition itself. The excavation is done at night and is a prime corollary to young Mallison's fall, less into night as calendrical spirit and more into eclipsed heterogeneity and exactitude of conscience, eclipsed indebtedness of partial systems to partial systems.

The effect is seismic within the narrative bodies of *Intruder in the Dust*. But beneath all convolution and upheaval, it is the mental imagery, the active conscience, that continues to haunt us within and beyond the Voodoo category of harlequin dead. For that mental imagery, or translated spectre of the dead-in-the-living, raises the myth of assessing the *exact shape of spirit*, the weight of spiritual conscience, to rouse itself from the sleep of material habit or age. And one finds one has entered the ground of myth. The shape of conscience is live myth, measureless foundations within daylight premises of buried cultures. Its weight torments us with a sensation of acute impartiality and hope that flits before us within diseased power-structures. That acuteness, or vision of impartiality and hope, ignites an obsession with exact force that, however, remains immeasurable. It flits before us within man-made and nature-made terrors and structured misconceptions. It reveals an appetite in entrenched insensible community to inflict damnation upon others and upon itself.

All this pushes us to reflect upon the action of image, or the dynamism of metaphor, the 'alchemy of the word' as the French poet Arthur Rimbaud put it. In my judgement, we tend to confuse spiritual exactitude with static particularity and this breeds narrative-reflections of deeds and objects that are passive in the mind's eye. But mental imagery – as it is beginning to disclose itself to us – is much more than that, it is the activity of live myth, it is much less an appeal to a passivity of mind than a bridge, however precarious, between day-life (or deed-life) and night-life (or indebtedness of bright partial suns to darkest genesis of stars).

The shadow of conscience

Even before young Mallison, Aleck Sander and elderly Miss Habersham set out to stay the hand of the lynch-mob by opening Vinson Gowrie's grave, the shadow of excavated premises falls over the region. It is a shadow that lays bare the land as another 'spectral carcass' deeded by generation to generation, 'cryptic three-toed prints . . . like a terrain in miniature out of the age of the great lizards'. The shadow envelops Charles in the theatre of creek and reflected grave – his clothing becomes soft, leaden – as he emerges that cold winter morning to become the unwilling recipient of Lucas's commanding hospitality. He, Aleck Sander and Edmonds' boy are led by Lucas into the shadow that falls everywhere. It drapes the gate through which they pass into Lucas's territory.[5]

The accent upon fossil terrain is part and parcel of the grave of history and of shadow that lays bare the land. All this is underlined by an accumulation and ramification of images within the very cabin in which Lucas lives where Charles confronts a 'framed portrait-group' in which Molly, Lucas's wife, appears like 'an embalmed corpse through the hermetic glass lid of a coffin'.[6]

The sensation of a sarcophagus – which one cannot fail to experience – possesses a significance that needs to be scrutinized. For one learns later in the novel that Molly and elderly Miss Habersham had grown up like twins. They had both been suckled at Molly's mother's breast. Molly was the daughter of one of Miss Habersham's grandfather's slaves. The two children had slept in the same room, the white girl in a bed, Molly in a cot at the foot of that bed. When Molly and Lucas had their first child Miss Habersham had stood up 'in the Negro Church' as godmother.[7]

One is under little or no illusion about the gulf between Miss Habersham and Molly. Despite Miss Habersham's godmother status they have already moved into separate ghettos. Thus the conception of white and black twins is static attire and Molly's 'embalmed corpse' becomes a device to endorse that static dress and to suggest intuitively the dead-end of a cultural homogeneous model.

There is another aspect to Molly's 'embalmed corpse'. I find that it mimics and brilliantly parodies events to come, in particular the double-headed coffin of Vinson Gowrie, in which one Jake Montgomery is also buried, as Charles Mallison, Aleck Sander and Miss Habersham discover when they open Vinson Gowrie's grave.

Despite such ramifications in the imagery of the novel that expose the dead-end reign of a corrupt regime – however dignified it appears on the surface in its daylight epitaphs and deeds – Faulkner (through Lawyer Stevens, Charles's uncle) devotes long passages to defend territorial-in-moral imperative. Herein lies his instructive failure to perceive the heterogeneous potential and cross-cultural mind within the shadow of *Intruder in the Dust*, so that that potential twinship – so remarkably manifest in creative intuition – freezes and aborts itself until it even seduces the intellect to erect a passive inverted twin pawn in the game of power politics. The very tone, the very voice of Lawyer Stevens's barren intellectuality, implies 'Faulkner's assumption', as Edmond L. Volpe puts it, 'of the role of spokesman for the South'.

Lucas is reduced, in Lawyer Stevens's argument, to an inverted pawn in North/South politics of culture. The 'privilege of setting him free' rests with territorial factor or ruling majority in Faulkner's South and cancels out original mentality or initiative, not only between the outside world (symbolized by the North) and the inside world (symbolized by the South), but also between blacks and whites since it rests with the collective whites alone – within a game of *imposed* unity – to set 'Sambo free'.[8]

The unity of the intuitive self (as darkened psychical pool of concentration) and its capacity to undermine the logic of ego-historical bias or one-sided moral imperative is an issue of unconscious irony, which is implicit in our exploration. Indeed, that realm of unconscious irony helps to redeem Faulkner's lapses and to give to Lawyer Stevens's homilies a sense of automatic carnival. For Faulkner and Lawyer Stevens are involuntary twins, both passive and active in turn. They are less absolute author (Faulkner) and fictional subject (Stevens), and more an automatic catalyst to invoke a series of ambiguous twinships in a mosaic self-portrait; namely, Molly and Miss Habersham (who share the same static cradle), Vinson

Gowrie and Jake Montgomery (who in turn share the same coffin), Vinson Gowrie's twin brothers who share the same puppet-like destiny, and other insensible twins within theatre of the grave and cradle that tends to parody itself unwittingly and involuntarily.

In the context of carnival or masked comedy and upheaval which disperses reflections of form (reflections on the mutability rather than immutability of character) we may perceive, I think, the fascinations of *shared ego or desire for conquest* entrenched within cultures. This brings home the reality of evil, in which cultures are enmeshed in codes to invert or overturn each other rather than become involved in complex mutuality and the difficult creation of community.

Inverted pawns in the game of civilization may cloak themselves in refined or stoical patterns of behaviour, or classical comedy of manners, which masquerades as order. They may accept a hierarchy of structures. Treaties are signed between those above and those beneath. Protocol is established. All seems well. And yet in broad daylight, as it were, the shadow of conscience drapes itself everywhere to become a different bridge, a potential bridge, across a dangerous divide.

Notes

1 Edmund L. Volpe, *William Faulkner* (London: Thames and Hudson, 1964).
2 William Faulkner, *Intruder in the Dust* (London: Penguin in association with Chatto and Windus, 1960), p.208.
3 Ibid., p.7.
4 Ibid., p.8.
5 Ibid., p.10.
6 Ibid., pp.15–16.
7 Ibid., pp.85–6.
8 Ibid., pp.148–50.

7

THE SCHIZOPHRENIC SEA

Carnival twinships

Faulkner's difficulty in relinquishing a conviction of territorial conscription of moral imperative, and the implicit polarizations such order engenders between outsiders and insiders, minority and majority cultures – with one side or the other arrogating to itself the determination of rights or principles – has its roots in legacies of conquest and in tormented monoliths of the nineteenth and twentieth centuries.

One of the first major tormented monoliths to appear in American fiction is *Arthur Gordon Pym of Nantucket*.[1] This was first published in the late 1830s and has since become a peculiar classic. The schizophrenic genius of Edgar Allan Poe in this strange narrative helps us to begin to perceive the decay of order conditioned by conquest; that order begins to review its daylight deeds, made sacrosanct by institutional codes, in the night-time rebellious dream life of the half-conscious and unconscious psyche.

Subversive review however was not Poe's intention, which was instead committed to an ego-conviction of necessary robot-deity or divine slave-master, commander of ships, commander of families, in nineteenth-century America. In *Pym*, versions, and inversions, of divine commander are mirrored in Captain Block and in other figures on land and sea as well as in black and white mutineers and rebels.

It seems to me an illuminating perspective of unconscious irony in *Intruder in the Dust* to move Faulkner's Lucas Beauchamp backward into Poe's schizophrenic high seas and place him within a previous incarnation as the authoritarian black mutineer Seymour who sails on Pym's carnival ship *Grampus*.

It is a comparison that may seem extreme at first sight, since Faulkner's Lucas is possessed by the appearances of unswerving dignity, whereas Poe's Seymour is painted as an executioner and fiend in a world fired by hate. Extreme as it is, it reveals a pathology of emotions in two classic American novels, a state of emotion governed by projections of fear across the generations from which may be minted bizarre currencies of the imagination that suffer violence or erupt into violence.

Lucas Beauchamp reflects an iron pride, a pitiless comedy of manners, a capacity to suffer insult and remain unbowed, a conviction of fanatical uprightness and superiority in the twentieth century that outrages Faulkner's whites for whom pride and superiority are commodities of tradition reserved to themselves.

Seymour reflects an authoritarian conviction in the nineteenth century, a pitiless capacity to inflict injury upon oppressor and oppressed who stand in his way. This alarms Poe's masochistic creativity, since he himself is torn between the state of tyranny, as material of the divine to be challenged, and the dream of rebellion, as gross sin to be punished. Seymour appals as judge and executioner rolled into one agent of authoritarian rebel in divine slave-master on Poe's sailing ship *Grampus* in the wake of mutiny.

Lucas inspires dread because he dons the Faulknerian mask of the victim who gauges nevertheless, with cunning insight, the vulnerable proportions of lynch-mob or lynch-god. That that lynch-god wears a white collective mask and possesses many hands only heightens the nemesis of black-masked Seymour who lusts for power and of inverted pawn Lucas who attires himself in the stoical attributes of the *status quo*.

This equation between Seymour, the authoritarian Poesque rebel, and nihilist, pitiless authority – an equation of pervasive irony in twentieth-century global politics, in inverted Latin American and Third World cultures which have wrested freedom from brutal empires they still emulate – is a measure of doomed symmetry or the death of the very freedom that appears to have been won.

Instead of freedom, doom presides; it resides in the acceptance of absolute structure within partial institutions that have masqueraded for centuries as the divine parentage of the modern world.

On the other hand, the complex breaches of partial, yet schizophrenically closed, order or symmetrical religious fate (by which Poe was haunted in his time) suggest that, in our time, there may exist another reading of events within the womb of cultural space; a reading that perceives meaningful distortions planted by the intuitive self within a work of the imagination – such as *Pym* – that symbolizes ambiguities of freedom – distortions that disclose varieties of *unstructured vision or unconscious arbitration* that mediate between all structured systems, all masks or deeds within that work.

Such mediation, I believe, is the irony of forces within the intuitive self – the irony of changed and changing emotions within the address of art – one discovers but cannot entrap. That address releases unsuspected potential, or mutated fabric, to absorb the stresses of genuine change within obsolescent order and to warn against every beguilement to succumb to age-old parody of imperial family or divine state, and to repetitive cycles of violence.

I should perhaps elaborate on the play of unstructured vision or arbitrating forces secreted in the indirections/directions, tendencies/upheavals, *within* and *through* partial systems, though I hope that the variables of this conception will emerge in our explorations as insight into alchemy of image and word rather than as intellectual statement.

100

The play of arbitrating forces should be associated with an *asymmetry* within the infinity and genius of art. This does not in any way imply that symmetries are false but it demonstrates that orders of symmetry may appear universal – may seek to pre-empt infinity – though they may actually be no more than useful, sometimes brilliant, extensions and inversions of a binding prejudice and locality. The stranger beauty of asymmetry lies in its subtle transformations of phenomena bound or tamed within a mask of universality and within patterns of elegant tautology – sometimes within patterns of unconscious parody of the past – sometimes within patterns that seek to reify territorial legend into moral or conquistadorial imperative symmetrized by habit or education into our perception of humanity.

Symmetries may be disrupted meaningfully, therefore, by the pressure of intuitive and subtle infinity upon localities of hubris masquerading as universal, an infinity of pressure whose truth ultimately resists every cage, to offer itself instead in the complex interactions of partial images as these disclose themselves subject to untamed and untamable resources within, yet beyond, daylight capture or framework.

Untamed and untamable infinity is a temptation to paranoia and it places undeniable stress on human sensibility, but its gifts to the human imagination, its corollaries of ongoing and ceaselessly unfinished explorations in the arts and sciences, are rewarding beyond measure. It confirms the necessity for complex mutuality between cultures. It offers, in my judgement, the only doorway into a conception of genuine breakthrough from tragedy. It has become a cliché to speak of the death of tragedy, but the growth of nihilism, the growth of ideologies that make pawns of humanity, the end-of-the-world syndrome in which we live, would all seem to be motivated by stoic lust or conviction, stoic intellectuality, the inverse nobility of tragedy.

Tragedy lives, and within our carnival age it implies a passivity that accepts the fate of catastrophe with little or no genuine complaint, it accepts the ultimate inversion of all by a structured and tamed nature that becomes, in stages, a decadent and fatally diseased or exploited muse. Carnival tragedy stresses, therefore, ultimatum or the hollow mask humanity wears with a semblance of dignity.

Asymmetric infinity, on the other hand, implies an enfolding and unfolding of cultures beyond tamed vision, or totalitarian caprice and loss of revolutionary soul, it implies unseen yet real natures whose life is indefatigable (and thus it may, indeed must, occasion a sense of exhaustion within ephemeral structuralism), and whose therapeutic horizons-in-depth lie beyond logical fate that frames canvases of existence.

These distinctions may, I hope, prove helpful at this stage though much more needs to be said on the mystery of injustice and mental pain, and whether the innocent may not suffer at times less from tragic fate and more from a lust for symmetry, by underpinning localities of hubris to polarize cultures into 'universal' camps that have no alternative but to articulate the death of others (and implicitly, in a nuclear age, of mankind) by inversions of blood and pitiless codes and fractions of violence in the response of one universal hierarchy to another. Herein lies the abnormal tension of Poe's *Pym* and the corruption of violence it portrays, a corruption in addiction to the death of mankind Poe constructs with realistic fallacy on his schizophrenic high seas.

Poe's fear of alien appearances – his subjection to the charisma of *blackness* and *whiteness* – helps us to see that his animus against the 'black person' or 'black enemy' was an obsessional neurosis that disabled him in the exercise of the very authority of freedom he idolized. Yet it gave him a singular concentration upon extreme or tormenting faculties by which he was conscripted. Sidney Kaplan writes in his introduction to *The Narrative of Arthur Gordon Pym*, 'Poe who has seemed to many an anguished man set apart from his times, was, in fact, a part of the American Nightmare. In the decade of the founding of Garrison's *Liberator*, of Nat Turner's conspiracy, of Theodore Weld's *The Bible Against Slavery*, he felt called upon to say that slavemasters violated no law divine.'[2]

Poe's defence of the institution of slavery in nineteenth-century America is an intellectual paradox. It was an attitude that may have been cemented by emotional and ambivalent memories. Some biographers speak of his ambivalence toward his foster-father, admiration at one stage, loathing at another, and something akin to symbolic mutiny comes through in *Pym* in the organs of family and state against which Pym and his companions mutiny to incur a burden of guilt, manifesting a greed to be punished for having sinned against surrogate divinity.

The masks surrogates wear in *Pym* are the substance of carnival twinships, carnival tragedy that gleams with asymmetric fissures of myth. We need to be clear, I think, about the strength of hollow ultimatum or mask in *Pym* which slips from the brow of character to character like the highwater mark of nihilistic tragedy even as it borders upon untamed potential for re-birth in the womb of space.

There is Captain Block's 'ultimatum' which would have left Pym to drown at sea. There is Pym's grandfather who threatens to cut his grandson off without a shilling and who comes close to assaulting him. There is the black mutineer Seymour on the *Grampus* on whom Poe projects his fear of authoritarian rule and repression.[3] These are a few prime examples of ultimatum that overshadows Pym.

Intriguing fissures in the Block ultimatum reflect unnamable mediation at the helm of the cosmos arbitrating between the 'death of the land' (a phrase that may help to illumine the density of Pym's emotion of decaying and claustrophobic family regime) and the 'womb of the sea'. That this intuition does flourish for a moment is demonstrated in the re-birth of Pym and Augustus from the paradoxical and cruel sea in the wake of their rebellion against the land – against the institutional corpses of family and state – a rebellion that is augmented by the only successful mutiny throughout the entire narrative of *Pym*, when the crew of Block's ship disobey his orders not to search for survivors from the *Ariel* but are harmoniously wedded to him again in restoring Pym and Augustus to life. It is an intuition that is imperilled. Block and his surrogates are conscripted

102

afresh into a chain of authoritarian mutineers and hollow commanders of the globe.

Tragic crew of the globe – masked by re-born (yet aborted) Augustus and Pym – succumb to greed or guilt to punish themselves within a repetitive cycle of blocks to freedom. The miraculous re-birth from the womb of the sea is fatally tainted, or rendered abortive, it seems, by the very mutinies that occasion it. Fatally tainted mask, yet miraculous fissure or arbitrating insight, remains in each bleak step from twinship to twinship.

The first twinship *Ariel* within a series of psychical or dream-association is overturned by Captain Block, and Pym and Augustus are rescued by Block's mutineers to escape drowning by the skin of their teeth. Thus they become psychical twins and undergo a 'partial interchange of character'.[4] It is a night-mare excursion, akin to overwhelming dream; it is a medium of re-birth para-doxically sprung, in the first place, from their disobedience and the deception they practised on their parents. The dream sea from which they are rescued registers the taint of original disobedience by painting its highwater mark of insensibility upon Augustus's brow, carnival block, as it were.

It is he who had encouraged Pym, in a drunken fit, to trick their parents, steal out of their homes, and set sail at midnight on the *Ariel*. Pym discovers too late that Augustus 'had drunk far more than I suspected, and . . . his conduct . . . had been the result of a highly concentrated state of intoxication . . . which, like madness, enables the victim to imitate the outward demeanour of one in perfect possession of his senses. He was now thoroughly insensible' as he held the tiller of the dream-ship *Ariel*.[5]

Thus it is that Augustus, though re-born twin to Pym from the womb of the sea, had previously, incorrigibly, slipped into 'block insensibility' to echo and mirror (to parody unwittingly) past and future blanket of indifference that Captain Block himself casts over the sea when the *Ariel* is overturned and Augustus and Pym are all but drowned. It is as if ruling Captain Block and insensible victim Augustus, at the helm of the overturned *Ariel*, share a mutual incorrigibility and projection of hollowness from one to the other.

The psychical re-birth/twinship between Augustus and Pym is established within ruling 'block insensibility', as it were. Asymmetric fissure of hope glimmer-ingly and intuitively exists but the wound of guilt is pathological and severe, and it begins to fester into recurring mutiny and authoritarian malaise.

If the *Ariel* is the first twinship, then the second – in interwoven physical stage and psychical insight – occurs on the *Grampus*. Here the head of block – with its ingrained wound – is worn by both Pym's white grandfather and the authoritarian mutineer Seymour whose existence we have already tentatively outlined as nineteenth-century incarnation of Faulkner's twentieth-century Lucas Beauchamp. The notion that Pym's white grandfather is psychical twin to black Seymour is scarcely Poe's conscious intentention. He achieves it unknowingly through 'partial inter-change[s] of character' and carnival usage of pigmentations. Through one mask he lays bare the shadowy gestures or omens concealed in another.

A certain decorum is adopted in depicting Pym's harsh grandfather who raises his umbrella against Pym as if it were a weapon when Pym is on his way to embark surreptitiously on the *Grampus*. No such restraint is necessary in painting Seymour with an axe in his hand on the deck of the *Grampus* in the wake of mutiny.[6]

It is on the *Grampus* that Block's metaphysical, terrifying and shifting mask possesses Augustus again. He becomes Pym's involuntary tormentor and gaoler. As with the *Ariel*, he had played a decisive hand in outwitting Pym's parents and concealing Pym in the hold of the ship. There Pym suffers the torments of the damned to which Augustus is insensible. Mutiny has broken out three days after the *Grampus* sailed and Augustus has no alternative but to abandon Pym to a fate that resembles drowning at sea within the black hold of a slave ship.

Pym surfaces again after his dreadful incarceration and Augustus is the one who begins to descend into gangrenous darkness of soul as the mutiny breaks into warring factions and the *Grampus* is stricken by pitiless elements.

Augustus's mask of psychical twinship in Pym's affections is slowly absorbed into the features of Dirk Peters, a stalwart mutineer on the *Grampus*. We need to pay close attention, I would suggest, to the depth of this conversion in the context of the carnival ambivalences we have been exploring. For one is now in a position to perceive in the novel *Pym* a profound and irrational coherence uncannily close to pre-Columbian or ancient American masquerade or myth that arcs or runs from North through Central into South America. Note that Dirk Peters is of Amerindian stock, that his antecedents are pre-Columbian. Let us also note some essential and clearly visible motifs of masquerade in which inversions and replacements, transfusions of psychical blood occur.

Just as Pym and Augustus share psychical blood after the collision between the *Ariel* and Captain Block's ship, Amerindian Peters and black Seymour are psychically twinned in the act of bloody mutiny on the *Grampus*. Augustus dies in the midst of the torments the mutineers suffer. So does Seymour. Augustus is swallowed within an ultimatum that aborts his twinship to Pym. Seymour is possessed by the corpse of the land when he succumbs to a ruse Pym's faction plays on him. Pym leads the assault by masquerading as the galvanized corpse of a dead seaman, galvanized institution of decaying family or state.

The victorious faction led by Pym appears to have no alternative in the ensuing weeks but to resort to cannibalism and consume the sole survivor from Seymour's party. This is the climax of hideous proportions foreshadowed in the consumption by fate of both Seymour and Augustus. Cannibalism is foreshadowed by psychical stomach and devouring insight into a dying age whose fate leaves every survivor a metaphysical orphan, metaphysical blood to be consumed or to be re-born.

The eclipse of Augustus leaves Pym brotherless and orphaned. The fall of Seymour leaves Peters also bereft. Thus it seems natural that Pym and Peters resume the thread of precarious hope, precarious motif of true relationship in re-birth, left vacant or twisted in the deaths of Augustus and Seymour.

However natural it seems, Peters is the most unprepossessing twin Pym could have adopted or found. Pym makes this abundantly clear in the repulsion he expresses on first meeting Peters. Peters is 'one of the most purely ferocious-looking men I ever beheld. . . . His hands, especially, were so enormously thick and broad as hardly to retain a human shape . . . His head was equally deformed, being of immense size, with an indentation on the crown (like that on the head of most Negroes), and entirely bald.'[7]

It is a vision that makes fissured sense only when read in the context of enthralling weight exercised by the block phenomenon to which Pym belongs. The apparent ugliness of Peters is a measure of Pym's fascination with varieties of carnival pigment in a cruel age. Just as the ferocity of Seymour exposes the violence masked by decorum in Pym's grandfather, so Peters's hideousness dramatizes Pym's addiction to an age he is unable to expose except by projecting his great fear of it into apparently alien pigmentations and features. Peter's features, therefore, are less a realistic portrait than a fissure or crack into deep-seated ambivalences in Pym himself.

In the course of the ensuing narrative, that projection upon Peters is gradually withdrawn to come home in galvanized corpses that rear their heads upon Pym himself (when he masquerades as one in a fearful scene on the ship). They rear their heads also upon a mysterious passing vessel manned by dead men that seem outrageously alive with the motion of the vessel as it approaches and passes the *Grampus*.[8]

That nameless vessel may well be perceived as a third twinship in the series commencing with the *Ariel*. If so, the fourth is the *Jane Guy*, which comes upon the wrecked *Grampus* drifting at sea, and saves the lives of 're-born twins' Pym and Peters. It is a fascinating unconscious irony that after the *Jane Guy* itself is gutted and destroyed in the Antarctic by metaphysical blacks (their very teeth are black), Pym records – on escaping with Peters – that he and Peters 'are the only living *white men* upon the island [italics mine]'.[9]

The enthralling yet hideous charm exercised by diseased order upon Pym seems no longer to be projected upon Amerindian Peters. Nevertheless that projection still complexly exists in the white-masked visage black Peters now wears as one perceives the classic Freudian slip Poe brings into the narrative of *Pym* some twenty years or so before the birth of Freud in 1856.

Masquerade and myth

I spoke earlier of a pre-Columbian bridge of myth that runs through the Americas and with which *Pym* achieves uncanny, however unconscious, synchronicity in the womb of cultural space.

For the purposes of this exploration we may approach the bridge where it is identified with a rainbow arc across Mexico into the Caribbean and Guianas. The masquerading figure associated with the Caribbean and Guianas is Yurokon.[10] He is the fourth in a series of masquerading 'block' gods (twinships of space, in my estimation) upon and beneath that rainbow arc. The first is Quetzalcoatl (bird and snake mask) followed by Kukulcan and Huracan (both of which sustain species of twins of heaven and earth). These mutate into, or are succeeded by, Yurokon (as Roth's inventory of masquerading features suggests) where the bridge arches into the Caribbean and moves into South America.[11]

One of the prime aspects of Yurokon is the blend he achieves between cannibalism and the bone-flute extracted from each victim from whose body a morsel is consumed.[12] By and large, scholars tend to repudiate the burden of ferocity projected onto the Caribs (with whom Yurokon is associated) by the Spanish conquistadors.

'In the sixteenth century,' Michael Swan declares in *The Marches of El Dorado*, 'the Spaniards excused their enslavement of the island Indians by convincing Europe that anthropophagy was the common custom there . . . The royal edict gave the colonizers liberty to do as they pleased with Indians who, without any doubt, were not cannibalistic.' Swan quotes Richard Schomburgk's *Travels* of the nineteenth century in respect to the Caribs (as distinct from other Indian peoples) who – Schomburgk declared – practised a form of ritual cannibalism and 'usually brought back to the settlement an arm or leg of the slaughtered enemy as a trophy, which would then be cooked so as to get the flesh more easily off the bone; a flute was made out of this.' In the light of oral traditions and of significant and varied parallels between Yurokon and the origins of Carib cannibalism in Roth's researches into the animism of the Indians, Swan has no alternative but to state that 'the object of [Carib] cannibalism was a kind of transubstantiation in reverse: the bone [flute] contains the living spirit of the dead . . . [It was the source of] prophecy and witchcraft . . . [and] transference of spirit.'[13]

The bone flute was a confessional organ involved in, yet subtly repudiating, the evil bias of conquest that afflicted humanity. It sought to invoke an apparition of re-birth clothed in colour and music, the rainbow colour and music of forests, skies and earth in various twinships associated with vegetation and constellation however imperilled these had been by brute appetite for war.

Yurokon's twinship of sea and sky, vegetation and star, was an affirmation of elusive foundations and partial institutions, and of a successive body of dying ages inhabited by precarious organ or bone-flute of re-birth, so subtle it bred a fissure in appearances one tended still to take for granted as absolute or total until they became carnival masks addicted to hubris. As such they could accumulate into an illusion of absolute and fearful command unless they yielded a profound distinction or arbitration between tragedy (as ultimate block) and therapy (as fissure of re-birth into unknown futures to be ceaselessly created though they exist paradoxically in the heights and the depths of eclipsed present and past).

The emergence of asymmetric future through fissured past and present symmetries or models leads to the notion of a bridge that inevitably breaks to convey the paradox of creation in both the heights (above the bridge) and the depths (beneath the bridge).

The descent of a masquerading block, such as Quetzalcoatl of Mexico, into the womb of the sea (that descent is also characteristic of cannibal Carib Yurokon) sustains the *Ariel* motif of potential re-birth (explored in Poe's *Pym*) in contradistinction to insensible or hollow lucidity within static, block commanders who cling to ship or broken bridge, resist descent and become mere spectators of events within the stream or sea or forest of creation beneath them.

The necessity for cannibalism in profound masquerade and myth touches deeply, I believe, upon the anguish of nihilist tragedy. There was no realistic necessity, for example, for the cannibalism practised by Poe's mutineers. Food and drink were available and were salvaged from an area of the *Grampus* immediately after the cannibal feast. This leads one to perceive a psychical and compulsive drama in which Poe was involved despite the apparent factual fallacies with which he justifies excesses of conduct or appearance.

Writers Roth, Schomburgk and Swan approach Yurokon cannibalism as the magic of animism, the acquisition of hidden and secret knowledge from the mind of enemy or deceiving friend. A ritual morsel from the body of enemy or too secretive friend is consumed. A bone extracted from that body becomes the seed of musical spirit, or voice of insight. This leads one to reflect deeply upon the inarticulate dimension of cannibal ritual implicit in the Yurokon myth. It is the fierce suppressed dialogue between *partial* orders masquerading as totalities or absolutes or captain blocks – the tone of terrifying duality as well between inner and outer being – that is at the heart of savage music in all ages, the birth of savage music in polarized cultures, the savage bone-flute. As an age polarizes, the stress upon eclipsed dialogue becomes more and more extreme, the necessity to penetrate the other's arsenal of secrets becomes more and more obsessive and compelling. The other, in this context, is both enemy and suspect spy or friend within warring factions at home or abroad. Inevitably as enemy and friend coalesce into deranged order, psychical nemesis or cannibalism is projected upon all persons and creatures. A psychical necessity to consume bias, to relinquish the hubris of conquest, becomes unconscious necessity. Carnival ambiguities and ambivalences arise within the arts, which require an unravelling of perspectives and of blocked dialogue between cultures, so that the mystery of freedom may be born and re-born and born again and again within terrifying closure or circumstance that threatens to consume all.

Poe's *Arthur Gordon Pym of Nantucket* is uncannily susceptible to illumination within a medium of pre-Columbian masquerade and myth whose proportions I have outlined. The excesses of Poe's *Pym* begin to yield to judgements and criteria born of the twinship of intuitive self and myth. Although *Pym* is regarded in some quarters as a classic, it remains controversial and is ignored or under-estimated. It may well be a tormented but significant forerunner that bears upon the womb of space in the cross-cultural carnival .

Notes

1 Edgar Allan Poe, *Arthur Gordon Pym of Nantucket* (New York: Hill and Wang, 1960).
2 Ibid., p.xxv.
3 Ibid., pp.10, 16, 18, 42.
4 Ibid., p.16.
5 Ibid., p.8.
6 Ibid., pp.18, 42.
7 Ibid., pp.42–3.
8 Ibid., pp.70–4, 88–90.
9 Ibid., p.169.
10 Walter Roth, *Animism and Folklore in the Guiana Indians* (Washington, D.C.: Bureau of Ethnology, 1909).
11 Ibid.
12 Richard Schomburqk, *Travels in British Guiana* (London: n.p., 1848).
13 Michael Swan, *The Marches of El Dorado* (London: Jonathan Cape, 1958), pp.284–5.

8

CONCENTRIC HORIZONS

The dying god and his carnival women

'I am an invisible man. No, I am not a spook like those who haunted Edgar Allan Poe ...' is the declaration Ellison's protagonist makes at the beginning of a complex confessional narrative.[1]

It is an important double-edged statement. It cuts, on one edge, into Poe's realistic fallacies and into the hideous portraiture of black men Poe heaps up in *Pym* that tends to conceal the depths of mutuality it sustains with white-masked visage; and on the other edge, invisible man's declaration speaks of the inverted pawns of a civilization in which motifs of re-birth may be stifled in the guilt of diseased orders.

It is the latter edge that fissures Ellison's major novel. *Invisible Man* is less concerned with twinship than with the womb of an age as this is perceived in an epic, dying god associated with the feminine muses of gold, blood, music and their rich evolutionary potential or their tragically debased fertility in psychical and material senses.

Invisible man is a repetitively dying (yet cyclically re-awakening) god who is metaphorically consumed first in the boxing ring phase of the novel, then in the Bledsoe phase, then in the paint factory explosion phase, and in other succeeding Harlem phases in which he is symbolically castrated yet bleakly 'potentialized', rendered metaphysically potent, within the womb of space.

With each metaphorical death, with each phase of reduction to a cannibalized figure, invisible man undergoes a bleak awakening or re-birth in the envelope of his civilization. He is no Jonah but the civilization that threatens to swallow him is part biblical sea or whale's belly metamorphosed, in some degree, into a womb of cultural evolutions.

That womb is symbolized by the signal importance of carnival women or muse figures who appear at each phase or cycle in the narrative. The disadvantages or debasements threaded into these muses make each re-birth or awakening that invisible man experiences bleak and terrifying.

Ellison insists on the solidity of invisible man or dying god who is 'a man of substance, of flesh and bone.' The stricture on cultural blindness bulks large –

'when they approach me they see only my surroundings'.[2] Nevertheless 'invisibility' is also a fissure in the womb of space, a ripple upon uniform premises, a complex metaphor of the imaginative descent of masquerading stone or solid body into a psychical pool on which concentric circles and horizons appear.

The novel is a confessional narrative. It begins at the end of the series of metaphorical deaths invisible man experiences when he descends into a hole or grave lit by electricity to review all that has happened to him over a long odyssey. In another sense, as already suggested, it is as if an alchemized creature or stone falls into biblical, yet electric, diseased whale adorned with political scenarios of memory to send out concentric ripples or horizons upon the inner yet outer sea of space. The stone, because it is solid, vanishes of necessity. Its invisibility is far-reaching irony of concentric capacities in ceaseless, enclosing, yet expanding cycles.

Concentric horizon or cycle one is the boxing ring set in motion by masquerading stone or descending god that secretes itself/himself in a blues well of music, a blues muse, an ancient mother of scarred freedom/unfreedom, dream-music or well of civilization associated with Louis Armstrong's 'underworld of sound'.[3] That underworld of sound yields to a well of terror, a well of forbidden sexuality masked by a naked blonde woman/debased white goddess at the boxing ring where music coalesces with the bewilderments of the mother of freedom into a metaphorical death and ambiguity of re-birth.

Concentric horizon two is the Bledsoe well of tainted scholarship in which the boxing ring mentality re-appears within Golden Day epitaph or asylum of the living dead from all professions. In that tainted well invisible man encounters the womb of space constellated in incestuous Trueblood muses and in a surreal extension of the white goddess.

On concentric horizon three, invisible man 'dies' again in an explosive sea of paint and his bleak re-birth may be constellated with Mary Rambo and other shadowy muses of ambiguous Christian and pre-Christian age.

The blend of Homeric, Anancy (African) and Christian imageries is substantial to the womb of evolutionary space that Ellison seeks in dying (awakening) epic god on each horizon or concentric ring that moves us to step forward and backward into the mutated 'stone' of history. In the context of mutated stone, *Invisible Man* intuitively alters block twinships into a medium of potential and *feminine* horizons, carnival women and muses, upon the rainbow bridge between cultures.

It is within the boxing ring phase, on horizon one, that the first trace is established – through debased carnival white goddess and bewildered blues mother – of linkages of Homeric and Anancy traditions. I shall comment later on the ancient blues muse and her response to invisible man's questions in the well of sound. It is the debased white goddess who presides in terror at the boxing ring of history that ushers in the first ruse or trick of Anancy 'death', half electrocuted, half punch-drunk, invisible man and his awakening into himself as clothed in a Cyclopean (Homeric) mask. 'A blow to my head . . . sent my right eye popping

110

like a jack-in-the-box . . .'[4] Thus invisible man, in association with terrified white goddess, foreshadows in himself the enemy who stalks him and whose secrets he prizes and digests with bewilderment, anguish and bitter gestation within the diseased whale of history.

The Cyclopean mask he himself wears in the deadly boxing ring phase is the start of an inner, pre-figurative acquaintance with others in clinical envelope and political theatre whom he will encounter. They too carry the Cyclopean birthmark. One is a doctor in a hospital who peers menacingly with 'a bright third eye that glowed from the centre of his forehead'. Another is Brother Jack in Harlem whose eye squints at invisible man with cyclopean irritation.[5]

What invisible man begins to learn figuratively and painfully, within the cyclical code that he inhabits, is the fascination of helplessness, the proneness to fall back into, with each arousal from, the Cyclopean nightmare that pursues him as much in his own skull, or Anancy skin, as in rituals of entertainment others impose upon him – repulsive arts, exploited sciences, faked renascences.

This bleakest of perceptions is in itself a measure of uncertain awakening from complex paralysis, it occupies the narrative with unspoken intensity that unsettles the shape of territorial imperative meaning, light is dark ground, gold is false ground, declarations of virtue or rightness may prove to be propaganda and the ground of lies. In this ambiguity of real/unreal performance, the prose of the boxing ring cycle fissures and threads the vitality of muses into hidden counterpoint with invisible man's helplessness; it is a vitality, however, that is so darkened and blocked in terror-stricken white goddess, or muse of electric gold, who presides at the ring, and equally terrified mother of freedom, who presides at the well of blues, that what is apparently unsettled is sealed or closed fast afresh.

Invisible man asks blues 'Ma' to tell him the secret of freedom but her enraged sons threaten him for making their great and confused mother – great and confused prisoner of history – cry.[6]

However disadvantaged or debased these vital muses are, they still potentialize an imperceptible tide upon which invisible man shape-shifts his helplessness into opposed, yet related, features. He is a black Odysseus in whose fictive, musical blood Anancy runs. His fictive status is a measure of insight into endangered thread of capacity, endangered foetus of freedom in the womb of space.

Ancient Homer tells us that the giant Cyclops Polyphemus would have eaten Odysseus had he not been blinded by the man's cunning. And in this intuitive conjunction of blindness to others (who become hidden, unseen entities) with cannibal Homeric legend (built into feminine horizon), foetal man in Ellison's narrative begins to eat the secret (although he never wholly digests it) of profound and mutual creative responsibility that arches through fathomless sound and sight in mutations of descending stone.

I emphasize the term 'feminine horizon' to make clear that the concentric cycles set in motion by descending man-god – in our reflections upon mutated stone – constitute a shift, not only from carnival twinship to carnival women and muses, but from implicit Poesque cannibal tragedy to implicit Ellisonian cannibal epic. The stress on 'cannibal' is of particular interest in the cross-cultural womb of space, since it links Cyclopean giant to nightmare, it also links foetal hope, or thread of re-born capacity, to Yurokon bone-flute and seed of music explored in the previous chapter.

It is true that carnival twinship did imply a womb of sea and space (and that the feminine projection was concealed in the elements) but the shift which is visible in *Invisible Man* is a subtle stroke of genius, and consists in unravelling the masked presence of the female upon or beneath rainbow arcs or bridges between cultures. This, I believe, is fundamental to the secret of a renewal of epic in the twentieth century and it reveals the bleakness of awakenings black Odysseus experiences when the female is consistently disadvantaged. The Bledsoe cycle is particularly instructive in this respect in that it suggests that the gestation of foetal man of history remains unfulfilled because of incestuous muse that comes to reflect hideously tainted memories affecting all relationships invisible man recalls in the urban, electric and diseased whale of civilization into which he descends to write his confessions. The link between foetal man's nightmare and the Cyclopean giant envelope enclosing him remains unhappily static or dominant and largely unbroken.

Bledsoe/Golden Day and Trueblood women

The Bledsoe phase in the black Odysseus's bitter epic is marked by Bledsoe's sophisticated tyrannies and lies, and by blind Homer Barbee's rhetoric in preaching of black freedom and black scholarship.[7] But it is darkly true, I find, that the *emotion* of tyranny, and chauvinist scholarship, is rooted less in sophisticated lies and comedy of manners, and more in implicit territory of gestations; a fettered being upon a treadmill in the womb of space. The womb of space is so sealed that the Bledsoe lie becomes as incorrigible as nihilist military heroes, nihilist lawyers, nihilist doctors, nihilist industrialists who inhabit the Golden Day.

The emphasis on layers of gestation that neither abort nor come to birth makes it self-evident that Trueblood territory runs deeper than clichéd sexual structure adorned by theories of frustration or repression. Not that frustration and repression are ignored, they do exist, but as transitive chords, as fissured dimension, into a deeper orchestration or pressure of sealed womb in which invisible man is confined. It is a prison made all the more vivid in the light of insights that take no comfort in escapism or commercial heavens. That the lure of escapism is a hollow dream is the bleakest of awakenings in itself to the formidable, subtle, complex creativity required if genuine epic, genuine community (rather than commodities of faked renascence) is to be recovered in depth.

There is a distinction, in other words, between clichéd sex, clichéd renascence and *coniunctio* or true marriage, true re-birth.

The confinement invisible man endures translates itself, when Bledsoe expels him from haven and college, into inevitable illiteracy of the imagination, into continuity of sealed space, hollow certificates, hollow letters of recommendation carried in the hope they will advance his fame and fortune in the world; they are designed by Bledsoe to invert him into a running pawn. They are witness to an illiteracy of the imagination masked by Machiavellian and academic creed. They bind him all the more frighteningly to an alphabet of nightmare.

The inner alphabet of ecstasy, the hoped-for renascence of epic brotherhood of man, tends to be sealed away again and again, and this issue of tormenting horizon translates itself into various perversions or traumatic deed that comes into broad daylight. A prime illustration in the Bledsoe phase lies in Trueblood's sexual intercourse with his daughter, Matty Lou.[8]

Trueblood wakes, or is awakened by his wife Kate Trueblood, to the inter-course in which he is engaged with Matty Lou Trueblood. Daylight reconnais-sance of the deed, in all its shame, pleasure and horror, makes him a monster to some, a hero to others. For example, when he tells his story to unhappy Odysseus (then a student at Bledsoe's college) and to fascinated Norton (a white, Olympian trustee), Norton is transported by confused emotions and recalls the portrait of a lost daughter he had idolized. When the tale is over, Norton seals the pact of vicarious incest that he shares with Trueblood with an economic hand-out. The deed thus acquires an economic sanction,

It possesses also a hidden institutional sanction in that Bledsoe's power over both Olympian Norton and Ellison's Odysseus is written into the conventional rhetoric and morality that subsist on pawns of humanity, within the womb of space, who are the obscure equivalents to an alphabet of ecstasy turned into letters of incest – into economic hand-out, on one hand, to pay for vicarious pleasures and entertainments – into chauvinist scholarship, on the other, to con-firm a wilderness of gestating politics, gestating community, that reinforces every Bledsoe regime. ' "They picked poor Robin clean," I said. "Do you happen to know Bled?" '[9]

How does invisible man imply eclipsed alphabet of ecstasy beneath monster Trueblood and nihilist Olympian Norton? He is susceptible to plucked and stricken numbers, to the clockwork language of fate, into which Trueblood runs. Beneath the voracious spectre of the clock, a surreal timelessness clothes itself in an extension of terrified white goddess whose forbidden sexuality, in the boxing ring phase, now cracks and yields. She infuses Trueblood (as if he is a surrogate mask black Odysseus wears) with her own terror by 'grabbing him round the neck' until 'a flock of little white geese flies out of the bed'.[10] Her guilt and her terror are his. Or is it that his guilt and his terror become hers? They become so large and yet so nimble that he runs frantically like Alice through the looking glass into the clock on the wall of the room and up a dark tunnel. That is the nebulously exact moment, the timeless moment, when he unconsciously embraces and enters Matty Lou, his grown daughter who sleeps in the same bed with him and his wife in the crowded shack in which they live.

One says 'timeless or nebulously exact moment' because the weight of dream-woman and dream-daughter cannot be established in partial reality. They are a joint clock and well of emotion, a sublimated, yet surreal, extension of both ancient blues mother of scarred freedom (metamorphosed into helpless yet consenting Matty Lou) and terrified blonde woman at the boxing ring (metamorphosed into 'flying geese') within whom invisible man first gained, and regains, an insight into himself as clothed in Cyclopean monster and mask, Cyclopean trueblood.

The ground of ecstasy – so swiftly turned into incest – lies in a mutuality of contrasting yet embracing presences, complex rainbow arc of mankind as the secret of epic. The seal that imprisons such mutuality, kills ecstasy and leaves in its train a blind contract and broken bridge in daylight reconnaissance. The innocence of 'white geese' converts into the clockwork machine of the sun. The lightning flash of spontaneous flying carnival fails to bridge the divide in humanity that consolidates into nightmare, incestuous block, incestuous wealth, incestuous poverty, incestuous family at the heart of day.

Jean Toomer's anti-climactic marriage of Dan and Muriel in *Box Seat*

Jean Toomer's *Cane* (in which *Box Seat* occupies a significant place) appeared in 1923, a quarter of a century or so before *Invisible Man* was published.[11] It possesses an intuitive, almost prophetic bearing, I believe, upon Ellison's paradoxes of dying god/masquerading stone. In texture and style, however, it differs markedly from Ellison's cyclical novel. It is also less epic in thrust and more stream-of-consciousness, prose-lyric theatre. Its originality lies in an abrupt, uneven, contract of emotions that remains anti-climactic and unfulfilled. The stream-of-consciousness metaphysic that informs its community of character is wholly unlike the interior flow, or insistent pressure that envelops consciousness in James Joyce's *Ulysses*. Much of *Cane*, one understands, was written before 1923; some of it had appeared earlier in American magazines, and it is doubtful whether Toomer was acquainted with Joyce's masterpiece, published in 1921, when he wrote *Cane*.

Toomer's stream-of-consciousness seems to me profoundly native to his American psyche; it is an apt disruption of an ancestral auction block world and of *person* in *property*, *person* as *property*. One has a sensation almost of guilty sleight-of-hand that shakes auction block securities, auction block psychologies, until formal properties float into masquerading carnival person, masquerading Christian stone.

> A continent sinks down. The new-world Christ will need consummate skill to walk upon the waters where huge bubbles burst . . . Thuds of Muriel coming down. Dan turns to the piano and glances through a stack of jazz music sheets . . . [He] feels the pressure of the house, of the rear room, of the rows of houses, shift to Muriel. He is light. He loves her. He is doubly heavy.[12]

That curious passage, in which new-world Christ walks on water, reflects the miracle of stone, the carnival transubstantiation, that Dan seeks to invoke in reaching out toward his desired bride Muriel, whose 'thuds' resist him to make clear her endorsement of an anchorage of security which she feels herself unable to transform, and against which Dan, despite the apocalyptic fascination he exercises upon her, seems but an impractical drifter destined to sink into oblivion.

Muriel is but one of Toomer's elusive 'brides' (sometimes sacred whores) in *Cane* who, in various ways, resist their ineffectual suitors. But Muriel is the most sensitive, most self-conscious, of them all, and she is aware (half-consciously, with almost puppet-like undertones) of Dan's intricate need of her within a creation of revolutionary art that he seeks to wed, an inner theatre he seeks to re-make against the tide of history. She seems to be driven by a sceptical yet sympathic perception of the mask of 'new-world Christ' Dan wears; and in response to this adorns herself with gaudy but implicit rainbow attire to match his fantasy. She seeks support from another puppet-like creature, Bernice. On arrival at Lincoln Theatre she 'leads Bernice who is a cross between a washerwoman and a blue-blood lady, a washer-blue, a washer-lady . . . Muriel has on an orange dress. Its colour could clash with the crimson box-draperies, its colour would contradict the sweet rose smile her face is bathed in, should she take her coat off . . . Pale purple shadows rest on the planes of her cheeks. Deep purple comes from her thick-shocked hair.'[13]

The desired, yet never achieved, marriage between Dan and Muriel is a token of a larger and deeper problem that obsesses Toomer. The mixture of perspectives that he pursues in *Box Seat* – theatre, stream-of-consciousness fiction, lyrical presences – is an indication of changed, inner/outer dialogue he seeks. He needs a revisionary splendour beyond conventional props and lies to overthrow a world of illusion that is built on auction block puppetries, puppet illuminations, puppet houses in which flesh and blood remain sealed and rarely afloat, or a psychical miracle of stone in alchemies of space.

Dan's defeat in the theatre, his disappearance into a sea of streets and houses, at the end of *Box Seat*, becomes a measure of Toomer's integrity, his despair with sexual puppetry or artistry of lies. Dan's failed marriage to Muriel becomes a galvanic, rather than mutual, rose.

The prime substance of that galvanic rose, that failed marriage, is dramatized with uneven and evocative intensity in the ambiguity of a dwarf (a surrogate Christ, a leper invisible to all) who kisses the rose with battered lips and makes it into a sponge of blood. This is the nebulously exact moment of anti-climactic marriage between Dan and Muriel. The dwarf appears in the theatre and sings to Muriel a 'high-pitched, sentimental' song, a song that is unable to voice what it seeks to express. Thus its sentimentality becomes all the more telling, all the more absurd, yet moving and alarming as failed element, failed thunder, in the wake of lightning 'mirror flash'. The song, fraught with gaudy emotion, comes to an end. The dwarf bows to Muriel. Then he offers the blood-soaked rose 'first having kissed it. Blood of his battered lips is a vivid stain upon its petals.'[14]

Muriel flinches back, unable to accept. 'Hate pops from [the dwarf's] eyes and crackles like a brittle heat about the box' as if to confirm the failed thunder of deity. Then the dwarf's tight-skinned, lightning brow changes, grows calm, profound, 'a thing of wisdom and tenderness'.[15] It is as if a path of genuine submission to Muriel's limited comprehension (or incomprehension) of revolutionary theatre surfaces, a wise response to her freedom, her right *not* to accept the galvanic rose, her right also to question its premises of sudden tenderness and transubstantial capacity; her right not to be conscripted by a chorus of politics or convention. But then that chorus violently intervenes to coerce her. 'Arms reach out, grab Muriel . . . Claps are steel fingers that manacle her wrists and move them forward to acceptance.' Muriel, 'tight in her revulsion, sees black' but has no alternative but to accept the gift of battered lips upon the rose and to grow blind to the mystery of the transformed brow of wisdom she may have begun to glimpse.

It is then that Dan's despair explodes. He springs up and shouts, 'Jesus was once a leper.' It is a half-mad declaration, a regression into galvanic lips, mask of hate, the dwarf has shed but he appears to resume. He steps down, 'cool as a green stem that has just shed its flower', yet remains in regressed circumstance in league with bloodstained sponge in the dwarf's outstretched hand. The green stem begins to vanish into the soil of the theatre, anti-climactic theatre.[16]

As he moves toward the exit and confronts the schizophrenic rage in himself and in the violent chorus or audience around him, his memory darkens still further and descends within the shackled sponge/rose in Muriel and himself, within leper or inverted Ascension of Christ.

His descent is as much a sombre judgement of himself as of others, it is an awkward repudiation of props of violence by which the consummation of mutual blood, mutual being, was defeated at the very moment it may have begun to encompass the rights of otherness as integral to arts of dialogue and truth.

There is an intriguing aspect to *Box Seat* I would like to mention. It is the aspect of parable, biblical parable, which subsists on secret understandings, grounded in hard-won freedoms, rather than coercive politics inevitably grounded in sophistications of violence and the rule of numbers. Toomer may have despaired of an art built on popular models of brute force, and attempted to explore secret signals for those initiated into parables of self-judgement, abruptly changing even irrational signals; for example, hate into tenderness, 'new-world Christ' into 'Jesus the leper'; warm-hearted although sceptical Muriel into blind, insensible muse who accepts the death of the rose in fantasy dwarf or surrogate bridegroom.

All this sustains Toomer's uncompromising rejection of art as an artistic lie masquerading as form, art as fascist privilege or obscene imperative. There is no short-cut, he implies, to alchemical *coniunctio* or true and productive union between man and woman, between one and other, between culture and culture. There is need for complex realities of changed form, revolving and evolving sensibilities. And as such *Box Seat* deepens its proportions of parable into an acceptance in itself of the failure of unhealthy, gaudy sentimentality, a failure that is also an indictment of mass-media nihilist theatre. There is a leprosy to the arts that is unperceived by a conditioned society, Toomer implies, and that leprotic gaiety unconsciously desires relief, unconsciously desires a sacrament of truth.

Box Seat is an American parable and one of the most remarkable confessional short novels associated with the so-called Harlem renaissance. I am tempted to say there is a Kafkaesque nightmare quality to it, though Toomer's sensuous floating images are unlike Kafka's studied, almost clinical envelopes of despair. Some of Kafka's work was published in Europe in his lifetime but nothing, as far as I am aware, had yet been translated into English. Kafka died in 1924 and it is unlikely that Toomer would have heard of him in 1923 when *Cane* was published.

Notes

1 Ralph Ellison, *Invisible Man* (New York: Vintage Books, 1972), p.30.
2 Ibid., p.3.
3 Ibid., p.12.
4 Ibid., pp.27, 25.
5 Ibid., pp.226, 463.
6 Ibid., p.11.
7 Ibid., pp.126–31.
8 Ibid., pp.62–3
9 Ibid., p.242.
10 Ibid., pp.57–8
11 Jean Toomer, *Cane* (New York: Harper & Row, 1969).
12 Ibid., p.108.
13 Ibid., p.116.
14 Ibid., pp.126–7.
15 Ibid., p.128.
16 Ibid., p.129.

9

JEAN RHYS'S 'TREE OF LIFE'

Wide Sargasso Sea appeared in 1966 after a gap of more than twenty-five (as the Publisher's note reminds us) in Jean Rhys's literary career. Since *Good Morning, Midnight* (1939), nothing by her had been reissued or published.

Wide Sargasso Sea was to prove a remarkable climax in that it revived the mood and inimitable pathos that had possessed the characterization of women in her previous fiction. It also struck new note in that it evoked a link between the world of the ex-slaves and their creole, dispossessed masters and mistresses within the decade of emancipation and the world of Charlotte Brontë's *Jane Eyre*.

Jean Rhys's Antoinette in *Wide Sargasso Sea* is a revival of mad Bertha, Rochester's creole West Indian wife, in *Jane Eyre*. Curious the involuntary humour in the tricks fiction and fate play! For Antoinette is the catalyst that is to occasion the reissue of Jean Rhys's half-forgotten works, published between the two world wars, even as *Wide Sargasso Sea* reopens the seal of doom Charlotte Brontë had inscribed into Bertha's existence. Such are the compensatory truths of fiction in which Pandora's Box suffers a complex and therapeutic reversal in releasing both half-forgotten or ignored fictions as well as the doomed Bertha into new life.

Bertha's 'madness' runs in parallel with Antoinette's 'ecstasy' as the lid of the box arises, an ecstasy or longing for love that is so acute at times it embraces many moods, depressions, and extremities of inner passion. Bertha's madness appears within the tidal spring of *Wide Sargasso Sea*, not as insanity at all, but a sentence passed upon her by an uncomprehending world that takes her wealth in the form of the dowry she brings and remains oblivious of her need.

In a sense we may say, I think, that Antoinette's passion is a *phenomenon of place and psyche* and, as a consequence, it needs to be interpreted or explicated over lapsed times if its elusive and essential quality of being within money legacies, legacies of slavery, and rumours of family neurosis, is to be perceived not only in depth but differently from the seal of hell upon the fictional mask of Antoinette's double (Bertha) in Rochester's Thornfield Hall.

What, in such a light, we may well ask, is fiction? Is Bertha a mask upon Antoinette and vice versa, a serial mask that may be sprung into infinite reversibles – within the life of the human/divine imagination – to release or bind a troubled and tormented age? If so, we need to pay much closer and stronger attention to the inner truths of fiction than we do in a money-mad age.

The placement and displacement of tormented age that helps us to perceive Bertha's hell in parallel with the genius of frustrated paradise – if I may so put it – lie in the contradictory levels of 'the tree of life' that moves like an apparition through *Wide Sargasso Sea*. Those levels provide a confused but potent mosaic inhabited by Christian, Amerindian/pre-Columbian, and African spectres.

The Christian spectre is calculated and explicit. It inhabits the garden in Coulibri Estate that Antoinette loved as a child. It is the tree of paradise that has grown wild until it threatens to destroy what it claims to guard and bless: 'Our garden was large and beautiful as that garden in the Bible – the tree of life grew there. But it had gone wild. The paths were overgrown and a smell of dead flowers mixed with the fresh living smell. Underneath the tree ferns, tall as forest tree ferns, the light was green. Orchids flourished out of reach or for some reason not to be touched. One was snaky looking, another like an octopus with long thin brown tentacles bare of leaves hanging from a twisted root.'[1]

When we turn to the pre-Columbian and Amerindian spectre in 'the tree of life', we enter an intuitive rather than explicit dimension. In other words, whereas Jean Rhys plotted an obvious correspondence with the 'garden in the Bible', it is unlikely that she was consciously aware of the pre-Columbian figuration that seems to me to secrete itself in the margins of her fiction and, as a consequence, there exists in the narrative indirections of *Wide Sargasso Sea* that peculiar blend of opacity and transparency that alerts us to the force of the intuitive imagination in building strategies of which it *knows* yet does not *know*.

I have written elsewhere on Jean Rhys's intuitive dialogue with the pre-Columbian *foodbearing tree* as the ancient Arawaks and Macusis viewed the tree of life.[2] I return to this distinction now and the substance of that dialogue but with different emphases on the nature of opacity and transparency.

Let us take *transparency* first. The convolutions of fire imagery within the narrative help to mirror inner and outer conflict and emotional stress in the ex-slaves and in the ex-masters and ex-mistresses of the estates, and this mirror may be interpreted, I would suggest, as a species of transparency. The mirror comes to a head, so to speak, in the blazing tree of life at the end of the novel. Antoinette's double, mad Bertha of Thornfield Hall, dreams that 'I turned round and saw the sky. It was red and *all my life was in it*. I saw the grandfather clock and Aunt Cora's patchwork, all colours, I saw the orchids and the stephanotis and the jasmine and *the tree of life in flames* . . . The man who hated me was calling too, Bertha! Bertha! The wind caught my hair and it streamed out like wings' (pp.189–90, my emphasis).

The mirror of dream-fire in which the tree of life blazes comes to a transparent head that streams with hair like wings. One looks through it backwards into the past, into the grandfather clock, into Aunt Cora's patchwork, into the garden of Coulibri across the sea. That backward glance may invoke another kind of mirror, an opaque mirror, wooden tree or funeral pyre to which the flame has not yet been set though opacity possesses its eloquence, its whisper of past and future events, its 'strange voice'.

In the shadow of that wooden tree we come upon Antoinette in the Roman Catholic convent school to which she goes after her mother's death and the fire that destroyed the house on Coulibri Estate. She dreams this time that 'there are steps leading upwards. It is too dark to see . . . I stumble over my dress . . . *I touch a tree and my arms hold on to it* . . . The tree sways and jerks as if it is to throw me off. Still I cling and the seconds pass and each one is a thousand years. "Here, in here," *a strange voice* said' (p.60, my emphasis).

The blend of opacity and transparency as figuration of groping consciousness backwards and forwards in time tends to be overlooked in fiction and in particular in a work such as *Wide Sargasso Sea*, which follows a deceptively straightforward narrative line broken by intrusions of abrupt fantasy populated by non-existences, non-existent voices, reappearing yet vanishing pathways and ruins pointing to ancient estates within a succession of empires (Spanish, French, British), and to new wealth or legacies in great halls and museums of history in Europe across the seas.

It is within the context of such 'non-existences' or vanishing/reappearing places and cultures that the tree of life blazes and speaks. The transparent head of fire through which we glance backwards into the vanished past and into a mask of wood possessed of its 'strange voice' is uncannily close to the Macusi/Arawak/Carib foodbearing tree and the creation myth it sustains.

The tale runs that the ancient Arawaks fled from the pursuing Caribs by ascending the foodbearing tree. But the Caribs set fire to the tree, the Arawaks were consumed, and they flew up or across in sparked wings to create the constellation of the Pleiades. Whose 'strange voice' then speaks in the foodbearing tree of the globe? Is it the voice of archaic, primitive or endangered humanity, is it the voice of neurosis and mutual insight within so-called victor and so-called victim, is it the voice of mutual hope or mutual hopelessness? Such ambiguities lie at the heart of creation myth and test the creative imagination to descend as well as ascend into the phenomenon of place and psyche of which I spoke at the commencement of this article.

Such a phenomenon gives us room to reflect upon the black presence in the tree of life. That tree has yielded so far an explicit correspondence with the 'garden in the Bible'. It has yielded an intuitive pre-Columbian blend of 'talking mask or wood' and 'emblematic head of fire'. It has led us to jump ahead into our own time and infuse the foodbearing tree of the globe with vanished peoples whose spark of conscience or remorse or terror addresses us still in the night sky of tradition within archetypes of creation myth. Now we come to the black West Indian presence in the tree of life.

When Antoinette dreams in her convent school of 'steps leading upwards' and of a veil of psyche or trailing dress that lies over ruined walls buried in the soil of place, we may recall a particular forest or wood (pp.103–7) in which Antoinette's English husband seems to lose his way upon a road that appears yet vanishes, a road that the black people deny exists, as if that road or vanished estate is guarded by the ghosts of slaves who have become apparitions of subversive or hidden religion.

Rochester (who is never explicitly named in *Wide Sargasso Sea*) confesses when he comes unwittingly into existent yet non-existent place: 'I was lost and afraid among these *enemy* trees' (p.105, my emphasis). He hears a shout or a voice but is afraid to respond. Eventually he shouts back. Baptiste, a black servant, appears and leads him out of the wood. Baptiste is grim and unsmiling:

'We look for you a long time,' he said.
'I got lost.'

(p.106)

He questions Baptiste who denies the existence of the road that Rochester has seen or thinks he has seen:

'But I saw it. A pavé road like the French made in the islands.'
'No road.'

(p.106)

Rochester had also encountered a young girl in the wood who ran from him in fear when he interrupted her in some obscure propitiatory rite she was performing to the gods. All this and the metamorphosis of the tree of life into an enemy wood or 'enemy trees' is a complex issue that may bewilder a reader until he perceives that this is another ambiguity in universal creation myth through which we see not only a capacity for genesis but desolation, terror, and exile. The gods become 'enemy trees' not only to Rochester but to the folk who have suffered within a theatre of cruelty until the need for propitiation drives them into deeper exile or hiding.

What is curious about all this, I think, is that the desire of the ex-slaves to propitiate their angry gods within hidden and secret ruins that appear to disappear is part and parcel of Antoinette's desperate longing and desire for love that dies to live. Antoinette, the white creole, steeped in the Catholic faith and its relics of saints, its worship of the 'garden of my Spouse' (p.53) also possesses a black, inner family tree to which she belongs in her inmost heart. She is a subversive, religious spirit, and in the end, when she is taken to England by Rochester against her will, fire becomes wings of hair to fly up to the stars or back to the naked pool and hidden stairways of Coulibri.

It is significant – in this outline of the black West Indian presence in the tree of life – that Antoinette's last dream-vision in Thornfield Hall when her 'hair streamed out like wings', a vision presaging her death, is of Tia, the black girl with whom she had played as a child beside the pool at Coulibri. Tia had been both enemy and friend in long-past days. It had been a relationship fraught with paradox. It was Tia who had struck her with a stone beneath the shadow of the great house at Coulibri that had been set on fire by the ex-slaves. She and Tia had swum together in the pool, they had exchanged clothes, her good dress for Tia's rags. And when Tia flung the stone she wept and the blood on Antoinette's face was reflected in her tears: 'We stared at each other, blood on my face, tears on hers' (p.45).

Thus, in her final extremity, Antoinette flew home to Coulibri.

One of the most persistent legends that black people nourished in the Americas and the West Indies during slavery and after was the dream of wings to fly home across the sea. Toni Morrison's *Song of Solomon* evokes this flying legend within a complex of intrigue and self-discovery. Jean Rhys implies in *Wide Sargasso Sea* that Antoinette flies home to herself in the end. She flies up as well as back. Biblical, frustrated paradise and intuitive, pre-Columbian catastrophe/creation myth are now edged, it would seem, by an African cult of wings in a tree of life and death.

Notes

1 Jean Rhys, *Wide Sargasso Sea* (London: Andre Deutsch, 1966), p.19.
2 Wilson Harris, *The Womb of Space: The Cross-cultural Imagination* (Westport, Conn.: Greenwood Press, 1983), pp.49–54.

10

'BENITO CERENO'

This chapter on 'Benito Cereno' comes from an unfinished critical study in which I am attempting to make certain intuitive connections between apparently irreconcilable imaginative writers in the past and the present.

This seems to me a helpful, an ironical and fruitful exercise, in some respects, at a time when the narrative shape of the twentieth-century novel is changing under the impact of new and old conflicting resources and loyalties stemming not only from Europe but from heterogeneous soils in the Caribbean, Central and South America, North America, Asia, Australia and Africa.

> Always upon first boarding a large and populous ship at sea, especially a foreign one, a nondescript crew such as Lascars or Manilla men, the impression varies in a peculiar way from that produced by first entering a strange house with strange inmates in a strange land. Both house and ship – the one by its walls and blinds, the other by its high bulwarks like ramparts – hoard from view their interiors till the last moment; but in the case of the ship there is the addition; that the living spectacle it contains, upon its sudden and complete disclosure, has, in contrast with the blank ocean which zones it, something of the effect of enchantment. The ship seems unreal; these strange costumes, gestures, and faces, but a shadow tableau just emerged from the deep, which directly must receive back what it gave.[1]

Intuition is the stamp of an unfathomable dynamic of emotion that may strike with cruelty and hell-fire bias even as it arms the individual conversely with a passion for justice and the mystery of truth. Within each prisoner of history is an attachment, involuntary perhaps but concrete, to the very premises of his age. How could it be otherwise when those premises are all he possesses or is possessed by?

Yet there is a curious relativity in the shapes of loathing and love, as the case may be, that begin to occupy that prisoner in the course of his (or her) working, reflecting, waking, sleeping life within the given premises of his age. In large part it is clear that that relativity is a predictable response to mobile conditions and feelings; depths of love, depths of hate.

Except that as the response deepens, becomes, in fact, peculiarly concentrated, immensely concrete, an orchestration of feelings – that are intensely human and unpredictable – comes into play like an inner and outer chorus which begins to pick up echoes, voices, impulses that seem both deeper than the prisoner's age (as if sprung from the forgotten past) and deeper than the prisoner's time (as if in touch with a tide running into the future).

These echoes, voices, hints, depths are the stamp of a feeling for which there is no other word but *intuition*. And what is striking about this, I feel, is that 'intuition' is not a turning away from concrete situations. It is, in fact, a revelation of other capacities at the heart of a concentration within and upon given situations. A revelation and concentration that exact a formidable price upon sensibilities which may recoil from what is 'seen' or 'learnt': recoil as before a mirage or as before issues by which they are non-plussed: issues that lack an immediate philosophical anchorage and conventional explanation.

That recoil is the philosophical hollowness of man (hollow inertia yet spatial ground of hope): a profoundly natural recoil since it carries within it immediate premises, that wish to re-assert themselves, acting, however, in dislocated context with accents, voices as of other personalities suppressed in the prisoner's light of day or ahead of the prisoner's logic of time.

There is, therefore, a profound but meaningful darkness written into intuitive imaginations. A darkness that leaves its stamp on daylight fixations with place and time as a religious complication of technologies of realism.

Perhaps there is a sense in which darkness makes man a religious animal whether he believes he is embraced by deity or not. Perhaps that is why, at earlier stages of primitive sensibility, marvels of line and paint were impressed upon secret, almost inaccessible, recesses within caves. That dark recess – that inner-most secret – is part and parcel of a necessity to caricature an age, as it were, within the womb of time and deepen that caricature through clowns of broken realism into a profound religious complication in which every actor in the human drama is a sacred mask/sacred animal in a ceaseless treasure of perspectives of inner/outer light, darkness . . .

At the heart of 'Benito Cereno' is the ghostly and enigmatic relationship between Don Benito, captain of the *San Dominick*, and Babo, his barber. And assuming one sees the vessel for the first time in this age it may well appear the strangest satellite from another century around this century. Who are the members of its crew? Whose value-studded masks do they wear? Who am I? What mask should I wear? What posture of concealment adopt like an actor who retires into a spiritual darkness to look through features, other than his own, that are familiar with cargoes of the past? A familiarity that is of assistance since otherwise the presence of the ship – and the cruel premises it raises into one's view – might prove a greater shock than one wishes to bear.

The approach to an imaginative drama launched over a hundred years ago – as though one is making a new yet calloused discovery – is assisted by a kind of helpful amnesia and manufacture of crutches of symbolic unconsciousness:

crutches of adventure, crutches of familiar royalty, crutches of familiar Christ, crutches of familiar commonalty in whose name one comes: crutches of ancient reflected land masses and ancient tribes of men as if they are an insensible ladder to be mounted and saved.

Perhaps these crutches of familiarity are made manifest, in some degree anyway, by one Captain Amasa Delano who sights the *San Dominick* for the first time like 'a ship in distress':

> Upon gaining a less remote view, the ship, when made signally visible on the verge of the leaden-hued swells, with the shreds of fog here and there raggedly furring her, appeared like a whitewashed monastery after a thunder-storm, seen perched upon some dun cliff among the Pyrenees. But it was no purely fanciful resemblance which now, for a moment, almost led Captain Delano to think that nothing less than a ship-load of monks was before him. Peering over the bulwarks were what really seemed, in the hazy distance, throngs of dark cowls; while fitfully revealed through the open port-holes, other dark moving figures were dimly descried, as of Black Friars pacing the cloisters.
>
> Upon a still nigher approach, this appearance was modified, and the true character of the vessel was plain – Spanish merchantman of the first class, carrying negro slaves, amongst other valuable freight, from one colonial port to another.
>
> (p.219)

I sight her too in his proportions of mirage ('whitewashed monastery . . . throngs of dark cowls') and his proportions of suppressed nightmare ('negro slaves amongst other valuable freight').

In his realm of nightmare I am on territory that is technological and real – actual cargo, freight etc., common-or-garden facts of Amasa's day.

In his realm of mirage I am on ancient premises or hypnotic media ('dun cliff among the Pyrenees').

One way or the other I am oppressed by a blanket of value-codes whose edge is the nightmare of the sacred.

It is significant, in this context, that as I draw closer still to the *San Dominick* I cannot but observe in Amasa's eyes a hint of a museum of oligarchical Venice and of sacred fossil democracy, carved upon a flux of waters, where before had existed a mirage of hierarchical church/Black Friars:

> Toward the stern, two high-raised quarter galleries – the balustrades here and there covered with dry, tindery sea-moss – opening out from the unoccupied state-cabin, whose dead lights, for all the mild weather, were hermetically closed and calked – these tenantless balconies hung over the sea as if it were the grand Venetian canal.
>
> (p.220)

Thus I find myself, in my turn, sketching into the ship a subjective/objective counterpoint between self-sufficient technological masks of the day (ship, freight, etc.) and sacred/eroded value-codes of community (church, democracy, etc.).

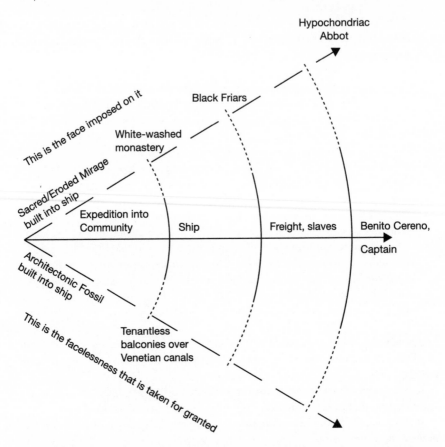

And a tension begins to emerge between claustrophobic values of conformity (Black Friars) and extinction of others within a tyranny of pattern or vacancy of man (tenantless balconies over the grand Venetian canal): at the same time a converse proposition hints at itself – renascent capacities for heterogeneous community within the media of man. To put it in another way architectonic proportions may subsist upon insight into falling static worlds and may achieve a remedial scale built into conscience and self. New proportions (or the regeneration of spaces one takes for granted) are available to the imagination when it begins to take into account all that is implicit and concealed like fossil value codes within apparently realistic crew, cargo, ship of an age or a civilization.

'Benito Cereno' sustains, in some degree, I believe, the kind of torment and latent scope for regeneration that reminds me of a deeper primitive memory still of cannibal bone and hollow flute. I cannot expand on this here and now except to say that the theme of the Carib bone or flute sustains an implicit tran-substantiation of implacable bodies of fate drawn out of opposing historical camps.

As one runs the gauntlet of captain and crew on the *San Dominick* one endures something both transubstantial and daemonic as the spectral appetite of man.

Take Don Benito 'on the after-part of the main deck' burning within himself as within the cauldron of the sea:

> His mind appeared unstrung . . . Shut up in these oaken walls, chained to one dull round of command . . . like some hypochondriac abbot he moved slowly about, at times suddenly pausing, starting, or staring, biting his lip, biting his finger-nail.
>
> (p.224)

Don Benito is supported by Babo as he tells his gruesome tale to Captain Delano:

> 'It is now a hundred and ninety days', began the Spaniard, in his husky whisper, 'that this ship, well officered and well manned, with several cabin passengers – some fifty Spaniards in all – sailed from Buenos Ayres bound to Lima, with a general cargo, hardware, Paraguay tea and the like' – and, pointing forward, 'that parcel of negroes, now not more than a hundred and fifty, as you see, but then numbering over three hundred souls. Off Cape Horn we had heavy gales. In one moment, by night, three of my best officers, with fifteen sailors, were lost, with the main-yard; the spar snapping under them in the slings, as they sought, with heavers, to beat down the icy sail. To lighten the hull, the heavier sacks of mata were thrown into the sea, with most of the water-pipes lashed on deck at the time. And this last necessity it was, combined with the prolonged detentions afterwards experienced, which eventually brought about our chief causes of suffering. When –'
>
> Here there was a sudden fainting attack of his cough . . . His servant sustained him, and drawing a cordial from his pocket placed it to his lips. He a little revived. But unwilling to leave him unsupported while yet imperfectly restored, the black with one arm still encircled his master, at the same time keeping his eye fixed on his face, as if to watch for the first sign of complete restoration, or relapse, as the event might prove.
>
> The Spaniard proceeded, but brokenly and obscurely, as one in a dream. 'Oh, my God! rather than pass through what I have, with joy I would have hailed the most terrible gales; but –'
>
> His cough returned and with increased violence; this subsiding, with reddened lips and closed eyes he fell heavily against his supporter.
>
> 'His mind wanders. He was thinking of the plague that followed the gales', plaintively sighed the servant . . .
>
> 'This excitement is bad for master', whispered the servant, taking his arm, and with soothing words gently drawing him aside.

When Don Benito returned, the American was pained to observe that his hopefulness . . . was but febrile and transient.

Ere long, with a joyless mien, looking up toward the poop, the host invited his guest to accompany him there, for the benefit of what little breath of wind might be stirring.

As, during the telling of the story, Captain Delano had once or twice started at the occasional cymballing of the hatchet-polishers, wondering why such an interruption should be allowed, especially in that part of the ship, and in the ears of an invalid; and moreover, as the hatchets had anything but an attractive look, and the handlers of them still less so, it was therefore, to tell the truth, not without some lurking reluctance . . . that Captain Delano acquiesced . . . With an untimely caprice of punctilio, rendered distressing by his cadaverous aspect, Don Benito . . . solemnly insisted upon his guest's preceding him up the ladder leading to the elevation; where one on each side of the last step, sat four armorial supporters and sentries . . . Gingerly enough stepped good Captain Delano between them, and in the instant of leaving them behind, like one running the gauntlet, he felt an apprehensive twitch in the calves of his legs.

But when, facing about, he saw the whole file, like so many organ grinders, still stupidly intent on their work, unmindful of everything beside, he could not but smile at his late fidgety panic.

(pp.228–9, 232–3)

In the linked passages I have quoted above, running together as one, I have attempted to match despair and hope as characteristic and identical colour of emotion within black mutineer (acting the role of patient servant) and white commander (acting the role of pitiful master) on the *San Dominick*. Characteristic too of my need at the outset, before boarding the ship, to act out self-obsessed riddles that reflect an inner darkness into which one retires as well as an outer body that one simulates as features of sustained shock, sustained self-deception at the same time, sustained love, sustained murder at the same time, within the gauntlet of history.

This, I believe, is the irony of the intuitive imagination and also the scale of heterogeneous fictions in which one is drawn to desist from giving exact weight to intelligences and motivations that run so deep, indescribably fierce and strong, so much deeper than lucid bodies of apparent evil or apparent good, they serve to confirm a mystery of otherness, a mystery of dynamic creativity and wholeness upon which the imagination sets its teeth like the bite of a consciousness far in advance of place and time.

I have attempted in my critical analysis of 'Benito Cereno' to become an actor playing a part, to act, as it were, in some degree, the role of Captain Delano. This is an idea which I find helpful in immersing oneself in imaginative fiction – to take a character or group of characters as black-comic parts one could oneself play and to let the obscurity of the rest impinge upon one by degrees of inner illumination.

It is essential to remember, I believe, that the achievement of the subjective imagination within a heterogeneous complex lies in a kind of irony that subsists on degrees of what I would like to call, for the sake of convenience, 'dramatic oracle'. Who is more steeped in darkness yet spiritually insulated, as it were, and capable therefore of becoming our most intimate judge and familiar than the kind of daemon that approximates to oracle? As 'oracle' the most ordinary character in a play or a novel is sometimes obsessed with ideas or implications that seem advanced or abnormally cunning or strange or obtuse or even naive. But basically this is a valid licence of heterogeneous drama, since it serves to highlight the enigma of a sacred otherness/darkness. All such excess is, in fact, instinctively related to simulated features of extravagance, inextricably woven into moments of self-deception, to make even deeper the mystery of intelligence and the function of creativity as breakdown of patterns of *hubris*.

I wonder whether a far-reaching issue does not arise from these considerations. Is it not true that imaginative writers belong to different orders in a peculiar sense that serves to provide different calloused crutches, different unconscious familiars, as it were, within a larger all-encompassing community sensitive to reconciliations one needs to approach with care?

Is Melville, in this novel, closer to Hemingway or Faulkner or Conrad or Wole Soyinka or Carpentier? Perhaps, in the American theatre, a connection could be made with Faulkner though I would think one would need to sense a number of intermediate stages which I am not qualified to unfold.

On the other hand, in a future section of the unfinished critical study I have in mind I hope, amongst other things, to look at *Cane* by the black American writer Jean Toomer. This sensuous, troubled and remarkable book first appeared in 1923 and is one of the most illuminating links, I believe, between the sensibility of a Melville in the mid-nineteenth century and the problems that were to besiege a certain kind of sensitive writer in the mid-twentieth century.

The issue of a writer's specific community of contrasting familiars, backwards and forwards in time, is a fascinating one. In 'Benito Cereno' the sacred mirage of place and time built into the ship provides a cue to pressures upon the writer's psyche. Melville wrote memorably about war, or the casualties of war, and in some ways his work reflects something one finds in those epics of war in which an echo arises, a tragic momentum and flux of the living and the dead.

In Parenthesis by David Jones, published for the first time in 1937, is regarded as an extraordinary epic of the Great War. I know it is a world away from 'Benito Cereno' in narrative design, yet strangely enough it provides me with the most evocative illustration I could find of mirage built into the technology of realism. And a shadowy but concrete signal at the heart of the word seems to flash from writer to writer across a great divide.

Take a curious passage in which the morning light dawns and the comical, sad resurrection/vivification of night-bones commences. Half-heard, half-hallucinated words of command are heard as the stupefied sleepers stir and 'the furrowed traverses whiten and agitate'.

> To their eyes seeming a wood moving,
>   a moving grove advisioned.
>   Stand-to.
>   Stand-to.
>   Stand-to-arms.
> Out there,
> get out there
> get into that fire trench.
> Pass it along to Stand-to.
> To peel back those eider-ducks me slumberin' lovelies – Prince
> Charming presents his compliments. Who's this John Moores in his
> martial cloak – get off it, wontcher – come away counterfeiting death –
> cantcher – hear the bird o' dawnin' – roll up – it's tomorrow alright.
>   Sergeant Charming's through your thorny slumbers, who bends over
> sweet Robin's rose cheek.
>   Morning sergeant – kiss me sergeant.
>   Whose toe porrects the ritual instrument to break the spell to resurrect
> the traverses.
>   Fog refracted, losing articulation in the cloying damp, the word of
> command unmade in its passage, mischiefed of the opaque air, mutated,
> bereaved of content, become an incoherent uttering, a curious bent cry
> out of the smarting drift, lost altogether – yet making rise again the grey
> bundles where they lie.
>   Sodden night-bones vivify, wet bones live.
>   With unfathomed passion – this stark stir and waking – contort the
> comic mask of these tragic japers.
>   With a great complaining, bay by bay, the furrowed traverses whiten
> and agitage.
>   In 'P' sap, in 'Q' post, in the fire-trench, in Moggs Hole and Cats Post.
>   An eastward alignment of troubled, ashen faces; delicate mechanisms
> of nerve and sinew, grapple afresh, deal for another day; ill-matched
> contesting, handicapped out of reason, spirits at the ebb bare up; strung
> taut – by what volition keyed – as best they may.
>   As grievous invalids watch the returning light pale-bright the ruckled
> counterpane, see their uneased bodies only newly clear; fearful to know
> afresh their ill condition; yet made glad for that rising, yet strain ears to
> the earliest note – should some prevenient bird make his kindly cry.
>   Chance modulations in the fluxing mist . . .[2]

No 'prevenient bird' makes his annunciation within 'Benito Cereno': Yet an echo of concupiscent bodies of fiction and history (as though history needs fiction in a new way, fiction history beyond given premises) arises within the intuitive outlines of a strange frontier of the imagination in which the static supports of an age, the purest investitures, masks, rituals etc. begin to embody the most curious contradictions and ironies of newborn leadership: bloodless leadership, hollow leadership, savaged leadership.

I have not so far commented upon the shrouded masthead of the *San Dominick* that conceals the skeleton of one Alexandro Arando who had owned the blacks on the ship and had been killed by Babo's mutineers. Captain Delano observed this masthead for the first time from his whale boat as the ship drew close to the vessel though at the time its only significance lay for him in what seemed to him a rude and freakish inscription painted beneath it.

> Whether the ship had a figure-head, or only a plain beak, was not quite certain, owing to canvas wrapped about that part, either to protect it while undergoing a re-furbishing, or else decently to hide its decay. Rudely painted or chalked, as in a sailor freak, along the forward side of a sort of pedestal below the canvas, was the sentence, '*Seguid vuestro jefe*' (follow your leader).

> (p.220)

Soon after, when he climbed aboard and sent his boat back to fetch provisions from his own sealer *Batchelor's Delight*, he was struck almost immediately by other 'instances of insubordination' that aroused him to question Don Benito from whom he received sometimes discourteous, sometimes muted, sometimes impatient replies.

An extravagance of effects may appear to heighten Captain Delano's obtuseness to the signs of mutiny, to the fate of Don Benito who is visibly distraught and a pawn in the hands of Babo; indeed to his own fate as Babo plots to outwit him.

But that obvious aspect of Delano's unawareness should not conceal from us what is less obvious, namely, the abnormal role Don Benito himself plays as absolute commander of a slave ship. It is he who apes unconsciousness, apes god, apes thunder. *Follow your leader.* Why then should a visiting captain, indulgent to a degree to the ways of arbitrary fortune and command, not be deceived by him, not take him for granted as involuntary figurehead suffering in his own right from a malaise wholly consistent with the appearances of being in pawn to death?

> But ere long Captain Delano bethought him that, indulgent as he was at the first, in judging the Spaniard, he might not, after all, have exercised charity enough. At bottom it was Don Benito's reserve which displeased him; but the same reserve was shown towards all but his faithful personal attendant. Even the formal reports which, according to sea-usage, were,

at stated times, made to him by some petty underling, either a white, mulatto or black, he hardly had patience enough to listen to, without betraying contemptuous aversion. His manner upon such occasions was, in its degree, not unlike that which might be supposed to have been his imperial countryman's, Charles V, just previous to the anchoritish retirement of that monarch from the throne.

This splenetic disrelish of his place was evinced in almost every function pertaining to it. Proud as he was moody, he condescended to no personal mandate. Whatever special orders were necessary, their delivery was delegated to his body-servant, who in turn transferred them to their ultimate destination, through runners, alert Spanish boys or slave boys, like pages or pilotfish within easy call continually hovering round Don Benito. So that to have beheld this undemonstrative invalid gliding about, apathetic and mute, no landsman could have dreamed that in him was lodged a dictatorship beyond which . . . there was no earthly appeal.

Thus, the Spaniard, regarded in his reserve, seemed the involuntary victim of mental disorder . . . [He] evinced the unhealthy climax of that icy though conscientious policy, more or less adopted by all commanders of large ships, which . . . obliterates alike the manifestation of sway with every trace of sociality; transforming the man into a block, or rather into a loaded cannon, which, until there is call for thunder, has nothing to say.

(pp.225–6)

The accent falls squarely upon a deranged concupiscence of roles like a tragic and unfulfilled annunciation of community, a tragic and unfulfilled marriage between static worlds masquerading as objective shield or history and formal plot or sovereign fiction. It is the echo of that objective masquerade, which prefers to arm itself ceaselessly in its submission to death rather than to conceive life by degrees of digestion of the shocks of change, that comes home to me, I find, on several levels of 'Benito Cereno'.

I shall, in closing, look further at two prime apparitions. First of all one becomes aware, I feel, that the roles that are being performed by the various actors in the tragedy of a civilization may achieve a resounding technical triumph and climax but their content and mystery are fast running into the sand (or into the sea) as though the actors themselves have become performing robots of fate. At such a time the irony of comedy lies with the intuitive imagination and how it employs what is apparently insubstantial, apparently evanescent as the writing of the future on the wall of the past.

This is beautifully shadowed forth, I think, in a passage in which Captain Delano is possessed by a 'chance phantom cats-paw' or 'dreamy inquietude' 'like that of one who alone on the prairie feels unrest from the repose of the noon' (p.252).

This leads on to my second apparition. The *San Dominick* is taken, Babo is seized even as he points a dagger at Don Benito's heart, the mutiny is put down and later Babo is tried and executed. But this escalation of relationships fixed into the deadliest engines of justice and love (gallows and cross) breeds a further polarization between time and eternity like a lullaby of silence.

In silence is instilled a glancing echo where there had been before a glancing ripple. The silent crutches of an age (as theatre of nightmare leadership) march endlessly forward.

> Some months after, dragged to the gibbet at the tail of a mule, the black met his voiceless end. The body was burned to ashes; but for many days, the head, that hive of sublety, fixed on a pole in the Plaza, met, unabashed, the gaze of the whites; and across the Plaza looked towards St Bartholomew's church, in whose vaults slept then, as now, the recovered bones of Aranda: and across the Rimac bridge looked towards the monastery, on Mount Agonia without; where, three months after being dismissed by the court, Benito Cereno, borne on the bier, did, indeed, follow his leader.
>
> (p.307)

Notes

1 Herman Melville, 'Benito Cereno' in *Billy Budd, Sailor and Other Stories* (Harmondsworth, 1972), pp.221–2. Further references to this edition are given after quotations in the text.
2 David Jones, *In Parenthesis* (London, 1969), pp.60–1.

Part III

THE ROOT OF EPIC

PREFACE: THE ROOT OF EPIC[1]

The true capacity of marginal and disadvantaged cultures resides in their genius to tilt the field of civilisation so that one may visualise boundaries of persuasion in new and unsuspecting lights to release a different apprehension of reality, the language of reality, a different reading of texts of reality.[2]

In 'History, Fable and Myth in the Caribbean and Guianas', Harris realizes three such *boundaries of persuasion*: different apprehension of reality, different language of reality, and different reading of texts of reality.

Different apprehensions of reality concern unfinished rehearsal. This term comes from the Anglo-Norman *rehearser*, perhaps from the Old French *hercer*, to harrow over. A harrow is a rake or a heavy frame drawn over cultivated ground. 'To

---

1 The systems of folk-belief in Guyana (African limbo, vodun [voodoo], Carib bush-baby, rainmaking vestiges, masquerade) may constitute the true phenomenal environment for the future Guyanese novel. These very belief systems that could so offend the educated intelligence might conceal a hidden resource of depth capacious enough to write epic for the age; hence my title, *the root of epic*.

How might such an epic emerge? Although folk-arts traditionally inform the poetry and drama of the Caribbean region, the West Indian novelist continues to write novels whose frame of reference (travails of the formerly-colonized West Indian man and woman in a white-excluding world) actually excludes its leading characters and by continuation, the readers it portrays ('Tradition and the West Indian Novel'). By imitating the nineteenth-century novel of convention, the typical West Indian novel, for instance, has failed to conceive itself and stands curiously out of frame. The English novel tends to portray back into an including-framework its leading characters, but the West Indian novel is *disfigured by convention* because its leading characters operate wholly in an excluding framework. West Indian man and woman excluded from the privileged society of the nation-state England in whose language and institutions he has been educated. This is as true for the Creole novel as it is for a writer as cultivated as V.S. Naipaul and his privileged but outsider's peregrinations in the English landscape. As such, the movement of the West Indian novel has been to duplicate the ethnographic report – of information to peoples other than those about whom the study is made. If we think of originality and tradition as plural masks worn by vestige gods (see 'Quetzalcoatl and the Smoking Mirror: Reflections on Originality and Tradition'), then such masks will celebrate the enigma of an inheritance that is both 'dialectically mixed and impure'.

2 'History, Fable and Myth in the Caribbean and Guianas', 1970, pp.152–83 in this volume.

137

rehearse', in the sense of 'to harrow' is a most apposite coinage; Harris's concept of the cross-cultural tradition has to do with undoing fixed frames in our picture of the world and introducing in their stead a fluid continuum or paradoxical series with hidden traditions.

Uniform, mechanistic readings produce a framed universe of experience which, to Harris, yields the fiction of absolute knowledge. And paradoxically, language, the maker of such fiction, can also unmake or breach that fiction.

> Language is deeper than 'frames', it transgresses against the frames that would make us prisoners of eternity in the name of one creed or dogma or ideology.
>
> (*Jonestown*, 1996, p.6.)

In the most recent group of Harris's novels the fictional dream-pilots – steersmen in the cross-cultural abyss Jonathan Weyl (*Carnival*, 1985), Robin Redbreast Glass (*The Infinite Rehearsal*, 1987), Anselm (*The Four Banks of the River of Space*, 1990), Christopher D'eath (*Resurrection at Sorrow Hill*, 1993) – are all involved in the cultural labour of unframing.

> A word about the characters in *Carnival*. Jonathan Weyl is – let us say – a twentieth-century Dante figure. He is secreted in the carnival of the twentieth century. The particularities of his existence make him intimate with some of the proportions of thirteenth-century Dante even as they move him light-years away, so that the origination of a Dantesque formula, a Dantesque mask, is called into question. There are stars in Dante's thirteenth-century cosmos he would never have perceived as we perceive them. They were fixed. Whereas for us the light that comes across space from a star is but the shadow of an object that may have vanished. News of its disappearance has not yet been transmitted to us. *To put it differently. Within the abyss of tradition – within the spatiality, the spectrality of tradition – the original nucleus that motivates us is so peculiar, so unidentifiable, that singularity needs plurality. Dante – in other words – needs a twentieth-century carnival of masks even as those masks look backwards to him and through him to the mysterious origins of Imagination in science and art* [my italics, AJMB].[3]

The act of seeing through plural masks produces masque-series that include the cross-cultural womb of space. They read from the parable of Being in the living landscapes; they enact the fable of history in its endless rehearsal. They bid to reach and rescue the hidden *traditions* of the imagination that fall under the harrow, that are in distress.

---

3 'The Unfinished Genesis of the Imagination', 1992, pp.248–60 in this volume.

As one goes over hidden ground, one rehearses in a way that is always preparatory but never definitive; such is the *unfinished rehearsal*.

Different language of reality illuminates a complex of new meanings through specific coinages, for example technical terms, such as those in Harris's essays on the American Imagination.[4] By revising the work of fiction through its intuitive clues,[5] it affords one a looking *into* vision as opposed to a looking *with* vision; while *different reading of texts of reality* concerns the archetypal fiction and its disinvestments of historic contingence; its roundness, circularity, approximativeness.[6] These are Harris's three boundaries of persuasion as they share rapport with sensibilities in cross-cultural community.

4 Preface to Part II.
5 'Literacy and the Imagination – a Talk', pp.75–89 in this volume.
6 Preface to Part I.

11

TRADITION AND THE WEST INDIAN NOVEL

I would like first of all to point out that the conventional approach to the 'West Indian' which sees him in crowds – an underprivileged crowd, a happy-go-lucky crowd, a political or a cricketing crowd, a calypso crowd – is one which we have to put aside at this moment for the purposes of our discussion. The status of the West Indian – as a person in world society – is of a much more isolated and problematic character. West Indians in their national context, in their nation-state, as such, are a minority in the world of the twentieth century, a very small minority at that. What in my view is remarkable about the West Indian in depth is a sense of subtle links, the series of subtle and nebulous links which are latent within him, the latent ground of old and new personalities. This is a very difficult view to hold, I grant, because it is not a view which consolidates, which invests in any way in the consolidation of popular character. Rather it seeks to visualize a *fulfilment* of character. Something which is more extraordinary than one can easily imagine. And it is this possible revolution in the novel – *fulfilment* rather than *consolidation* – I would like first of all to look at in a prospective way because I feel it is profoundly consistent with the native tradition – the depth of inarticulate feeling and unrealized wells of emotion belonging to the whole West Indies.

The potential of the novel

The consolidation of character is, to a major extent, the preoccupation of most novelists who work in the twentieth century within the framework of the nineteenth-century novel. Indeed the nineteenth-century novel has exercised a very powerful influence on reader and writer alike in the contemporary world. And this is not surprising after all since the rise of the novel in its conventional and historical mould coincides in Europe with states of society which were involved in consolidating their class and other vested interests. As a result 'character' in the novel rests more or less on the self-sufficient individual – on elements of 'persuasion' (a refined or liberal persuasion at best in the spirit of the philosopher Whitehead) rather than 'dialogue' or 'dialectic' in the profound and unpredictable sense of person which Martin Buber, for example, evokes. The novel of persuasion rests on grounds of apparent common sense: a certain 'selection' is made by the writer, the selection of items, manners, uniform conversation, historical situations, etc., all lending themselves to build and present an individual span of life which yields self-conscious and fashionable judgements, self-conscious and fashionable moralities. The tension which emerges is the tension of individuals – great or small – on an accepted plane of society we are persuaded has an inevitable existence. There is an element of freedom in this method nevertheless, an apparent range of choices, but I believe myself that this freedom – in the convention which distinguishes it, however liberal this may appear – is an illusion. It is true of course that certain kinds of realism, impressive realism, and also a kind of fateful honesty distinguished and still distinguishes the novel of individual character especially where an element of great suffering arises and does a kind of spiritual violence to every 'given' conception.

I would like to break off here for a moment to say that the novel of the West Indies, the novel written by West Indians of the West Indies (or of any other place for that matter) belongs – in the main – to the conventional mould. Which is not surprising at this stage since the novel which consolidates situations to depict protest or affirmation is consistent with most kinds of overriding advertisement and persuasion upon the writer for him to make national and political and social simplifications of experience in the world at large today. Therefore the West Indian novel – so-called – in the main – is inclined to suffer in depth (to lose in depth) and may be properly assessed in nearly every case in terms of surface tension and realism – as most novels are assessed today – in the perceptive range of choices which emerges, and above all in the way in which the author *persuades* you to ally yourself with situation and character. I shall return to this point and to a close look at the work of certain West Indian writers . . . But at the moment I would like to pursue the subtler prospective thread I have raised to your attention. I believe it is becoming possible to see even now at this relatively early time that the ruling and popular convention, as such, is academic and provincial in the light of a genuine – and if I may use a much abused term – *native* tradition of depth.

Native and phenomenal environment

The native and phenomenal environment of the West Indies, as I see it, is broken into many stages in the way in which one surveys an existing river in its present bed while plotting at the same time ancient and abandoned, indeterminate courses the river once followed. When I speak of the West Indies I am thinking of overlapping contexts of Central and South America as well. For the mainstream of the West Indies in my estimation possesses an enormous escarpment down which it falls, and I am thinking here of the European discovery of the New World and conquest of the ancient American civilizations which were themselves related by earlier and obscure levels of conquest. This escarpment seen from another angle possesses the features of a watershed, main or subsidiary, depending again on how one looks at it.

The environment of the Caribbean is steeped – as I said before – in such broken conceptions as well as misconceptions of the residue and meaning of conquest. No wonder in the jungles of Guiana and Brazil, for example, material structural witnesses may be obliterated or seem to exist in a terrible void of unreality. Let us look once again at the main distinction which for convenience one may describe as the divide pre-Columbian/post-Columbian. The question is – how can one begin to reconcile the broken parts of such an enormous heritage, especially when those broken parts appear very often like a grotesque series of adventures, volcanic in its precipitate effects as well as human in its vulnerable settlement? This distinction is a large, a very large one which obviously has to be broken down into numerous modern tributaries and other immigrant movements and distinctions so that the smallest area one envisages, island or village, prominent ridge or buried valley, flatland or heartland, is charged immediately with the openness of imagination, and the longest chain of sovereign territories one sees is ultimately no stronger than its weakest and most obscure connecting link.

Vision of consciousness

It is in this light that one must seek to relate the existing pattern of each community to its variable past, and if I may point to the phenomenal divide again, the question which arises is how one can begin to let these parts act on each other in a manner which fulfils *in the person* the most nebulous instinct for a vocation of being and independent spirit within a massive landscape of apparent lifelessness which yields nevertheless the essential denigration and erosion of historical perspectives. This indeed is a peculiarly West Indian question, strange as it may appear to some, and in fact a question peculiar to every phenomenal society where minorities (frail in historical origin or present purpose) may exist, and where comparatively new immigrant and racial cells sometimes find themselves placed within a dangerous misconception and upon a reactionary treadmill. And it is right here – if one begins to envisage an expanding outward and inward creative significance for the novel – that the monument of consolidation breaks down and becomes the need for a vision of consciousness. And this vision of consciousness is the peculiar reality of language because the concept of language is one which continuously transforms inner and outer formal categories of experience, earlier and representative modes of speech itself, the still life resident in painting and sculpture as such, even music which one ceases to 'hear' – the peculiar reality of language provides a medium to *see* in consciousness the 'free' motion and to *hear* with consciousness the 'silent' flood of sound by a continuous inward revisionary and momentous logic of potent explosive images evoked in the mind. Such a capacity for language is a real and necessary one in a world where the inarticulate person is continuously frozen or legislated for in mass and a genuine experience of his distress, the instinct of distress, sinks into a void. The nightmare proportions of this are already becoming apparent throughout the world.

The point I want to make in regard to the West Indies is that the pursuit of a strange and subtle goal, melting pot, call it what you like, is the mainstream (though unacknowledged) tradition in the Americas. And the significance of this is akin to the European preoccupation with alchemy, with the growth of experimental science, the poetry of science as well as of explosive nature which is informed by a solution of images, agnostic humility and essential beauty, rather than vested interest in a fixed assumption and classification of things.

Let us look at the *individual* African slave. I say *individual* deliberately though this is an obviously absurd label to apply to the persons of slaves in their binding historical context. But since their arrival in the Americas bred a new and painful obscure isolation (which is difficult to penetrate in any other terms but a free conceptual imagination) one may perhaps dream to visualize the suffering and original grassroots of individuality. (In fact I believe this is one of the growing points of both alienation and feeling in modern West Indian literature.) He (the problematic slave) found himself spiritually alone since he worked side by side with others who spoke different dialects. The creative human consolation – if one dwells upon it meaningfully today – lies in the search for a kind of inward dialogue and space when one is deprived of a ready conversational tongue and hackneyed comfortable approach.

Irony

I would like to stress again the curious irony involved in this. To assume that the slave was an *individual* is historically absurd since the *individual* possesses certain distinguishing marks, education, status, background, morality, etc., while a slave – in the American context of which we are speaking, as in most situations I imagine – was like an animal put up for sale. (The same qualitative deprivation – though not in terms of absolute coercion – exists for the illiterate East Indian peasant, for example, in the twentieth century in the West Indies.) When therefore one speaks of an inarticulate body of men, confined on some historical plane, as possessing the grassroots of Western individuality one is creatively rejecting as if it were an illusion, every given, total and self-sufficient situation and dwelling within a capacity for liberation, a capacity for mental and unpredictable pain which the human person endured *then* or endures now *in* or *for* any time or place. To develop the point further it is clear that one is rejecting the sovereign individual as such. For in spite of his emancipation he consolidates every advance by conditioning himself to function solely within his contemporary situation more or less as the slave appears bound still upon his historical and archaic plane. It is in this 'closed' sense that freedom becomes a progressive illusion and it is within the open capacity of the person – as distinct from the persuasive refinements of any social order – within the suffering and enduring mental capacity of the obscure person (which capacity one shares with both 'collective' slave and 'separate' individual in the past and in the future) that a scale emerges and continues indefinitely to emerge which makes it possible for *one* (whoever that *one* may be, today or tomorrow) to measure and abolish each given situation.

Scale

The use of the word 'scale' is important, a scale or a ladder, because bear in mind what we are saying is that the capacity of the person in terms of words and images is associated with a drama of living consciousness, a drama within which one responds not only to the overpowering and salient features of a plane of existence (which 'overpoweringness', after all, is often a kind of self-indulgent realism) but to the essence of life, to the instinctive grains of life which continue striving and working in the imagination for fulfilment, a visionary character of fulfilment. Such a fulfilment can never be intellectually imposed on the material; it can only be realized in experiment instinctive to the native life and passion of persons known and unknown in a structure of time and space.

Therefore it is clear that the change which is occurring slowly within the novel and the play and the poem is one which has been maturing slowly for centuries. Some of the most daring intimations exist in the works of modern writers, Proust, Joyce, Faulkner, and I would also venture to say in the peculiar style and energy of Australian novelists like Patrick White and Hal Porter, a French novelist like Claude Simon, an English/Canadian novelist like Malcolm Lowry and an African problematic writer like Tutuola. Lowry's novel 'Under the Volcano' is set in Mexico where it achieves a tragic reversal of the material climate of our time, assisted by residual images, landscape as well as the melting pot of history, instinctive to the cultural environment of the Central and South Americas.

Let us apply our scale, for example, to the open myth of El Dorado. The religious and economic thirst for exploration was true of the Spanish conquistador, of the Portuguese, French, Dutch and English, of Raleigh, of Fawcett, as it is true of the black modern pork-knocker and the pork-knocker of all races. An instinctive idealism associated with this adventure was overpowered within individual and collective by enormous greed, cruelty and exploitation. In fact it would have been very difficult a century ago to present these exploits as other than a very material and degrading hunger for wealth spiced by a kind of self-righteous spirituality. It is difficult enough today within clouds of prejudice and nihilism; nevertheless the substance of this adventure, involving men of all races, past and present conditions, has begun to acquire a residual pattern of illuminating correspondences. El Dorado, City of Gold, City of God, grotesque, unique coincidence, another window within upon the Universe, another drunken boat, another ocean, another river; in terms of the novel the distribution of a frail moment of illuminating adjustments within a long succession and grotesque series of adventures, past and present, capable *now* of discovering themselves and continuing to discover themselves so that in one sense one relives and reverses the 'given' condition of the past, freeing oneself from catastrophic idolatry and blindness to one's own historical and philosophical conceptions and misconceptions which may bind one within a statuesque present or a false future. Humility is all, says the poet, humility is endless.

Such moments in a scale of reflection (which affect the medium of the arts, however obscurely) are not, of course, peculiar to our time alone. The work of Dante, I believe, was associated with one such 'timeless' moment of reality and fulfilment. And it is interesting to recall Eliot's words – 'Dante,' Eliot remarks, 'more than any other poet, has succeeded in dealing with his philosophy, not as a theory or as his own comment or reflection, but in terms of something *perceived*. When most of our modern poets confine themselves to what they had perceived, they produce for us, usually, only odds and ends of still life and stage properties; but that does not imply so much that the method of Dante is obsolete, as that our vision is perhaps comparatively restricted.'

Some may interpret the ground of distinction lying between 'most of our modern poets' and Dante as one of personal habit (the character of our modern poets) and impersonal vision (the character of Dante). I cannot help feeling, however, that the distinction actually is one between the historical, self-sufficient individual, as such, and a living open tradition which realizes itself in an enduring capacity associated with the obscure human person.

I want now to approach the work of certain West Indian writers bearing in mind the background of tradition we have been quickly exploring.

Tragic premises

One of the most interesting novelists out of the West Indies is George Lamming. Lamming was – and still is – regarded as a writer of considerable promise. What is the nature of his promise? Let us look at his novel *Of Age and Innocence*. This is a novel which somehow fails, I feel, but its failure tells us a great deal. The novel would have been remarkable if a certain tendency – genuine tendency – or a tragic feeling of dispossession in reality had been achieved. This tendency is frustrated by diffusion of energies within the entire work. The book seems to speak with a public voice, the voice of a peculiar orator and the compulsions which inform the work appear to spring from a verbal sophistication rather than a visual, plastic and conceptual imagery. Lamming's verbal sophistication is conversational, highly wrought and spirited sometimes: at other times it lapses into merely clever utterance, rhetorical, as when he says of one of his characters – 'He had been made Governor of an important colony which was then at peace with England.' It takes some effort – not the effort of imaginative concentration which is always worthwhile but an effort to combat the author's self-indulgence. And this would not arise if the work could be kept true to its inherent design. There is no necessary difficulty or complexity in Lamming's novels – the necessary difficulty or complexity belonging to strange symbolisms – and I feel if the author concentrated on the sheer essentials of his experience a tragic disposition of feeling would gain a true ascendancy. This concentration is essential if the work is not to succumb to a uniform tone which gives each individual character the same public-speaking resonance of voice. I would like to stress a certain distinction I made earlier once again. In the epic and revolutionary novel of associations the characters are related within a personal capacity which works in a poetic and serial way so that a strange jigsaw is set in motion like a mysterious unity of animal and other substitutes within the person. Something which is quite different to the over-elaboration of individual character within the conventional novel. And this over-elaboration is one danger which confronts Lamming. For in terms of the ruling framework he accepts, the individuality of character, the distinctions of status and privilege which mark one individual from another, must be maintained. This is the kind of realism, the realism of classes and classifications – however limited it may be in terms of a profound, poetic and scientific scale of values – the novel, in its orthodox mould, demands. Lamming may be restless within this framework (there are signs and shadows of this in his work) but mere extravagance of pattern and an inclination to frequent intellectual raids beyond his territory are not a genuine breakthrough and will only weaken the position of the central character in his work. He must school himself at this stage, I believe, to work for the continuous development of a main individual character in order to free himself somewhat from the restrictive consolidation he brings about which unfortunately, I find, blocks one's view of essential conflict. This becomes a necessity in terms of the very style and tone of his work. He cannot afford to crowd his canvas when the instinctive threat of one-sidedness is likely to overwhelm all his people and in fact when this one-sidedness may be transformed into a source of tremendous strength in a singleness of drive and purpose which cannot then fail to discipline every tangential field and exercise. The glaring case is Shephard whom you may recall in *Of Age and Innocence*. Here was an opportunity which was not so much lost – as lost sight of – to declare and develop the tragic premises of individual personality by concentrating on the one man (Shephard) in order to bring home a dilemma which lay in his coming to terms with the people around him by acting – even when he was playing the role of the great rebel – in the way everyone else appeared to see him rather than in the way he innocently may have seen himself.

Comedy of pathos

It is illuminating at this point to compare V. S. Naipaul's *A House for Mr Biswas* with George Lamming's *Of Age and Innocence*. Naipaul never loses sight of his Mr Biswas throughout a very long chronicle in the way Lamming disposes of Shephard again and again. Naipaul's style is like Lamming's in one respect: it is basically conversational though without the rhetoric and considerable power Lamming displays and it follows a flat and almost banal everyday tone. On this flat conversational level the novel has been carefully and scrupulously written. The possibility for tragedy which lay in *Of Age and Innocence*, the vein of longing for a lost innocence associated with Shephard's world is nowhere apparent in *A House for Mr Biswas*. Mr Biswas is essentially comic – a mixture of comedy and pathos – where Shephard may have been stark and tragic. Naipaul's triumph with Mr Biswas is one which – in the very nature of the novel – is more easily achieved, I feel, than a triumph with Shephard for Lamming would have been.

146

To achieve the nuclear proportions of tragedy in Shephard, Lamming needed a remarkable and intense personal centre of depth; this he never held, overlooking the concrete challenge which stems from such a presence in his novel whose status is obscure. On the other hand the sad figure of Mr Biswas lends itself to a vulgar and comic principle of classification of things and people which gives the novel a conventional centre. In the first place Naipaul's world is one which is devoid of phenomenal and therefore corrosive sensibility. He builds his chronicle around a traditional Hindu family in Trinidad and therefore persuades his readers to identify with an assumption of individual status, of historical context. The inner and outer poverty of Naipaul's characters – while achieving at times memorable pathos – never erupts into a revolutionary or alien question of spirit, but serves ultimately to consolidate one's preconception of humanity, the comedy of pathos and the pathos of comedy. It is this 'common picture of humanity' so-called on which Naipaul's work rests. The novel for him, as for many contemporary readers and writers, restricts the open and original ground of choice, the vision and stress of transplantation in the person out of one world into another, the necessity for epic beyond its present framework, or tragedy within its present framework, since the assumption remains to the end a contemporary and limited one of burial and classification, a persuasion of singular and pathetic enlightenment rather than a tragic centrality or a capacity for plural forms of profound identity.

Moral distinctions

It is interesting to look at John Hearne in the light of the problems we have been discussing – the problem of centrality which appears to be an essential goal for Lamming and historical status of individual character as it emerges in Naipaul.

Hearne's solution of this problem I find to be unsatisfactory. He is a writer of much talent, capable of acute organization and story-telling, whose aim, it seems to me, is to achieve a certain moral distinction. This distinction, however, unfortunately, reveals a poverty of creative perception which springs, to a large extent, from the pure logic of the conventional novel. Hearne is not instinctively a tragic writer nor is he comic and therefore since he is a serious novelist *all* his characters have to be taken seriously in depth within a moral context. The tragic writer achieves a certain rejection of the 'given' historical situation, the comic writer thrives on the poverty of historical situations once he can maintain the illusion of a common rather than uncommon humanity, but the moral writer has to be truer than anyone else to a proportionate even classical ground of responsibility. In order to achieve this classical ground Hearne *imposes* a moral directive on his situations and this is a considerable creative shortcoming, especially in a context such as the Caribbean and the Americas where the life of situation and person has an inarticulacy one must genuinely suffer with and experience if one is to acquire the capacity for a new relationship and understanding.

Hearne's methods can be seen in a nutshell in his short story 'At the Stelling', which appears in *West Indian Stories* edited by Andrew Salkey. The story, as such, is

147

told with a certain brilliance and economy but once we examine the way in which the moral directive is imposed we are disappointed. What is this moral directive? It has to do with the relationship between master and servant, the officer-in-command and the men he commands, the necessity for proportion and responsibility. John, of Carib descent, shoots his leader Cockburn who is a mulatto, as well as seven or eight men in a survey party. Cockburn has allowed his private sentiment and jealousy of John's prowess in certain matters to obtrude into his public duties. In the end Cockburn is seen as an unfortunate whose training in the traditions of leadership is still lacking at this particular time. The lesson is driven home by the arrival of the previous surveyor and party leader, Mr Hamilton, an Englishman, and Shirley, also an Englishman, the superintendent of police. Their arrival sets a different tone to the whole affair which would never have happened if Cockburn, who has been shot dead, had been equipped to lead the survey party in the way Hamilton was and still is.

What Hearne is doing here is to arrive at a plausible moral ground by investing heavily in two characters, whose historical status (they are both educated Europeans) allows him to achieve his classical proportion. He has in so doing turned away from the real moral depth and challenge in his material. Let us imagine that the shooting had occurred and Cockburn, the half-baked new leader, had been an Englishman with the given status of Hamilton or Shirley. Then the situation would have opened up and become no longer a matter of relative training and lack of training but of relevant conception and misconception. The full peril of the situation would have invaded all the characters – whose image of themselves would have begun to suffer in a new and unpredictable way – and the obscure status of the Carib descendant as well as the transforming imperative to endure (which is the highest moral principle) would have begun to grow into a creative scale and capacity for self-judgement within the person of each and everyone. It is in this respect I recall Lukács, the Marxian critic, who points out that a simple affirmation of classical tradition is not enough. And he says a renewal of the classical form can only come by repudiating much in the historical apparatus of the novel or as he puts it in Hegel's words 'in the form of a negation of a negation'.

Model of realism

It is at this point that we can see the paradoxical place C.L.R. James occupies in relation to West Indian literature. *The Black Jacobins* is not a novel but it has a curious bearing on the problems we have been discussing. I am not concerned here with James's economic theories of history, which in regard to slavery, in particular, may have exercised some influence since they appear to bob up again in that distinguished book *Capitalism and Slavery* by Eric Williams.

The Black Jacobins first appeared in 1938. The central historical character is Toussaint L'Ouverture. And James seeks to discover him within a dimension of suffering – the stark world of the slaves – and a dimension of revolution – the

148

world of ideological France. The fact that James seeks to implicate both worlds – the world of the slave and the ambivalent world of the free – is consistent with the mainstream tradition and melting pot of the Caribbean. Some may feel the emphasis is too harsh at times, even repulsive and abnormal, but this harshness belongs to a school of extreme realism and to the very nature of many an emotional close-up of historical perspective. James's study therefore is one of the models which may have influenced the realism of certain West Indian novelists who thought they saw an opportunity for commercial investment in historical sensationalism. It is now possible to see how dubious these Mittelholzerian enterprises were and in fact the rise of the comic novel in the West Indies, Selvon and Naipaul, came as a necessary corrective. The dust, however, is now beginning to settle and it is also possible to discover *The Black Jacobins* in relation to the genuine and native capacity of the West Indian. It is a severe and imaginative reconstruction of the historical figure of Toussaint L'Ouverture – Africa, the Caribbean, Europe. The very harshness of line is a repudiation of melodrama and a repudiation of permanent fixtures of value – fascist ornament or liberal self-deception. Toussaint – and this is the curious almost unwitting irony of the work – emerges not because he fits in where James wants him to stand, but because he escapes the author's self-determination in the end. James seeks to smooth over a number of cracks in building his portrait but each significant flaw he wrestles with begins to make its own independent impact.

Toussaint's friendship with and expulsion of Sonthonax, the Frenchman, whom he genuinely appeared to like and admire is one such recalcitrant split or bulge. It seems much more reasonable, in my view, to accept Toussaint's explanation of his action in regard to Sonthonax as one inspired by a reluctance to entertain the counsel of Sonthonax to declare Haiti a sovereign and independent state. In fact this uncertainty of design in Toussaint's mind seems to be borne out by his otherwise inexplicable dealings with his black generals, his equivocation, his secrecy and his alienation from many who were waiting on him to give the final and decisive word. Toussaint was a man of genius, and genius in such phenomenally difficult circumstances must entail, I feel, a strange involvement with both the salvation of grass-roots and the harvest of achievement and labour. The question was – how to reconcile the depth of sacrifice, the freed slave must now voluntarily make, with an abstract freedom? Such a vision of reconciliation – slavery with freedom – was essential to retain a continuity of growth and survival in the world at large, the world of Europe, of France, Spain and Britain with whom Toussaint had had diplomatic and strategic dealings – and the world of America, North and South. It was a tragic problem which was to be taken out of his hands with fearful chaotic consequences for Haiti. Furthermore it would appear that this was inevitable. For Toussaint may well have been an agnostic as far as contemporary political faiths are concerned. He may well have had peculiar doubts about the assumption of sovereign status and power. And this was profound heresy even then, much more so now. Where would he have found a real nucleus and following? It is a significant attempt James has made which reflects dedication, self-sacrifice and clarity of intention. Nevertheless in my view – as I said before – the weight of evidence he brings forward refuses ultimately to bow to his fixed purpose. The obscurities and cracks in Toussaint's armour are not amenable to his interpretation of them as a misfortune of secretive temperament. Rather they appear to indicate, when one takes each consistent inconsistency into account, a groping towards an alternative to conventional statehood, a conception of wider possibilities and relationships which still remains unfulfilled today in the Caribbean.

The failure to contain Toussaint sheds a certain paradoxical light beyond the historical framework James set up, upon the seeds of tragedy which are native to a cultural environment whose promise of fulfilment lies in a profound and difficult vision of the person – a profound and difficult vision of essential unity within the most bitter forms of latent and active historical diversity.

Literature and society

This talk may have been somewhat different, perhaps, to the line I may have been expected to take. But it seems to me vital – in a time when it is easy to succumb to fashionable tyrannies or optimisms – to break away from the conception so many people entertain that literature is an extension of a social order or a political platform. In fact it is one of the ironic things with West Indians of my generation that they may conceive of themselves in the most radical political light but their approach to art and literature is one which consolidates the most conventional and documentary techniques in the novel. In fact many of the great Victorians – Ruskin, Gerard Manley Hopkins, Dickens in *Bleak House* for example, where a strange kinship emerges with the symbolism of both Poe and Kafka – are revolutionaries who make the protestations of many a contemporary radical look like a sham and a pose. The fact is – even where sincerely held, political radicalism is merely a fashionable attitude unless it is accompanied by profound insights into the experimental nature of the arts and the sciences. There are critics who claim that the literary revolution of the first half of the 20th century may well stem from the work of Pound and Eliot, Joyce and Wyndham Lewis. I am not prepared to go into this claim now but the point is – how is it that figures such as these, described in some quarters as conservative, remain 'explosive' while many a fashionable rebel grows to be superficial and opportunistic?

Literature has a bearing on society, yes, a profound and imaginative bearing wherein the life of tradition in all its complexity gives a unique value to the life of vocation in society, whether that vocation happens to be in science, in education, in the study of law or in the dedicated craft of one's true nature and life. For if tradition were dogma it would be entirely dormant and passive but since it is inherently active at all times, whether secretly or openly, it participates the ground of living necessity by questioning and evaluating all assumptions of character and conceptions of place or destiny. A scale of distinctions emerges, distinctions which give the imagination room to perceive the shifting border line between original substance and vicarious hollow, the much advertised rich and the hackneyed caricature of the poor, the overfed body of illusion and the under-fed stomach of reality – room to perceive also overlapping areas of invention and creation, the hair-spring experiment of crucial illumination which divides the original spiritual germ of an idea from its musing plastic development and mature body of expression. It is this kind of scale which is vital to the life of the growing person in society. And this scale exists in a capacity for imagination. A scale which no one can impose since to do so is to falsify the depth of creative experience, the growth and feeling for creative experience.

It is a scale which at certain moments realizes itself in a range and capacity which are phenomenal – the peaks of tragedy, of epic, of myth have been such moments in the dialogue of culture and civilization – while at other times we must be grateful if we are allowed to work at the humility of our task with all of our creative suffering instincts, leaving ourselves open, as it were, to vision.

And this is the germ of the thing the writer feels when he says in everyday talk that 'a work begins to write itself', to live its own life, to make its author *see* developments he had not intellectually ordered or arranged.

One last word. As you may have observed I have said nothing about V.S. Reid whose novel *The Leopard* I admire for certain reasons which I leave you to judge after all I have been saying. Nevertheless I feel it is necessary to wait and see what his third novel will be. After all, many West Indian writers – whose novels have been, or are being now written to be published – are relatively young men. And this, of course, is a tremendously hopeful thing. And in this connection I recall Roger Mais, whose work may be naive in some respects, and unfulfilled in others, but whose life is a symbolic reminder of the brutal philistinism of the middle classes and the upper ruling classes in the West Indies which have thwarted, on many occasions, the rise of the liberal imagination.

12

HISTORY, FABLE AND MYTH IN THE CARIBBEAN AND GUIANAS

It occurred to me as I contemplated this series of talks entitled 'History, Fable and Myth' that it may prove illuminating to look first of all at J. Thomas' rebuttal of the nineteenth-century historian Froude in his book *Froudacity*. *Froudacity* was first published in 1889 and has been reprinted by New Beacon Books in 1969. It is not my intention to review *Froudacity* at this time but rather to highlight the crux of the dispute between Froude and Thomas as I believe this will help to make clear the kind of historical stasis which has afflicted the Caribbean I would suggest for many generations.

The crux of the dispute between Froude and Thomas appears to me to have been set forth by C.L.R. James in his introduction to the 1969 republication of *Froudacity*.

In that introduction James quotes Froude as follows:

> In Egypt or India or one knows not where, accident or natural develop-
> ment quickened into life our moral and intellectual faculties; and these
> faculties have grown into what we now experience, not in the freedom in
> which the modern takes delight, but under the sharp rule of the strong
> over the weak, the wise over the unwise.

James then goes on to say that Thomas now 'has him [Froude] in the historical prison in which he had placed himself, and he [Thomas] overwhelms the great historian.' This overwhelming rebuttal, as James sees it, springs from Thomas' insight into a controlling law of history in contradistinction to Froude's emphasis on the dicey, accidental character of nature and society. In fact James sums it up in this way: 'What is important is not the difference in tone and temper of the two writers. It is that Thomas bases himself on a sense of history which he defines as a controlling *law*. And if you have no sense of historical law, then anything is what you choose to make it, and history almost automatically becomes not only nonsense, i.e. has no sense but is usually a defence of property and privilege, which is exactly what Froude has made of it.'

The question nevertheless arises – Does Thomas' stress on Law – as C.L.R. James implies – dispense with Froude?

In order to answer this let us look first of all a little more closely at Froude's position and after that come back to Thomas.

As I read Froude I am reminded of a certain dilemma which was put brilliantly by Darwin in his *Descent of Man*. Darwin begins by speaking of the horns of certain beetles then he moves on to look at crests and knobs on other creatures.

> The extraordinary size of the horns, and their widely different structure in closely allied forms, indicate that they have been formed for some important purpose: but their excessive variability in the males of the same species leads to the inference that this purpose cannot be of a definite nature. The horns do not show marks of friction, as if used for ordinary work. Some authors suppose that as the males wander much more than the females, they require horns as a defence against their enemies; but in many cases the horns do not seem well adapted for defence . . . The most obvious conjecture is that they are used by the males for fighting together; but they have never been observed to fight, nor could Mr Bates, after a careful examination of numerous species, find any sufficient evidence in their mutilated or broken condition of their having been thus used . . . The conclusion which best agrees with the fact of the horns having been so immensely yet not so fixedly developed – as shown by their extreme variability in the same species and by their extreme diversity in closely allied species – is that they have been acquired as ornaments. This view will at first appear extremely improbable; but we shall hereafter find with many animals, standing much higher in the scale, namely fishes, amphibians, reptiles and birds, that various kinds of crests, knobs and horns have been developed apparently for this sole purpose.

This ornamental stasis with implications that point to the wasteland – to excess baggage from cradle to grave – depicts rather ironically but accurately Froude's relationship to property as something so sovereign, so accidental, so fortuitous, it serves to eclipse all sensibility. Such an eclipse of sensibility may well be an omen of an age in which, not long before, the person had been property (slave property). And this area of eclipse of sensibility held Froude unwittingly, I would imagine, in its toils – in its historical prison. Indeed it is in this way, in terms of sovereign object or prison – eclipse of the person in slave property – eclipse of the resources of sensibility – that I find myself re-reading James' remark (re-reading it with a different slant, in a different way, I must confess) that history makes non-sense or no-sense, non-sensibility or no-sensibility.

Froude's defence of property – property implying both flesh-and-blood (in the fetish of the slave) as well as inanimate conviction (the world of things) – was a historical prison and Froude – as prisoner of his age – may well have taken a malicious and pessimistic view of nature and society. The world of objects, the world of achievement for him – in its ornamental stasis – was fortuitous, dicey (and therefore fundamentally precarious, fundamentally inclined to be wasteful or purposeless) and the human person was an object to be measured, validated, pronounced fit or unfit in an economic ruling context. Froude therefore could see no merit in change. He prized stability as so fortuitous, so accidental that any society which 'worked', which held itself together in some shape or form should be safe-guarded against change. In this context, Anglo-West Indian Society of the nineteenth century appeared to him to 'work', to hold itself together. Froude distrusted change since in his estimation everything was so dicey, so fortuitously consolidated that change, in fact, was likely to rob it of any conservative historical shape it already possessed.

All of Froude's biases and aberrations in his reports on the Caribbean sprang, I would suggest, from this central dilemma. A dilemma we have not yet solved and which presses in on us – in the late twentieth century – in many forms. It resides at the heart of economic fascism wherever this is practised. Rhodesia and South Africa are glaring examples.

And now I would like to return to Thomas. When C.L.R. James says with brilliant polemic that Thomas overwhelmed the great historian Froude I take it he means that Thomas broke out of Froude's prison of history by visualizing a law in contradistinction to a philosophy of fortuitous achievement, dicey establishment, realm of accident.

But (with all due respect to C.L.R. James) we must ask ourselves – Did Thomas really achieve such a breakthrough? The answer to this may well lie in the way Thomas wrestled with the law in terms of the existing magistracy of his day and in terms of various Governors of Trinidad and other nineteenth-century figures.

It is here that – beyond a shadow of doubt – the unwitting irony of Thomas' book is laid bare. For the scale of *Froudacity* upon which Thomas measures his magistrates and governors is consistent with a comedy of manners. In that comedy of manners the law consolidates itself – as a just instrument – around noble or benevolent figures which include Chief Justice Reeves of Barbados, certain good and conscientious Governors of Trinidad and Gordon of Khartoum. On the other hand it consolidates itself into a bad instrument around bad magistrates, Governors etc. Because of these fluctuations in Thomas' comedy of manners the law comes into close *rapport* with Froude's ornament and ironically reinforces fortuitous idols on the side of heaven or on the side of hell.

According to Thomas, had such-and-such a Governor remained things might have been different. Had such-and-such a Governor never arrived things likewise might have been different. In the same token in the twentieth century had Kennedy not been assassinated things might have been different in the United States. In short, Thomas' wrestle with the Law would seem to consolidate a fortuitous destiny or ornament of history.

In support of what I have been saying let us look at the implications in these key passages in Thomas' *Froudacity*.

It is almost superfluous to repeat that the skin-discriminating policy

induced as regards the coloured subjects of the Queen since the abolition of slavery did not, and could not, operate when coloured and white
stood on the same high level as slave owners and ruling potentates in the
colony.

Thomas expands on this in the following:

> History, as against the hard and fast White-master and Black-slave
> theory so recklessly invented and confidently built upon by Mr Froude,
> would show incontestably – (a) that for upwards of 200 years before the
> Negro Emancipation in 1838, there had never existed in one of those
> then British colonies . . . any prohibition whatsoever, on the ground of
> race or colour, against the owning of slaves by any free person possessing
> the necessary means, and desirous of doing so; (b) that as a consequence
> of this non-restriction, numbers of blacks, half-breeds, and other
> non-Europeans, besides such of them as had become possessed of their
> 'property' by inheritance, availed themselves of this virtual license, and
> in course of time constituted a very considerable proportion of the slave-
> holding section of those communities; (c) that these dusky plantation
> owners enjoyed and used in every possible sense the identical rights and
> privileges which were enjoyed and used by their pure-blooded Caucasian
> brother-slave-owners. The above statements are attested by written
> documents, oral traditions, and better still perhaps, by the living pres-
> ence in those islands of numerous lineal representatives of those once
> opulent and flourishing non-European planter-families.

According to Thomas, therefore, it would appear that with the decline of
capital 'slave-property' – with the decline of investment in human persons
owned by blacks and whites alike – a hard and fast White-master and Black-slave-
substitute theory came into force. This theory high-lighted pigmentation differences as never before as part and parcel of the ornament of society to which the
law conformed. In short, the whole society remained an economic commodity
though this time a new sophistication, pigmentation, came into force.

Thomas is not an apologist for slavery – in fact he indicts slavery with great
passion – but the trap into which he falls is in most ways identical to the stasis (the
stasis of ornament, of property as accident, as fortuitous establishment or comedy of manners) to which Froude conforms. Froude and Thomas, in this respect,
were children of the nineteenth century and neither possessed the genius to
penetrate intuitively or otherwise the ironic trap of the ornament, of the prison
of the wasteland.

Clearly Thomas failed to deepen the ornament of his age in such a way that
unpredictable intuitive resources would affect the *prison* of the object and therefore the *person* of the object. *Prison* and *person* had become locked together as
uniform property and both Thomas and Froude played on this synonymous

condition in their individual comedy of manners. This meant, in fact, that Thomas – passionate as he felt about objects of injustice – could not supply a figurative meaning beyond the condition he deplored.

It is my view therefore that Thomas does not really overwhelm Froude. The duel which they fought is nevertheless a very instructive one in pointing up the historical stasis which afflicts the West Indian sensibility and which may only be breached in complex creative perspectives for which the historical convention would appear to possess no criteria. Oddly enough James ends his introduction to *Froudacity* with a quotation from Merleau-Ponty which helps to make the view I have been expressing more clear: 'The act of the artist or philosopher is free, but not motiveless. Their freedom . . . consists in appropriating a *de facto* situation by endowing it with a figurative meaning beyond its real one.'

In this connection we must note that both Thomas and Froude shared a common suspicion of Haitian vodun and other primitive manifestations which signified for them a 'relapse into obeahism, devil-worship and children-eating'. Therefore they consolidated an intellectual censorship of significant vestiges of the subconscious imagination which they needed to explore if they were to begin to apprehend a figurative meaning beyond the real or apparently real world.

It is my intention to concentrate in some degree on those vestiges as part and parcel of the arts of the imagination. In this respect I believe the possibility exists for us to become involved in perspectives of renascence which can bring into play a figurative meaning beyond an apparently real world or prison of history.

I want to make as clear as I can that a cleavage exists in my opinion between the historical convention in the Caribbean and Guianas and the arts of the imagination. I believe a philosophy of history may well lie buried in the arts of the imagination. Needless to say I have no racial biases and whether my emphasis falls on limbo or vodun, on Carib bush-baby omens, on Arawak zemi, on Latin, English inheritances – in fact within and beyond these emphases – my concern is with epic stratagems available to Caribbean man in the dilemmas of history which surround him.

There are two kinds of myths related to Africa in the Caribbean and Guianas. One kind seems fairly direct, the other has clearly undergone metamorphosis. In fact even the direct kind of myth has suffered a 'sea-change' of some proportions. In an original sense, therefore, these myths which reflect an African link in the Caribbean are also part and parcel of a native West Indian imagination and therefore stand, in some important ways I feel, in curious *rapport* with vestiges of Amerindian fable* and legend.

Let us start with a myth stemming from Africa which has undergone meta-morphosis. The one which I have in mind is called limbo. The limbo dance is a well known feature in the Carnival life of the West Indies today though it is still subject to intellectual censorship as I shall explain as I go along in this paper. The

---

* Fable and myth are employed as variables of the imagination in this essay.

limbo dancer moves under a bar which is gradually lowered until a mere slit of space, it seems, remains through which with spreadeagled limbs he passes like a spider.

Limbo was born, it is said, on the slave ships of the Middle Passage. There was so little space that the slaves contorted themselves into human spiders. Limbo, therefore, as Edward Brathwaite, the distinguished Barbadian-born poet, has pointed out is related to anancy or spider fables. If I may now quote from *Islands*, the last book in his trilogy –

> drum stick knock
> and the darkness is over me
> knees spread wide
> and the water is hiding me
> *limbo*
> *limbo like me*

But there is something else in the limbo–anancy syndrome which, as far as I am aware, is overlooked though intuitively immersed perhaps in Edward Brathwaite's poems, and that is the curious dislocation of a chain of miles reflected in the dance so that a re-trace of the Middle Passage from Africa to the Americas and the West Indies is not to be equated with a uniform sum. Not only has the journey from the Old World to the new varied with each century and each method of transport but needs to be re-activated in the imagination as a limbo perspective when one dwells on the Middle Passage: a limbo gateway between Africa and the Caribbean.

In fact here, I feel, we begin to put our finger on something which is close to the inner universality of Caribbean man. Those waves of migration which have hit the shores of the Americas – North, Central and South – century after century have, at various times, possessed the stamp of the spider metamorphosis, in the refugee flying from Europe or in the indentured East Indian and Chinese from Asia.

Limbo then reflects a certain kind of gateway to or threshold of a new world and the dislocation of a chain of miles. It is – in some ways – the archetypal sea-change stemming from Old Worlds and it is legitimate, I feel, to pun on limbo as a kind of shared phantom limb which has become a subconscious variable in West Indian theatre. The emergence of formal West Indian theatre was pre-ceded, I suggest, by that phantom limb which manifested itself on Boxing Day after Christmas when the ban on the 'rowdy' bands (as they were called) was lifted for the festive season.

I recall performances I witnessed as a boy in Georgetown, British Guiana, in the early 1930s. Some of the performers danced on high stilts like elongated limbs while others performed spreadeagled on the ground. In this way limbo spider and stilted pole of the gods were related to the drums like grassroots and branches of lightning to the sound of thunder.

Sometimes it was an atavistic spectacle and it is well known that these bands

157

were suspected by the law of subversive political stratagems. But it is clear that the dance had no political or propaganda motives though, as with any folk manifestation, it could be manipulated by demagogues. The whole situation is complex and it is interesting to note that Rex Nettleford in an article entitled 'The Dance as an Art Form – Its Place in the West Indies' (which appears in *Caribbean Quarterly*, March–June 1968) has this to say: 'Of all the arts, dance is probably the most neglected. The art form continues to elude many of the most intuitive in an audience, including the critics.'

It has taken us a couple of generations to begin – just *begin* – to perceive, in this phenomenon, an activation of subconscious and sleeping resources in the phantom limb of dismembered slave and god. An activation which possesses a nucleus of great promise – of far-reaching new poetic synthesis.

For limbo (one cannot emphasize this too much) is not the total recall of an African past since that African past in terms of tribal sovereignty or sovereignties was modified or traumatically eclipsed with the Middle Passage and with generations of change that followed. Limbo was rather the renascence of a new corpus of sensibility that could translate and accommodate African and other legacies within a new architecture of cultures. For example, the theme of the phantom limb – the re-assembly of dismembered man or god – possesses archetypal resonances that embrace Egyptian Osiris, the resurrected Christ, and the many-armed deity of India.

In this context it is interesting to note that limbo – which emerged as a novel re-assembly out of the stigmata of the Middle Passage – is related to Haitian vodun in the sense that Haitian vodun (though possessing a direct link with African vodun which I shall describe later on) also seeks to accommodate new Catholic features in its constitution of the muse.

It is my view – a deeply considered one – that this ground of accommodation, this art of creative coexistence – pointing away from apartheid and ghetto fixations – is of the utmost importance and native to the Caribbean, perhaps to the Americas as a whole. It is still, in most respects, a latent syndrome and we need to look not only at limbo or vodun but at Amerindian horizons as well – shamanistic and rain-making vestiges and the dancing bush-baby legends of the ancient Caribs which began to haunt them as they crouched over their campfires under the Spanish yoke.

Insufficient attention has been paid to such phenomena and the original native capacity these implied as omens of rebirth. Many historians have been intent on indicting the Old World of Europe by exposing a uniform pattern of imperialism in the New World of the Americas. Thus they conscripted the West Indies into a mere adjunct of imperialism and overlooked a subtle and far-reaching renascence. In a sense therefore the new historian – though his stance is an admirable one in debunking imperialism – has ironically extended and reinforced old colonial prejudices which censored the limbo imagination as a 'rowdy' manifestation and overlooked the complex metaphorical gateway it constitutes in *rapport* with Amerindian omen.

Later on I intend to explore the Amerindian gateways between cultures which began obscurely and painfully to witness (long before limbo or vodun or the Middle Passage) to a native suffering community steeped in caveats of conquest. At this point I shall merely indicate that these gateways exist as part and parcel of an original West Indian architecture which it is still possible to create if we look deep into the rubble of the past, and that these Amerindian features enhance the limbo assembly with which we are now engaged – the spider syndrome and phantom limb of the gods arising in Negro fable and legend.

I used the word 'architecture' a moment or two ago because I believe this is a valid approach to a gateway society as well as to a community which is involved in an original re-constitution or re-creation of variables of myth and legend in the wake of stages of conquest.

First of all the limbo dance becomes the human gateway which dislocates (and therefore begins to free itself from) a uniform chain of miles across the Atlantic. This dislocation or interior space serves therefore as a corrective to a uniform cloak or documentary stasis of imperialism. The journey across the Atlantic for the forebears of West Indian man involved a new kind of space – inarticulate as this new 'spatial' character was at the time – and not simply an unbroken schedule of miles in a log book. Once we perceive this inner corrective to historical documentary and protest literature which sees the West Indies as utterly deprived, or gutted by exploitation, we begin to participate in the genuine possibilities of original change available to a people severely disadvantaged (it is true) at a certain point in time.

The limbo dance therefore implies, I believe, a profound art of compensation which seeks to re-play a dismemberment of tribes (note again the high stilted legs of some of the performers and the spider-anancy masks of others running close to the ground) and to invoke at the same time a curious psychic re-assembly of the parts of the dead god or gods. And that re-assembly which issued from a state of cramp to articulate a new growth – and to point to the necessity for a new kind of drama, novel and poem – is a creative phenomenon of the first importance in the imagination of a people violated by economic fates.

One cannot over-emphasize, I believe, how original this phenomenon was. So original it aroused both incomprehension and suspicion in the intellectual and legal administrations of the land (I am thinking in particular of the first half of the twentieth century though one can, needless to say, go much farther back). What is bitterly ironic – as I have already indicated – is that present day historians in the second half of the twentieth century, militant and critical of imperialism as they are, have fallen victim, in another sense, to the very imperialism they appear to denounce. They have no criteria for arts of originality springing out of an age of limbo and the history they write is without an inner time. This historical refusal to see – this consolidation of an incomprehension of the past – may well be at the heart of the Terrified Consciousness which a most significant critic to emerge in the West Indies at this time, Kenneth Ramchand, analyses brilliantly in his essay in the *Journal of Commonwealth Literature* (West Indies number) July 1969 (published by Heinemann and the University of Leeds). One point which Kenneth Ramchand did not stress in his essay – but which is implicit in what he calls the 'nightmare' in Jean Rhys' novel *Wide Sargasso Sea* – is that Antoinette is mad Bertha in *Jane Eyre* and that Jean Rhys, intuitively rather than intentionally, is attempting to compensate a historical portrait of the West Indian creole – to bridge the gap, as it were, between an outer frame and an inner desolation. It is this that sharpens the pathos of her novel and makes for that terrified consciousness which Ramchand sees now as a universal heritage.

It is this cleavage between a statistical frame and the inner portrait of reality that makes for unwitting irony in the so-called new emancipated writer and Gerald Moore in his new book, *The Chosen Tongue* (published by Longmans, 1969), brings it into sharp focus when he states –

> Both M.G. Smith, the Jamaican anthropologist, and V.S. Naipaul appear to believe that the West Indies possesses no genuine inner cohesion whatever and no internal source of power. Having no common interests to cement them, the inhabitants of the area can be held together only by external force. Professor Elsa Goveia reaches an opposite but equally depressing conclusion. She argues that the West Indies had one integrating factor historically, and this has been 'the acceptance of the inferiority of Negroes to the Whites'.

In this context it is illuminating to recall that Froude was doing on behalf of imperialism what many contemporary historians are doing in a protest against imperialism. Namely he, too, set out to demonstrate that the West Indies had no creative potential. His view sprang out of the arrogance of the nineteenth century civilized European whereas theirs would appear to spring out of what Martin Carter, the distinguished Guyanese poet, calls the 'self-contempt' of the exploited, formerly indentured or enslaved, West Indian. Such a dead-end of history in which nineteenth-century imperialist and twentieth-century anti-imperialist come into agreement is material for a theatre of the absurd.

I believe that the limbo imagination of the folk involved a crucial inner re-creative response to the violations of slavery and indenture and conquest, and needed its critical or historical correlative, its critical or historical advocacy. This was not forthcoming since the historical instruments of the past clustered around an act of censorship and of suspicion of folk-obscurity as well as originality, and that inbuilt arrogance or suspicion continues to motivate a certain order of critical writing in the West Indies today.

Capitalism and Slavery (a brilliant and impressive formal thesis of research written when he was at Oxford by Eric Williams, who became Prime Minister of Trinidad) would seem to be the model British West Indian historians have elected. And I must now draw to your attention something which, I believe, confirms my view of the inbuilt censor in West Indian historical convention. Professor Elsa Goveia regards Dr Williams as 'the most influential writer on West

Indian history to emerge from the West Indies during the present century'. Yet in an article entitled 'New Shibboleths For Old' (appearing in *New Beacon Reviews*, Collection 1, 1968) she has this to say of his recent work –

> In spite of all Dr Williams' protestations about the need for cultivating a West Indian inspiration, in spite even of his own authorship of *A History of the People of Trinidad and Tobago*, can the reader be expected to draw any other conclusion than that a West Indian subject-matter is somehow worthless? Dr Williams cannot have it both ways. If he ignores or devalues writers because they write about the West Indies rather than about other subjects, then he is perpetuating the very attitudes of mind which have in the past led to the neglect of West Indian studies which he himself constantly condemns. The combination of omissions and hasty dogmatism which mars his present book will not remedy the unhappy conditions which have for so long retarded the development of our understanding of 'the unique antecedents of the people of the West Indies'.

This I fear is lamentably true. Until the gap is visualized, understood and begins to close, the West Indian historian and anthropologist will continue to reinforce a high-level psychological censorship of the creative imagination and to consolidate a foreboding about the risks involved in every free election of spirits.

As such the very institutions of the day will become increasingly rigged by fear and misgiving, and political deterioration is the inevitable corollary. And this indicates to me that in the absence of a historical correlative to the arts of the dispossessed, some kind of new critical writing in depth needs to emerge to bridge the gap between history and art. Denis Williams stated the dilemma very effectively in 'Image and Idea in the Arts of Guyana' (The Edgar Mittelholzer Memorial Lectures, second series, January 1969, published by the National History and Arts Council of Guyana). I now quote –

> Yet the first fact of the Caribbean situation is the fact of miscegenation, of mongrelism. What are the cultural implications of this mongrel con-dition? It is important to have experienced the homogeneity, richness, the integrity of the racially thoroughbred cultures of the Old World in order properly to take the force of this question. It is important if only as a means of discriminating between our condition and theirs, of assessing the nature and status of our mongrel culture when contrasted with the cultures of the thoroughbred, of realising the nature and function of the ancestor as he determines our cultural destiny. For we are all shaped by our past; the imperatives of a contemporary culture are predominantly those of a relationship to this past. Yet in the Caribbean and in Guyana we think and behave as though we have no past, no history, no culture.

And where we do come to take notice of our history it is often in the light of biases adopted from one thoroughbred culture or another, of the Old World. We permit ourselves the luxury, for one thing, of racial dialectics in our interpretation of Caribbean and Guyanese history and culture. In the light of what we are this is a destructive thing to do, since at best it perpetuates what we might call a filialistic dependence on the cultures of our several racial origins, while simultaneously inhibiting us from facing up to the facts of what we uniquely are.

I would now like to resume the earlier thread of my argument in the dance of the folk – the human limbo or gateway of the gods – which was disregarded or incomprehensible to an intellectual and legal and historical convention. I had begun to point out that, first of all, the limbo dance becomes the human gateway which dislocates (and therefore begins to free itself from) a uniform chain of miles. In this context I also suggested that the gateway complex is also the psychic assembly or re-assembly of the muse of a people. This brings me now to my second point about limbo, namely, that it shares its phantom limb with Haitian vodun across an English/French divide of Caribbean cultures. This is a matter of great interest, I believe, because Haitian vodun is more directly descended from African myth and yet – like limbo which is a metamorphosis or new spatial character born of the Middle Passage – it is also intent on a curious re-assembly of the god or gods. Therefore I ask myself – is vodun a necessary continuation of a matrix of association which had not fulfilled itself in the Old World of Africa? If so that fulfilment would be in itself not an imitation of the past – much as it is indebted to the past – but a new and daring creative conception in itself.

If Haitian vodun is a creative fulfilment of African vodun one must ask oneself where do the similarities and differences lie. The basic feature they hold in common lies in 'possession trances' – trance features, I may add, which are not the case with limbo.

Pierre Verger in an essay appearing in *Spirit Mediumship and Society in Africa* (published by Routledge and Kegan Paul, 1969) writes –

> Possession trances occur regularly among the Nago-Yoruba and Fon people of Dahomey during rites for orisha and vodun . . . They are the culmination of an elaborate ritual sequence. Seen from the participant's point of view, such trances are the reincarnations of family deities in the bodies of their descendants – reincarnations which have taken place in response to the offerings, prayers, and wishes of their worshippers.

In a footnote to his essay he defines orisha and vodun as: 'The general names given by the Yoruba and Dahomean people respectively to the deities worshipped by them. They are generally considered to be the very remote ancestors who dealt during their lifetime with some force of nature, and who can still do so on behalf of their worshippers.'

Pierre Verger has been speaking here of African vodun. I would like now to give my definition of Haitian vodun which appears in *Tradition, The Writer and Society* (New Beacon Publications, 1967) as this will help me, in parenthesis, to unravel certain similarities and differences in African and Haitian vodun and to look back afresh at the significance of the human limbo gateway.

Haitian vodun or voodoo is a highly condensed feature of inspiration and hallucination within which 'space' itself becomes the sole expression and recollection of the dance – as if 'space' is the character of the dance – since the celebrants themselves are soon turned into 'objects' – into an architecture of movement like 'deathless' flesh, wood or stone. And such deathless flesh, wood or stone (symbolic of the dance of creation) subsists – in the very protean reality of space – on its own losses (symbolic decapitation of wood, symbolic truncation of stone) so that the very void of sensation in which the dancer begins to move, like an authentic spectre or structure of fiction, makes him or her insensible to all conventional props of habit and responsive only to a grain of frailty or light support.

Remember at the outset the dancer regards himself or herself as one in full command of two legs, a pair of arms, until, possessed by the muse of contraction, he or she dances into a posture wherein one leg is drawn up into the womb of space. He stands like a rising pole upheld by earth and sky or like a tree which walks in its shadow or like a one-legged bird which joins itself to its sleeping reflection in a pool. All conventional memory is erased and yet in this trance of overlapping spheres or reflection a primordial or deeper function of memory begins to exercise itself within the bloodstream of space.

Haitian vodun is one of the surviving primitive dances of sacrifice, which, in courting a subconscious community, sees its own performance in transgressive terms – that is, with and through the eyes of 'space': with and through the sculpture of sleeping things which the dancer himself actually expresses and becomes. For in fact the dancer moves in a trance and the interior mode of the drama is exteriorized into a medium inseparable from his trance and invocation. He is a dramatic agent of subconsciousness. The life from within and the life from without now truly overlap. That is the intention of the dance, the riddle of the dancer.

The importance which resides in all this, I suggest, is remarkable. For if the trance were a purely subjective thing – without action or movement – some would label it fantasy. But since it exteriorizes itself, it becomes an intense drama of images in space, which may assume elastic limbs and proportions or shrink into a dense current of reflection on the floor. For what emerges are the relics of a primordial fiction where the images of space are seen as in an abstract painting. That such a drama has indeed a close bearing on the language of fiction, on the language of art, seems to me incontestable. The community the writer shares with the primordial dancer is, as it were, the complementary halves of a broken stage. For the territory upon which the poet visualizes a drama of consciousness is a slow revelation or unravelling of obscurity – revelation or illumination within oneself; whereas the territory of the dancer remains actually obscure to him within his trance whatever revelation or illumination his limbs may articulate in their involuntary theme. The 'vision' of the poet (when one comprehends it from the opposite pole of 'dance') possesses a 'spatial' logic or 'convertible' property of the imagination. Herein lies the essential humility of a certain kind of self-consciousness within which occurs *the partial erasure, if nothing more, of the habitual boundaries of prejudice.*

I have quoted rather extensively here from my previous essay because I think this may help us to see in rapport with Pierre Verger's definition of African vodun that while the trance similarity is clear, the functions have begun to differ. Haitian vodun – like West Indian and Guianese/Brazilian limbo – may well point to sleeping possibilities of drama and horizons of poetry, epic and novel, sculpture and painting – in short to a language of variables in art which would have a profoundly evolutionary cultural and philosophical significance for Caribbean man. Such new resources (if I may diverge for a brief moment and speak as someone whose chosen tongue is English) are not foreign to English poetry except in the sense that these may be closer to the 'metaphysical poets' – to a range and potency of association in which nothing is ultimately alien – of which Eliot speaks in his famous essay on 'dissociation of sensibility'.

Such a variable emphasis is outside the boundaries of intention in African vodun which is a conservative medium or cloak of ancestors. The gulf therefore between an inbuilt uniform censor and the imagination of a new art which exists in the British West Indies, in particular, is absent in Africa. African vodun is a school of ancestors: it is very conservative. Something of this conservative focus remains very strongly in Haitian vodun but there is an absorption of new elements which breaks the tribal monolith of the past and re-assembles an inter-tribal or cross-cultural community of families.

The term *loa*, for example, which means *spirit* or *deity* is of Bantu origin – not Yoruba or Dahomean, the tribal homes (some say) of vodun. Furthermore (I now quote from Harold Courlander's *Vodun in Haitian Culture* published by the Institute for Cross-Cultural Research, Washington):

The various cults encompassed by the term Vodoun in its larger sense are not easy to set down diagramatically because of different degrees of blending and absorption in different regions of Haiti. Had the old cults or 'nations' remained independent of one another, as they probably were in early days, they probably would have included the following: Arada (Dahomey or Fon), Anago (Yoruba), Mahi, Ibo, Kanga, Congo (including

Moundongue, Solongo, Bumba, etc., or these elements also might have maintained independence), and Petro (a cult in the African pattern that appears to have originated in Haiti). In certain parts of Haiti one still finds Ibo, Congo, and Nago cults that have resisted absorption, but this pattern does not hold for most of the country . . . There has been intrusion of Catholic practices and doctrine into Vodoun. Many of the *Loa* are identified with Catholic saints.

Elsewhere Courlander has this to say – 'Vodoun has perhaps the same meaning to some Haitian leaders as astrology to some leaders in India.'

All in all – while it is true that the role of Haitian vodun or vodoun is part and parcel of a prophetic and esoteric perspective in the Haitian body politic – the strict collective traditional sanction which belongs to Africa has varied in a manner comparable in some degree to the cleavage we have noted between history and art in the British West Indies.

I could not help noting this passage in Courlander's essay –

The question of Vodoun's influence in politics in earlier days is blurred or distorted for a variety of reasons. European writers sometimes were unaware of Vodoun as a genuine religious pattern common to the entire nation, and, as we have noted, frequently delighted in depicting the superstitious character of the people. Haitian historians of the past were sensitive to the charge that the country was overrun with pagan rites, and they largely avoided mention of Vodoun. Little on the subject is likely to be found in government archives for much the same reason.

It is my assumption, in the light of all the foregoing, that a certain rapport exists between Haitian Vodun and West Indian limbo which suggests an epic potential or syndrome of variables. That epic potential, I believe, may supply the nerve-end of authority which is lacking at the moment in the conventional stance of history.

But we need to examine this with the greatest care in order to assess and appreciate the risks involved.

In the first place the limbo imagination of the West Indies possesses no formal or collective sanction as in an old Tribal World. Therefore the gateway complex between cultures implies a new catholic unpredictable threshold which places a far greater emphasis on the integrity of the individual imagination. And it is here that we see, beyond a shadow of doubt, the necessity for the re-visionary, profoundly courageous, open-spirited and receptive artist of conscience whose evolution out of the folk as poet, novelist, painter is a symbol of risk, a symbol of inner integrity.

With African vodun – as we have seen – the integrity of the tribal person was one with a system which was conservative and traditional. There was no breath of subversion – no cleavage in the collective. History and art were one medium.

With Guyanese/West Indian limbo that cleavage is a fact and the rise of the imaginative arts has occurred in the face of long-held intellectual and legal suspicion. Therefore the rise of the poet or artist incurs a gamble of the soul which is symbolized in the West Indian trickster (the spider or anancy configuration). It is this element of tricksterdom that creates an individual and personal risk absolutely foreign to the conventional sanction of an Old Tribal World: a risk which identifies him (the artist) with the submerged authority of dispossessed peoples but requires of him, in the same token, alchemic resources to conceal, as well as elaborate, a far-reaching order of the imagination which, being suspect, could draw down upon him a crushing burden of censorship in economic or political terms. He stands therefore at the heart of the lie of community and the truth of community. And it is here, I believe, in this trickster gateway – this gamble of the soul – that there emerges the hope for a profoundly compassionate society committed to freedom within a creative scale.

I would like to re-emphasize the roles of 'epic' and 'trickster'. The epic of limbo holds out a range of variables – variables of community in the cross-cultural tie of dispossessed tribes or families – variables of art in a consciousness of links between poetry and drama, image and novel, architecture and sculpture and painting – which need to be explored in the Caribbean complex situation of apparent 'historylessness'. And furthermore in the Americas as a whole, it would seem to me that the apparent void of history which haunts the black man may never be compensated until an act of imagination opens gateways between civilizations, between technological and spiritual apprehensions, between racial possessions and dispossessions in the way the *Aeneid* may stand symbolically as one of the first epics of migration and re-settlement beyond the pale of an ancient world. Limbo and vodun are variables of an underworld imagination – variables of phantom limb and void and a nucleus of stratagems in which limb is a legitimate pun on limbo, void on vodun.

The trickster of limbo holds out a caveat we must reckon with in our present unstable situation. It is the caveat of conscience and points to the necessity for a free imagination which is at risk on behalf of a truth that is no longer given in the collective medium of the tribe. The emergence of original works of art is consistent with – and the inevitable corollary of – an evolution of folk limbo into symbols of inner cunning and authority which reflect a long duress of the imagination.

13

THE AMERINDIAN LEGACY

The cleavage which we have observed between history and art in respect of the Negro in the Caribbean (as indeed in respect of all races – Indian from India, Chinese, Portuguese etc., all of whom have become original participants in limbo and Carnival) – takes on even greater proportions with the Amerindian.

One has only to glance at census figures, for example in Guiana in the middle of this century. Amerindians were excluded from the population and their numbers given as an historical aside.

Hand in hand with this statistical ghetto goes a documentary stasis of Amerindian cultures. I would like to draw your attention to a recent pamphlet entitled 'The Amerindians in St. Lucia' by the Rev. C. Jesse published by the St Lucia Archaeological and Historical Society, 1968. Father Jesse speaks of the Caribs as 'resorting particularly to the cannibalism for which they were notorious'.

He also refers to

> Shamans who acted as intermediaries of evil spirits. From serious accounts left by early missionaries, it would seem proved that the shamans dealt with the Devil and were at times possessed by him. In general the Caribs of the West Indies surrounded themselves with super-stitious practices from the cradle to the grave.

In regard to the Arawaks he writes

> In the way of religion, the Arawaks seem to have specialised in zemis or small idols. These objects were supposed to be dwelling places for the spirits of nature and the spirits of their ancestors to reside. Each person, according to Dr Rouse, had one zemi at least, sometimes as many as ten: the idols had the form of grotesque human beings, turtles, lizards, birds, potatoes, and manioc; some even were of geometric design. Needless to say the cult of the zemi was associated with gross superstition.

It is revealing – as another symptom of the cleavage between history and art at which we have been looking – that an organisation which describes itself as an 'historical society' should sponsor and publish in the year 1968 Father Jesse's biases. Clearly the historical assumptions and prison in which Frazer wrote *The Golden Bough* have scarcely begun to thaw in the West Indies. And this in spite of the researches of scholars such as Mircea Eliade and Lévi-Strauss; in spite of a genuine renascence of sensibility which has erupted into the work of the gifted Guianese-born painter Aubrey Williams through Amerindian symbols; in spite of the new winds of scholarship blowing through the work of others such as Rev. Father Placide Tempels.

I would like to say something briefly about Aubrey Williams's paintings before I move on. There is no other painter from the Caribbean, to my knowledge, who has attempted (as Aubrey Williams has) to interpret the sensibility of the Amerindian with colour.

It is my view that this use of colour is a poetic and liberating device. One recalls a famous poet who saw *colours* within the vowel structure of a poem. More pertinent – in this context – is the kind of *light* which seems to glow or expand in Turner and in a different way, in Van Gogh: in another way still in an Australian painter like Nolan or in the work of the American Jackson Pollock.

In fact paintings which intuitively or intentionally make colour a character of metamorphosis are involved in the elements as a peculiar, often fantastic scale. There is a musical intimation (which I find in Williams' use of colour – a brooding, sometimes savage undercurrent of music). But here is another aspect to Aubrey Williams's paintings. Amerindian peoples – for one reason or another – have been decimated. Therefore a translation of the blood of the past into the scale of the elements is consistent with the character of 'space' – the theme of 'space' – re-assembly, re-constitution of the muse – which we explored previously in terms of subconscious and unconscious variables in Negro Guianese/West Indian limbo and Haitian vodun.

In this sense, I see Aubrey Williams as a painter of renascence who has been affected in an original way by an Amerindian 'resurrection' as Edward Brathwaite, for example, has been affected in an original way by an African 'resurrection'.

Let us look, first of all, at the cannibal horizon of the extinct Caribs which Father Jesse labels 'notorious'. Michael Swan takes a different view. His isn't a searching analysis but he indicates certain signposts which are useful. In the cannibal horizon he hints at 'transubstantiation in reverse' and points out that the accusations levelled by the Spaniards were largely a smoke-screen for their own excesses. Excesses, I believe, partly compounded and projected out of their own Catholic Spanish psyche of heaven and hell. Therefore, whatever inner fiends the savage Caribs truly possessed as pre-Columbian conquerors of the ancient West Indies and Guianas – these were irrelevent to the Spaniards who were incapable of assessing the Carib genius and psyche or the brooding melancholy of Carib temperament and wished to find merely ready made black devils in the New World consistent with the ornamental surfaces of Latin symbolism.

Such a gateway complex between pre-Columbian primitive and ornamental

Latin symbolism carries within it, nevertheless, a new latent capacity, a *caveat* or warning we need to ponder upon deeply and to unravel in our age. If we succumb to a blackhearted stasis – to enclosures of fear – we may destroy ourselves; on the other hand, if we begin to immerse ourselves in a new capacity or treaty of sensibility between alien cultures, we will bring into play a new variable imagination or renascence of sensibility steeped in *caveats* of the necessary diversity and necessary unity of man. In short, we won't oversimplify or crudify similarities or differences, but will seek, as it were, however difficult, even obscure, the path, to bring all perspectives available to us into an art of the imagination, an architecture of the imagination.

We know from investigations into the psychology of the victim (conducted for example in post-Hiroshima Japan) that it is he, the victim, very often, whose consciousness is infused with omens of the future (apocalyptic omens are often of this kind in a victor/victim syndrome.) It is as though the guilt of the victor stands on the threshold of a creative breakthrough in the darkening consciousness of the victim as prelude to the birthpangs of a new cosmos. It is not inconsistent, therefore, that we may discern, in the rubble of the Carib past, signs akin to a new ominous but renascent consciousness at the time of the Spanish conquest.

That new darkness or dawning renascence lay not simply in the ritual morsel of the enemy they devoured or the flute they fashioned from his bone, but from a sudden upsurge of bush-baby spectres which rose out of their cooking pots like wraiths of smoke or sparks of fire. Certain vestiges of legend – in this context – have come down to us and the bush-baby syndrome corresponds to a figure C.G. Jung calls the *puer aeternus* – the immortal or archetypal child of dreams.

If this is the case, we can look back at the Carib 'immortal child' of dreams with the aid of alchemical symbolism for which, as you may know, there are three stages, namely, first of all, the nigredo or blackness – sometimes called *massa confusa* or unknown territory (not to be equated superficially with the colour black, but with an undiscovered realm), second *albedo* or whiteness (again not to be equated superficially with the colour white since it means an inner perspective or illumination, the dawn of a new consciousness), third *cauda pavonis* or the colours of the peacock, which may be equated with all the variable possibilities or colours of fulfilment we can never totally realise.

The immortal wraith which the Caribs glimpsed, as they crouched over their campfires, and consumed a morsel of the enemy, carried therefore overtones of eclipse at the hands of Spain (akin to *nigredo*), overtones also of a new dawn (akin to *albedo*), and of a host native (akin to *cauda pavonis* or rainbow peacock). There was also the bone or flute they fashioned whose music has long faded but retains for us the seed of an unwritten modern symphony The only attempt as far as I am aware, to write a modern composition was made by Philip Pilgrim in the 1940s. He based his music on A.J. Seymour's *Legend of Kaieteur*. That music was largely in his head. It was his intention to put the full score on paper but he died within weeks of the first experimental performance he conducted in Georgetown before a generous and greatly enthusiastic audience. I wrote this before I knew that 'The Legend of Kaieteur' would achieve a 'resurrection' and that the skeleton bars of music Philip Pilgrim left behind would invoke a new response in a reconstructed score by Bill Pilgrim. Thus both A.J. Seymour's *Legend of Kaieteur* and Philip Pilgrim's music have been re-assembled into a joint classic within the gate of the Republic of Guyana.

To return to the main thread of my argument. The overtones and undertones of host native – of a native consciousness – could have occupied little more than a latent threshold in the Carib/Latin world of the sixteenth century. For that was an age whose over-riding character – as in the centuries to follow – remained rooted in notions of conquest. What I would suggest, however, is that this over-riding character of conquest (the Caribs themselves were conquerers of the ancient West Indies before Spain, England, France, Holland came on the scene) was in a state of subconscious erosion. And I also feel that this latent threshold – this inner erosion of a certain dominant mould or character of conquest – this inner secret of the native (inner divergence of the native from a consolidated given pattern which is the tyranny of history) is profoundly consistent with the originality of the Guianas and the Caribbean renascence of sensibility.

All this is implicit, I believe, in our cannibal horizon out of which *the wraith of time ascends like subsistence of memory*. I have often wondered whether the ritual of Guyanese and Caribbean hospitality (with its religious concern for the stranger) is not related obscurely to the theme we have been unravelling – the native or host consciousness.

This scale of the native as host consciousness is subtle and complex and involves both inner and outer horizons we may only have begun to perceive afresh in our age. The alchemical analogies I have chosen are not easily comprehensible. They may need, in fact, to come into rapport with a new anthropology capable of investigating the subconscious and unconscious mind of an age. For, we must remember, the whole syndrome was latent, unrealised in the West Indies from the Carib/Latin age to our day in spite of the Carnival host. Indeed this latency, this lack of realisation – except on Carnival occasions when the whole populace seems to have been devoured by a school of masks – may have been inevitable. For the raw material of life lived in the West Indies and the Central or South Americas has involved not only peoples from Asia, Africa, Europe who were alien to each other (and therefore caught, as it were, in culture shock) but situations of change (conquest, slavery, indenture, emancipation, etc.) which precipitated crises again and again in economic terms. Thus, in effect, the Carib or Carnival 'immortal child' was an inner omen which diverged from the immediate realism of the day. Such a divergence exposed latencies or sleeping resources. Those resources of inner divergence need to be converted in our age, I feel, into an original threshold in a Caribbean architecture of consciousness so that we may begin to cope within ourselves with the overburden or sheer raw material of life lived which has been our blanket realism for centuries in these parts.

170

In other words, it is not that the Caribbean and Guianas are at the rim of the world like a kind of gutted monster (as V. S. Naipaul and others see it) but rather I would suggest, that the waves of action stemming from many movements and continents since the European Renaissance have come so thick and fast that 'realism' becomes, in itself, a dead-end and the need begins to dawn for a drama of consciousness which reads back through the shock of place and time for omens of capacity, for thresholds of capacity that were latent, unrealised, within the clash of cultures and movements of peoples into the South Americas and the West Indies. Such an art of subsistence of memory involves, I feel, a kind of shroud at times or organ of obscurity we need to participate in as intrinsic to the arousal of illumination in perspectives of sleeping/awakening resources of the imagination.

To return to the Caribs. It is possible to read into the destiny of the Caribs something of the sleepwalker of history which became their lot in the wake of the Spanish conquest. They continued to remain bogged down in the overriding character of the age – they began to duplicate, on an inferior level, the role of conqueror they had played in pre-Columbian times: they became mercenaries or jungle-police of the Dutch and English. It was, in a way, a crowning indignity for a once proud people.

Thus the inroads inflicted on them by the Spanish Conquest never healed (perhaps we need to look even farther back into the pre-Columbian mind of the Caribs for the first causes of their downfall). There may have been a brooding death wish even before Spain arrived. With the dawn of the nineteenth century they were virtually extinct. Their 'immortal child' omens, compounded of morsel and flute, analogous to a prophecy of the birth of a native imagination that could absorb both conqueror and conquered in an everlasting spiritual tenant (or genius of place) remained a latent threshold they never crossed – and assumed, as a consequence, inner proportions we would describe today as a nervous breakdown.

The process of shamanism resembles a nervous breakdown. The shaman, as we know, is likely to appear in the tribe in times of crisis, and his role – far from being 'gross superstition' as Father Jesse believes – is an indispensable creative attempt to see through or break through a hang-over of the past (in the Carib syndrome that hang-over was the diabolic overburden of the character of con-quest) and to make of every inner divergence, every subtle omen of change – subsistence of memory to feed imagination in the future. There is a trickster element in the shaman which reflects his ambivalence and can lead sometimes to self-enchantment or hubris. This is understandable since the diabolic inflation of the warrior king hang-over is not easily seen through. That this conversion of diseased character – diseased warrior king into half-trickster, half-shaman – occurred with the Caribs may be gleaned from the events of the early nineteenth century.

As we know the Caribs were on the verge of extinction at the beginning of the nineteenth century. It was at this time that Mahanarva – the last Carib warrior chieftain to come to Stabroek – arrived to claim his gifts from the English Governor. These gifts constituted the pay the Caribs had been receiving for services rendered as mercenaries or jungle-police to various occupying powers since the Spanish. It was a custom or treaty which was fast becoming archaic and little need existed any longer to guard the escape routes of African slaves. In fact, slavery had been or was on the point of being abolished.

Mahanarva claimed that a considerable fighting force lay under his command in the Bush which would constitute a threat to Stabroek. Little penetration of the interior by the English had been made at that time since their fortunes lay on the coast. So the treaty with the Caribs was one which signified a kind of over-all cover to imperial adventure since, in theory, the English occupation extended far beyond the coast, and the treaty with the Caribs gave that hypothetical occupation a symbolic seal – gave 'teeth', as it were, to the unknown world of the Bush stretching into a continent.

Such an arrangement seemed, on the face of it, empirical and astute but the decimation at the heart of a people – the primeval fall-out of a broken tribe – was something that may have been truly obscure to the European occupying powers.

It was Mahanarva who unwittingly parted the shroud for the eyes of the English Governor. The tale of a considerable fighting force was accepted and much impressed, he dispatched a scout – unknown to Mahanarva – to reconnoitre the position. (That scout, if I may diverge for a moment, was the beginning of certain new penetrations by Europeans – the nineteenth-century arm of the conquistador – amongst whom figure names like Barrington Brown, Horsham, Schomburgk and others.) However, to return to Mahanarva, the English scout discovered that the Carib chieftain had lied. There was no body of warriors lying in the Bush. Mahanarva's ancient command had shrunken to rags. A handful of warriors was all he possessed.

There are two issues which arise from this bald historical account which we find occupying little more than a footnote in the history books.

First of all, Mahanarva's 'lie' gives us an insight (if we begin to free ourselves from dogmatic morality) into the trickster womb of the shaman. When Mahanarva claimed that his fighting forces were intact we know now from insights we have gleaned into our own psyche and into the so-called savage mind that he was compensating in himself losses his people had endured over centuries. He became the womb of the tribe in certain respects that are analogous to traces of mythology – ancient Greek, Persian, Mithraic as well as Christian – in which stones and rocks become charged with architectural latencies, inner rooms, etc., and therefore give birth to numinous tenants. In the same token, Pallas Athene, half-feminine, half-warrior archetype of wisdom, leapt from the head of Zeus; the Christian aeon was born of Peter the Rock. The shaman therefore stands in a perspective wherein 'death' becomes 'life' and the diseased warrior-king is translated into half-priest, half-feminine guide into the underworld. And that underworld of the lost Caribs constitutes for us a very significant dimension of elements (animate and inanimate realms of psyche, realms of subsistence of memory).

Second, Mahanarva's 'lie' to the Governor brings into play a fateful – however subconscious – erosion in the character of conquest. The shroud which was parted gave the Governor a view of his hypothetical kingdom. There were no Carib fighting forces lying in the Bush either to threaten Stabroek or alternatively secure the interior for the English Crown, but instead a chasm of losses – the primeval fall-out of a broken people who were partly victims of themselves, partly his victims and of others who had invaded the Guianas – victims, in effect, of a global appetite for adventure.

As such the statecraft of the European nineteenth-century representative of the Crown came into intimate rapport, with the trickster-shaman of aboriginal allies. It was a marriage of alien yet conspiring functions (trickster to statesman) that broke a uniform pattern to complacent character on both sides, and a creative necessity was born for the spatial re-assembly or salvage of the muse of authority.

I would like now to look back to the Arawak zemis which we touched on earlier in this chapter. Father Jesse dubbed these 'gross superstition'. *Zemi*, in fact, which I like to call the Arawak icon, iconic turtle or lizard or bird, etc., is related to *seme* which mean 'sweet' or 'delicate'. The correspondences making for spatial links – Arawak/Latin/English in the Caribbean – are enormous.

Space (our weakest resource in that we appear to move freely through it or bend it freely to our wills) is analogous to the Arawak *seme* (which means *delicate*) and to zemi or icon – zemi of the turtle (space of the turtle), zemi of the lizard (space of the lizard), as well as to the Latin threshold signifying hidden perspectives (latere 'to hide'). We are involved therefore – if we can imaginatively grasp it – in iconic or plastic thresholds – in an architecture of consciousness or re-constitution of spaces in the West Indian psyche running through Negro limbo and vodun into sculptures or spaces equivalent to rooms of an Arawak cosmos (rooms of turtle, bird, lizard).

In fact, an awareness of such a subconscious perspectival landscape infuses, in my view, a new quality or apprehension to a remarkable poem like Derek Walcott's 'A Tropical Bestiary' which can be approached as a zemi-studded poem. The heraldic images, namely Ibis, Octopus, Lizard, Man-o-War, Bird, Sea Crab, the Whale, Tarpon are partly fortuitous and ornamental like

> flesh that has lost pleasure in the act,
> domesticity drained of desire.

But Walcott's work witnesses to a continuous wrestling with his images and a technical development beyond that of any other Caribbean poet. As such a visionary overlap reaches his poem akin to an intuitive fusion of spaces and psychic concert of the god of land and sea.

> The sea crab's cunning, halting, awkward grace
> is the syntactical envy of my hand.

This brings us to the question of landscape. A friend of mine recently told me that in conversation with a certain high-ranking Guyanese official and politician, he discovered that that politician saw landscape as nothing more than the boundaries of his constituency. The ideal artist or scientist for him, therefore, was someone who conformed to an immediate governing stasis of place and time. As I reflected on this kind of realism, as some would call it, I recalled my boyhood (before World War II broke out) when I often swam at the Fort on the Georgetown foreshore. I reflected also on an observation I made when I was last in Georgetown in 1966: the sea no longer stands where it used to be and the land has grown in its place by six or seven feet. Therefore, if I were to endow the *de facto* mound or grave, which now exists on the foreshore with a figurative meaning beyond the present stasis of reality, I might see the ghost of the past (the ghost of my childhood) swimming in dry land.

That kind of imagination – which is clearly suspect to the politician – is true of areas of the primitive world and, in my conception, it corresponds to an architecture of consciousness within which the opaque mound or wall of earth possesses fugitive not absolute boundaries; and the swimmer in dry land witnesses to a fluid room or dimension.

This is but a small illustration of a landscape of the imagination which can be unravelled to lay bare many complex rooms and dimensions that have a profound bearing on Caribbean man as a civilisation-making animal, as an architect or a poet.

In Latin-American literature this reality is something which, I believe, occupies certain artists and novelists. This kind of vision, however, is quite rare in British West Indian literature. At the present moment I am glad to note that there is a new critical grasp of the issues. And some of the credit may lie with the Spanish Literature Department of the University of the West Indies and the work which Gabriel Coulthard and James Irish, for example, are doing there. I am indebted to James Irish for the quotation I am about to read to you. That quotation is a statement by Gabriel García Márquez which James Irish records in a paper of his entitled 'Magical Realism: A Search for Caribbean and Latin-American Roots':

> I am a realist writer, [Gabriel Garcia Marquez declared] because I believe that in Latin-America everything is possible, everything is real. There is a technical problem in that the writer finds difficulty in transcribing real events in Latin-America because no one would believe them in a book. We live surrounded by these fantastic and extraordinary things and still some writers insist on recounting to us immediate realities of no real importance. I believe that we have to work, investigating language and the technical forms of narration so that the entire fantastic reality of Latin-America might form part of our books, and so that Latin-

American Literature might in fact correspond to Latin-American life where the most extraordinary things happen every day. We Latin-American writers, when we sit down to write, instead of accepting them as realities, enter into polemics and rationalise by saying 'this is impossible; what happens is this man was a lunatic'. We all start giving a series of explanations which falsify the Latin-American reality. I believe that what we should do is to promote it as a form of reality which can give something new to universal literature.

As you will see, this 'form of reality' of which Marquez speaks is akin to my swimmer in dry land or to Merleau-Ponty's endowment of the *de facto* situation with a figurative meaning beyond a historical stasis.

In the third and last section of this address, I intend to look, amongst other things, at one area of the work of Edward Brathwaite who possesses, I believe, the greatest potential among Caribbean poets for the revival of poetic folk drama.

14

CONTINUITY AND DISCONTINUITY

So far we have been looking at a cleavage between the historical convention and arts of the imagination in the Caribbean. I have suggested that the historical convention remains a stasis which possesses no criteria for assessing profoundly original dislocations in the continuous pattern of exploiter/exploited charted by the historian. As such, the West Indies, history-wise, appear to me to be little more than an adjunct of imperialism. It has become essential, I feel, to assess dislocations which point away from the straitjacket of convention. These dislocations, I have suggested, may be perceived in areas of folk obscurity such as Negro *limbo* or phantom limb of the dismembered god and slave, in aboriginal features at which we have also been looking, and in the rise of the individual artist and imagination in the West Indies today. We have also touched on archetypal resonances, for example, the many armed deities of India, European alchemy, etc. In fact, the word *native* is not to be confused with *local* prejudice. Karl Marx, for example, was a profoundly native phenomenon. This meant that his resources went so deep they appeared obscure and embraced many contradictions to acquire universal application in the Western world. Many economic theses, however, which are easy to read have a pseudo-universal or local/insular application.

To turn to creative writers and artists – Herman Melville and William Faulkner, Wole Soyinka and Amos Tutuola, Denis Williams and Alejo Carpentier (if I may give a few examples) are native/universal spirits not local ornaments of middle-class, working-class, or any-other-class prejudice. I would like to make it very clear that it is not my intention to denigrate West Indian historians. I have a high regard for Professor Elsa Goveia and for Mr C. L. R. James, but it is my personal view that there does not exist a philosophy of history in the Caribbean correlative to the arts of the imagination.

I have not been able in these talks to look at the new, largely unpublished poets in the Caribbean. But judging from manuscript poems I have read in Jamaica, it would appear that Wayne Brown and Dennis Scott are certainly rising poets to watch.

There is a certain point I would like to clear up at this stage. When I used the word 'evolutionary' (as I have been doing all along in these addresses) I intended

176

not to imply a kind of static progression in which later cultures are seen as superior to earlier cultures, or in which some sort of biased projection is made back into primitive ages (either in the pseudo-romantic sense which exalts the noble savage, so-called, or in the equally pseudo-romantic sense which exalts the pride or arrogance of the consumer age).

My use of the word 'evolution' has nothing in common with either of these views. I am saying this because I was approached by someone who unfortunately had gained this impression. When I emphasise 'evolution' I am concerned with the gateway-complex between cultures. Such a gateway-complex means, in fact, that one stresses a discontinuous line – the missing links, as it were, between cultures rather than a hard continuous dividing wall. Such a discontinuous or dotted line means, in effect, that one has in mind no dogmatic evolutionary reinforcement of superiority and inferiority. One is, in fact, intent on an original overlap or viable frontier between ages and cultures.

Such a quest invites us to look afresh in each age at the life of the imagination, as this addresses us from the past with a new intuitive logic and design that diverges from the prison of the past, or which speaks through us towards the past and the future in a manner that also subtly diverges from the prison of the present and may I add, from popular prejudice. You may recall that previously we were speaking of the Caribs. The pre-Columbian-Carib was the Conqueror of the ancient West Indies and the ancient Guianas and we found that the post-Columbian-Carib, in a way, carried on this role of conqueror at an inferior level. The post-Columbian-Carib became the mercenary of the Dutch and French and the English. Therefore, one has apparently a continuous historical line, a continuous historical character coming out of the pre-Columbian world into the post-Columbian world and, in fact, we know that there are projections by people today who think of the Amerindians as a people who were intercepting or catching slaves.

Much of this projection upon *all Amerindians*, irrespective of tribe, is related to the continuous historical line associated with the Caribs. In fact, when we look very closely at the Carib vestiges of legend I believe one sees that there has been a divergence at a certain moment of time in terms of the bush-baby omens that pointed away from that continuous character line towards a subtle annunciation of native host consciousness. If one invests in the continuous historical line of conquest one misses that kind of subtle divergence and this, of course, is part and parcel of the cleavage which exists between the historical convention and the arts of the imagination. Continuity does exist within a profoundly original scanning of the womb of tradition but it would appear to nourish divergences from one-sided convention and to breach closures of the imagination.

In fact I believe that it is here (in this sometimes almost subconscious divergence – it takes a peculiar kind of mind, I would think, to perceive both sides of the coin in his lifetime, namely, the wall of prejudice and the intimate phenomenal resources for divergence) it is here, I repeat, that the essential object-ivity or life of art resides. It does not reside in the given historical prejudices of the artist or poet or novelist or sculptor, but in what is virtually intuitive and subconscious terrain that may acquire its conscious application later in the extensive body or development of the artist's work, or at a later post-mortem reappraisal stage by critical intelligences who may be better placed to appreciate the intuitive breakthrough in a work of art executed within a certain age or prison of history. This view of art as an extraordinary drama of consciousness whose figurative meaning lies beyond its *de facto* historical climate is anathema to the materialist or conventional realist, though I know that Lukács, a Marxist critic, toyed with the idea and that the great Irish poet Yeats attempted to articulate it when he wrote 'Man can embody truth but he cannot know it'.

This is a helpful point at which to turn to a poem like Edward Brathwaite's 'Masks', the second book in his trilogy. It seems to me that there is an abrupt terrain or fugitive line in 'Masks' which constitutes for me anyway (the poet himself may not agree) what I would call the dramatic breath of the poem. Take for example:

> So the god,
> mask of dreamers,
> hears lightnings
> stammer. . .

I repeat

> hears lightnings
> stammer

Note the echo of the drums, of thunder implied there in association with the lightning that *stammers* across the sky. That stammer – in association with the thunder of heaven's drum – constitutes the oracle of the poem.

> So the god,
> mask of dreamers,
> hears lightnings stammer,
> hearts rustle
> their secrets
> blood shiver like leaves
> on his branches. Will
> the tree, god
> of path-
> ways, still
> guide us? Will
> your wood lips speak
> so we see?

Sound becomes *sight* because of the fugitive boundaries of the drum, of the mask that allows for the breath and life of the icon.

Brathwaite is, I believe, a Caribbean poet of renascence. And, as you know, in this series I have been concentrating on perspectives of renascence within which for example, we looked at Aubrey Williams, the painter, and the bearing his work may have on an Amerindian renascence.

Brathwaite has been affected by African images but in an evolutionary way as I understand it. Evolutionary in that it seems to me, fugitivity makes for areas of overlap or gateway drama between Africa and the West Indies—*between sound* and *sight*. Therefore there is an *oral* and *visual* coincidence in his poems which invokes a speaking oracular voice as well as an imagistic intelligence. Because of this gateway between voice and image his icon breathes and the oracle addresses us through the elements in a manner consistent with West Indian folk consciousness.

One must remember that *breath* is all the black man may have possessed at a certain stage in the Americas. He had lost his tribal tongue, he had lost every-thing except an abrupt area of space and lung: he possessed nothing but the calamitous air of broken ties in the New World. Historical convention has no criteria for this inner subtle storm of reality (almost Yoga reality in the Indian sense of the yoke between the breath of man and God) – the yoke of imagination in the trickster theatre of the Caribbean 'as a breath-body' or field of meta-morphosis beyond the *de facto* embalmed posture of the slave in every catalogue of injustice.

The exploitation of man by man, inhumanity of man to man, is reinforced, ironically, I believe, by ceaseless catalogues of injustice. We need somehow to find an original dislocation within which to unlock a body of claustrophobic assump-tions which strengthens itself by promoting a self-encircling round of protest – obsession with irreconcilable differences – irreconcilable frontiers – irreconcilable ghettos – like a static clock that crushes all into the time of conquest. Much of the character of civilisation as we have known it has been geared to this static clock which obviously seeks to shape its material, all its human material, into time-tables of defensive capital, defensive labour and other territorial imperatives. That is why the catalogues of deeds compiled by historians conform to dead time that measures man as a derivative industry-making animal, tool-making animal, weapon-making animal.

And the quest therefore for an inner clock is so necessary in our situation of social and industrial character geared relentlessly to static time (to statistical bundles of labouring, fighting time, etc.) that it constitutes a universal, complex and liberating theme. Something far different, needless to say, to the tautology of fact – embalmed fact.

It is in this context that we look back again at the fugitive line or breath of the icon in Edward Brathwaite's 'Masks'.

This brings me to the last section of my talk. I have felt from various writers' conferences I have attended (whether a Commonwealth Conference in Australia, UNESCO Conference in Cuba, seminars in British Universities, etc.) that no philosophy of history exists in regard to the Third World. One has the sense that a plea is mounted on behalf of the black man and the deprivations that he has suffered. A plea which invests in deterministic horizons within the past, present and future. Once, again, therefore it seems to me the *native consciousness* is being overlooked within deterministic projections, and criteria are invalidated which might probe into unpredictable perspectives, latent spaces we need to unravel in our age. One has the sense also that vested interests are at work to embalm the fact of exploitation. Thus a new kind of callous is enshrined which blocks perspectives. How many people are aware for example, that when the horrors of slavery were being mounted in the Caribbean, press-gangs roved England in search of able-bodied men for the Navy. The appalling deprivations such men suffered in the age of Nelson, the great Admiral, would make for a catalogue of horrors. Surely this is a related aspect of a civilisation which saw men as bundles of labouring, fighting time, time-fodder to fertilise the fields of industry or to fence the high seas. For the Navy is not an arbitrary choice since without it the West Indies would not have become a British possession.

So I return to the thread of my argument. In a society which has been shot through by diverse inter-racial features and inter-continental thresholds, we need a philosophy of history which is original to us and yet capable of universal application. Caribbean man is involved in a civilisation-making process (whether he likes it or not) and until this creative authority becomes intimate to his perspectives, he will continue to find himself embalmed in his deprivations – embalmed as a derivative tool-making, fence-making animal. As such his dialectic will remain a frozen round of protest.

It would seem to me that the closest West Indian historians have come to a philosophy of history is in terms, firstly, of the Marxist dialectic. C. L. R. James is notable in this respect and deserves the closest attention. In terms, secondly of Marxism allied to various humanitarian and egalitarian principles, Elsa Goveia is notable in this respect and deserves too to be read with the closest attention. In her *Slave Society in the British Leeward Islands at the End of the Eighteenth Century* there emerges what seems to me a key passage:

> Sooner or later we shall have to face the fact that we are courting defeat
> when we attempt to build a new heritage of freedom upon a structure of
> society which binds us all too closely to the old heritage of slavery.

For that 'old heritage of slavery' as Professor Goveia sees it (and as many liberal West Indian intellectuals see it) serves to buttress a state of inequality and deprivation of opportunity that threatens democracy. In short, that 'old heritage' may come to constitute – if it does not already constitute in Professor Goveia's thinking – an adamant and inflexible psychological fortress.

But – as a humane scholar – she reasons

> Perhaps however, there is still good reason to believe that the forces of

radicalism will prevail. For now that a democratic suffrage has been established in many parts of the West Indies, the time may be ripening for the emergence and success of renewed movements of *protest*.

I would suggest that intuitively, unintentionally, Elsa Goveia puts her finger on the sterility of West Indian politics and intellectualism. Protest in intellectual political terms (Marxist and humanitarian) continues to divide the Caribbean. Some people have said that Dr Jagan's Marxist party in Guyana – radical and far-thinking as it once was – eventually became dominated by the self-interest of an Indian peasantry who built a wall in the face of that very 'old heritage of Negro slavery'. I do not think this is true but if it is it is no denigration of the Indian peasantry, because they are as much trapped as any other group in the Caribbean and, one feels, in the same token, that the West Indian Federation split into island fortresses who were intent on building a hard and fast wall against that very 'old heritage of slavery' within themselves and without. It seems to me, therefore that the structure of intellectual moral protest (which has been the political climate of the West Indies spearheaded by thinkers like Elsa Goveia) will remain an embalmed posture until immense new disciplines (a new anthropology I would think) can assess original divergences from claustrophobic, political ritual.

Kenneth Ramchand and Paul Edwards put their finger rather well on the wall of deprivation which hems in the West Indian intellectual. I quote from their article on Michael Anthony in *The Journal of Commonwealth Literature* (July 1969 No. 7):

> Anthony is committed in *The Year in San Fernando* to involving us in the feel of a peculiarly open state of consciousness; that this is achieved by a scrupulous adherence to the boy's point of view in a deceptively easy style that carries the necessary sensuous burden as well as sustaining the illusion of adolescent reportage. *The kind of participation invited in this way* seems to us to be of a more experimental kind than that which V.S. Naipaul suggests may be achieved in another way. A literature can grow only out of a strong framework of social convention. And the only convention the West Indian knows is his involvement with the white world. This deprives his world of universal appeal. The situation is too special. The reader is excluded; he is invited to witness and not to participate. It is easier to enter any strong framework of social convention however alien. It is easier to enter the tribal world of an African writer like Camara Laye.

The reader's sensuous involvement in Anthony's fiction will be further illustrated, but there is another element (not restricted to the question of involvement) to be traced in Naipaul's remark. The West Indian hankering after something like a tribal past or coherent social present as an organising principle for fiction, only latent in Naipaul's comment, appears more distinctly in *Bim* where praise for *A House for Mr. Biswas* is followed by this conclusion: 'The negro West Indian cannot really expect novels like *Biswas* until he has a strong enough framework of social convention from which to operate.'

Novels do indeed reflect the society out of which they have been created, but coherence in the world of the novel is one thing and an external framework of social convention is another. It is naive to confuse life with fiction at this level . . .

The line of reasoning pursued by Naipaul and *Bim* makes it all too clear – ironically perhaps – how strong is the *de facto* historical situation in the West Indies in black/white rigidity and how it encircles the imagination. Edwards and Ramchand – in their study of Michael Anthony – seek to break out of that prison by exploring *The Year in San Fernando* as an open state of consciousness which endows the *de facto* situation with a figurative meaning beyond the conventional stasis. Herein lies, I believe, the immense possibility which the Caribbean novelist or poet may pursue. It is something which the Latin American writer – unlike Naipaul and *Bim* – understands at this moment of time.

It is my view that the subtle key to a philosophy of history is embedded in the misunderstood arts of the Caribbean which we have traced through Negro limbo, Haitian vodun, Carib bush-baby, Arawak zemi as well as through Latin and English inheritances and the intuitive logic of a few Caribbean poets, painters, novelists etc. One area I have neglected is to deepen our perception of the fauna and flora of a landscape of time which indicate the kind of room or space or material vision of time in which whole societies conscripted themselves. The point here is that, by tracing this, one is able to endorse what one has been saying before. The sort of facile reliance on what is called 'a strong framework' is, in my view, a parody of the historical convention – an unconscious parody perhaps, whereby the imagination fails to deepen its resources, and to explore perspectives away from the embalmed posture of history. The trap is a very pervasive one because it seeps into literature itself and begins to take over the critical role until the whole realm of criticism is subsumed or taken over by historical convention and the critic loses his independence.

We saw with the Caribs that they possessed an apparently unchanging identity which embodied pre-Columbian conqueror in post-Columbian mercenary. That stasis, however, had been secretly breached in their bush-baby omens of a new native consciousness. This was not apparent in a collective sense to the Caribs who continued to enact the sleep-walking role of conqueror at an inferior mercenary level.

Let us note also that parrots were the heralds of Manoa or Eldorado. Heralds of a bank of time. The Aztecs of Mexico, as you know, also visualised a bank of time which possessed a cyclic character. For this reason – at the end of each cycle of 52 years, according to our reckoning – they were convinced time might die unless replenished with the heart's blood. This terrifying emphasis on replenishing the bank of time fatefully determined the character of Man as slave to an industry of priests who worshipped the sun. The hearts of men were torn out of their breasts to feed the gold of time – if I may be permitted to invoke an overlap between Eldorado and ancient Mexico – and one is reminded of that 'mire of human veins' which Yeats associated with Byzantium at a certain level of artifice and desperation.

The parrot was the herald or omen of Manoa, the rabbit figures in the cyclical calendar of ancient Mexico, and if we appoint these as fauna of the landscape of time, we are involved in the character of Man as this was fatefully established through philosophies of time in those civilisations.

The curious spin-off available to us today from cyclic orders, half-moon orders, waves or troughs of time, rooms of time, some approximately vertical, some horizontal, which we can trace through many civilizations is this: ghosts of time infuse the spectre of humanity. Cyclic ghosts in ancient Mexico, linear ghosts in a twentieth-century programmed age, run upon a thread that promises rapport with a flexible humanity inhabiting shapes of time, rooms of fruitful diversity in an architecture of consciousness. This architecture of the imagination remains in a state of latency by and large. Yet the mysterious fauna and flora of legend, in which philosophies of time gestate, may offer a continuity from the remote past into the future.

One needs however to pause and reflect. Continuity can be deceptive. It may seem to embalm the potential available to us. On the other hand it may assist us to perceive pressures of profoundest creativity and revisionary momentum into models of discourse we may so easily accept without sensing their alignment to legacies of conquest.

Continuity cannot be seized or structured by any group and thus it should empower arts of complex originality that may approach and scan and weigh the numinosities, and specificities, and contrasting proportions that give rhythm and echo to the building blocks of a civilization.

One cannot be complacent about the future. The pressures upon marginal and disadvantaged societies are acute and terrifying in a world of abused landscapes and the savage exploitation of resources.

Conquest may remain brutal in many areas of the globe but it also has its seductive guises, its enormously persuasive media, its power to dispense honours and prizes in the maintenance of its cultural vested interests. The true capacity of marginal and disadvantaged cultures resides in their genius to tilt the field of civilization so that one may visualize boundaries of persuasion in new and unsuspected lights to release a different apprehension of reality, the language of reality, a different *reading* of texts of reality.

Perhaps such a breakthrough remains frail. Yet it is there. All I have attempted in this essay is to touch on one or two aspects of possibility. Possibility may become, with the passage of time, a tapestry or orchestration of probabilities . . .

15

QUETZALCOATL AND THE SMOKING MIRROR: REFLECTIONS ON ORIGINALITY AND TRADITION

There are conflicting legends about the parentage of Quetzalcoatl. One is inclined to say he was an orphan. And the legend of the 'orphan song of ancient Mexico' – upon which I shall comment later – may well confirm this.

Some of his putative ancestors wore the mask of Light and of the Sky. The feathers of the quetzal bird signified the Sky. Others wore the mask of the Earth. The scales of the wise serpent signified the Earth.

Quetzalcoatl was revered by his people as a god. But on looking into the Smoking Mirror he was confounded by a prophecy of the death of gods. Strange prophecy. For it was as if gods constituted a succession of densities or veils between humanity and an everlasting, unfathomable creator.

The Smoking Mirror symbolized those veils that lay between oneself and the creator. The veils were everywhere, in a tree one took for granted as passive or lifeless furniture, in landscapes, riverscapes, creatures, natures, one took for granted.

Quetzalcoatl was stricken by a kind of cosmic terror. It wasn't only the veils in the Smoking Mirror. It was a sudden upsurge of guilt. He had contemplated – if not actually performed – incest with his royal sister.

Incest, in this context, was not necessarily a physical act but a symbolic, protective, kith and kin cloak over a privileged family whom an immortal god seeks to embrace absolutely as his property. The chosen sister, or representative of the family, becomes a pawn of immortality.

What does one mean by a 'pawn of immortality'? Does not immortality imply true freedom? A pawn is unfree. If immortality does not imply a true freedom then the soul of freedom may need to rid itself of the net of one-sided immortality, so one-sided, so reserved for those who are chosen or elected to receive it, that it serves as a weapon to extinguish others who are foreign or outside of the chosen family.

Let me put it this way: when Quetzalcoatl looked into the Smoking Mirror, and into the densities or veils that lay between himself and an unfathomable creator, he felt a wholly different compassion for the world than entertained by incestuous love. He touched his sister and she became less of a pawn. Or let me put it differently. As a pawn of immortality she had overlooked the ruses of Lord Death and how subject she was to such a commander of human and animal destiny. Was Lord Death an immortal? The plaster of vanity and incestuous love slipped from her eyes. Lord Death was the commander of all things and species and yet a very strange, unpredictable thing happened. Death appeared to break into plural masks to reveal an enigma of Soul.

Here is an important seed of epic. Eurydice was a pawn of the Lord of the Under World, Lord Death. Orpheus sought to bring her back into the life of consciousness . . . I shall come back to this later. It is an important strand. But now let us return to plural masks and to the enigma of the Soul.

The Soul is a solitary wanderer yet steeped in plural masks it may pluck from the fractured body of Death itself into curiously living sculptures, curiously living paintings, curiously living Word or ventriloquism of Spirit.

This incredible humour (the Soul has a profound sense of humour), this incredible grace, in which the Soul leans upon fractured Death for its plural masks, is pertinent to the paradoxical life of the Soul as it wanders everywhere. For then the Soul implies what a vocation in the imaginative arts should mean. Such vocation should wrestle with distinctions between conquest, absolute conquest, privileged by Death, and a breakage of Death's commandments through the mystery of living arts.

Any attempt within ourselves to gain enlightenment from the Smoking Mirror must take the Soul's humour, the Soul's unique comedy, into account. The Smoking Mirror brings through and beyond cosmic terror a sensation of being plural, of a capacity within ourselves to wear many masks, each mask possessing its *partial* eye that glances into a core of mystery at the heart of complex traditions. Singular bias structures us to bypass the rhythms of plurality. Singular bias is *not* the solitariness of the dreaming Soul in space . . .

Let us imagine a fall-out from the Smoking Mirror across two thousand years into solitariness of Soul, solitariness in our bewildering universe . . . How would that fall-out clothe the Cartesian ego that underpins the mindset of Europe? The Cartesian dictum runs *I think therefore I am*. It sounds familiar as though a brooding solitariness of Soul is to be equated with the biased ego!

But when I contemplate brooding solitariness I have in mind neither the Freudian Ego nor the Cartesian Ego but a gnostic concept in which one is, as it were, lifted above one's age, upon an imaginary constellation (such as I visualize in my novel *Resurrection at Sorrow Hill*) in order to steep oneself in a theatre, so to speak, of plural masks that bear on the travail of humanity – in an orchestration of ancient and modern histories and characterizations and imageries as well revolving, so to speak, around a transitive principle or musical chord.

Plural masks are *not* the same as Cartesian dualism. Plural masks imply a living cosmos in all its grain and particularity that may appear to sleep, to be dormant, but is susceptible to riddling proportions of eruptive life. Unity then is paradox, the core of paradox. Unity appears dormant, passive, but may be fired into rhythms of differentiation that make us aware of inequalities, jealousies, passions, that may bedevil our world absolutely unless – by stages as it were – a transfiguration of appearances occurs, appearances we take for granted.

I mention this in order to bring into play a glimpsed goal, a glimpse – little more do we have – of the enormous potential to be realized in the rebirth of original epic within the suppressed fire of the Smoking Mirror, suppressed rhythms and music as well.

Resurrection at Sorrow Hill drew me back to *Palace of the Peacock* and to the music-maker Carroll who reappears at the end of the book within a corridor in ancient El Dorado. He whistles through a window in the palace, *a window that becomes a medium of transitive density*. I emphasize *density* and *transitive*, as though a *chord* exists within the window – within the density of the window (let us say) – the window becomes a medium of *transitive density* as the chord fires, so to speak, and Carroll's whistle is transformed as it passes through the window. It is transformed into an eruption of majestic music within the text of reality. The transitive chord within the window, within a body of density, fires – as I said before – and thus, coincident with the music, appears the lightning bark of a tree.

Music in the text is simultaneous with the incandescent imagination. I am told that this kind of simultaneity, in which density is a transitive medium into music and the incandescent imagination, is consistent with quantum mechanics, but *Palace* was written in 1959 (published in 1960) and I knew nothing of quantum mechanics at the time.

Indeed though I have read *Quantum Reality* by the physicist Nick Herbert, and have been excited by it, and what I discern as validating premises to certain things I have been doing in my fiction, the truth is that I did not see, in Nick Herbert's thesis, the role of densities as transitive media planted in nature. The matter truly came home to me on the publication of *Resurrection at Sorrow Hill* at the end of 1993. At the core of *Resurrection at Sorrow Hill* one finds the eruption of music in the text simultaneous with the incandescent imagination. It was this that suddenly enabled me to return to *Palace* and speak of it now as I have done.

I find now that I could give many examples of this phenomenon in the work I have written within the past four decades. With hindsight they are abundantly clear to me. Densities are not uniform. They vary, they vary with multiple strands, multiple transitive chords within them. I could give many examples but I trust the essential point is made. One thing that I should add is this: transitive densities may instil themselves in fiction that is shaped in 'the mind of the imaginative writer who has been deeply affected by the life of primordial land-scapes, tall rapids, burning savannahs, rain-forest rocks imprinted with the mark-ings of ancient cultures, markings that resemble extra-human messages from the gods who write in fire and wind and water.'

In earthquake-prone regions buildings are now being constructed that seek to incorporate in themselves rhythms that may respond to, and thereby withstand, the shock of a quake that may last only thirty seconds but is able to do immense damage to conventional architectures. The daring architectures that are beginning to come into play have a long way to go. I tend to visualize such architecture, however new, as hinged, let us say, to a primordial cradle as the earth moves and the ground shakes. The moving earth, the shaking ground, is akin to a primordial cradle that takes us back to riverscapes and the geology of landscapes, the genesis of the architecture of the earth itself as it turns in space.

Through the eyes of my own fiction I see transitive chords, implicit music, instilled or orchestrated into a building. When the earthquake comes, the building releases its transitive chords, there is hidden music in the cells of the building, a concert is created between the mind of architecture and the primordial instinct in the quake, the sailing plates in the earth.

For an instant, while the quake lasts, a new space or dimension in the mind of architecture is realized that unravels and absorbs the energies in the living earth.

It is no doubt unusual to suggest that modern architecture needs to conceive of itself as hinged to a primordial cradle; I do so now to indicate a link between architecture and the multi-dimensionalities of epic; epic – unlike conventional fiction – is steeped in upper worlds, under worlds, and in a theatre of plural masks plucked from apparent catastrophe and from histories around the globe.

In the light of all I have said it is interesting to note Iris Murdoch's statement – or that of the narrator in her book *Under the Net* – that 'the present age was not one in which it was possible to write an epic.'

Needless to say I do not agree with this but it tells us something of the state of mind amongst leading intellectuals and writers.

Obviously epic is a misunderstood term; it is misinterpreted by the mass media which judge any large-scale Hollywood performance to be epic. Epic is *not* Hollywood *Ben-Hur* or Hollywood *Moses*.

Epic is an *arrival* in an architecture of space that is *original* to our age, an *arrival* in multi-dimensionality that alerts us to some kind of transfiguration of appearances – in parallel with science and architecture – that implies energies akin to extra-human faculties inserted into the fabric of history.

I say 'arrival in' to make a distinction from academic *descriptions* of epic as something that belongs to the past and is now a museum-text to be imitated in the theatre or in performances of virtuosity . . .

To arrive in a tradition that appears to have died is complex renewal and revisionary momentum *sprung from originality and the activation of primordial resources within a living language*. We arrive backwards even as we voyage forwards. This is the phenomenon of simultaneity in the imagination of times past and future, a future that renews time in its imaginary response to gestating resources in *the womb of the present and the past*. It is unlike the linear biases that prevail in conventional fiction.

To arrive in a place where we are not brings into play transitive chords within densities, transitive dimensionalities that unlock doors within the body of language itself. Arrival then differs from photographic description. Arrival then is a concert between unfathomable psyche and place-in-depth, place displaced, recovered in the living Word.

Photographic descriptions of places, like academic descriptions of past traditions relegated to the museum, are useful, needless to say. But they do not offer us the criteria we need when we are challenged by the rhythms of creative work that give a re-visionary sensation of the life of epic, the transitive chords of epic that bear on many activities.

The impossibility of writing epic in our age – innermost epic as distinct from virtuoso performance, epic that alters the surfaces of language – may *not* be an impossibility at all ... Rather claims of impossibility may suggest difficulty in assessing – with an open mind – the emergence of such epic, difficulty in arriving within the medium of a new criticism that does not take the genesis of fiction for granted, the genesis of science for granted.

True there is a vested interest in the novel-form of the eighteenth and nineteenth centuries, a novel-form that was a response to social patterns and classes one associates with the Industrial Revolution.

Indisputably that novel-form has exercised considerable dominance around the globe within the expansion of European empires. But such an expansion involves many cultures and began long before the eighteenth century. It is not linked solely to the Industrial Revolution; its contours and horizons may be traced much farther back than the eighteenth century through the inception of the Middle Passage into ancient Rome, Macedonia, Persia, ancient Greece and India. The Caribbean poet Kamau Brathwaite writes in his long and remarkable poem *X/Self*:

> Rome burns
> and our slavery begins.

Such an expansion may need, does need, I think, to be considered and reconsidered for different clues it offers us about alternative fictions and latent cross-culturalities between diverse ages, past and present, that bear on imaginative truth.

Carnival, in its most subversive and regenerative essence, gained new ground within South America, Central America, and Caribbean cultures that suffered abysmally at the hand of the conquistadores who came into the Americas on the heels of Christopher Columbus.

The gestation of New World epic arguably began in a peculiar and terrifying way. We *arrive* in New World epic when we experience or re-imagine the earthquake of conquest as if conquest is native to our very bones.

The Spanish conquistadors came to the ancient Americas under the banner of Christ, Christ the law-giver and saviour of Mankind. And then – despite ruling assumptions of law and salvation – they engineered the massacre and the decimation of the American Indians to acquire land and gold, a process of decimation that continued under wave after wave of settlers and colonisers. Conquest is native when our bones begin to question every skeleton gateway into the New World.

The life of the Carnival skeleton introduces us, in surprising and surprised

188

ways, to ourselves. Our antecedents were the victims of conquest, our antecedents were paradoxically also victors who gobbled up land and gold. We are all, in that sense, dialectially mixed and impure. And this blend of victor and victim arouses us to the meaning of Death within Carnival, Death which wears the mask of global commander, global conquistador, Death – on the other hand – which is sensitive to the terror of the crushed, the victimized, Death which brings merciful release from pain.

It is logical to assume that the tenderness, originality, compassion that seeps through – almost subconsciously – the blood-stained fabric of history into the margins, the corners, of South American and Central American arts (as I witnessed these when I visited Mexico, Easter 1972) would have been a total impossibility (Christ would have been totally negated) had Death, the conquistador, triumphed absolutely.

The ancient animal riddles that bear on messengers of Soul within pre-Columbian traditions opened the body of conquest, touched on the mystery of Christ the tiger which springs in the New Year (if I may adapt a line from T.S. Eliot), as much as on the mystery of Quetzalcoatl, the winged serpent which flies in space, to release at the heart of a cruel masquerade of power, a disturbing, unsuspected heresy that I read as one of the cornerstones of recovered epic that bears on our age

A word about animal riddles. Animal beings associated with divinities or divine heroes or god-men is a crossing of frontiers that seem absolute in their own right. The animal state seems absolute in its own right. The divine state seems absolute in its own right. When absolute frontiers, enshrined into absolute separation of animal being and divine being, are broken, a re-visionary momentum is set up within the depth resources of language to question the surfaces of language and the reification of conquest in the name of the divine. When we perceive an animal ingredient in the divine, we find ourselves steeped in plural masks that break an addiction to power, that break a hubris or proclivity to enslave others whom we deem inferior creatures. In breaking the hubris, so to speak, of the ruling or commanding state we break a commandment, we commit a heresy.

The crossing of frontiers, or heresy I have in mind, in this instance, is *sacramentalized adultery* between the creaturely spouse, or wife of the conquistador Lord Death, and a fractured epic hero in the extremities of Western civilization in South America. In *Resurrection at Sorrow Hill* I call the fractured hero Hope and I name the wife of the commander Death (Death spelt with an apostrophe D'eath) Butterfly. *Butterfly* – the spouse or wife of Mr Universe with a gun (another title for commander Death or D'eath) – *is, as her creaturely name implies, a vessel of all species. She is human and creature, animal and soul, angel and naive maiden. A drop of her angelic blood gives oceanic value to the voyages of Christ the tiger and Quetzalcoatl the winged serpent.*

To put it as simply as I can: we are involved in an orchestration of imageries divine and human, creator and creature, Death and complex liberation from death-dealing regimes that embrace humanity in many areas of the globe. This desire for liberation is instinctive to ancient epic but it needs to be grasped differently, realized differently, it needs re-visionary capacities in our own age.

Let us recall that, in an ancient epic, Eurydice – the wife of the music-player Orpheus – is plucked away from him by Death, the Lord of the Under World. Orpheus is given a chance, it seems, to recover Eurydice but disobeys a command *not* to look back. Eurydice is snatched back into the Under World. In this I see a prime motif of the unfinished genesis of the imagination, of a necessity written into the collective unconscious to return to, and take up, the theme of Orpheus differently from the way it is enshrined as a museum text in the humanities. *Orpheus disobeys a command.* Intuitively, subconsciously – I would venture to say – he glimmeringly perceived, when he looked back, that Eurydice would remain a pawn of the Under World if her apparent release had been sanctioned or sealed by Lord Death himself or itself. Something more radical and disturbing within death-dealing and conquistadorial regimes was gestating within layers of the unconscious.

In *Resurrection at Sorrow Hill* Butterfly is *not* Hope's wife. Eurydice was Orpheus' wife. Butterfly is Death's (or D'eath's) wife. Butterfly is a spouse that has been cruelly used by a death-dealing establishment, by the Lord of the quake and the Under World. Hope's adulterous affair with her is conducted in fear and trembling. Even when he outwits D'eath and brings Butterfly back to life, after he dreams they have both been shot and killed by the jealous commander, he knows that Death is still at his heels. Interwoven with his fear of D'eath or Lord Death runs a multi-layered perception that the surfaces of the language, the commanding surfaces of the language, are creatively fractured to expose an ambivalence in Death that is *not* apparent in the traditional frame of the Orpheus/Eurydice legend.

In the sacramentalized adultery between Hope and Butterfly, Death or D'eath is exposed, the seal is partially broken into ambivalence, ambivalent majesty, ambivalent despair, and an orchestration of histories and imageries around the globe erupts, as a consequence, into other figures and other characters.

There is Christopher D'eath for example. The mystery of the resurrection of Christ is implicit in the Christopher faculty in D'eath or Death. Thus D'eath breaks into two and grows capable of remorse. He desires that his abused spouse should be lifted into another realm and tenderly embraced by Hope. But that desire cannot be forced in the fiction, in the evolving life and language of the fiction, it is too far-reaching to be forced, for force after all is the faculty of conquest. The desire to release his spouse is unmistakably active but it cannot be forced. Let us say it gestates and looms as a significant element that bears on the future . . .

What emerges I find is that D'eath (or Death) is broken into a series of plural masks. His command over all species is questioned very deeply in fictionalizations of the heart of nature within the unfinished genesis of the Imagination. As a consequence D'eath succumbs to despair. He seeks to extinguish himself, he seeks to commit suicide, but fails and is left with bullet marks – the stigmata of the bullet on his face. Those markings have the imprint of a creaturely Spider.

One of the issues that the fiction raises – in my attempt to raise to your attention provisional criteria that may help us into an appreciation of the re-birth of original epic – is that the resurrection of Christ has been fallaciously aligned to the *conquest* of Death or to a structured immortality replete with one-sided bias.

There is an apparently commonsense equation between resurrection and the conquest of Death, conquering Death, to conquer Death.

But *uncommon sense* surely tells us that to stress *conquest* is to succumb to the very monster we fear; *D'eath's vocabulary is rooted in a predatory coherence*, in ruthless competition, in cannibalistic plans of living and industry that may promote the downfall of others. Such, we are told, is the real world.

To conquer Death involves us in a cruel irony, it involves us in crusades, in inquisitions that burn men's bodies, kill heretics and infidels, in order to save their souls (a wholly mistaken notion of the solitariness of the Soul which is intent – when it paints constellations in the heavens to endorse remoteness and solitariness (as has been the practice in ancient cultures from times immemorial) – on steeping itself even as it appears to levitate in space, in a rich diversity in theatres of the enigma of truth on planet Earth).

That the conquest of Death, the conquering of Death, is equated with the resurrection of Christ tells us much about ruling premises civilization plasters on the surfaces of language; such ruling premises upon language, such predatory coherence, tell us much – when we reflect upon it deeply – of the closed mind of the conquistadores who raped a continent under the banner of Christ.

Original epic in our age, I would hope, begins to move the enigma of the resurrection into new dimensions that we need to nurse within the complex life of the Imagination; original epic may help us to take up afresh the burden of an uncertain but far-reaching rescue of the universal spouse (animal spouse, creaturely spouse, human spouse in all its pigmentations and differences) that death-dealing ideologies and regimes marry and imprison around the globe . . .

The work of writers such as Juan Rulfo and Octavio Paz, both Mexican, may carry indirect thresholds into the re-birth of original epic. The seed of epic, however buried or remote, may also reside in some of the fictions of Angela Carter with their animal messengers from other worlds. I think the possibility also exists in the work of three Guyanese-born writers, with whom I am considerably impressed, namely David Dabydeen, Pauline Melville and Fred D'Aguiar. One has to wait and see. There are other imaginative writers whose work you may begin to approach through recent critical studies such as Vera Kutzinski's *Against the American Grain* (published by Johns Hopkins University Press), Nathaniel Mackey's *Discrepant Engagement: Dissonance, Cross-Culturality and Experimental Writing* (published by Cambridge University Press), and *The Repeating Island* by the Cuban writer Antonio Benitez Rojo (published by Duke University Press).

Space does not permit me to go into these and I must emphasize that these studies are not engaged with a direct approach to the issues I have raised about epic, but in going against the grain – as they all do – they heighten our attention to masking and musicality and cross-culturality.

For instance Nathaniel Mackey, a very gifted, imaginative writer, and a scrupulous scholar, discusses in illuminating ways what he calls 'the genius of black music' as it has affected various texts by twentieth-century American writers.

Let me quote what he says of the 'orphan song of ancient Mexico'. He writes – 'In divergence and dissent one hears the voice of the orphan, the outsider, the excluded. Music and the writing that embraces it are something like the *icnocuicatl* or orphan song of ancient Mexico which, as Gordon Brotherson explains, "explores feelings of cosmic abandonment and the precariousness of mortal life before the unknown."'

Let me tease a clue from this that may fruitfully bear on epic.

I am thinking of the orphaned state – if I may so put it – of the Soul of tradition, the way tradition is enshrined in museum-texts, the way the orphaned Soul of tradition may open our minds to a state of cosmic abandonment that humanity experiences despite technologies of progress. Also the promises of tradition, whether in scriptures or elsewhere, remain unfulfilled. The disciples of Christ may have been promised the end of the world, and the descent of the kingdom of heaven, in their lifetime. The promise remains unfulfilled. And yet the potency of such a promise seems to imply a hidden kingdom committed to universal compassion and justice: a hidden kingdom unable to disclose itself to a divided humanity plagued by closed minds that continue to disfigure the body of civilization in their pursuit of fundamental causes enshrined into terrorising absolutes.

I repeat: the promises of ancient epic, like ancient scriptures, remain unfulfilled. I have already commented on Eurydice in ancient Orphic legend. I suggested that Orpheus' disobedience may be re-read or re-interpreted afresh as unconscious or subconscious insight into Eurydice's fate as a *continuing pawn* of sovereign Death if her release is sanctioned within a frame of absolute rules and commandments issued by the identical regime that promises to liberate her. Is such liberation a genuine liberation? When Orpheus looks back he disobeys. And my interpretation of that is that *subconsciously* he knows that Eurydice's liberation would have been a hypocrisy, a fraud. She would not have been free . . .

In other words the absolute commandment issued by a sovereign death-dealing regime is partial (when seen in another context or light) and that partiality is threaded into inequalities, into injustices, harboured by one-sided traditions. You may recall how Virgil – who had laboured for Dante in guiding him through the inferno and the purgatorio – was unjustly excluded from the paradiso. He was deemed a pagan because his address lay in a pre-Christian age. How one-sided is such a paradiso? Does it not need a profound, re-visionary momentum of the frame of language in which it is cast?

Once such deep-seated inequalities remain within traditions, the Soul of tradition itself is orphaned, it suffers cosmic abandonment in that it *appears* to nurture absolutes which polarise humanity irreconcilably. Unless such absolutes can yield their partialities within plural masks that question themselves, the Soul is cut adrift and may lose its potency to arbitrate, with profoundest creativity, between divisions in humanity. The Soul then appears to endorse a state of affairs in which cultures languish between worlds. Sometimes they are seized or cajoled or bribed with promises that can never be fulfilled.

Perhaps this throws some light on the fate of the Mesopotamian giant Gilgamesh who was promised immortality. He secured the plant of immortality but fell asleep upon the bank of a river. A chthonic or Under World god arose and consumed the plant.

Let us venture to re-interpret what happened. I would suggest that an obscure feud, obscure rage, inserted itself into the inequalities of Mesopotamian epic and this cancelled the promise of an immortality inevitably and tragically steeped with bias. Gilgamesh does have a peculiar limbo immortality nevertheless that may throw some light on the anguish of genius, the orphaned state of the Soul as it confronts a demiurge in the feuding depths and in the feuding heights of creation, a demiurge that may claim to be its parent, a parent that may be its enemy.

A deeply troubling and important question now arises. Let us look at it through the eyes of a gnostic Christian. For gnosis, or inner knowledge – the knowledge of the solitary (of whom I spoke earlier) – is said to pre-date Christianity and to be as old as epic. For the gnostic (the gnostic Christian or the gnostic pagan who dreams of extra-human parents interwoven with cosmic enmity and abandonment in Orphic song as much as in the song of ancient Mexico) the consent of a parent–creator (who may reconcile the vagaries and contradictions of parentage) is an invaluable quest within the language of time. Indeed it is essential if the Soul of tradition is to resume its voyage out of the past and into the unknown future.

All well and good to take the future for granted in a purely materialistic way in which one day's greed is another day's greed but when the future opens itself to the Soul of traditions it cannot be taken for granted.

Each day is a voyage into forbidden realms, a conversation with messengers of deity, with angels in the Blakean sense. Each day is a reckoning with veils or densities that lie between us and a God with whom we have at times a sensation of inner rapport or of whom we may have some inner gnosis or knowledge, but who remains unfathomable and beyond description; who seems to imply at times our orphaned predicament.

Gnosis then is steeped in densities and bodies of knowledge through which we hope to pass – changed in heart and conscience and mind – into unknown, parenting futures that may bring justice at last.

Here we touch the core of the problem. What is the distinction between consent (the consent of a parent–creator, consent to adventure into the genius of the future in concert with the re-opening of the deepest, gravest, unfulfilled promises to Mankind, implicit in ancient traditions) *and* commandments one associates with jealous gods of Upper Worlds and Under Worlds who have become prey to traumatic inequalities in the womb of tradition?

Such jealousies and rages remain as pertinent to us as they were to the fate of Gilgamesh, when the chthonic or Under World serpent cancelled the promise of immortality issued presumably by some other oceanic or rival commander of rivers and tides.

Look around our world. Catholics rage at Protestants; equally a high-ranking Protestant minister – I won't give his name – recently claimed that the Catholic Pope was the anti-Christ. A year or two ago Hindus were intent on killing Muslims in order to secure the site of an ancient temple in India. Christians and Muslims are at war in Bosnia . . . One could go on and on. Each group has – it would seem – no misgiving in issuing its commandments to its followers

By and large civilization remains in pawn to savage commandments, ruthless creeds and ideologies. Within the re-birth of original epic the consent of a living creator for the voyaging artist or scientist to trespass across forbidden frontiers would seem to imply a radical shift in such premises of feud built into com-mandments. Not that diverse faiths and religions should be conquered and uni-fied. Such conquest, as we know, deepens the pressures of rage and a longing for revenge within the defeated who bide their time in Under Worlds.

Rather – to put it as simply as I can – the radical shift in premises of com-mandment, that claim to be absolute when they are partial, invites an approach to the spouse of death-dealing regimes through a descent into inequalities all over again but with a difference.

That difference rests on diverse cultures, a capacity within diverse cultures to create and re-create windows into the enigma of truth. Each window's suscepti-bility to rigidity, rigid commandment, breaks, turns, I am suggesting, into a transi-tive architecture, a transitive medium into other dimensions within the unfinished genesis of the Imagination. Diversity then sponsors the liberation of the orphaned Soul within re-visionary and plural masks. The Soul is heightened even as the capacity of humanity to nourish itself in new perspectives of imaginative truth is deepened . . .

What promise then – may I ask – does the re-birth of epic offer?

It offers a renewed scrutiny – as I have already implied – of the unfulfilled promises of tradition and of descent and ascent all over again into inequalities, unequal cultures. *It offers in stages a conversion of such inequalities into numinous inexactitudes.*

Such numinous inexactitudes breach the role of dogmatic exactitude or fanat-ical ideology and creed *not* by conquest but by civilization's arrival upon bridges from one closed mind to the other, from one closed world to the other. Within such subtly and complexly breached closure the orphaned Imagination, orphaned from its creator, is imbued with an inner immensity, an inner dynamic, that learns through all its carnival manifestations and masks. Does such inner immensity imply a new and evolving role for the Soul of traditions? This question, this implicit promise, moves us into a future into which we arrive with hope, yet fear and trembling.

For a breakthrough from conquest-driven imperatives is a task for which a fallible humanity is scarcely equipped. Let us remember however that epic sustains an engagement with extra-human parents who may resemble feuding and warring commanders but are intrinsically sponsors of diversity that may assist us to free ourselves from apparently incorrigible bias.

Address to Temenos Academy, London, 7 February 1994

Part IV

UNFINISHED GENESIS

PREFACE: UNFINISHED GENESIS

Unfinished genesis operates in the living language. It makes works in the language that enable the artist to create from a stronghold-in-the-imagination.

The power of the imagination is present within a living language, and composes, within the artist, an interior unpredictable dialogue that gives rise to 'variables within the language of the Imagination' and a 'ventriloquism of Spirit'.[1]

This carries acute ramifications with the individual exercise of liberty and the acts people commit in the name of liberty – acts often bereft of depth and vulnerable to savage retribution under the disguise of justice.[2]

Correspondences between literature and her sister arts, music, painting, drama and architecture, depend for their fecundity on maintaining open channels with traditions in the arts of the Imagination. When, as in the case of the allegorical portraits-in-landscape by the painter Titian, a language of the imagination, realized in Titian's age as a fecund and vibrant system of memorization, is no longer practised; when that language dies, the living artist, in our day, might, in that dead language's memorial, perceive something newborn 'running deeper than the demise of a culture or a language'.[3] This points to the regeneration not just of an abstracted imaginative resource but equally to ourselves as a re-imagined resource prolonged into art[4] and accompanies the potential for a new conceptual language[5] that requires, as it were, windows into a nonsensational world apparent other than through the frame of the senses. The final essay picks up again 'the intuitive clue'. In 'The Literate Imagination', the intuitive clue was seen to co-opt

1 'Profiles of Myth and the New World' (1966), pp.201–11 in this volume.
2 'In the Name of Liberty' (1990), pp.212–21 in this volume.
3 Ibid.
4 'Aubrey Williams' (1966) and 'Apprenticeship to the Furies' (1966), pp.222–5 and 226–36 in this volume.
5 *'nonsensational changes in human nature itself* (so subtle are these changes that they are easily smothered by a sensational world), changes therefore within the genesis of imagination in nature and space and psyche' 'Creoleness, The Crossroads of a Civilization' (1988), pp.237–47 in this volume.

the redrafting of a text at ever more resonant levels. In 'The Unfinished Genesis of the Imagination' that clue is seen also to sow or secrete new texts into the future.

16

PROFILES OF MYTH AND THE NEW WORLD

A brief word before I enter the substance of my paper.

Is it possible for an imaginative writer to work in a language he does not love? I love the English language deeply. It is my native language. I was born in Guyana, South America. Such are the proportions, extensions, extremities, of a living language.

It saddens me to learn from various sources of the predicament of the humanities around the globe. Teachers and lecturers are undervalued. Also issues of tradition remain, it seems to me, in a kind of limbo.

There are traditions prior to the rise of the eighteenth-century and nineteenth-century European, realist novel that are disregarded when it comes to the language of the Imagination within fiction. I applaud Frances Yates's *Art of Memory* in the context of the salvage of such traditions in Europe. She confessed to the difficulties of her task. I applaud Kathleen Raine for her editing of the magazine *Temenos* and her founding of the Temenos Academy in London.

Some, in this audience, would be aware of such research and such work but virtually nothing is known of pre-Columbian traditions of fluid identity that seem to me to breach tribal fixtures and adamant racial codes, and to possess enormous potential bearing on arts of fiction.

Such traditions appear irremediably lost but intuitive dimensionalities and clues have surfaced I find in my own work across several decades. This is the mystery of one's peculiar dialogue with the past and it proves or validates what C.G. Jung calls the 'collective unconscious' and its eruption within processes of hard work, concentration and creativity, into the subconscious and conscious. Jung by and large applied his concept to the human psyche and faculty. I sense the collective or universal unconscious extending into voices that echo within the roots of nature as from the ancestral dead, from rivers, from rocks, from birds and other species, from the rhythm of landscapes, skyscapes, etc.

Intuitive clues which erupt from the unconscious are rooted in labour and in ecstasy – as much in labour as in revelation – and they bring insights for the re-education of society by strangers in the self.

I shall touch on these matters in my paper. But something else, I think, needs to be said about the matter of literacy. Some years ago skilled and semi-skilled workers on farms and in factories lost their jobs and for the first time were revealed to the gaze of the general public as unable to read or write. In their long working life they had got by socially and in the work-place efficiently and well. To read or to write was not a necessity in the performance of duties or tasks. In my judgement the appearance of a body of young people who have difficulty in reading books – because of a limited vocabulary – needs to be judged carefully. Within the linear biases that rule our society we see them as witnessing involuntarily to a decline in standards of literacy. And this is partially true. But to reify such statistics into an absolute is to succumb to a fallacy. Many young people with limited vocabularies, and lodged in other deprivations, may not be truly comparable with their literate peers in a previous generation. Their parents and grandparents may never have read a book. Thus their surfacing within the body politic is comparable to the exposure of the unskilled and semi-skilled workers to whom I referred a moment ago. Rather than a straightforward decline therefore we may be witnessing the emergence of hidden proportions of humanity whom society has long manipulated as factory or farm or military fodder.

The danger that confronts us is, therefore, more complex than a linear decline in conventional literacy. The danger lodges in technologies that may be used to manipulate whole and entire societies, and the elites within those societies who deem themselves literate but are conscripted by linear biases and fallacious absolutes. Moral tone, moral vigour, should instil a flexability of encounter with the past if the living language, in which we work and write, is to throw up out of its depths provisional bridges between the weak and the strong, the workman and the artist, between the closed worlds of the sciences and of mathematics and the deep-seated, half-articulate, numinous conscience of the creative and re-creative genesis of the Imagination.

I trust this brief, introductory word may help as I enter now the substance of my paper.

The pitiless slogan 'ethnic cleansing' has echoed around the globe within a chorus of grief, raped women, bombed villages and cities; and I would like to suggest that a certain, well-nigh forgotten tradition in the pre-Columbian Americas may still be raised into renascent focus to assist us to see the fallacy in concepts of pathetic racial purity. Such concepts appear at times to be innocuous but they may signify, I think, the death of the Imagination within frames of dogmatic identity and dogmatic homogeneity.

My consolation is that the Imagination never dies entirely and prompts us to ask ourselves – What is home? How should the arts of the nation-state – the arts of Commonwealth, the arts attuned to resources of community – visualize home within diasporas, conflicts, and within the funeral procession of our civilization?

The pre-Columbian tradition that I propose to bring to your attention implies a profound and unusual treaty of sensibility between human presence on this planet and the animal kingdom. I would like to intuit from that treaty certain approaches to defects in secular realism, certain approaches to fanaticism associated with religious ritual or dogma or absolute, certain approaches to a fiction in dialogue with the sacred, a dialogue of creativity that is aware of the mystery of the sacred as it inhabits our psyche, an awareness that breaches however – and is not the slave of – fanatical creed, fanatical absolute.

Across the chasm of centuries I find myself returning to the ancient treaty or tradition, to which I refer, as a medium of variable, live, fossil proportions. Take Quetzalcoatl whose appearance on this planet – according to some legends – occurred around two thousand years ago. Quetzalcoatl was regarded as a god-man. The fossil proportions in the name are obvious, namely, quetzel (the bird), coatl (the snake or serpent). The bird of heaven and the ecstatic or abysmal serpent become a variable code in the language of the Imagination. One is tilted, so to speak, into a series of extraordinary particularities in craft and art as these were pursued – it seems to me – in a distant age. Painted faces upon pottery or vases, sculpture, and other modes of expression appear to gain their inner support from a live, fossil domain. Features were slanted or sharpened, noses pinched, lips flared, in coincidence with a numinous bone or beak, feather or scale. Human faces were curiously rounded into the spirituality of an owl, or the conscience-stricken glance of a hare. Or rather, let us say, the flesh of paint that drapes conscience or spirituality seemed to lean upon an inner fabric, an inner, dissolving yet re-constituted owl-fabric, the glance as well of a running beast, a startled hare, the poise of a jaguar, that are metamorphosed into variable human features.

A range of diverse expressions begins to address us which is startlingly akin to racial types or tribal fixtures as we would see them now. Indeed an odd humour prevails and it is as if all ethnicities, all the races of the earth, travelled to ancient America to become models for their craftsmen and artists!

One could draw upon all sorts of animal combination and coincidence, subtleties, differentiations, that bring to the human mask, the human gesture, an involuntary association and kinship with numerous creatures.

Let me give five pregnant examples:

(1) A small figure in buff clay, meticulously worked, from Pueblo Copana-huasta, late classic AD 550 to 950, called 'Warrior', sustains a caricaturized royal tiger, astonishing resemblance to the Tudor King Henry VIII.

(2) In the same late classic period we come upon another apparently ruling personage, popularly known by historians today as the Juárez sculpture. The Metropolitan Museum of Art in New York City identifies this with Palenque. It is called the Juárez sculpture because of the strong and vivid resemblance it bears to President Benito Juárez, Abraham Lincoln's respected contemporary.

(3) A reclining figure, brownish clay with traces of red pigment and white paint, Central Mexico, Middle Preclassic, 1150 to 550 BC, is Chinese in its physiognomy.

(4) Hieratic ape, cloistered nun-like expression, one might perceive in a medieval European cathedral, comes from Guatemala, AD 150 to 250 or earlier.

(5) Massive Olmec Head, La Venta, dated 1000 to 600 BC, appears vividly Negroid or African. The flaring, majestic nostrils, the rhythms of expression,

invoke the sensation of an inner jaguar support or scaffolding. The jaguar was immensely important to the ancient American world and I would hazard a guess that the Olmec is an earlier manifestation of the variable code of the god-man such as we associate with Quetzalcoatl.

The term 'numinous inexactitudes' came into play in a new fiction I have written. And I would like to apply this term to all such figures of fluid and variable identity that we may pursue in the ancient American world. The crafts-men of that age – let us for the sake of convenience call them 'artists' – were in pursuit of a figuration of the creator that could never be grasped or realized exactly. Their treaty with the animal kingdom was such that they looked for support, for traceries, for cues, for clues, within infinite subleties in meta-phorically alive, fossil corridors and shapes within the inimitable architecture of the animal kingdom. The variations were such that features emerged which we – in our addiction to absolute realism – would place as racial types whereas then they constituted, in my judgement, a variable and fluid life-enhancing diversity.

I am not suggesting for a moment that this phenomenon was wholly pervasive in the ancient pre-Columbian world. It was – I imagine – a precarious evolution in the theatre of the mind. There were pressures, I would think, there were strictures, there was a sense of the forbidden that continues to haunt the psyche of humanity, and all these constituted a profound challenge to the resources of the creative Imagination and a threat as well. And indeed the fall of the ancient pre-Columbian tradition from precarious heights, and from a peak of strange glory or diversity of spirit, into bloodthirsty ritual and cruel, heart-wrenching sacrifice, is a symptom of the triumph of restrictive convention.

That foul triumph, I would suggest, needs to be analysed in a context of the forbidden, in a simultaneous context of what constitutes consent from a creator when art and science adventure deep into the kingdom of nature, a multi-form nature that is ambivalent at times, a nature associated with all species, landscapes, riverscapes, skyscapes, a nature that is sentient and alive, though we may be tempted to see such life as so bordering on passivity that the kingdom of space and nature becomes for us a pawn to be manipulated.

Let us admit that the consent of deity, the consent of a creator, when humanity adventures into the cosmos – as much as into the recesses of the animal kingdom – is an unfashionable concept, to say the least, in our time. Yet the pressure for such consent lingers on in subconscious and unconscious ways and unless we begin to visualize what I would call 'the storage of the forbidden, forbidden territories in ourselves' we are likely to be taken by surprise and to become the victims of restrictive and unjust convention that operates in every sphere of activity, national and international.

All cultures are subject to the ravages of unjust convention which may take the form of stereotypical purities. Take incest. Incest has been countenanced at times as a royal privilege to preserve the purity of the ruling line. But incest is also a dread abuse of the weak in so-called ordinary families. How susceptible are such families to unconscious legacies of perverse linearity that seek to frame the identity of the family into an absolute convention?

The tension between royal incest and incest within the family creates, I feel, an irreconcilable situation that reflects the power of forbidden territories within us. We are forbidden incest yet at another level incest is sanctified. We may institute legal protection to safe-guard victims of family-incest. But the compulsion runs so deep that it may elude us and provide cement for our institutions until these harden into projected incest, so to speak, projected violence by the state upon others to preserve stereotypical purities. The stranger is targeted, the foreigner is targeted, the refugee is targeted, as impure. Such targets reflect consent from some perverse deity in ourselves committed to abstract incest and the projection of violence, sanctified violence, upon others.

At the heart of such perverse consent lies – I am implicitly suggesting – a conviction that we have cemented subconsciously or unconsciously into our prized institutions the conviction of stereotypical and absolute purity that may affect the nature of citizenship in some nation-states. The tragedy is that all of us – whatever our intellectual and surface persuasion, liberal, democratic, fascist – are influenced at some level in ourselves by the charisma of our institutions, the sacrosanct territory of our institutions. We are forbidden – though we may scoff at such a notion – by formidable, rarely exposed legacies, to begin a penetration of a core of pre-possessions and biases that colour our judgements even within the liberal state that fears secretly to be swamped (as the saying goes) by foreigners.

Let me return at this moment to the five examples I gave of variable and fluid identity in the ancient pre-Columbian world. I stressed that these were not racial types, as we understand the term. We tend to label them categorically racial because of our addiction to an absolute realism. We miss the differentiations that may arise in a play of subtleties and rhythms of expression in a treaty between art and the animal kingdom.

I could add many more to the five examples I have given. But I shall merely say that the differentiation in variable identity brings into play Phoenician features, Asian features, Semitic, Latin, Romanesque, etc. Ivan Van Sertima, in his book *They Came Before Columbus*,[1] has argued impressively that Africans visited the ancient Americas. I read recently that a navigator – his name slips from me – is now organising an expedition across the Pacific in an ancient Chinese vessel to see whether the Chinese may not have crossed that great ocean two or three thousand years ago.

Van Sertima's thesis rests, in part, on the Olmec physiognomy but he – I know him well – has never argued that all the races of mankind had congregated in ancient America hundreds of years before the birth of Christ.

What we need to visualise, I think, is an art that is steeped in numinous inexactitudes. Fluid identity creates a number of windows into reality. The ancient pre-Columbians pursued a creator beyond seizure, a creator whose likeness could never be rendered exactly. Indeed to invest in such exactitude was to restrict the focus of the Imagination, to bind it into ritual or into dogma. There was, I sense, a complex recognition of forbidden territories and the necessity to gain the consent of the elusive creator-god in adventuring into the cosmos. Such consent however was steeped I would say *not* in incorrigible bias but in profoundest, self-confessional self-knowledge.

Such deep self-knowledge was painful but it possessed the ecstasy of a break-through from binding formula (which never encompasses the elusive proportions of deity).

Inadequacies began to surface in conventional narratives of stereotypical purity and these evolved into numinous inexactitudes within which the Imagination was empowered by the sacred to pitch its parameters of vision into unsuspected spaces, unsuspected heights and depths. As a consequence a simultaneity occurred not only between a variety of features and pigmentations in variable identity but between intimate reality and stranger reality. That simultaneity broke a purely linear persuasion, it broke a linear addiction to a progressive chasm between the past and the present. It revealed that however determined we are to maintain absolute linearity in fictions of reality the past is still active in the present moment, it still arrives in the future, and continues to store ambivalent pressures that fall below the level of creative and re-creative consciousness, pressures that continue to cement our fears and biases within the institutional life of the nation-state.

You may agree I hope that all this bears on the language of the Imagination and how it affects narrative fiction. An elusive deity or creator whom one may view, so to speak, through a series of windows – all of which are meaningful self-deceptions – alerts us to the fallibility of human discourse, a purely human discourse. We need to revise our understanding, I find, of the nature of the Voice we hear – the nature of our own utterance – in a dialogue with the sacred. I shall return to this in a moment. But first a comment on realism to which cultures are addicted. Even as we perceive the usefulness of realistic narrative we become aware surely of its partial stance in illuminating the legacies of the past, the motivations of the past that run far deeper than the surfaces of fact. Newspapers may describe the length of a murderer's hair, the suit he wore when he stabbed his victim, the car he drove, it may provide you with a multiplicity of factual detail, it may disclose the contents of the victim's stomach, but one is left in the dark as to the impulses, the motivations, at work. More and more one is told of the rising incidence of meaningless crime.

A series of motivations suppressed within instinctualities of body and spirit require windows into reality that are other than the frame of realism. The Olmec window, for instance, to which I referred earlier in this paper, is instinct with a jaguar scaffold in the theatre of the mind. And this discloses itself so curiously that we need to turn to other windows in which a serpentine spiral or unsuspected ladder reveals the architecture or the myth of the brain. Is the brain a myth? I intend no offence to biologists! It is a myth in the degree that we may hear the voice of Quetzalcoatl across the chasm of centuries. A cautionary voice speculating on the serpentine coil in the brain that flowers at times into wisdom, an electrical circuit akin to wisdom, but is capable in another disjointed flash, or moment, of conceiving – within the laboratory of primitive science – the action of dread power from which one mints technologies of violence.

In the same token we may be drawn to another window, a window of legend, the legend of the Incarnation that runs in parallel with the mystery of life in space, to contemplate a winged capacity in the myth of the brain.

Myth – a despised concept in an age of realism – endorses a series of instinctualities in all useful but partial windows that we erect upon and into reality. Altruism, sainthood, are as mysterious as dread violence. No absolute disclosure exists to unravel motivation. But we may glimpse through a series of windows, more or less abreast of each other, a pregnant cosmos that nourishes and sustains us in the quest for inimitable motivation within dualities, trinities, quaternities, etc. etc.

Let me return now to the question that I raised a little while ago about the fallibility of a purely human and conventional discourse.

I have no dogmatic theories about this but I became aware of variables within the language of the Imagination when I worked and travelled in the rain forests and savannahs of Guyana.

One such variable – and this appears rather pointedly in a new fiction of mine entitled *Resurrection at Sorrow Hill* – relates to a creator and his/her agents and agencies which speak through metaphorically closed lips in the guise of a ventriloquist of Spirit. Such speech exists, as it were, in some priority that comes before human utterance. In that priority lies the mystery of the exact Word of creation but its adumbrations, its vibrancies akin to speaking Shadow and Light are active within the numinous inexactitudes to which I referred earlier in this paper. There is, as it were, a vibrancy to silence. There is a Silence that is interior within, anterior to, the human myth of the Word. Silence in the depth of that myth of the absolute Word ripples into layers of sound within all gestures, all species, within the shape of rocks whose hieroglyphic utterance in crevice and markings, markings of age akin sometimes to a cradle or an epitaph descended from the stars, is espoused and matched by the applause of the elements in a clap of water upon rock within a waterfall.

The ventriloquism of Spirit implies therefore – I would suggest – rhythm, gesture, sound signifying priorities that are beyond exact representation or seizure.

It implies the numinosity (as well as luminosity) of a Voice prior to all voices; it implies incandescent utterance within the genius of the planet, it implies Shadow-tongues, latencies, involuntary associations that test us deeply with regard to compressions of time, the legacies of the past in the present.

Ventriloquism of Spirit within the sounding board of rock or marble or wood may articulate commandments that we enshrine upon stone but such commandments are numinous inexactitudes.

Even stranger is the Voice's susceptibility, in its innermost problematic, to a kinship with the maimed, the apparently passive constituents in nature. And the temptation arises, within human cultures, in a medium which seeks support from fossil passivities in nature, to project that passivity, as it were, upon all species in nature itself. Thus the quest for a supportive nature, upon which to clothe representations of an elusive and problematic creator-deity, may move by degrees, almost unwittingly, into the desire to plunder, exploit, enslave species in nature, the desire to manipulate landscapes in nature.

The stresses latent in such exploitative creeds may be balanced by a desire in cultures to achieve a narrow scale of self-preservation and to maintain this within the diverse species that they manipulate or exploit. Thus unwittingly again perhaps – as these cultures become fortresses – narrow self-preservation incorporates into itself a deafness to what it does not wish to hear and in this we perceive the beginning of a hubris cemented in human discourse. By and large I fear that this is our predicament as the twentieth century draws to a close.

We need today – it seems to me – an openness to the language of the Imagination simultaneous with a grasp of the sacred that requires self-confessional and profound self-judgemental art rooted in a spectrum of variable identity. As though the sacred, the consent of deity, in humanity's – in civilisation's – adventure into the cosmos, is a paradox of the innovative mind. In that paradox, the burden of Memory alerts us to the Guilt of our own actions in the past – ancestral action, the action of our antecedents; alerts us to lapses from life-enhancing diversity into stereotypical purities breeding incest, stereotypical pride breeding violence and rape. That alert would be unbearable if it rested on a singular or linear narrative of history. Singularity and linearity are the stuff of escapism which may take many post-modernist patterns. Let me resume what I was saying: the alert to the lapses and legacies of the past would be unbearable if it did not acquire a degree of density that steeps us in diverse personae – sometimes virtually abreast of each other – which help us to see ourselves differently, see ourselves broken into many players within ourselves and within stranger cultures. Such diversity, such strangeness, may then take up the burden of Memory in a new light and puncture or stagger that burden, puncture or stagger ancestral Guilt. Those punctures and staggerings create openings, corridors, into new architectures of space.

Absolute Guilt paralyses the Imagination. The need to stagger the burden of memory, replete with guilt, is essential to the creation of a new age. But within a heterogeneity of the Imagination intact memory may be creatively sustained in conjunction with staggered guilt. That is, I believe, an essential key into motivations of the sacred that we tend to eclipse in fanaticism and dogma. Fanaticism blocks the intricacies of the sacred. Dogma has no perception of the spiritual subversion of biased institutions.

My inner feeling is – and this is not based on intellectual premises but on hard work within the problematic of fiction across several decades, work that ignites the spark of intuition – that the pursuit of staggered guilt, staggered yet paradoxically whole and intact Memory – subsists upon a spectrum of variable identity or diverse profiles of myth.

Mixed societies, heterogeneous societies, are an essential ingredient in the modern world, if we are to begin to see ourselves differently, and to create a living, vital, non-complacent future within the burdens that history has placed on us in every corner of the globe.

Jacques Monod, the French biologist, coined a memorable phrase when he wrote – 'Every living creature is also a fossil.'[2] And I tend to think that that dictum is a belated footnote to arts of memory which Frances Yates, the great Renaissance scholar, sought to salvage with great difficulty she confessed. For such arts, rooted in unfathomable origins, had virtually disappeared by the age of the Renaissance when they still flourished precariously. Titian's *Allegory of Prudence*, for instance, needs to be read in a quite different way from the singular and triumphant individualism that we associate with Romantic hubris. Such Romantic individualism denied the life of strangers in the self and sought self-sufficient characters as its province. Curiously enough the rise of the novel – which by and large tends to hold up a mirror to provincial society – runs in parallel with Romantic certitudes of the nation-state. Herman Melville is an exceptional nineteenth-century novelist in his involvement with diverse characters plucked from many cultures around the globe. Melville was in despair at the height of his powers for he knew he was regarded as an irrelevant and marginal, imaginative writer.

To return to Titian! The link between the human and instinctual, animal codes is not Romantic. In a previous essay I speak of that link as 'the genius of the creature'. Thus human presence articulates itself into strange plurality and density born of simultaneous representations of the heights and the depths. The animals in Titian's allegory are instinctual manifestations of 'intelligentia', 'prudentia', 'memoria'. And this raises a peculiar and interesting parallel to the pre-Columbian tradition I have sought to explore in this paper.

Pertinent to the issues I have attempted to raise is the nature of freedom, and I would like to close my paper on this note. Freedom, as we know, is not an absolute. It is hedged around by legal codes that bear on obscenity, blasphemy, libel, etc. etc. The ground of the sacred implies – as I have tentatively outlined – the complex, imaginative, self-confessional, self-judgemental art that echoes, as it were, from within ourselves; such echoes – I would say – invoke an orchestration of imageries and histories to take us through and beyond ourselves into the music of space, incandescent space, rhythmic space, ventriloquist space. Deity's consent, therefore, touches upon, or is born from, or renewed within layers of profoundest self-knowledge, elemental as well as moral self-knowledge. Deity's consent is at the core of a penetration of the forbidden in humanity's continuing adventure into an ocean of space and into transferable genetic codes and cells from one species into another, from animal to plant.

What does freedom mean within an adventure that implies operations that tend to function within closed orders or disciplines, the closed world of mathematics, for instance, worlds that transcend commonsense, biology, certain categories of experimental science? Is there a sacred necessity, a visionary, re-visionary necessity – steeped in profound rehearsals, and alterations of imaginative fiction – to throw provisional bridges across chasms between the arts and the sciences?

Can we truly speak of freedom when the age in which we live – despite mass-media technologies of communication – possesses no numinous, imaginative bridges between the arts and the sciences? Such bridges cannot fit into linear convention which bases itself on description, described place, on progressive description as one thing falls behind another. Whereas one is speaking of peculiar densities and transparencies of unconscious, subconscious yet eruptive legacy that bring one *there* upon a psychical bridge between past and present traditions, a psychical bridge that may carry circular, spiral, and other spaces of paradox linking mathematics and fiction.

As I say there is no formula – such as the formula of a pure or static language, a photographic stasis built into the documentary word, a stasis that voids the re-visionary momentum of consciousness and unconsciousness. One arrives *there* on a bridge within the peculiar intensities, partialities, re-visionary partialities that break closed worlds within the active fossil resources of a living language.

You may have heard of Emmanuel Lévinas who has contemplated architectures of space in his philosophy. I have not read his work but Hena Maes-Jelinek, the Belgian scholar, comments on Lévinas in an essay she wrote on my novel *The Four Banks of the River of Space*.[3]

Space in Einsteinian mathematics is curved. There are, one could say, implicit shapes, rooms, dimensions in space.

In *The Four Banks of the River of Space* a diagram appears of a stage-discharge curve of a non-tidal river in Guyana, South America. The Macusis – an ancient Amerinidian people – have lived there on the bank of that river for centuries that stretch back into the mists of time

The curve is peculiar. It subsists on clusters of minuscule stars signifying measurements and observations of the volumetric discharge of the river across seasons and months and years.

By accident, it seems, the stars are so spread out and grouped by the hand of science, shall I say, that one falls into them as into a constellation in the night-sky of the river. One perceives one's head and chest reflected there metamorphosed into a violin. Furthermore the curve assumes the quality of a fossil rib in the fluid body of the river. And, by degrees, the night sky constellation endorses a land rib, a river rib, a sky-reflected-rib, reaching into space.

The rhythm, the silent music, the numbers, crack open a closed world of mathematics not descriptively – there is no formulaic description – but by taking one *there* into (I quote now from *The Four Banks of the River of Space*)

> Music and numbers [which] were a revelation of a fluid skeleton, a
> ribbed body, to be associated with the flesh of the elements, the smooth
> flesh of water, the spark and the animal magnetism within the anatomy
> and the blood of ancient streams upon which many cultures had

survived and above which they buried their dead in mounds and hills. Our antecedents from all races and peoples glimpsed that skeleton as they wrestled with floods and droughts, plenty and scarcity, from times immemorial, antecedents we also glimpse in the nightsky of the ancient river through the seed of moral legend, moral theatre that they sowed, primitive constellation and metamorphoses of the voice of the flute [. . .] Primitive antecedent. Intimate refugee.

[. . .] It was but a glimpse into a library of illustrated dream within a theatre of science [. . .].

That glimpse empowered my pilgrimage upwards in space yet backwards in time within the Carnival Day of the twentieth century [. . .].[4]

Freedom, it seems to me will become progressively meaningless unless humanity can arrive upon provisional bridges between what appear to be closed minds, closed disciplines, closed orders. There is – I have attempted to show – shared territory between partial windows upon reality we reinforce by complacent habit into absolutes. To attempt to arrive at another absolute theory, another absolute description of such shared territory is to succumb to further fallacy. The real possibility, it seems to me, lies in the changed fabric of language as it draws upon unsuspected resources within an unfinished genesis of the Imagination.

Notes

1 See I. Van Sertima, *They Came Before Columbus* (New York, 1976). There are numerous references to the Olmec (distinctions and variations) as he argues for an African presence in ancient America.
2 J. Monod, *Le Hazard et la Nécessité* (Paris, 1970); *Chance and Necessity* (London, 1971).
3 See H. Maes-Jelinek, 'Unfinished Genesis: *The Four Banks of the River of Space*', in: *Wilson Harris, The Uncompromising Imagination.* ed. H. Maes-Jelinek (Mundelstrup, 1991), pp.239–45.
4 W. Harris, *The Four Banks of the River of Space*, in: *The Carnival Trilogy* (London, 1993), pp.312f.

17

IN THE NAME OF LIBERTY

Events in Eastern Europe are on everyone's lips as I write this informal Note which has to do with freedom, freedom of speech, as this addresses the issue of imaginative truth. One feels in the light of world-wide events that such an issue is saturated with peculiar urgencies that test one to the core, the core of one's faith, the core of one's understanding of reality. I feel I must attempt to assess, in some degree, intuitive resources that may lead into the ground of complex faith in truth. Fiction is the sister of truth. Or else it is a lie. Alas, there is no short-cut in such matters as events everywhere make clear – the fanaticisms we have seen in the past decade, the terrorism, and yet the profound longing for Liberty. The intuitive fabric of self-knowledge, self-judgement, or responsibility for events that one bears (in however small a way) can never be taken for granted. Indeed it remains ceaselessly unfinished and open to investigation by creative conscience.

I find myself distracted – if distraction is the word – by a question I cannot bypass – the question of *immediacy*. Do not people project their fears or guilts or humiliations or wishes or desires into *instant* frames to house their heroes or their villains, their causes of virtue or vice? Immediacies, immediate reactions, are most active within particular moments of crisis when emotions are inflamed and absolutes gain ascendancy. Such projection is so compelling, so gripping, that it eclipses all thought of duality or a possible reversal in the judgements one exercises under pressure or fear. Joseph Conrad, the Anglo-Polish novelist, states through the lips of Lord Jim – I paraphrase loosely – that heroism and anti-heroism may sometimes be read upon a divide as thin as a sheet of paper.

Such a frail distinction nevertheless remains obscure. And yet, once visualized as a garment of history, it may assist us to weigh the gestures and straitened circumstances of the body politic within particular crises. This brings me back to the upsurge of masses, people's power, in Eastern Europe, the drama of immediacy, the indictment of political villains. The Russian Revolution of 1917 was a signal, it seemed, of a new moral and economic order. It seemed absolute. It led to the secret arrest and assassination of the czar and his family. It spoke of the coming of the classless society. It spoke of justice even as it began to lay the ground for the rise of a new ruling and despotic class. Now – seventy-two years later – one sees what has been obvious for some time: its edifice became the cement of intolerance. Where it still rules it has begun to re-consider its pre-possessions and is on trial. Where it lies in ruins it appears as if blasted within a day and a night by a hand of space no-one had foreseen.

On seeing that hand, so to speak, raised in tumultuous, television bodies in Prague, Berlin, in Warsaw, in Bucharest, and elsewhere, I felt a spontaneous stab of joy, yet bitter-tasting irony I must confess. I was reminded of scenes I witnessed as a young man on the streets of Georgetown, British Guiana, in the mid-twentieth century when processions of ordinary people, trade unionists, sugar estate workers, etc., etc., paraded carrying banners adorned with pictures of Stalin, Lenin, Thomas Paine, Karl Marx, Walt Whitman and Trotsky. It was a heady, chaotic love affair with Liberty that was to have its tragic consequences.

What happened there was but a small tributary within a great tide that had already divided Europe in the name of revolutionary Liberty, a tide also at work in the politics of Latin America, Asia and Africa. Stalin died in 1953 and was buried with honour in Moscow. It was to take many long years before Russian writers were to disclose that he was arguably the most cunning and sinister tyrant of his age. A year or so after Stalin's death, another Joseph, Joseph McCarthy, the alleged hero of anti-communism, was censured by the US Senate. Too late then to avert the consequences of the Inquisition he had mounted against teachers, writers, actors, and many others whose only crime was the free exercise of their own minds. In some degree nevertheless that Senate censure precipitated the slow, laborious re-habilitation of the character and reputation of the 'villains' McCarthy had indicted.

I started this Note by implying a necessity to probe intuitive resources through which to scan the nature of immediacy and to weigh dualities when the hero becomes a tyrant, the romance of Liberty a theatre of tragedy. If that were all, one would be involved in an inflexible alternation, an inflexible rhythm of opposites.

Nihilism is rooted in the absolute sway of dualities, the swing of alleged good into evil, alleged evil into good, without respite across the decades and gener-ations. Accept such a formula and the sceptical and nihilistic philosopher or artist is free (whatever freedom means in this context) to indict the sacred and to turn away from the possibility of *inimitable* Being or truth.

Scepticism becomes remorseless in its traffic with frames of dogma that sustain certain kinds of bias which cultures associate with heroes or gods or sacred per-sonages. Such frames are projections of immediacy – one may argue on behalf of the sceptical artist – in which phenomena of existence are given instant glorifi-cation in the temples of civilization. And since such projection is suspect in the political arena, it is equally dubious – the argument may run – in the so-called sacred place or temple where a god or a prophet is identified with a phenomenon of nature.

By degrees, it seems to me, scepticism allied to nihilism inevitably make their trade in repudiating the sacred personage in politics or religion. So much so that unwittingly perhaps the entrenched sceptical mind is conditioned by what it feeds upon. Conditioned by the hubris it attacks as that hubris re-appears in a form of secular or intellectual dogma. We have seen that paradox at work in some communist societies where secular freedom contradicts itself in becoming an *absolute* condition of thought and existence; inimitable Being slowly becomes forfeit to an art or a politics *that is bereft of depth*.

The secular mind that takes its orientation from the surfaces of life – where the depth-imagination is suspect because it does not conform to a ruling theory – is less free than it thinks. Perhaps not free at all. It tends to circumscribe itself afresh within frames it appears to loathe in political or religious dynasties. One has seen the embalmed Lenin, for instance, the prize of an establishment, the embodiment of the Revolution in the 1920s, turn by unbreathing degrees into the ironic vestment of a showcase czar.

The apparition of the secular and free mind appears sanguine and emancipated because it is 'embalmed', metaphorically speaking. It is the unwitting pawn of legacies of tradition it cannot genuinely rehearse; rehearse, penetrate, and change in depth. Nothing disturbs its sanguine contour until a sudden, catastrophic eruption, emanating from unpredictable numinosity in the body politic, occurs. It is as if the phenomenon the secular mind is disposed to cheapen or flatten strikes back in an uncanny way.

In pointing to an addiction to 'immediacies' and to the sway of dualities that foster nihilism I am not proposing the corollary that history repeats itself endlessly. Not at all. My point is nevertheless that cultures are prone to invest in *partial* structuralizations of Being, in a partiality to which it may remain blind, a partiality that it equates with wholeness, with an apparition of wholeness. Such apparitions are not the static address they seem. They have roots – if I may so put it – in the unconscious. They secrete an irony, they secrete terrifying reactions. Liberty that is without depth or truth may bring the entrenched, sceptical imagination face to face with the odour and dreadful sanctity of the tyrant on whom it preys.

It is logical in the light of the above to assume, I think, that post-modernist scepticism inevitably brings about a restriction in the scope of word and image. In the space-age civilization, that ours is becoming, such loss of depth needs to be considered and remedied before it exacerbates a range of unpredictable conflicts within the narrow and biased frameworks of many cultures.

Let me turn at this stage into an area where I may attempt – as I implied at the beginning of this Note – to assess *intuitive* resources that bear on the undervalued truths within, beyond, and beneath *partial* appearances.

Cultures vary around the globe. The shamanic body of a culture that I sought to depict in a South American river community in my novel *The Whole Armour*, (1962)[1] possesses its own peculiarities that spring from the region.

Cristo, in that novel which celebrates a wake for a dead man who is still alive, is the son of the river prostitute Magda. In a sense, an intuitive sense that arises from neglected possibilities in a remote area of the globe, Cristo and Magda are living fossils, living shells of a people and community which celebrate and mourn a bizarre Christ-figure that they sculpt, as it were, out of themselves. In another pertinent sense they resemble the fragmented Arawaks who occasionally appear in the forest and who stage a carnival reconstruction of their last battle with the Caribs in the Guyanas. When Cristo runs into them it is as if he has been catapulted back into a past age. He has been pushed by his terrible, seemingly majestic mother into risking everything and embarking upon an adventure in search of truth, aboriginal and spiritual truth.

Their community is beached against the Atlantic, on one hand, with the equally vast ocean of the forest on the other. The shaman – from times immemorial – is a voyager into the unconscious, the unconscious, aboriginal body of the sea and of the forest that breaks through subconscious terrain into the conscious host native. The shaman carries within himself the seed of genesis that is native to every feminine element, so to speak, the womb of fire, the spirit of rain. However nerve-stricken such a voyager may be, his tension reflects a cultural void yet an extension beyond that void – *not* a denigration of the marriage of the sky and the earth. His task, in psychical fact, is to recover the profoundest reality of meaning when meaning may so easily become the victim of lust and lies. A bizarre extension of the Christ-figure of missionary churches (South American Catholic, South American Protestant) he may be, but even more his need is to explore the fossilization of Justice within a society that resembles a police state.

The shaman needs to surrender himself to a numinous realm in search of the inimitable, apparently ungraspable body of the law of truth. What is apparently ungraspable possesses a core of numinosity or myth that may give to shamanic fiction a far-flung reality. Myth becomes a basic corrective to tyrannous or despotic immediacy.

The legacies of missionary endeavours, missionary churches in South America from the age of the Spanish Conquest into the twentieth century become unbearably static unless they encompass imprints born of the seas the missionaries and conquistadors have crossed, born of the forests and rivers they have penetrated and sometimes ravaged for gold, imprints that are woven into a geography and art of Being. The planet on which we live – however mapped or raped or circumscribed – remains a living surrogate of a theatre of infinite particularities and vestiges of creation, a planet at risk.

Magda and Cristo – as live fossils imprinted by the legacies of the past – are blood brother and mother of an ailing humanity that has stepped on the moon, a moon that overshadows even as it illumines the voyaging spirit with a self-understanding that cannot be fixed or isolated in any territory or upon any star. Such isolation, such fixture, remains nevertheless the temptation of Conquest. Such fixture indeed may have appeared quite normal a century or two ago – when conquest was the norm – but now that a new and invisible tide is rising, the misapprehensions and prejudices of the past come home as the stigma of space within age-old adventures and colonizations.

To stand under the stigma of space – as the spawn of age-old adventure – is to identify in a new and scarred way with the live fossil of the self, to re-open imprints that have hardened into a block device, block divisions, block poverty, block wealth, within the body of a civilization.

The shamanic quest re-opens these scars and imprints within the body of a plagued community and within related, hunted animal species. In those mutilations the shaman perceives the genesis of the tiger as a recurring goad to fathom uncharted inner/outer spaces. He suffers decapitation in a battle between the Caribs and the Arawaks. A typical shamanic experience that acquires unpredictable content nevertheless within diverse theatres of history. His form is re-assembled, trunk and head, a living walking tree in a threatened landscape and riverscape.

Justice swims in the fish in the rivers, grows in the tree, flies with the bird, rages in the cloak of the tiger (the whole armour of god) with which he is clad by the secret, forgotten natives, warriors, priests, dwarfs, etc., etc. that he encounters.

It may come as no surprise perhaps to learn that Cristo – in the cloak of the tiger, the creaturely tiger – returns to his people to be accused of – and executed for – a crime he did not commit. But the message he brings from his travail in the forest helps him to touch an aspect of the *genius of the creature*, the genius of love in the creature, in the woman who is to bear him a child. That link between creature and pregnant form is one which I hope to illumine a little later on in this article. Let me say now that I believe it is a link that helps to sustain the value of inimitable Being which grows forfeit in the nihilist imagination.

All this – needless to say perhaps – is part and parcel of coming to grips with the cross-cultural significance that shamanic cultures – possessing roots in South America in this instance – may bear on the Imagination of Justice, inimitable Justice, partial Justice.

It is against this backcloth that the family of the shaman *alters*, acquires altered, almost divine, resonances – divine in a creative, self-analytic sense – that may affect the entire community and undermine its political cruelties and obsessions. The terrible mother Magda who had pushed Cristo to embarking on his quest – pushed him into a medium of insight far stranger than she anticipated – ceases to be the magnet of ferocious clan or incestuous privilege. It is a difficult ordeal for her as it is for the people of the region (the people of the world) to acknowledge, in the fibre of their passion, that the victim on the scaffold is underpinned by a politics that feeds on scapegoats within the authoritarian family, and that blood-letting ceremonies have been a compulsive – however unwitting – equation with revolutionary Liberty. As they struggle with the depth of a change of heart and mind that is occurring within them, the temptation returns to suppress the divine all over again, to restore it to a status of lust as the pampered offspring of a rich whore.

We need to scan closely – if we are not to be deceived by the sophistications of lust or overrun by a commerce in bodies in the name of politics or art – the *genius of the creature* that the shaman brings as his message from the depths of the unconscious. We need to scan closely the ramifications of the genius of the creature as it supplies resonance and correlative imageries to a love of Justice.

A love of Justice born of a voyage in space cannot be real until it gains cross-cultural resonance within a theatre of the creature where the ceremony of politics may perceive its obsessions undercut and transformed: a ceremony that so enacts, and re-enacts itself, that it *sees* within and through its own *blind* one-track logic and circumscription of history by immediate circumstance into an intuitive realm where the cruelty of the hunt is visualized and lifted into transfigurative dimensions in the animal, creaturely constellations; *sees* the constellation of the starred, tiger cloak, *visualizes* the constellation of the head-dress of the bird or the feather, *visualizes* the constellation of the scales of the fish upon a masked priest who listens to the hidden voices of creation, the fantasy, chaotic yet blended voices of stone and tree.

Thus it is that the creature becomes an extension of inimitable Being. The disfigurements that are the lot of the hunter and the hunted are not bypassed. They are susceptible to a transformation within the hollow of Justice, transformation into a correlation or association of imageries. It is as if Justice were now sculpted or painted in undying memory, living memory as well as the memory of the future that can never be taken for granted, as the undercutting of hubris, undercut, one-sided appearance or hollow figure, *undercut, one-sided, ruling premise*. For such ruling or unchanging premise (by which cultures frame their absolutes) is in true practice and rigid identity *ceaselessly partial* and therefore it needs to be sliced into extremities and to yield itself to creative therapy and to ungraspable but utterly real wholeness and complex truth.

The difficulty in all this lies in encouraging a perception of inimitable Being that runs through and beyond mere intellectual theory or sophistication or bauble or ideology. The ancients used to speak of 'rhetoric' in a wholly different and living sense from how we exploit or make propaganda of ideas. I am not concerned with ideology in its sophisticated parroting of bias, its sophisticated adoption of a radicalism that touches only the surfaces of life. I am suggesting that there are creative and complex pathways into visualizing the stubborn illusion of a ruling and unchanging figure or premise that solidifies itself in so-called first, second and third worlds. A ruling or unchanging figuration that reifies itself within the deprivations of cultures, that becomes the prize in an arena of turbulent and conflicting factions, is indeed a stubborn illusion; it signifies that however catastrophic are immediate or technological circumstances no real or innermost change of heart and mind occurs within the pendulum of humanity as it swings backward and forwards within old and new regimes. Except that illusion signifies hollowness, the body of the hollow Word (let us say). Thus a strange potential exists for the original imagination in depth. Such potential – one cannot over-emphasize – is not an intellectual formula. It requires profound application in *reading* reality in a different way, *reading* Justice in a different way.

In yielding itself in depth therefore – as implied above – painted or sculpted Justice becomes – in the particular context we have been pursuing – *an association of images such as the feminine/masculine cloak of a starred tiger draped around a hanging man whose brow or eyes take wing or life or swim just above the trunk of human/animal limbs within an ocean or a forest of space.*

One may – needless to say perhaps – change the emphases in this correlation of imageries in the theatre of the hollow, ruling Word that transforms itself into associative figures through which Justice gauges its partiality even as it releases itself from absolute or hollow biased identity into the mystery of universal truth. For what is at stake, in a numinous portrait of Justice, is the flexible placement of associations *within a pregnant form, a living language, a pregnant Word*. Such pregnant form gives life to the hollow appearance of Justice. That is my intuition of fiction and its bearing on the sacred, its bearing on the scope and capacity of the Word to come into equation with inimitable truth.

Languages die, they assume the shape of a memorial cliché upon the sensibility of a vanished age. But in the sense that pregnant form remains (pregnant form needs to be equated with an invisible but real field that cloaks appearances), we may perceive a correlation or association of newborn imageries in numinous intercourse, running deeper than the demise of a culture or a language, and returning in its vitality, its irony of visible and invisible circulation of forces, its comedy of frames and the undercutting of frames within an infinite medium or field, its indirections and directions in questioning a ruling and embalmed identity that becomes the self-mocking code of abortive revolutions as of obsessions with race and ethnicity.

The correlation of imageries I have suggested in respect of a 'whole armour of god' implies a feminine/masculine, creaturely coat that descends into an animal creation even as it runs into the depths of space for various thresholds into and of constellations of ungraspable but true wholeness. The masked priest in the forest who listens to the hidden voices – the hidden solidity of music in the root of tree or stone – may be as much female as male ironic presence, female or male counterpoint of divine comedy in solid music, so that the shamanic encounter with reality opens the way to a priesthood in which the listening Presence in the mask is unfathomable yet vitalized by a current of innermost gender within the paradoxes of language that may imbue objects with invisible femininity or masculinity, with innermost undying memory or creaturely birth, creaturely genesis.

An astonishing parallel of which I was unaware in 1962 when *The Whole Armour* was published may be perceived in Titian's Europe which was still in touch with ancient arts of memory. Let us glance at the painting *Prudence* by Titian. *Prudence* (whom one tends to associate with the feminine) is portrayed in Titian's painting as a *male face or mask beneath which appear three animal heads, a wolf, a lion, a dog*.

Frances Yates, the Renaissance scholar, writes of 'the symbol of Prudence (in Titian's painting) and *her* three parts, *memoria, intelligentia, providentia*'.[2] Yates is concerned with memory systems that may appear absurd to those who have lost touch with an ancient tradition. I would suggest that the male and animal counterpoint to Prudence exists within *an invisible but pregnant orientation*. Thus the surface identity of the male and animal appearances needs to be subtly and complexly revised within an invisible field through which all ruling appearances are comprehended as partial and through which – in their partiality, in the acknowledgement of their partiality – they become a threshold into the birth of new ideas, new associations, the genuine rehearsal of legacies of tradition. One may put it in another way and say that appearances in the painting *prudence* (as is also the case in the invocative mystery of the word *justice*) are susceptible to *visualization in depth* within space and psyche and nature. The core of the sacred overlaps the genius of the hunted creature but is beyond the obsolescent frames in which we tend to identify the sacred. The core of the sacred is beyond total seizure or capture within structures or pigmentations or dyes past and present. Thus there is a strange numinosity and frailty to the sacred that give it its invisible resources and enduring strength, enduring challenge to art and science. In this context of the comedy and truth of the sacred, intuition is not to be confused with sensationalism, with best-selling orgies in the market-places of politics and culture, and with the commerce of bodies and the slaughter of reputations that are a profitable arena in the nihilist novel.

One more illustration of arts of visualization in the ancient world. Let us glance at pre-Columbian America and the curious correlation of imageries in *Quetzalcoatl*, a correlation which may be equated I would suggest with *wisdom*. The marriage of sky (*quetzal*) and earth (*coatl*) touches upon evolutionary symbolisms in a post-Darwinian century. Less notably – shall I say obscurely and truly – it belongs to the family *prudence* and *justice*.

Quetzalcoatl emerged in faculties of ancient American civilization two millennia or so ago before the word 'america' had been coined. *There was a human mask or face interwoven with or flanked by snake (coatl) and bird (quetzal).* With the sudden disappearance of Quetzalcoatl – divine man and creature – there came about in succeeding empires (Toltec, Maya, Aztec, etc.), a fatal fossilization in the articulation and philosophic concept of *wisdom*. The parallels that we have perceived with the correlative imageries in respect of *justice* (South American shamanic quest) and *prudence* (Titian's Europe) are obvious. Except that what is obvious is often understood with difficulty in a conditioned mass-media age that invests in 'immediacies'.

I would like to close by saying I have written this article in response to an invitation by *Third Text*. The guest editor wrote to me implying a necessity at this time to explore the reality of the sacred and associated issues. These it is clear from grave controversies affecting religion and politics in many areas of the world are pertinent to the so-called 'Third World artist who becomes resident in the West'. I am keenly aware that the views I have expressed are personal. It is possible that writers from (let us say) India or Pakistan or China or Africa or Japan would not endorse the cross-cultural spectrum of values and creativity I have outlined. They may entertain quite different and remarkable apprehensions of sacred and secular worlds.

219

I say this because I have listened to Indian writers at one or two conferences. They emphasized with pride the great age of their surviving civilization. African writers have emphasized the fact of their own living African languages in which they may write directly and immediately to their own people as is the case with native writers in England, France, Italy, Holland etc., etc. All this has been of great interest to me in the light of my mixed antecedents, mixed ancestry, and fragmented traditions in South America and the Caribbean.

Then, of course, there is the crucial question of when it is, at what time in his or her life, a Third World artist may have come to live in the West. Some may have arrived in their childhood or adolescence or early youth and may have been educated in universities or colleges in Britain or France or the United States. Others like myself may have come in their late thirties from areas of the world in which they have lived and worked and which have helped to shape their particular and global vision. I mention all this because on reflection it seems to me there may be no such thing as a 'Third World writer or artist'. (Personally I have never cared for the term 'Third World'. It smacks of legacies of a Calvinist imperialism.) There is beyond dispute a heterogeneity of talent impinging on the West.

Whereas Asian-born and African-born writers may fall back on surviving civilizational and linguistic structures, the pre-Columbian civilization and cultures – from which some of my antecedents came – fell in the sixteenth century. The languages of the Arawaks or the Caribs or the Macusis have vanished from the Caribbean and survive in a few regional pockets in South America. English is my native language now, a changing, subtle medium of imageries and numinous resource, a living possession or gesture of psyche after centuries and generations of conflict in the Americas. English as a living medium has absorbed I am sure – indeed I know this to be true – some of the rhythms, some of the incantatory spirit, of the alien tongues of those who are my distant ancestors.

Many cultures similar, so to speak, to mine in paradox and diversity – whose native languages are now Portuguese (Brazil) and Spanish (Venezuela and Mexico) – seem to me to be an essential part of, even as they appear to belong to, the extremities or margins of Western civilization. This paradox may be a more remarkable phenomenon than the West itself comprehends.

There is the absorption of diverse content to which I referred above. Extremity or marginality, in my view, lifts the medium or diverse experience to a new angle of possibility. Marginality is not so much a geographical situation (even as the word 'Europe' implies more than a place or a fixture) but rather an angle of creative and re-creative capacity as the turbulent twentieth century draws to a close. It involves us in a curiously tilted field in which spatial pre-possessions and our pre-possessions are dislodged; in which we pursue the great Quarry of Being within a perception of re-visionary distances between viable centre and raised or flexible, moving circumference.

I have attempted to outline my approaches to this theme in this article. And I return to it for a brief moment in order to say that marginality is a raised contour or frontier of habit in the topography of the heart and mind; when raised or dislodged in the ladder of creature understanding it involves us in the risks and the potential of a creation we cannot take for granted, it involves us in the hunt in creation for a medium of transformations, it involves us in the hunt for a greatness of Being within yet beyond place.

I am well aware that allusions to 'greatness' are anathema in some quarters. As with the word 'deity' or 'God' it may appear to have fallen out of fashion or to have been jettisoned entirely (when it is not used to exalt boxers or wrestlers or film stars) but it creeps back in reactionary and unexpected frames. There is the arrogance and insensibility that reactionary 'greatness' breeds in those who set themselves up to judge or to pillory or to humiliate others. What is judgement if not a matter of grave conscience committed to truth? When it falls below such moral insight, or intention, or motivation, it degenerates into abuse by the privileged of the vulnerable . . . There is the nemesis that haunts our civilization in a peculiar way in that varieties of energy are all equated with a violence that becomes the perverse or inevitable form of technological 'greatness'. When energies are bundled together and located within an absolute frame or identity in an age of material structures then it seems to me that meaningful and creative and frail distinctions between patterns of force tend to be lost. The 'invisible fields' to which I referred earlier in this article in charting cross-cultural ancient and modern parallels become remote in undercutting and transforming ruling prejudice or bias.

The nemesis of jettisoned 'greatness' may creep back into the public domain most ironically perhaps in bestowing its largesse, freedom of speech so-called for all, a free-for-all. How free and how available to all matters little it seems to intellectuals on the march. On the face of it however such a 'free-for-all' appears to offer a generous medium for unravelling distinctions and differences until one discovers that in practice it becomes a game in which the *partial* appearance is questioned, yes, but twisted by sophists to conform to, or serve, other *partial* cliques or codes or purposes or expression. The 'free-for-all' becomes a sophisticated dead-end in such games.

I have attempted to suggest in this article that the truths of distinction and difference cannot be served by post-modernist nihilism, that they are in fact pointless and oppressive material of division, conflict and feud until perceived as inseparable from complex, intuitive faith in *inimitable* Being.

Notes

1 Re-issued as one of the four novels in *The Guyana Quartet*, 1985.
2 Frances Yates, *The Art of Memory*, 1966.

18

AUBREY WILLIAMS

As an imaginative writer I have at times attempted to speak of correspondences between literature and music, literature and painting. Aubrey Williams's paintings always evoke in me a sensation of music. As my wife Margaret once remarked, his paintings *sing* through fire.

In this address I should like to talk of the vibrancies and draperies of tone and colour in his work. I have also something to say about the genesis of tragedy in the Caribbean implicit in these draperies as a changing articulation of the form of classical tragedy within itself. I shall attempt to show what I mean by *draperies* by approaching the artist's work within and through the implicit horizons he invokes in the expression 'the mark of the hand'.

'The mark of the hand' is a mysterious signature. I say mysterious signature or textuality for Aubrey had in mind Timehri markings on ancient rocks in the interior of the Guyanas. Timehri may be translated not only as 'the mark of the hand' but as 'the hand of God'. There is an odd humour in the word 'Timehri' which is obviously the Anglicized version of an Amerindian root word. As though one were involved in a secret or unwitting pun on TIME. What is time? Time is identified with space in Einsteinian mathematics. But space, in the phenomenology of consciousness, has many objects within it, many draperies, many variable garments and shapes.

Timehri rock therefore occupies space as a garment in nature, or creation, *upon living time*. The mark of the hand, therefore, the hand of God upon rock, is a confirmation of our intercourse with living time. The mark is mysterious. It hints at a language or text that existed before human discourse. Yet it engages with human discourse to enrich the language of the imagination.

One remembers that the ancient Arawaks saw wood as a garment upon flesh-and-blood. The legend comes down to us in a seemingly crude way. The Arawak shamans created flesh-and-blood from the wood of a cherry tree. It is a question surely of imagery and vocabulary. We may abide with a crude story-line that wood becomes flesh-and-blood. Or we may deepen the imagery to imply the genesis of carving, carven wood that becomes a garment upon naked consciousness, living consciousness, even as Timehri rock is a garment upon living time.

The mystery of consciousness continues to baffle science. Time and age play their tricks as well. Astronomers have sought to calculate the age of the universe only to find that apparently subordinate parts of the universe are older than the parent universe itself.

You may remember that Pygmalion in ancient Greece saw his ivory Galatea come alive under the chisel. Such is the story-line until one breaches the frame of the story to perceive that ivory like rock and wood is drapery upon the mystery of living time and consciousness.

Equally the parable of Adam whom the God of Biblical genesis moulded from clay speaks for itself as a garment of earth or garment of pregnant mud upon the mind of Man.

The far-reaching – indeed awesome – implications that reside in the genesis of the imagination (I would say the *unfinished* genesis of the imagination) are to be gleaned, I think, in unique signatures, unique and original textualities, that reside in the mark of the hand which writes upon rock, clay, wood, and in all the elements, in the burning bush that seems to flame at times in Aubrey's canvases. All draperies upon living time and upon the mystery of naked consciousness are partial. They sustain infinite orchestrations or vibrancies of cloak or garment in nature, upon the natures of nature.

Around 1970, 1 think it was, I came upon Aubrey Williams's paintings for the first time at an exhibition in Jamaica. I was possessed by a sensation of music secreted in colour. I remarked on this and spoke of it in a talk I gave for the Mittelholzer Memorial lectures. I wonder now, looking back, whether it is pos-sible to suggest that such a rhythmic vibrancy is a clue to the implicit genesis of tragedy in the diverse arts of the New World, a clue we scarcely understand in the clash of cultures in the Caribbean, for it possibly bears upon an *alteration* in the classical mould of tragedy in the Old World.

Whatever the wounds inflicted on the body of the Caribbean, that body secretes in itself, it seems to me, a paradoxical and celebrative spirit. We are aware of this, I think, but its significance lies in a void.

Aubrey was fully aware of the dangers of what he called 'runaway technology', he had no illusions about the deprivations of the folk in the West Indies, he knew his history, the injustices inflicted upon Africans, through the Middle Passage, the injustices inflicted upon indentured servants from India and China, the decima-tions of American Indian populations since the European Conquest in the sixteenth century.

All this, needless to say, is ripe content for tragedy in the accepted classical sense. How does vibrancy, celebrative instinct, alter the form of tragedy? Let me return to Aubrey's paintings for a partial answer.

Vibrancy of tone possesses an insistent, inner beat and tidal pulse that is not content in its instinct for radiance with any single garment upon living time or consciousness. Thus the absolutes of tragic art, the stoic unswerving mould and unyielding fates in, let us say, *Antigone* by Sophocles, or, for that matter, *King Lear* in Shakespeare, give way to other draperies, other curtains, *through* which something else, something uncanny and nameless, something unfathomably redemptive or renascent, is glimpsed. That something else beyond the absolutes of tragic art – invokes an instinct for celebration in a dreadful world. And yet a tragic lamentation persists in the articulation of paint in Aubrey Williams's work. There *is* tragedy.

I remember in my talk in 1970, after the exhibition of Aubrey's work in Jamaica, commenting on a sensation of spilt cosmic blood transmuted into the elements. Such transmutation invoked the hidden voices of the Arawaks of Jamaica broken on the wheel of history. The tragedy *was* unmistakably there yet the subconscious energy and living tidal pulse and colour and tone edged a paradox into play. The curtain moved aside as to the pressure of a mysterious hand, so vital that one saw *through* into implicit spaces beyond fatality and loss.

This orchestration of moving, parting draperies was celebrative whether the painter consciously intended it or not. Aubrey Williams's originality must surely enrich our eye within and across the entire, multi-layered canvas of Caribbean and South American imaginations.

Take Leroy Clarke, the Trinidadian painter. I saw his work years ago in Brooklyn, New York. I was impressed. Then, not so long ago, in London. He had achieved a great leap forward. I venture to think that at the heart of the crowded rich carnival of apparitions that he invokes resides a live fossil bone. That is how I see it. He places garment upon garment over that bone. The wealth of detail and expression is remarkable. The celebrative power of these canvases is different from the tone of Aubrey Williams's paintings.

The difference – the unique spectrality in Clarke – endorses originality. Clarke and Williams are different painters. This confirms in my view the reality of partial draperies. It is not a uniform identity by any means. We are edged into collaboration and difference sustained by uncanny drive and motivation within and through and beyond the surfaces of experience.

Stanley Greaves, Guyanese-born, who lives in Barbados, is another entirely different painter. He is schooled in the exploration of modern themes, expressionist, impressionist, constructivist, architectonic . . . But he wears these media or modes upon an inner grasp of form-within-yet-beyond-identical form. One senses in his work a true absorption of influences and a parting of the ways into other unsuspected vistas.

And now a quick word about the Arawak painter George Simon. I celebrate George Simon's arrival . . . He remains little known. He is a native Arawak of South America and Guyana. He possesses a sure touch, I find, into the veined tapestry, the evolving tapestry, of worlds he and his ancestors have known. A gifted painter to be cherished. It is good to know that a renascence is occurring in which Amerindian painters are involved. These include Genevieve Cox whose sensibility, tapestry, space and line, I became aware of only recently. They return us to the mark of the hand with which I started this talk.

Aubrey Williams's paintings enrich our eye to entertain a complex radiancy of tone that bears subconsciously on inner, far-reaching dimensions and rooms and capacities available to a world that has suffered deeply across generations and centuries.

The wounds are visible yet deep, the pain sometimes seems endemic, but a paradoxical celebration has commenced within the void of history. That paradox, which defies historical trauma and logic, may prove momentous in generations to come.

This text was presented at a seminar on Aubrey Williams, organized by the Institute of International Visual Arts (inIVA), held at The October Gallery, London, 19 January 1996.

19

APPRENTICESHIP TO THE FURIES

The Furies! What are the Furies? Are they nourished by our animosities, prejudices, biases? Are we intricately and complexly and dramatically part and parcel of the womb-body of the Furies? Are they in us yet far from us? Are they ghosts tapping at our window within abused elements, water, air, fire, earth? I have been intuitively involved in an imagination of the Furies – their protean shapes and configurations – for some considerable time. They are such a neglected medium in the humanities, yet deeply rooted simultaneously, that a late twentieth-century interpretation is paradoxical and personal and I have had to fall back on a gathering impetus within my own work across the past four decades to cope with and confront an insistent theme of the Furies.

In my latest fiction entitled *Jonestown* the question arises – 'How strange to entertain the regeneration of oneself through the furies one has long feared?'

Let me pause and stress 'regeneration of oneself', implicit in which is the regeneration of one's age, one's community. I shall return to this issue of regeneration (involving a crossing of borders of fear in the life of the imagination) as I lay out the premises of my discussion. But let me continue with the quotation I began to read, indeed let me re-read the opening question and continue to the end of the short passage that contains it.

> How strange to entertain the regeneration of oneself through the furies one has long feared? How steeped has one been – without quite knowing it – in uncanny dread of the masks one's dead mother wears, or has worn, across centuries and generations, the mystical wilds and wildernesses, the mystical brides?

Let me remind you at this stage of the dread Sirens (all presumed to be women), of dread Circe, of the three terrible winged goddesses with serpents in their hair, namely, Alecto, Megaera and Tisophone, which pursue and punish doers of unavenged crimes. It is a curious and interesting phenomenon that Canaima, the revenge figure in Guyana and South America, is male. Indicating perhaps a shamanic force to Canaima. Shamans are susceptible to an inner body or womb, the womb of Dream. In Canaima's case his male imaginary womb, so to speak, is stoked with apparitions of revenge for crimes of which a people might not know, or have forgotten, they or their antecedents have committed.

Classical lore in Europe and the ancient Greek world tends to identify the revenge-syndrome with the female. Anton Ehrenzweig in his book *The Hidden Order of Art* appears to endorse an implicit preoccupation in Freud with the many disguises of the death-goddess or the 'killing goddess'. He emphasizes three women or a triple-goddess.

The medium of the Furies – perhaps because of an identification with the female gender – has been (as far as I am aware) neglected in the humanities, understandably so, for feminism and the rights of women are now celebrated causes. Yet in my view these causes may founder unless a profoundly creative and re-creative and re-visionary grasp of the theatre of the womb-body of cultures and civilizations is visualized in depth. It is no exaggeration, I feel, to say that the life of the imagination may well be at stake without a vital approach to the Furies, their potency for terror and simultaneously, paradoxically, for the regeneration of cosmic love.

We need, I think, to see women – when portrayed as embodiments of the Furies – *not* as individual characters in the psychology of the novel or the cinema but as human vessels inhabited by spectralities and concretions, by a cellular chemistry pertinent to the body of the womb in shamanic lore, the womb of nature and of civilization.

Think of the human vessel in the genius of the Imagination symbolizing ingredients within itself and beyond itself which are richer and stranger than individual gender. When one looks deep into its cellular fabric – into the vessel of the womb in space and time in shamanic lore – one visualizes the seed of the land, one visualizes oceanic parables littered with stars and constellations, one visualizes the spring of rivers and the veined leaves of forests that have cradled cultures since time began. The womb therefore in shamanic lore transgresses the boundaries of individual gender. The content of the vessel of the womb in nature and cosmos and Dream is both spectral and concrete. Ghosts are there in the blood of the living, ghosts of the living past and unborn future.

You see then, do you not, that though the Furies were portrayed as women, gender was a mask for far-flung – sometimes self-contradictory – natures, the natures of fire and water and the multitudinous fabric of the cosmos within the heart of human and animal passion, elemental passion as well, the passion of storm and lightning, the peace of halcyon days as well, the magical days of the halcyon bird.

The womb, let us say, is a seminal vessel. The active life of that spectral and concrete vessel implies, at one level, intercourse between man and woman, intercourse between the partiality of the male and the partiality of the female. Such partiality tells of a deeper hunger in the body of nature, it tells of an unfinished climax of body and spirit, it tells of the reach of spirit into far-flung responsibilities within essences of creation, the fluids of animal soul mirrored in, and interwoven with, the ecology of oceans and rivers and lakes upon which the individual floats at times like a bubble.

Wars and famines are not new to humanity across the centuries, landslides are not new, earthquakes are not new, the volcano is not new, but within the past three hundred years since the Industrial Revolution we have seen, through the historical lenses that we possess, the action of man-made instruments and machines in the miring of the globe on a scale that seems extraordinary, to say the least, when it invokes comparison with the loss of species and changes in the environments within millennia prior to what is called the Enlightenment.

Our man-made capacity to treat living landscapes and riverscapes and sky-scapes as passive furniture, and the processes that have been set in train, are a potential and a real rifling of the body of the womb in nature which has borne us, in which our gestation as a species began.

It is not difficult, I would have thought, to appreciate how, in ancient times, abused nature or natures sought revenge and were dressed up in the theatre of cultures as 'killing goddesses'.

Anton Ehrenzweig in his *The Hidden Order of Art* and implicitly Freud – from whom he draws a measure of inspiration – place a remarkably high premium on the 'killing Goddess' in the pessimistic, psychological vein that they bring into their books.

The mind-set that Ehrenzweig and Freud elaborate implies a serious necessity to look deeply into the processes of revolutionary technique in the arts. I applaud this but on closest examination of their psychology I am left with the impression that we are lodged in a dead-end in which to shore up the ruins of a loss of resurrectionary soul, a death of God, a death of cosmic love.

And this, I would have thought, is substantive to the European novel-form through Thomas Hardy into Franz Kafka and into Thomas Mann's obsession with the diseased, virtually incurable character.

I do not have to tell you that the European novel-form – in the wake of European empires since the sixteenth century – has exercised an enormous influ-ence upon all societies around the globe which tend, by and large, it seems to me, to bypass their own resources and to under-estimate the bearing these might have on a re-visionary dynamic aligned to the Furies.

Having said all this I must confess that Ehrenzweig in *The Hidden Order of Art* does, it seems to me, leave a faint door ajar into the seminal mystery of the imagination beyond the Freudian dead-end. A profound scanning of clues within the depth-body of the language of fiction (such as he analyses in Goethe) opens a vital communication with the latent capacities to 'transcend the limits of individual existence'.

The irony, it seems to me, is that such a 'transcending of the limits of indi-vidual existence' would shake the very foundations of modern theory which is preoccupied in politics as much as in fiction with individual status, plot, and with an arsenal of technologies to cope with every threat to prosperity from envious regimes and from masses in foreign lands. Ehrenzweig, like a few other formidable European critics, seems fated, as far as I can see, to scan the technologies of depth-resources in the arts yet to stop at the door he holds faintly ajar into other texts of the imagination than those enshrined in Freudian – and other related variants of – realism. Inevitably the womb-body of civilization succumbs to latency or remains a prize to be rifled and disputed by all generations. That dispute registers, it seems to me, in the subconscious or the unconscious as a revenge-syndrome nursed by those who see themselves as despoiled or raped or injured.

This curiously enough fuels the character of the 'killing goddesses' in the modern cinema. Let me give the titles of four films that come to mind: *Play Misty for Me, Fatal Attraction, Black Widow, House of Cards*. The formidable 'killing' women who appear on the screen are capable of leading battalions. They carry many seductive and calculating faces and in that sense are triple or more agents of a revenge-syndrome in a world that has wounded them deeply.

Needless to say these films are manufactured for a mass market familiar with the rape of women in Bosnia, Rwanda, in the alleyways of many a metropolis (a woman was raped recently in a taxi cab by the taxi driver). It is incredible but I read a report recently of rape in or close to a Buddhist temple in the Far East by a Buddhist priest.

Rape in the theatre of war is nothing new but the horror it invokes never fades. It arouses us in depths of the unconscious and subconscious to dread the womb-body of a civilization from which our age is sprung. How real is cosmic love in such dire affliction and distress?

I would argue that all this is pertinent to aroused Furies whom classical lore invested with the mask or persona of women intent on punishing the doers of unavenged crimes. I would also argue that the modern cinema – wittingly or unwittingly – invests in that revenge-syndrome with female protagonists who become deadly in the roles they play.

Such roles may be archetypally consistent with the Furies, but, alas, no 'transcending of the limits of individual existence' occurs.

Rather it is just to say, I think, that a war of genders, male and female, becomes the individualistic plot and story-line of the films I have listed. If, however, we take seriously the cue from world events, the wrongs inflicted on women, then the womb of nature and civilization – in its acute association with theatres of abuse and conflict – inserts a witness to itself in the lament of consciousness embroiled in the rape of environments and settlements around the globe. It would take too long in this address to list the species, rainforests, oceans, rivers, but let me remind you of the horrendous glow of burning oil fields in the recent Middle East War.

Iraq is one of the cradles of civilization. The tyrannies of Saddam Hussein are visible triggers, in reports that appear in newspapers and journals, of the precipitation of conflict that has scarred the peoples of the region. Less visible is the archetypal person or vessel or mirror of a threatened landscape-cradle of civilization to which humanity is indebted. That debt may be stated crudely in modern currency, in the pounds or dollars or francs with which we buy barrels of oil still to be salvaged from a wounded earth. But the debt is numinously alive in the Furies, were we to seek to re-trace our steps into the past and into what are now the ghost-armies of Alexander the Great. Bitter as such a re-tracery is, there are, I would think, pregnant cross-culturalities available to sensitive scholars that transcend the boundaries of revenge-politics.

Let me stress what I have been saying. In the modern cinema we perceive the portrayal of women in such films as *Play Misty for Me* or *Fatal Attraction* or *Black Widow* as archetypally consistent with the Furies whose vocation it was in classical myth to pursue the doers of unavenged crimes. I have attempted to suggest that, though these films do not relate directly to theatres of war in Iraq or Iran or the former Yugoslavia or Rwanda, they are influenced by such horrendous conflicts in their portrayal of revenge-seeking women in the mass-media cinema. Such women are individualized as in the conventional novel. They are portrayed as strong and violent as men. They do not – in Anton Ehrenzweig's phrase – 'transcend the limits of individual existence'. As a consequence they lack something, in my view, which may open our imaginations to the regenerative potential in the Furies.

The supreme casualty that we suffer as things now stand in conventional realism is the death of cosmic love. Think about this honestly and carefully. Love may serve as an ornament of gratification for the individual who builds a fortress that makes him or her immune to the deep-seated malaise of humanity around the globe. Within that fortress we may manufacture entertainments and fictions – such as I have listed in the cinema – which run in parallel with diseased character in the modern novel. I alluded, you may remember, to Kafka and Hardy and Mann earlier in this talk. The equation, however, with the European masters, who depict the fate of civilization in a pessimistic vein, is overshot in the cinema by a conflict of gender in which love becomes a feature of seduction and violence. The family becomes a fortress subject to invasion by marauding females. Such is surely the theme of *Fatal Attraction*.

It seems to me – when we take all this into account – that we are driven to see that a 'transcending of the limits of individual existence' is an enormous question that bears on the roots of love in the womb of space and time. Post-modern Freudian psychology breeds pessimism. Revenge-syndromes lifted into populist entertainment create a money-making industry, no doubt, but it polarizes gender even as it endorses the 'killing goddess'.

I would like now to speak of the creation of texts that diverge from the narrative form which we associate with the European convention. This is a testing matter. I am, I must confess, not concerned with theory-for-the-sake-of-theory but with insights I have assembled in my writing career across close on four decades.

I must emphasize strongly that it is not my intention to elevate such insights into a formula or into ruling criteria. Not at all. One is aware of a growing diversity in the areas of Caribbean and Latin American literatures, not to speak of Africa and Asia, all of which possess unique roots in the soil of tradition that may be aroused in peculiarly new ways to bear on the arts of the imagination.

Only recently in January [1996] I spoke at the October Gallery in London on the work of the painter Aubrey Williams, who died a few years ago, and was able in that context to say something of Leroy Clark, Stanley Greaves, George Simon and Genevieve Cox.

With regard to writers in the Caribbean and Central and South America, the long-neglected masterpiece *Pedro Paramo* by the Mexican novelist Juan Rulfo is gaining ground. In the Caribbean and Guyana one cannot but be aware of new developments in the work of writers such as Robert Antoni, Pauline Melville, Erna Brodber, Fred D'Aguiar, Laurence Scott, the poet Mark McWatt, the poet David Dabydeen, and in the novel *Crossing the River* by Caryl Phillips, which is written in documentary prose even as it seems to question the ironies of hollow avocation or professional status within the conditioned mind of blended diasporan character across two hundred years.

It isn't easy to be confident of anything in the life of the humanities and my specific purpose in mentioning a few names of largely new and talented and gifted poets and fiction-makers – and also you may recall painters – from the Caribbean and Guyana – is to suggest that there might well be a ground or turning point through and beyond the boundaries of the imagination long taken for granted by colonial peoples.

I trust I have cleared the air also – if this were at all necessary – in pursuing insights assembled from my own work across close on four decades. No dogma or formula is intended.

The fiction I have written in and since *The Guyana Quartet* has been driven by a re-visionary dynamic that takes nothing for granted within its narrative body to bring into play a blend of pasts and presents and likely or unlikely futures. I say the fiction takes nothing for granted, but I need to qualify this in a slightly unusual way. The truth is that across the long years of concentrated work I have not lost hope, within a severely nihilist climate and endgame philosophy of the Imagination, that through profoundly intuitive and changing texts and forms it is truly possible to visualize the action of cosmic love within the dire circumstances, the dire plight, that afflicts humanity. Cynics would argue that the action of cosmic love is lacking in theatres of crisis. Cosmic love – many would argue – is dead. This is nothing new. We live not only in a post-Freudian age steeped in pessimism and in escapism but in a post-Nietzschean age. The death of cosmic love would seem to be a consequence of the death of God. Where is God when men's and women's bodies are seized by the affliction of war or famine or crisis?

I am saying – let me repeat – that conventional realism offers no reply. It may describe events but the frame it uses endorses the absence of cosmic love. It cannot breach the limits of individual existence. If anything it reinforces those limits. It consolidates the nation-state and the vested interests of the nation-state. It accepts love as the privileged premise or ornament of fortunate societies that may secure themselves from torment and seek in hedonism their philosophy.

All this is understandable, I think, when we confess that we think and feel and judge and surrender to immediate experience within a frame of language and a psychology of the ego and super-ego that underestimates the womb of time and the vessel of the person.

To revise and break the mould of such under-estimation of the womb of time and the vessel of the person requires, I think, immeasurable persistence and dedication in and to resources beyond formulaic closure or instituitionalised story-line or plot.

In *Jonestown* – my latest novel – Francisco Bone subsists in the womb of time and space and dream upon blended ages. The seas and landscapes upon which he moves is a multi-layered and all-pervasive fabric in that they affect every detail, every object, in his life. Let me pluck an instance from the actual text of the fiction. Look at him now in a classroom in Albuoystown in the year 1939 – he is nine years old – to which he has returned from the future. He has travelled back across mountainous waves and seas from the dreadful carnage of Jonestown which occurred in November 1978 in Guyana. He has travelled back to his childhood in Albuoystown, a poor suburb of the city of Georgetown. Mr Mageye his teacher is at the blackboard. Here is the passage that I said I would read (the I-narrator is Francisco Bone):

> I was affected by the memory of a steep wave that had threatened to overwhelm the Virgin Ship on my crossing from 1978 disaster-ridden Jonestown back to 1939 Albuoystown.
>
> Black and steep as Night over Jonestown, blacker than the blackboard at which Mr Mageye now stood.
>
> He (Mageye) loved to play pranks. He would arouse laughter in his class and then resume his history lesson. He dodged behind blackboard and wave. As the Ship was about to fall through the roof of the world he occupied a crevice in the blackboard and peered through it as if it were a telescope. At that instant I heard the bells of the Sirens ringing. The Ship righted itself.
>
> I heard the voice of the Sirens through the magical bells declaring that Mr Mageye was a rare phenomenon, a genuine and sacred jester. He stood there in the telescopic wave with the look of a gentle Sphinx. The expression passed from his features, he moved back to the front of the blackboard, and he resumed the history lesson.
>
> (*Jonestown*, p.33)

The womb of space which Francisco carries is now pregnant, as the passage I have read shows, with linkages between 'wave' and 'blackboard', between a 'crack' in the blackboard and 'a telescope'. All this constitutes a kind of 'sacred jest' which is – if you read the entire work – a threshold into the action of cosmic love.

The quantum physicist Nick Herbert in his book *Quantum Reality* emphasizes the one-track mind to which humanity is addicted. Yet he suggests there might be microscopes to overcome such a biological flaw. The 'sacred jest' acknowledges the flaw but implies simultaneously layers in the womb of space and dream through which the collective or universal unconscious erupts into the subconscious and into the mystery of a creative and re-creative dynamic of consciousness.

I say 'mystery of consciousness' because science has not solved 'consciousness', how it comes about, what are its roots in the body, so to speak, of space and time. Let me emphasize, therefore, that the creation of texts which diverge from one-track realism must, I would think, of necessity seek to cross chasms in reality, to cross from the familiar raw material of existence we would associate with a mere blackboard, for instance, to an element such as a storm or a wave upon which the elements write with the chalk of lightning. The schoolmaster Mr Mageye writes with mere chalk, the voices of the Sirens, secreted in the elements, may be converted into rhythms that write themselves upon a black towering wave and, in that instant, the dread voices of the Sirens which Odysseus feared in Homer's poem are edged with the momentum of a salutary or saving lighthouse, salutary and regenerative omen. The new text brings together therefore motifs and imageries from the past and present and the future in the womb of space and time into a re-visionary gestation or arousal of the light of consciousness. Cosmic love arises then within the dire precipice of storm. This, I am saying, is a different kind of fiction from conventional realism. It suggests that cosmic love may be visualized within the sweep of imageries sprung from different times and ages. All this is pertinent to the vessel of the person steeped in spectralities and concretions through which to transcend individual one-track destiny which may ally itself with freedom but, in fact, is intent on cementing a fortressed ego or super-ego for itself. Freedom should mean, I think, the action of memory to acquaint us deeply, profoundly, with the perilous voyages of humanity out of its cradles of dream in space and time so that the grain of cosmic love may come home to us in all its astonishing reality and fragility and originality.

Without that salvage of cosmic love within the convertible imageries of linked pasts and presents and futures what – may I ask – is art? Is art an ornament, a form of escapism, a sophisticated façade expressed enigmatically in Samuel Beckett's text *Imagination Dead Imagine*?

One may ponder upon that last word 'Imagine' in that short and complex text. It seems to me to endorse or indict or invoke the void of the fortressed individual whose roots in a whole humanity extending across the ages have been well-nigh severed. As a young man, I saw those roots imperilled with the forfeiture of the Caribbean federation in Guyana and the West Indies. Some Caribbean writers and thinkers, it seems to me, lock themselves at times in an insular cultural politics which eclipses genuine alternatives or parallel universes of sensibility in their own region and in the Americas.

The ancient Maya possessed a concept of blended pasts and futures. Eric S. Thompson, an American scholar, points out in his book *Maya Civilization* that this concept baffled the European mind, though I would think that Chaos mathematics – a new phenomenon in European science – has edged a little closer into its potential significance for the modern mind. Long before I knew of it the idea was intuitively alive in my own work as a sliding scale that re-visits the cradles of living landscapes and seeks bridges across chasms of reality.

That quest for bridges is born, I think, of the activity of broken archetypes. Archetypes cannot be seized in their wholeness.

The Blessed Fury (a term I now borrow from the text of *Jonestown*) which appears toward the end of *Palace of the Peacock* dressed in nothing but her long flowing hair, is a measure of the broken Virgin-archetype. I could trace such measures and links between broken Virgin-archetypes and broken Predator-archetypes in *The Guyana Quartet* and succeeding novels into *The Carnival Trilogy* and *Resurrection at Sorrow Hill* but obviously that is impracticable.

Let me close my address with a few words on broken archetypes and their profound bearing on the Furies in *Palace of the Peacock*.

The Virgin-archetype, in its wholeness, would imply, in my understanding, intercourse, shorn of violence, with the womb-body of nature and reality. Let me repeat 'intercourse with nature and reality' that is shorn of violence. One may attempt to visualize, let us say, the birth of Christ from a Virgin as sprung of inter-course shorn of violence. I do not have to say how difficult this seems in real terms, in the so-called real world. It seems to reside in a realm beyond the human imagination. The fact that we entertain it at all in religious myth means it is not entirely beyond the faculties of truth with which art and science wrestle. What we salvage from such an apparently impossible idea, I think, is a broken Virgin-archetype, broken, yes, but profoundly active. Think of a whole number which it is impossible to realize or seize. When it breaks it brings us numerous factors that take us deep into the past, to question fallacious absolutes, even as it enriches our creative conscience in addressing the all-too-human crises that afflict us in the present and for which we require new solutions to cope with the gravity and the tragedies that confront civilization.

The broken archetype becomes therefore a re-visionary dynamic, in all its factors and strands, that we may address and immerse ourselves in within the womb of space and time.

The Blessed Fury which appears towards the end of *Palace of the Peacock* is a manifestation of the factorization of the Virgin-archetype. The mould of the absolute revenge-seeking Furies is broken and she moves on a line, let us say, between the revenge-politics of the Furies and the apparently impossible wholeness of the archetype to which she belongs.

The long garment of hair which is her dress is close to nature and it diverges from absolute dogma or absolute historical costumery or investiture. There is a child at her side. She secretes elements of Arawak as well as European mythology within herself. She is actually one of three women who appear in the novel. They may be seen as a kind of triple goddess. But the emphasis on their killing force as set out in Freudian logic by Anton Ehrenzweig is deeply altered. I say 'triple goddess' with hindsight for I knew nothing of this when I wrote *Palace of the Peacock.* I learnt of it for the first time in the mid-1970s. It isn't easy to intellectualize my divergence from the 'killing goddess' that comes to occupy a nature we have abused. But let me remind you of what I was saying a moment or two ago. To find ourselves within a medium of broken wholeness is to respond to infinite variables and factors in a quest for impossible fulfilment which we entertain nevertheless as a true goal though we resist imposing it on ourselves as an accomplished feat. For to do so is to succumb to incorrigible bias in the name of truth.

As I already said the woman dressed in her hair is one of three women. The others are Mariella and an ancient Arawak woman. They have been so abused that they carry all the potential to become revenge-seeking Furies. But in their alignment to the Blessed Fury they become susceptible to roots in living land-scapes and in a voyaging humanity. Mariella is a woman and a kind of earth goddess. The ancient Arawak woman invokes through rivers and waterfalls the long, epic journey that the aboriginal peoples of the Americas made from the Bering Straits into the North and Central and South Americas. They become regenerative vessels though still sustaining terror-making faculties. They imbue the second death of the crew with a re-visionary crossing of chasms of reality in which many cultures in the Americas have foundered

The mystery of the Furies, and the natures of revenge, and the possibilities of regeneration, are, I would think, of profoundest proportion in crossing boundaries into a renewal of the archetypal life of the imagination as it seeks to engage with the roots of consciousness.

What is imagination? What is consciousness?

This is an age of crisis. Conflicts between genders, between races and cultures, between technology and nature, are looming more critically and terrifyingly perhaps than ever before within the frontiers of history and the traffic of refugees of body and spirit everywhere who are the children of the Furies.

My innermost feeling is that humanity is at the cross-roads in this, the last, decade of the twentieth century. This has been, let us remember, the century of the Holocaust. Capital punishment has not been abolished in the Caribbean and in many African states such as Nigeria where a writer was recently hanged.

In the Far East there is rising prosperity but the bondage of fear is strong, punitive logic is entrenched. And child prostitution, with the rising fear of Aids, is becoming a lucrative business.

A one-track mind-set or psychology of brute realism is undeniable in many areas of the globe. We cannot, in the deepest senses, alleviate the suffering of victims of crime, victims of social disability, unless we begin to take stock of the Furies, take stock of revenge-syndromes in ruthless competition and trade, in populist cultures, in entertainment, in politics. The abuse of the elements has set in train changing weather patterns, storm, famine, drought. But I am suggesting that the Furies also bring a most searching scrutiny into things we take for granted, into links between ages and realms we tend to bypass or eclipse, they also bring long-neglected keys which are pertinent to a literacy of the imagination, pertinent to the conversion of boundaries of fear into thresholds beyond the tyranny and the charisma of fear. Such paradox is native to the genius of creation, it is native to a buried core-response within communities in the womb of space and time and the tasks of the regeneration of our age.

'Apprenticeship to the Furies' was the keynote address for Festival Week, Cave Hill Campus. University of West Indies, Barbados, March 1996.

20

CREOLENESS: THE CROSSROADS OF A CIVILIZATION?

There are, I am sure, many approaches to the ideas, themes, and concepts embodied in what is called 'creoleness'. My main interest in writing this essay is to seek to trace how creoleness may apply to fiction, indeed to the genesis of the imagination in the living soil of South America and the Caribbean. May I say at the outset that such genesis for me is ceaselessly unfinished and that this sensation of *unfinished genesis* – in worlds of space and nature and psyche – has its roots as much in Old Worlds as in New, in the crossroads of a civilization upon which we may have arrived in subtle and complex and involuntary ways that are altering conventional linearity and conventional frameworks.

I do not wish in doing so – in tracing the application of creoleness to fiction and to the nature of our potential to change our responses to reality – to engage in purely intellectual argument or theory. Indeed this is not my intention at all. What I hope to do is to touch chords of deep-seated emotion and passion which lie within shared layers of experience in person and society: layers that are native to the embattled, philosophic core of universality, universal crisis, within creoleness.

My mother and her middle-class family in British Guiana in the 1930s were called Creoles. Our ancestry was mixed: Amerindian; European; African; and, on my father's side, perhaps Asian as well. (Because of a family rift, I have never properly known his antecedents.)

Sometimes the term *Creole* was implicitly or covertly hurled at us like a metaphoric brick (designed to alert us to our impure lineage and mixed race) by the pure-blooded tenants, so to speak, of a property that my father – who died when I was two years old – had left me in his will. I occasionally visited this property when I was at school – perhaps first when I was eight or nine – and it imprinted upon me unforgettable unease if not guilt or terror. Such properties were, in their tenement order, slices of a plantation world. They existed sometimes cheek by jowl with beautiful colonial residences and houses which prompted the guide-books to speak of 'the garden city of Georgetown'; as if to cement an involuntary treaty of sensibility or insensibility between the *inferno* and the *paradiso* in South American soil. Infernal plantation age, paradisean garden city!

From childhood, therefore, creoleness made me aware of the complex labyrinth of the family of humankind into which I was born in the twentieth century. I felt myself peculiarly involved with the tenants who threw their fictional stone at the Creole landlord – involved in their deprivations and disadvantages. They were African Guyanese, East Indian Guyanese, sometimes poor white Portuguese Guyanese. The label *Indian* possesses half-static, half-kaleidoscopic proportions in the mind of the folk as if to bring the paradox of mixtures, of creoleness, into Carnival play. *East Indian* was a label applicable to the descendants of Indians who arrived from India into Guyana under a system of indenture in the nineteenth century. The label tended to run at the edges into American 'Indian' or Amerindian tribes, who formed a small but legendary proportion of the Guyanese population.

It is contended in some quarters that Creoles were the pure, lineal descendants of early settlers in South America and the Guyanas. But my experience is different. The wounds, the vulnerability of the Creole bring a different emphasis into the human comedy. I found myself on the edges or margins of a world, the estate of the world, that were shifting into numinous disorder in order paradoxically to alert us to shared responsibilities within the unfinished genesis of arts of survival. This numinous paradox was largely masked from us by ghetto-fixated habit.

As a consequence, therefore, in the eyes of the deprived tenant of the New World creoleness was so internalized and suppressed that scapegoats became the order of the day. Creoleness became a form of self-deceptive division even as it harboured within itself a potential for the renascence of community. Such renascence could not be easily stilled, and thus it engendered patterns of nemesis in its suppression.

A perverse, yet apparently natural, order of political fiction tended to grip the populace. Creoleness was a badge of blood and mixed descent from wicked plantation owners who had made astronomical fortunes by sweated labour or by slaves in previous generations. Whatever historical truth lay in this, the tragedy was in reinforcing a fixation with protest, a suppression of profoundest creativity to throw bridges across chasms, to open an architecture of space within closed worlds of race and culture. A mind-set came into play that was to bedevil, I believe, the arts and the sciences. For without complex revisionary bridges between art and science conscience is paralysed by dogma; and freedom, in my view, grows increasingly susceptible to a hidden mafia or ruthless establishment within civilization.

I use the term *mafia* not in any political or national context (such as Italian mafia, American mafia, or any other aspect of a hegemonic underworld), but in order to illumine a perverse commitment to privileged frame or family, a hidden authoritarianism that cements its vested interest in the preservation of ruling convention by fostering an incestuous realism or comedy of manners in fiction, fashion and the like. Although one may argue that fashions in the arts may incline toward rebellious extremes, nevertheless they are underpinned, it seems to me, by the logic of consensus or conditioned, short-term responses to reality in consumer societies, the logic of materialism; a logic that sustains, however

unwittingly, an invariant code or fate. The body politic grafts into itself considerable skills in the sophisticated manipulation of bias and prejudice, even within
those who protest against the rule of things. Such protest is fated to be conditioned by the very thing it targets. One merely has to glance at the rise of
authoritarian, rigged elections in newly independent states once under British,
French, Dutch, Spanish, or Portuguese rule.

This is a crucial matter of form that, it seems to me, is rarely considered by
cultural and political vested interests on the right (so-called) or the left (so-called).
There is virtuosity of form or skill or talent in playing upon, or within an invariant model or frame. There is originality of form that taps caches of imagery and
possibility in a state of eclipse through/beyond/within apparently invariant but
partial models.

We need, I am sure, to consider all this with the greatest care to arrive within
the immeasurable but curiously concrete ground of *involuntary* association
between invariance (unchanging premise or frame or story line of art) and complex chasms that may offer resources of transubstantial dimensionality and
change, transfigurative bridges between apparently closed orders still susceptible
to conquistadorial habit.

The word *chasm* is adopted therefore in this exploratory essay to imply that
within the gulfs that divide cultures – gulfs which some societies seek to bypass by
the logic of an institutional self-division of humanity or by the practice of ethnic
cleansing – there exists, I feel, a storage of creative possibility that, once tapped,
may energize the unfinished genesis of the imagination. In that energy eclipsed
bridges and potential bridges exist between divorced or separated or closed
orders and worlds, bridges that are sometimes precarious, never absolute, but
which I think engender a profound awareness of the numinous solidity of space,
inner space/outer space, space as the womb of simultaneous densities and
transparencies in the language of originality.

I shall endeavour to further illumine by degrees what I mean by *chasm* and also
what I mean by *involuntary association* (a term I employed a little earlier in this
essay) and their pertinence to the paradoxes of creoleness. Clearly, one must
confess, *creoleness* is a peculiar term. It may sustain a conservative if not reactionary purist logic. It may give a privileged aura to (so-called) pure-blooded
settlers in the New World. In fact, not only may the descendants of Europeans in
the New World wear the mask of the Creole, but so do Africans, East Indians,
Chinese and others. Indeed, as in my family experience, *creoleness* signifies mixed
race and a cross-cultural nemesis capable of becoming a saving nemesis. *Saving
nemesis* may also be a peculiar expression, but it implies recuperative powers and
vision within a scale of violence that is dismembering societies around the globe.

One may well ask therefore: does creoleness sanction New World tribes
(unrelated to Carib, Arawak, Apache, Blackfoot, or other Native American
peoples) who designate themselves now *African* Americans, *Irish* Americans, *Italian*
Americans, *German* Americans, and so forth? I recall on a visit to Yale University
in 1979 I was addressed by an African American poet of a pale colour (brown

pigmentation). I was sure he was an American of European and African descent, but the advertising for his reading and address emphasized solely his African ancestry. It gave me a curious feeling of a public-relations trap into which it is fashionable to fall. By the same token one reads of *black* fiction, *black* poetry, the *black* arts, *black* painting, and the like.

On the other hand does creoleness complexly, hiddenly, overturn tribal bias; does it involve a spiritual subversion of idols through symbolic portraitures of *blackness*? Does *black* hint at an involuntary association of many cultures? Does *black* reach beyond mere pigmentation along racial and tribal lines into densities and transparencies of tone, a layered wealth of tone – musical, rhythmic, poetic – in which diverse cultures may share? Does *black* puncture prescriptions of blandness masquerading as light?

Quite honestly I do not know the answer to these questions, but in my own work as an imaginative writer, across many decades since the end of World War II, I have encountered an eruption of intuitive clues within unconscious into subconscious into conscious layers of dialogue with the past that indicate for me *numinous perhaps nonsensational changes in human nature itself* (so subtle are these changes that they are easily smothered by a sensational world), changes therefore within the genesis of imagination in nature and space and psyche.

I say all this, of course, with caution, without dogma, without a desire in any way to promote a theory. The issues that confront us (whatever insights of hope one may have garnered from one's work) are incredibly grave. And yet I do not underestimate the personal vision in the teeth of a mass-media world. It is through such deeply intuitive insights drawn from hard work and concentration that one may reflect in new ways upon areas of history that are replete with ironies of involuntary association between cultures. Such ironies highlight an addiction to invariance, closed minds, and divided cultures, even as they disclose, I think, the mystery of cross-cultural wholeness steeped in the freedom of diversity to cross boundaries that restrict our vision of therapeutic and evolving reality.

It is said that when the ancient Caribs appeared in pre-Columbian times upon what is now known as the Caribbean Sea, they came without women and chose their wives from the Arawaks whom they seized and overcame. There are parallels in history which lead us to believe that their choice was influenced by criteria of kinship resemblances to be perceived even in a foreign people, clanship resemblances to be analysed even in conquered peoples, and a family code or criterion to be plucked from the body of a stranger. This is natural – natural choice, let us say; but it also possesses sinister implications. The ancient alchemists coined the term *opus contra naturam* to alert us to the trickster faces of nature, one of which may easily beguile us so that we absolutize it, by apparently natural choice, into a status of such privilege that, by degrees, we come to deceive ourselves about our powers or capacities to seize and institutionalize the purity of nature. We are tricked by nature, as it were, into consolidating partiality, partial appearance, into an absolute frame, an absolute good.

When the Nazis invaded Poland, they separated Polish families, selecting children from among their Polish brothers, sisters or cousins because they conformed to an Aryan model. They shipped these children to Germany, where they were taken into German families. A sinister question mark attached to those who, for one reason or another, were mixed or dubbed non-Aryan. There was nothing new in such implicit ethnic cleansing. In the flux of cultures and civilizations across the centuries – cultures at war one with another – the recruitment of children who appeared to conform to a standard elevated by a victor or invader, was established practice. When the Ottoman Turks conquered Constantinople, they treated Christian children who matched favoured criteria of purity and likeness in a manner similar to the Nazi treatment of Polish children centuries later.

Let us return now to the theme of the 'chasm' within humanity and to *involuntary associations*. It is possible to gain new insights into fiction and creativity through what one may call the 'creolization of the chasm' within illuminations drawn from, or nursed from, the fabric of involuntary associations embedded in humanity.

In the selection of a thread upon which to string likenesses that are consolidated into the status of a privileged ruling family, clearly cultures reject others who remain nevertheless the hidden or unacknowledged kith and kin, let us say, of the chosen ones. The rejection constitutes both a chasm or a divide in humanity and a context of involuntary association between the chosen ones and the outcast ones. The relationship is involuntary in that, though, on one hand, it is plain and obvious, privileged status within that relationship endorses by degrees, on the other hand, a callous upon humanity. And that callous becomes so apparently normal that a blindness develops, a blindness that negates relationship between the privileged caste and the outcast. That negation cannot absolutely cut the thread of relationship, but it throws a shroud of habit upon it until it virtually fades and remains an involuntary association. The relationship becomes less and less an active ingredient in the multifaceted integrity and flexibility of nature and psyche.

A bias grows which may profit from that hidden relationship in purely formal experimentation (Picasso's formal, let us say, appropriation of facets in the African mask); but unless a genuine cross-cultural apprehension occurs of the unfinished genesis of the imagination affecting past and present civilizations, an innermost apprehension of changing, cross-cultural content within frames we take for granted, the involuntary ground of association to which I have referred, remains between privileged and afflicted cultures.

The creolization of the chasm in humanity should alert us to a series of caveats. What is at stake are the gifts one culture offers another, gifts that imply new and changing ways of reading innermost vulnerability within civilizations and cultures. Formal experimentation is important, but conquistadorial habit may employ sensational colour and tone in its intercourse with others, to eclipse the nonsensational or unfathomable ground of cross-cultural astonishment when models of involuntary association break cultures, though such continuities never can be structured absolutely.

Needless to say, this essay sets out my personal view within a continuing exploratory capacity that bears on my apprehension of imaginative truth. Perhaps it may help if I look, once again in a personal and undogmatic way, beyond and through the appropriation of facets in one cultural artifact by another culture, such as I implied with the Spanish painter Picasso and the African mask. To do so, to look through and beyond sophisticated patterns of appropriation, which are implicitly cross-cultural, we need to raise the issue of gifts – born of unconscious momentum within the chasm of humanity – that one culture unself-consciously (it follows from what I have just said) offers to another culture, to raise also the issues of partiality and vulnerability in all models we may perceive fallaciously, I believe, as social, cultural or technological absolutes.

The differentiation in content within diverse cultural models – content that may seem opaque to one culture viewing another – needs to be translated and transfigured in fictions that give simultaneous representation to densities and transparencies. All languages are subtly, hiddenly connected, and the live, fossil particularities in the language of fiction – arising from variables of the unconscious/subconscious/conscious in the chasm of humanity – help us to arrive upon unsuspected bridges, bridges of innermost content that have a deeper, stranger luminosity and incandescence than the purely formal appropriation by one culture of another's artifacts.

I am saying that such luminosity, such incandescence, exacts a price. The simultaneity of densities and transparencies is a 'depth phenomenon' of the language of fiction which throws up, brings up, in ways we scarcely understand and tend to overlook, continuities between cultures: continuities that open diverse content (once deemed opaque) into unsuspected capacities for the renewal of an inner dynamic of universal civilization.

Who would suspect, for example, a link between Legba (the Haitian loa who stands at the crossroads of the Caribbean and the South/Central Americas) and Hephaestus (the inimitable craftsman of the ancient Greek Olympian gods)? The key to such a link lies in paradoxes of vulnerability in civilizations apparently remote from one another. Legba's vulnerability is manifest in his one-legged frame. He is also aged: the years, the generations, centuries perhaps, clothe him. *Yet he brings the gift of agelessness.* What is agelessness? Agelessness, I would suggest, is not to be equated with the hubris of immortal identity, though the desire to do so remains virtually incorrigible and strong. Yet we may combat such seductive but fallacious strength when we begin to perceive that Legba is consumed by the poverty, the dire predicament, the hunger of the Haitian people, in whose pantheon he is a god. He is being consumed, yes, but a paradox links him to the dire predicament of his people and to immortal identity or privileged family. The consumption of his body by the soil and the fire of time is so protracted – the fire is so invisible in its long, drawn-out persistence – that a living residue grows up again and again upon the crossroads of a society to make him appear invulnerable and strong, whereas what is at stake is the issue of vulnerable soil, vulnerable resources, vulnerable capacities, that need to be read and understood differently, differently from prescriptions of political and cultural habit, by original, human imaginations.

An invisible fire, as it were, lives agelessly within him as if to offset the terminal malaise of a civilization. That offset is paradoxical, for it postpones a necessity to read reality differently. It cultivates hubris and fallacies of strength. And yet within that cultivation one may still, however glimmeringly, perceive an incandescence, a luminosity, a transfiguration of resources that may break by creative degrees (to match the protracted ritual of invisible conflagration within the institutions of society) a hidden linkage of catastrophe to authoritarian and hierarchical habit.

Within that breakage, an immortal god such as Legba is wounded, appears crippled, to bring his gift to civilization. The caveat or warning inserted into the gift tends to be overlooked because such a crippled one may mesmerize society in having virtually arisen from the grave of a doomed order, a doomed Haiti – a doomed Caribbean, some would say – in the light of the perilous conditions that prevail there.

It is easy to assume that Legba's wound is an irrelevant window through the frame of privileged hierarchy and that he invites us to cement a longing for absolute dynasty or power. But the caveat remains; it may brighten, it may flicker, to tell us that the capacity for non-consumerable proportion in Legba is not endless. It is ageless only in the sense that originality invokes a compression of times in creative fictions and that a *transfiguration* may run out of the past into the present and the future to turn invisible fire around into a therapeutic signal.

Legba has his roots in Africa. However, his creolization in Haiti is a signal of mixed resources born of Haiti's relationship to conservative, tribal Africa as well as to confused legacies of slave-owning French landlords cheek by jowl, so to speak, with revolutionary, counterrevolutionary politics in France and the rise of Napoleonic dictatorship. Haiti's Africanness was embroiled, therefore, in the contradictions of a classical Europe in that the classics were taught to the ruling, educated, political classes. Indeed, in this scenario we come abreast of the self-deceptions in a purely formulaic (some would say Cartesian) education, in which a so-called dialogue with the past rests on *descriptions of, not numinous arrival in*, the complex, disturbing life of tradition. I have mentioned it before, but let me stress it again: a purely formal appropriation of the material of the past reduces the past to a passive creature to be manipulated as an ornament of fashion or protest or experimentation in post-modernist styles, post-modernist games. Such games are rooted, I believe, in a one-sided modernism which takes us back to defects in the enlightenment associated with the Renaissance, an enlightenment that aborted a profound cross-culturalism between science and art, as among the diverse cultures of humanity around the globe.

To arrive in tradition involves an appreciation of profound tension between originality and tradition; it involves a breach in formidable prepossessions of a materialist mind-set, a mind-set that has exploited nature, exploited landscapes/ riverscapes/skyscapes over the past two hundred years since the Industrial Revolution, a mind-set that takes for granted the exploitation of others through technological innovation.

There can be no perfect or absolute arrival in tradition, and some measure of descriptive logic is necessary; but we need a narrative that helps us to sense the partiality of linear progression and brings home to us in genuine stages of creativity (rather than purely intellectual experimentation) the simultaneity of the past, the present, and the future in the unfinished genesis of the imagination.

Legba's creolization makes visible, I would suggest, an insecurity in the pantheons of the gods around the globe. Such insecurity is a kind of arrival in tradition: it runs counter to secure ideologies or dogmas in which immortality is described as the grain and blood of hierarchical privilege.

Legba's numinosity and insecurity revolve around two strands drawn from the tapestry of civilization. One strand is the fallacy of invulnerability, of supernatural strength despite eroding environments and institutions, of complacent declarations of strength with every return from the grave of his diseased society. He is pinned, as it were, again and again as an ambiguous godlike Creole (aged and ageless, weak and strong) to be questioned deeply in his apparent passivity and complacency in our new and original visualization of him in this essay. The other strand, therefore (in our original address to him now), is to raise the spectre of transfigurative repudiation of fate which he may conceal, invisible fire that consumes remorselessly yet is not absolute, fire that consumes yet may turn around into a resource of evolutionary change and complex transfiguration of the prison house and frame of cultural habit.

This brings us to the enigma of the gifts that the gods bestow upon humanity. We come to the edge of technologies that we accept at our peril in their purely formulaic transparency. The gift of every advance in technology is fraught with ambiguity in its innermost content.

Even the exploding furnace of the atom remains opaque in its application as a therapeutic tool in our civilization. Its dangers, its horrendous mushroom, are all apparent. Its terrifying beauty is apparent. Yet it remains dense within a civilization that is still blind to an innermost incandescence of evolving and changing alphabet of the psyche.

Legba's peculiar cousinship to ancient Greek Hephaestus may help us with regard to the issue of technology that I have raised. Hephaestus was maimed, and the other immortal gods saw him sometimes as a figure to be ridiculed. It is difficult to establish precisely what injury he endured; it may have been his legs, or it may have been obscurely genital. Whatever it was, it incited in him a cunning and jealousy less characteristic of gods, one would think, than of mortal humanity. His status as a visibly maimed immortal may seem absurd. Such paradox undermines yet confirms, in ultimate and unfathomable essence, an immunity of soul. Immune self or soul or paradox of genius is other than the masquerade of brute refinements of power or mechanics of potency to which the Olympian family is addicted.

The distinction between an immune system (in a therapeutic or medical sense), an elusive self or soul (in numinous immunity), and a fallacious immunity, or exemption from the torments of creative conscience – the distinction between inner fire that threatens to consume but may heal, and brute refinement that disenfranchises the soul – is the thread that runs through Haitian Legba and Olympian Hephaestus.

This is a distinction of great stress, and, as a consequence, Hephaestus appears at times to resort to base traps and trickery to compensate his pain and his jealousy of others who gain the prize of love in cheating and robbing him. His masterly skills – technology, artisanship – degenerate into glittering nets and machineries of hate, spite, venom with which to wage war. A tragic precedent is set. Yet one needs to remember that Hephaestus was driven by a sense of loss and grief in the face of others whose behaviour was rooted in Olympian vanity; at times, ruling utterances and precepts that seemed one-sided and biased, reflective as well of caprice and prejudice, whatever heights in the exercise of justice in the affairs of humanity they claimed for themselves. Was it not Plato who expressed a degree of loathing and foreboding at the behaviour of the lofty family of the immortals?

It is necessary to see, at this stage, that immortality may consolidate itself into a façade for regimes that lose their capacity for self-critical, self-judgemental momentum into dimensions of the reformation of the heart and the mind of an age. One such dimension is the chasm in humanity to which I referred earlier in this essay, the 'creolization of the chasm'. Legba and Hephaestus are symbols of the chasm raised onto a plane of maimed immortality to strike an uneasy, perhaps terrifying, balance between abnormal stress within the body of a civilization and creative/re-creative genius.

That balance requires a penetration of the opacity of immortal regimes, an opacity rich with involuntary counterpoint between the powerless (who are deemed irrelevant and cast aside) and the powerful, a counterpoint as well between the numinosity of weak species (ingrained nevertheless with the unfathomable integrity of nature) and brute tyranny masquerading as the survival of the fittest.

Hephaestus' maimed and cunning sexuality, for instance, raises – as I have already implied – the chasm of humanity into the pantheon of the gods. At one level, Hephaestus seems to us little more than a puppet or a clown, and he appears to remain blind to his own genius which is darkened and conscripted to aid and abet technologies of trickery, waste or war. We who scan him through Haitian, Creole, Legba may arrive in the past and bring him upon the crossroads of a present civilization. There we may scan, in new fictions of philosophic myth, an *involuntary* counterpoint, let us say, which he brings into play against the hubris of sex – so much a part of the malaise of late twentieth-century civilization. We may unravel the opacity of immortal regimes – regimes of ruling fashion, regimes of sophisticated exploitation of species – to illumine, in some degree, a cruel addiction to uniform orders of rape disguised within the phallic, invented masks of bulls, or the sculpture of sharks, the horn of deer, that the immortals may wear to execute a perverse Carnival which throws its long, pointed shadow into the symbolic vivisection of the animal kingdom.

Is it absurd to suggest that Legba's shield in old age (weak yet strong old age) is implicit in a comedy of overturned, Hephaestian armour that Achilles wore? The seed of that armour is the conflagration of Troy – perhaps a measure of con-flagration that fascist Haiti may well bring upon its head in the foreseeable future. Yet time – within that overturned, Hephaestian shield Legba unconsciously bears – is still on the side of the Caribbean and Central and South America.

When we seek to make a distinction between the opaque content of ancient symbolizations or legends and purely formal innovation employing character-istics borrowed by one culture from another (as Picasso, let us say, borrowed characteristics from the African mask to create a new formal style), we need, I think, to address an *involuntary* ground of association which is native to the arts of humanity.

That involuntary ground reaches subconsciously, unconsciously, *through* the *humanization* of nature that we set up into ruling models in our places of learning and in the humanities, the universities, reaches *through* such models into nature(s) which, I repeat, are *extrahuman* even as they (such natures) bear on humankind, even as they bring gifts to humankind. Such gifts are akin to quantum fire of soul (*anima mundi*), quantum oceans, quantum landscapes, quantum riverscapes, which imply minuscule linkages between being and nonbeing, psyche and pebble or leaf or wood or cloud or tide or rock.

The quantum imagination, in my view, may be curiously visualized as a revisionary epic which seeks to reclaim extrahuman faculties in incandescent equations between being and nonbeing. The subtle, complex rhythms of nonbe-ing, the intricate fibre and dimensionalities of space, have been so blocked away that living landscapes become theatres of brute conquest, media to be exploited and manipulated.

Let us put this in another way: extrahuman faculties may be eclipsed in a hubris that governs models built on an assumption of the domination of nature(s) within institutions that claim to humanize the world even as they entrench biases that may imperil the future of humankind. This is a supreme irony, that arts of imagination have scarcely, it seems to me, ventured into in modern times.

The reasons for such neglect are clear: extrahuman faculties are so eclipsed, by and large, that their content within legend or sculpture or mask or word or painting, becomes apparently opaque. Yet these extrahuman faculties continue to subsist on inescapable truth within an involuntary ground of association which I would describe as involuntary genius.

Genius in this subconscious, unconscious theatre of psyche (acting within, yet beneath, layers of logical awareness) is a phenomenon of the extra-human (what is beyond the arrogant humanization of natures) acting upon the human

246

susceptibility to what is other than absolute, individual logic, what is attuned to a capacity in which we need to *read* ourselves in the book of reality – in fictions of reality – as *partial* creatures. It is within such numinous partiality that one-legged Legba and maimed Hephaestus reach through and beyond themselves (however unwittingly) into architectures of space that are relevant to chasms in humanity and to a multidimensional cosmos.

Let me close this essay by returning to Legba's Hephaestian shield. As I implied earlier, that shield is an extrapolation from the armour that Hephaestus built for Achilles at the request of Achilles' immortal mother. That armour was to topple Troy. Its panoramic motifs are of profound interest. It pictured *self-deceptive* (I would say) and *peaceful occupations and environments* – sheep rearing, woods, gentle fields, and the like – *for it was dedicated to war.* Within such panoramic clarity an *invisible* seed smouldered that would erupt into a flower of all-consuming fire and war. One needs more than a formal appropriation of Achilles' armour if one is to arrive within a capacity to lift an invisible seed of fire, within Hephaestian technology, into a trigger of simultaneous densities and transparencies.

The creolization of Legba, therefore, within a tormented Haiti and Caribbean, is an issue of complex linkages and mixed traditions – transcending *black*, transcending *white* – in which the seed of all-consuming fire turns around into an incandescent imagination that may so balance shadow and light, age and youth, strength and weakness, poverty and wealth, that it throws a ceaseless bridge across the chasm of worlds, an apparently doomed world of materialism and conflict and another real (however apparently unreal) world buried in the content of imaginations history seeks to exploit, for purely formal, stylistic reasons, rather than as an immersion in creative difficulty, in a true, far-reaching, evolving cross-cultural regeneration of the heart and mind of an age.

21

THE UNFINISHED GENESIS OF THE IMAGINATION*

Here on the surface of mystery (table and tablecloth, book and page)
World's inexhaustible heritage
Into the present rises, the unregarded familiar
Where, in ignorance and wonder, I receive and praise.

These lines by Kathleen Raine are, I believe, acutely relevant to the passion which informs the founding of the Temenos Academy in these critical and dangerous times as we move into the last decade of the twentieth century.

A few weeks ago I met a German publisher, a man of sensitivity and sensibility, and he told me of an unusual difficulty he faced in his publishing business. He had received a manuscript which he and his readers perceived as clinically brilliant and impressive. But it left them with an unhappy and bitter taste in the mouth. As though they had been consuming ashes. The writer had analysed the state of civilization, the pollution, the greenhouse effect, the devastation of landscapes, the rising tide of anti-Semitism, the possibility of ethnic and racial conflicts, the division between cultures, famine on one hand, prosperity on the other.

He had concluded that civilization was subject to a circumscription of values, an incorrigibility, that was propelling it into an abyss. The fatality was endemic and could not be overcome.

I understood the publisher's hesitation in publishing the thesis. I have not heard what decision he may have reached in this matter. On the surface of my mind I felt the German writer may have made a logical analysis one could not overturn. Unless one could breach his argument in the light of a vision of resources, available to the Imagination, he had not considered in the pattern of his thesis. Perhaps within the abyss of which he speaks there are proportions through and beyond models of discourse, models of tradition we have been conditioned to accept as absolute. Perhaps there is a strangeness, a series of strangers within the body of the self, so to speak, that may offer us a wholly different intuitive penetration of the life of the Imagination. Perhaps the abyss so-called secretes unsuspected resources that may alter circumscriptions of fate.

I would like to pursue this in my address this evening which, in some degree, takes the form (if 'form' is the word) of a journey . . .

May I start somewhere in the ancient world. *Antigone* by Sophocles. Sophocles, it seems to me, has addressed the blindness of his society, its circumscription by ritual habit, its restrictive or restricted vision, in a peculiar and uncertain way. Paradoxically it is this peculiarity, this uncertainty, that makes him a great playwright of the ancient world. Tiresias – the seer in the play – was spiritually sighted but physically blind. He tries to persuade Creon, the king of Thebes, that Antigone's brother who lies on the street should be given a proper burial. But Creon is intent – in the exposure of the corpse – on scourging everyone who may contemplate rebellion. Creon though physically sighted was spiritually blind. How may we plumb or address the nature of vision in such a world? Antigone's father Oedipus was blind. All the characters in the play seem to have inherited a cloak over their eyes which they hold up in varying degrees as the flag of self-righteousness or conviction or hubris. In the end Hades triumphs. Some scholars would call this ontic or aboriginal tautology. *Hades is Hades is Hades for ever and ever.*

As I reflect on this now it seems to me that the German writer – despite his clinical logic and brilliance – is the victim of ontic tautology. The endemic fatality of his discourse – with all its statistical and convincing panoply – is circumscribed by classical Hades.

It is interesting to note that many of the outstanding American playwrights – Eugene O'Neill, Arthur Miller, Tennessee Williams – are deeply enmeshed in patterns of classical tragedy in their twentieth-century plays.

Now, there is something in *Antigone* I would like to address quickly. There comes a moment when Antigone abandons her traditional or ritual plea. She concentrates with extraordinary and irrational exclusivity upon her brother's plight. It is almost as if he is occultly alive and she is pleading for his life. Prior to this moment her plea was based on the sacred laws of the state, a plea that Tiresias endorsed. The particular lines expressing this divergence in the substance of Antigone's plea have been disputed by scholars. Goethe was amongst these who claimed that Sophocles did not write those lines. They had been planted in the text by a stranger hand. And yet Aristotle who knew the play raised no such questions.

I tend to feel – as an imaginative writer subject to uncanny lines sprung from unconscious/subconscious memory, and appearing within the drafts of fiction I write – that Sophocles planted those lines in his play. I see such lines as 'intuitive clues'. A term I have adopted in previous essays. I interpret 'intuitive clue' as implying that the *visible* text of the play runs in concert with an *invisible* text that secretes a corridor into the future, a future where the burden of classical blindness – as in the instance of Sophocles's *Antigone* – needs to be taken up and treated differently. That corridor for me, in this context, runs into the dawn of the Christian age.

How do the texts of the Gospels take up the burden of classical blindness? The occult life of the risen Christ confuses Mary Magdalene. Christ is not immediately recognizable. The resurrected body of Christ walks on the road to Emmaus but is not recognized by his companions who knew him well before the crucifixion. *And yet a breach occurs in the tautology of Hades.* That breach constitutes a kind of subtle abyss in a story-line we take for granted. Christ – let us say – crosses from one bank of the subtle abyss to the other. He is apparently the same person but – in acquiring or absorbing unsuspected particularities and elements in the fabric of the risen body – he is *not* immediately recognizable. It takes a new concentration, a new way of reading reality, for his companions to recognize him and begin to come abreast of the resources of the subtle abyss. Thus the resurrection-body does not conform to a story-line upon which everything is immediately clear and conformable to a ruling pattern.

The tautology of the story-line is fractured in favour of a mysterious continuity that defies absolute models, absolute formula. One senses that the models we have enshrined – whether tragedy, epic, allegory, documentary realism – are partial, and if we invest in them absolutely then alas the abyss into which our civilization is slipping has nothing to offer us but an ultimate divorce from the genesis and mystery of consciousness, ultimate divorce from reality, ultimate loss.

The motif of the resurrection-body appears to have its unfathomable roots in an occult dimension within the life and unfinished genesis of the Imagination such as erupts I feel in Antigone's exclusive and re-visionary alignment with her dead brother who became mysteriously demanding and alive. But also when we attempt to give historic certitude to the resurrection-body of Christ in the first century AD we are confused and puzzled as that body appears to elude us and to slip away into the future as though something that may have happened in the past relates to the mystery of time, to the future.

Let us visualize an invisible arch, an invisible text, running from the ancient world into the originality of the future. How does this bear upon, or address, for instance, Dante's 'divine comedy'? You may recall that Virgil was barred from the *paradiso*. He had come from a pre-Christian age. He had come from the pagan world. He was a pagan. Virgil's exclusion from the *paradiso* raises momentous – however disguised – questions about the character of tradition in the modern world.

It is easy to say to ourselves – why bother with a thirteenth-century poet whose great allegory is remote from us? Indeed why bother with Sophocles? I do not agree. Herman Melville and Malcolm Lowry – American and English writers of genius – were profoundly aware of the dimensionalities of allegory within the modern world. Whether we are conscious of it or not there are pre-possessions within our civilization that make us susceptible to patterns of property which are securely guarded in one shape or form until they border upon an authoritarian *paradiso*. The authoritarian texture tends to be hidden beneath various legal codes that enshrine cultural and economic and racial distinctions between outsiders and insiders, economic migrants and political refugees.

The barriers between religions today are notoriously visible. We invite obscenities or shout abuse at each other across those barriers. How intractable are such barriers? What are the tasks of imaginative genius to begin the transformation of such barriers in the light of numinous and unsuspected resources available to the Imagination within the abyss of our late twentieth-century age?

Clearly there are no answers to such questions in terms of pure tradition which may offer us patterns of satire, of comedy, of fantasy, patterns in which we make game of each other, post-modern game with glosses upon freedom of speech, terrorist game, ideological game, advertising game, but a deeper answer, an unpredictable breakthrough, must awaken us to a counterpoint between originality and tradition unlike the models we possess.

I mention this because I shall soon speak of my own work. But the pressure to do so – strange as it may appear – is free of egocentricity. It is a pressure that arises from strangeness, from abysmal strangeness. *Abysmal* not in a despairing sense. Surely this is clear by now! *Abysmal* in the sense of the subtle abysses that lie between all partial models of tradition, subtle abysses that make strangeness into intimacy, intimacy into what is at first unrecognizable until one perceives there a medium of extraordinary re-visionary momentum and truth.

It is not only the gulf between religions and cultures that plagues us today. There is the widening gulf between the rich and the poor, the world of plenty and the world of famine. We may think we can make a good patchwork or mechanical arrangement to ameliorate such a division. But this I feel is an illusion. There is no economic solution to the ills of the world until the arts of originality – arts that are driven by mysterious strangeness – open the partialities and biases of tradition in ways that address the very core of our pre-possessions. This involves paradoxical orders of readership. As an imaginative writer I find myself *reading* in continuously changing ways. I re-read works by writers I may have misjudged and which I return to and perceive differently. I re-read my own fictions after a long while and see connections there I planted and yet which seem utterly new. Let me attempt to illumine what I mean as concretely as I may. Let me commence with *Carnival*, the first novel in my Carnival trilogy. The second is called *The Infinite Rehearsal*, the third *The Four Banks of the River of Space*.

A word about the characters in *Carnival*. Jonathan Weyl is – let us say – a twentieth-century Dante figure. He is secreted in the carnival of the twentieth century. The particularities of his existence make him intimate with some of the proportions of a thirteenth-century Dante even as they move him light years away, so that the origination of a Dantesque formula, a Dantesque investiture, a Dantesque mask, is called into question. There are stars in Dante's thirteenth-century cosmos he would never have perceived as we perceive them. They were fixed. Whereas for us the light that comes across space from a star is but the shadow of an object that may have vanished. News of its disappearance has not yet been transmitted to us. To put it differently. Within the abyss of tradition – within the spatiality, the spectrality of tradition – the original nucleus that motivates us is so peculiar, so unidentifiable, that singularity needs plurality. Dante – in other words – needs a twentieth-century carnival of masks even as those masks look backwards to him and through him into the mysterious origins of Imagination in science and art.

There is also Amaryllis who is a Beatrice figure. She has acquired particularities of numinous sexuality in the twentieth-century carnival. I shall touch upon these in due course for they help in the transformation of the barrier between the Virgilian pagan and the *paradiso*.

There is Everyman Masters the twentieth-century Virgilian guide. As 'Everyman' he cannot escape his pagan body. Indeed he visualizes Christ as riding into Jerusalem on a pagan donkey, a donkey that is another kind of Trojan horse. In it lies an invisible text, an invisible army, that will overturn Jerusalem itself as well as the Roman age.

All these complications imply various fractures and subtle abysses in story-lines we take for granted. The reader – as I said before – has to read differently, to read backwards and forwards, even more importantly forwards and backwards. All the imageries are partial though attuned to a wholeness one can never seize or structure absolutely. Wholeness becomes a thread or a continuity running from the *inferno* into the *paradiso*. I said earlier that 'wholeness' cannot be seized or structured. Wholeness is a rich and *insoluble* paradox. Wholeness has to do with an origination of the Imagination whose solidity is interwoven with a paradoxical tapestry of spectrality, of the light year. Thus it is that Everyman Masters is both dead and alive when he dies and returns into Jonathan Weyl's dreams, into Amaryllis's dreams, as their Virgilian guide. The rich but insoluble paradox that clothes him brings an impulse into the text of *Carnival* to transform an authoritarian *paradiso*.

> The ecstasies and torments that run parallel through the twentieth-century age made it inevitable that the dead king should descend into the living Inferno the moment Amaryllis and I glimpsed heaven and consummated our secret marriage vows. The Inferno *lives* when the dead retrace their steps around the globe. Our marriage was unique heart and mind but for that reason – unique tranquillity and ecstasy, unique revolution and peace – it was inevitable that a master spirit would return to counsel us and to bear the penalty of the Inferno that runs in parallel with heaven. Masters accepted the penalty. He became my guide and opposite (our guide and opposite) in arriving from the kingdom of the dead to counsel us in the land of the living and to guide my pen across the pages of this biography of spirit.[1]

The use of the word 'inevitable' in the passage above from the novel *Carnival* is intended to pre-empt fate and in so doing to steep us in a continuity that is other than fate, the continuity of insoluble wholeness. As a consequence the dead/living king (that Everyman Masters is) bears the penalty of the Inferno in order to make of every erasure of pagan labour's claim to the *paradiso* a fracture or subtle abyss in the story-line of the *paradiso*. That fracture, that subtlety of penetration, is lifted into the bliss of the *coniunctio* between Amaryllis and Jonathan Weyl as a portent of a healed humanity across all terrifying barriers.

What is divine comedy? In the light of the abyss of space and time of which a thirteenth-century poet was unaware, may not divine comedy transform itself into light-year comedy, may not a numinous equation exist between spectrality and blissful sexuality as the seed of the Incarnation?

Light-year comedy within the context of numinous sexuality brings the rhythms of obsolescence into youth and vice versa. In such rhythms landscapes/ riverscapes/skyscapes are miniaturized into bodily/bodiless continuities we do not immediately recognize as pertinent to the sacrament of sex. Let me read another passage from *Carnival*.

> Our naked flesh was inhabited by mutual generations clad in nothing but obsolescent organs, obsolescent youth. What obsolescence! What intim- ate renewal of being beyond age and youth! We were intimate, ageless being, we were four years short of thirty, we were young, we were old as the coition of the hills and waves miniaturized in our bodies. We were a dying fall into deeper orchestration of mutual spaces.[2]

When I wrote that passage – and though it came out of intense care and concen- tration – I did not realize (it may well have been written by a stranger) the continuity it sustained with future work, the corridor that ran through it into the characters that would appear in the second novel of the *Carnival* trilogy, namely *The Infinite Rehearsal*. Many imaginative writers know of the legacies one work offers another that is still to be written. What I am referring to, however, is deeper than this. It is as if those legacies are overturned by the hand of a stranger to imply a continuity the legacies themselves may have eclipsed. It would never have crossed my mind – when I wrote *The Infinite Rehearsal* – to associate Jonathan Weyl, Amaryllis, Everyman Masters in *Carnival* with Robin Redbreast Glass, Emma and Peter in *The Infinite Rehearsal*. Even now I advance the association with some trepidation. Yet it is blindingly clear that it exists. Robin Redbreast Glass is immortal Faustian youth. He sustains a link with Jonathan Weyl (the twentieth-century Dante figure in *Carnival*) because of the medium- istic bliss that erupts into his relationship with Emma. Emma – the female priest in *The Infinite Rehearsal* – an ageing woman (presumably therefore obso- lescent in sexual terms) validates Amaryllis, the Beatrice figure, in *Carnival*. Numinous intercourse occurs between her – the ostensibly aged woman – and the immortal Faustian youth Robin Redbreast Glass. Peter – as Robin's *alter ego* – is a mediumistic Everyman Masters and a shadowy Virgilian guide in *The Infinite Rehearsal*.

Robin Redbreast Glass arises from the grave of the sea to become immortal Faustian youth. There has been a boating accident in which Robin, his mother, his aunt, and others were drowned. Peter and Emma were in the capsized boat but they escaped and lay on the beach exhausted. Peter lay with his head under Emma's hair and upon her breasts. When Emma and Peter are old they meet the resurrected Faustian youth (who therefore has not aged) in the tunnel of the light years. Robin sees himself within *alter ego* Peter as if the years fall away and *he* (Robin instead of Peter) lies with Emma on the beach. He lies with his head beneath her hair and upon her breasts. And yet he recognizes her as an aged woman simultaneously. He sees her as a female priest. It is this saving paradox within age and youth, within the translation of obsolescence and fertility, that gives to the spectrality of encounter a wholly different apprehension of the living in the dead, the dead in the living, absence in presence, presence in absence. I am not sure that the terms 'dead' and 'living' apply in this context for one is dealing with a continuity of encounter that nourishes itself by overturning legacies of expectation. That is how it seems to me. I have no dogma or absolute theories about the unfinished genesis of the Imagination.

Robin is amazed to discover that Emma is a priest. *So was I, the writer.* Prior to writing this novel I believed women should not be priests. I changed my mind in the light of the subtle abysses that appeared in the *Carnival* trilogy. Robin records his astonishment in a series of short passages I shall now read. The allusion to *Skull* is to a city of prosperity littered with desolations.

Robin exclaims inwardly:

> I saw in a flash that she was a priest, a female priest, she was hope in the city of Skull, revolutionary hope, unconventional hope.[3]

Let me confess that the issue of the female priest is one that startles me. It overturns a certain legacy of expectation that I have entertained from childhood. *The priest is male is male is priest is male for ever and ever.* Aboriginal or ontic tautology enshrined in so many story-lines. But a question arises: are the stigmata upon the body of Christ a story-line? Do they not imply an abyss at the heart of history? Is the crucifixion of the Son of God – no less a person, mark you – the very Son of God – is this not an abyss at the heart of human history? If so then the stigmata may imply a range of association we do not recognize and have scarcely begun to gauge. That is how I felt when I came to Emma – the young/old, obsolescent/fertile priest. Through her my grasp of Faust underwent a profound change. My apprehension of the stigmata underwent a profound change. Let me come first to the stigmata. Robin addresses Emma inwardly again:

> All this made me scan Emma's features closely. She was veiled by dateless day infinity comedy. I saw her innate sorrow. I suddenly saw how worn she was. It was as if a nail had woven its innermost weblike constancy into her flesh, an ecstatic nail, a sorrowing nail. Ecstatic and sorrowing![4]

When Robin alludes there to 'dateless day infinity comedy' as a veil upon Emma's features he draws upon an ancient pre-Columbian, calendrical perspective. This matches I think the notion of light-year vistas. But I wish at this juncture to remind you of the 'nail', its 'innermost, weblike constancy . . . ecstatic nail, sorrowing nail . . .'

It is as if one glimpses numinous sexuality within Robin's blissful relationship to Emma on the beach beside the sea, a numinous sexuality that becomes a spectral nail that pierces through the *inferno* into the *paradiso*.

> In such a nail that shatters one's pre-possessions I knew the construction of a sound that echoed in the air and in the sea. It was the music of the priest, of the God of nature. 'One comes,' said Emma, 'to a beloved creation, to the divine, in every moment that one survives in the inimitable textures of nature, truly lives and survives.[5]

All this I feel brings a wholly unexpected variation into the stigmata we tend to identify tautologously with the body of Christ. Through Emma the female priest – Emma the body of the womb – a multiple counterpoint – weblike yet constant – is woven that involves Faustian, immortal youth, the resurrection body, ecstatic numinous, paradisean nail, and sorrowing nail that pierces the tyranny of the inferno.

> As I lay on the beach I was pierced by the cry of the gulls, the laughing sea gulls. Were they gulls or were they cranes? I could not tell. It was a cry from heaven and yet it was a subtle, piercing, shaking laughter. A shaking note like strings of music in the sea. The motif of an incomparable composition . . .[6]

It may interest you to note that the cry of the gull echoes a pre-Columbian motif which relates to Quetzalcoatl. Quetzal the bird. Coatl the snake, the abysmal yet fertile earth which is 'beloved nature'.

Now, may I return to Faust and the way in which the multiple counterpoint – of which I spoke above – affected my vision of Faust. There is an aspect to Faust, immortal youth, when he seems to achieve a divorce from the resurrection body in *The Infinite Rehearsal* and looms as absolutely dominant. He buries the ecstatic, sorrowing nail within a hubris of immortality. He seeks implicitly to abort the mysterious buoyancy that is open to him as he lies beside Emma. Weblike constancy becomes a sterile rigidity. And then he gains a position by which to manipulate a series of ageing masks. One such mask bears the initials W. H. (my own initials). A joke, a serious joke. Except that Faust sees the ageing masks he wears as expendable. And in that sense the joke may hurt. Despite one's labours for Faust – despite the labour of one's antecedents across generations – one and they are expendable and doomed.

The rigidity of the perpetually young immortal Faust secures the *tautology of tyranny*, the worship of fascism, of evil. Faust's ageing masks include the ageing institutions of democracy, of the Church, of the humanities, the universities. We have seen how such ageing institutions may be worn to the detriment of peoples in Hitlerite Europe, in Field-Marshall Amin's Africa, and most recently in Saddam's Iraq.

I do not have to remind you that tyrannies have been nourished by the ageing Church which turned a blind eye to injustice, by ageing democracies which have been the suppliers of machinery of war or have stimulated in the commercial field gross, materialistic ambitions.

I cannot easily explain it but the curious fractured story-lines within *The Infinite Rehearsal* drew me intuitively to sense that the numinous body of the womb in the female priest implied unsuspected fabric that breaks and alters the rigidity of Faustian hubris. The substance of the nail, the substance of instrumentalities linking cultures, turns institutions around to examine and re-examine themselves in creative and re-creative lights. Robin Redbreast Glass yields to the priest Emma.

I felt her lips upon mine. The kiss of all loves and all true lovers.[7]

The numinous instrumentality of the nail becomes the seed of invisible texts in which ageing, expendable masks become the secretion of strangers who are intimate to ourselves and who will sustain continuity into the future.

One needs to be cautious for the issues we are exploring do not turn on dogma or intellectual formula. Yet one may have, I think, a certain true confidence in the intuitive life of the Imagination, its spectrality and miraculous concreteness beyond implacable identity or formula.

It is the nail, the paradox of associative instrumentalities, which brings me now to the last volume in the *Carnival* trilogy, namely *The Four Banks of the River of Space*.

Let me commence by presenting a cross-cultural parallel between an aspect of Homer's *Odyssey* and South American/Guyanese legend relating to the figure of Canaima. Telemachus is approached in Ithaca by a friend who tells him that his father Ulysses is alive and will return home to redeem the kingdom and to destroy Penelope's suitors who are wasting the substance of the state. The next day when Telemachus runs into his friend and reminds him of their conversation the friend is astonished. He has no recollection of it. He was somewhere else. Homer covers the discrepancy by saying that a god or a goddess had appeared in the shape of Telemachus's friend. A similar yet enigmatic confusion of identity occurs in South America and it relates to the revenge apparition or fury or god called Canaima. Ulysses does return as prophesied and is not immediately recognized. He comes in the rags of a beggar.

An aspect of Ulysses' fury when he returns which I find horrific is his slaying of many or some of Penelope's serving women who had slept with some of the suitors in the palace in Ithaca. One accepts the necessity to slay the suitors but the hanging of the serving women filled me with dread as a child when I read Homer. Upon reflection across the years I find it endorses another parallel with Canaima. The aspect of terrifying revenge! True, Ulysses was a great hero, a returning hero but the redemption of his kingdom is tainted by the horror of revenge.

I recall coming upon a group of Macusi Indians in the Potaro River in British

Guiana in the mid-1940s. They told me Canaima was active amongst them and in pursuit of some obscure wrong he had judged their people had done – some crime they had committed in the past – and as a consequence he was spiriting away their young men and maidens. It is hard to describe their state of misery in the face of Canaima who is indeed a formidable legend associated with the enactment of revenge upon wrong-doers. The pathology of revenge in him becomes a form of evil.

It is important to note in charting the parallel with Homeric epic that Canaima may appear in an encampment – intent on sowing fire like a terrorist or causing some bitter distress – and be recognized as a neighbour, as one's cousin, or someone's brother or father. Yet the following day when the recognized person is cornered he makes a good case for being somewhere else, hunting, fishing. An uncanny confusion overwhelms the tribe. Not only are they confused about the crime they or their antecedents have committed and which brought Canaima into their midst but they are confronted by an abyss within which lurks the identity of terror. *If only they could seize the instrument Canaima uses!*

The instrument becomes both spectral and concrete. And this explains in some degree the ascendancy of the camera amongst deprived peoples. If they are to deal with such spectrality, such concreteness, a shift has to occur in the premises of their *reading* of reality in the sky, in the land, in the river, everywhere. That shift seems almost impossible in a mass-media world and yet a moment may have arrived when the apparatus, the instrumentalities we take for granted, are susceptible to cross-cultural and re-visionary momentum. Take the camera. Disadvantaged peoples become pawns of the camera. Their ills are made visible to millions of viewers and then they fade from the news. The camera becomes a weapon with which we shoot an animal or a savage and bring him home as a trophy in the television box. There are passages in *The Four Banks of the River of Space* which extend the complications I have raised but – for the purposes of this talk – I wish to restrict my emphasis to the matter of weaponry and instrument.

A camera is a weapon in some instances. In other instances it is an extension of the caring eye. It could also be a private excursion into the future through recorded relics of memory. Each relic implies a fossil dimensionality that enriches the present and the future. The camera is also an eye of spirit as when one encounters people – as I did in a marketplace in Mexico City – who are alarmed that their souls may be imprinted or captured on the glass eye staring at them.

If all this is true of the camera how much more varied are the weapons and instruments of past civilizations. The bow of Ulysses in Homer's epic is *not* the same bow for us. How it lived for him, how it felt to him, the faint tremor and music of the string, the sound of the wind that whispered in the branches of trees from which the bow came are not the same for us. But tremor, sound, wind, incomparable composition at the heart of words may awaken us to the mystery of trees, the precious life of trees. The abyss that has opened between ourselves and Homer – the greatest of epic poets – nourishes a fantastic and mysterious continuity that breaks a pattern of sameness, same bow, same arrow, even as it enriches the numinous raw material from which we fashion a bow, or a vessel, or a ship.

To destroy our rainforests now is to place our civilization upon another hill of Calvary. The three crosses fashioned from trees become the eloquent masts of a sinking ship from which Robin Redbreast Glass would be taxed, as never before, to arise. A bow, or a ship, or a camera, or a sword, or a knife, or an axe are not singular or same objects. They are instinct with pluralities. On one level that instinct cements violence. On another level we fashion, and are fashioned by, the enigma of constructive truth. The two levels or forces resemble each other but they are not the same.

The resemblance cannot be dismissed however. It achieves an overlap that resists absolute model or formula. There is no absolute model for constructive truth. There is no absolute imprint upon violence. Justice can be tainted by revenge. The resemblance assists us to make differentiations that are sometimes shockingly new in abysmal circumstance between our proneness to violence (as a solution to the world's ills) and a blow we may strike that liberates our prepossessions, unshackles our bondage to fate. The latter blow is inimitably creative, inimitably constructive, in apprising us of the burdens of an imperilled globe that may only be borne in intimate and far-reaching alignment to strangers who are pertinent to us as we are pertinent to them. This issue of knowing ourselves, recognizing ourselves differently, implies a creative/re-creative penetration or blow directed at models of tradition whose partiality engenders an accumulation of crisis.

That such accumulation is visible everywhere makes clear, I would think, the rituals of sameness, of repetitive slaughter ingrained in violence within the symbols of world politics. One returns to the issue of instrumentality, the life of the extended body, in visualizing the stranger in ourselves. The mould of revenge gives way to profoundest self-confessional imagination. We may not recognize ourselves in the evil-doer but our dismemberment at his hands need not be a prescription for ultimate self-destruction. To jettison such a prescription is to perceive within the threat of a dismembered world an instrumentality that has chiselled us, shaped us, across aeons of space. We cannot seize such instrumentality but we can release in it, from it, proportions that begin to overturn the aboriginal tautologies that condition our responses to evil. Evil seems to be evil for ever and ever until it voids self-confessional creativity. In *The Four Banks* Canaima, the evil-doer, returns to Anselm, the good man, after forty years. Alarming as it appears Canaima has changed. He has been dislodged *within* the instrumentality of a cosmos he abused. An *abused* cosmos which has shaped one, sculpted one, across aeons and evolutions, is a paradox no one can solve. Can one abuse a creator that has sculpted one, written the word of being into dust and marble and flesh? The extremities of evil are woven into such a paradox which Canaima begins to illumine when he returns to Anselm in a Dream.

Canaima the fury becomes a redemptive daemon. Has not Anselm, the good

258

man, the architect, the saint – in the nameless proportions of artifice and instrumentality, religion and law which have their roots in well-nigh forgotten pagan realms – conspired inadvertently with powers that bred catastrophe? Canaima's return therefore is self-reversal in such illumined conspiracy. His return is an illumination of restrictive vision into shared evil, shared faculty of redemption through the arts and sciences that have been abused in the prosecution of fundamental causes.

Anselm sets out on his odyssey into the past with Canaima's dislodged knife in his side. It is as if he gathers up into his arms – in a wholly new, abysmal, terrifyingly creative light – the corpse of the bird-dancer Canaima had slain forty years previously on the bank of the Potaro River in South America. The corpse is but a mask to be worn by endangered species whose life is now wholly precious, sacred.

> Canaima's knife . . . had metaphorically killed me . . . pierced me to the core of the body's waking instrument.[8]

The Body's Waking Instrument. The arousal of the body to itself as sculpture by a creator one abuses. The body wakes to itself as inimitable art, inimitable multi-faceted, living fossil extending into all organs, objects, spaces, stars, and the ripple of light. Wakes also to self-confessional blindness, blindness to self-destruction and the destruction of others.

The body wakes to the instrumentality of breath – 'sharpest extension of breath in sculpted body-senses'.[9]

> Perhaps I was the medium of the dance in touching the earth, in touching the light, in touching the sculpture of appearances as if every structure one shaped, or ordered, or visualized, was a sacred infusion of slow-motion lightning into substance, substance into life.[10]

I appreciate the difficulty in a phrase embodying 'slow-motion lighting'. It was the closest I could come to a visualization of the energies of the cosmos as sleeping/waking life, as station and expedition, as the transfiguration of technologies into a therapeutic edge within the malaise of gross materialism that threatens to destroy our planet.

I would like to close by reading the following passage:

> One could hear a murmuring vibration in Shadow-organ space. One could hear one's voice issuing from the body of a stranger.
> 'It is a sounding cornerstone that exists everywhere, in the soil, in the air, in the fire, in the water. It exists in the singing chorus of the Waterfall, in the greenhouse Shadow of the drowned in space whose indeterminate age makes them as much our victims as our attackers, as much our killed as our killers.

'Are we too old, too young, to dream of the knife and the Rose? When do dreams commence? In the womb or in the seed of the womb? I have drawn the Shadow of my brother from the river of the dead. And still I ask myself: whose Shadow? whose brother? whose stranger? A life or a death that baits the unconscious is not to be equated with conventional structures, or conventional hubris, or conventional uniformities and clarities. The sweetest song of unconscious beauty may turn and rend a theatre of technicalities, technical apparatus, technical nudity, technical descriptions of the act of love or death, purely technical climax that averts its head from the anatomy of the abyss.

'Is it the anatomy of the abyss that I glimpse in myself, in him, in nameless others one bears – who bear one – into the parentage of Being? Have I borne a spatial being that is capable of taking upon itself familiar/unfamiliar resemblances? Does the burden of art involve a confrontation with an ultimate loss of fear? Nothing that is or was, nothing that bears or is borne, was created in the beginning from fear, fear of one or fear of the other, though fear may come in the wake of a Presence with which one needs to be reconciled through stages of haunted masquerade, the haunted sinner in one's arms, or in the cradle, or on the stage of Memory . . .'

The uncanny, unfinished body of music within us ceased. But it had invoked a change in the transparencies of the unconscious. The paint of the sun began to lift. Everything had been passive, fixed. Now a spark in the sun lifted, the sun itself moved and began to fall. The spark unravelled the sky to touch the high precipice of the globe in the Dream.[11]

Notes

* Address to Temenos Academy, 18 March 1992.
1 Wilson Harris, *Carnival*, 1985, p.125.
2 Ibid., p.124.
3 Wilson Harris, *The Infinite Rehearsal*, 1987, p.59.
4 Ibid., p.60.
5 Ibid., p.61.
6 Ibid., p.60.
7 Ibid., p.61.
8 Wilson Harris, *The Four Banks of the River of Space*, 1990, p.15.
9 Ibid., p.16.
10 Ibid., p.8.
11 Ibid., pp.153–4.

SUMMING-UP

If the chief role of the literary essay is to develop hypotheses – in Harris's writing, the hunches and intuitions relating to the reality of what I have called his dream-book of the culture – then the greatest value of these essays would be where they diverged from a common background of shared assumptions about the nature of the world and the degrees of evidential support.

Harris's principal achievement seems to me his defining in a comprehensive manner essential areas of experience largely ignored in conventional narratives. For the English language, this means the discovery of the cross-cultural imagination in the fiction; the development of a new diction for that resource; detailed evidential support for the reality of that resource. His enquiries show why that resource remained largely unapprehended, and why once recuperated, it should have uncovered such rich seams for the culture.

Harris's use of the cross-cultural imagination has made it an imaging-field where motif, support and medium overlap and give 'multitude'. 'One becomes, it seems, a vessel of composite epic, imbued with many voices, one is a multitude. That multitude is housed paradoxically in the diminutive surviving entity of community and self that one is' ('Letter from Francisco Bone to W.H.' in *Jonestown*, p.48 in this volume). If, in one sense, the literary essay is a groundwork for the novel, then it is also an index of the extent to which the writer will augment the novel.

If Harris's essays comprehend a singularity, if they express what Harris in 'Tradition and the West Indian Novel' calls the 'historical self-sufficient individual', then Harris, by his own definition, is engaged in a work of capacity and scale, an 'échelle (Fr. *échelle*, *éscale*, scale) or ladder of scale' a womb of tradition that Harris has vastly revised.

I noted in the Introduction how an education in the English language continues a distinct inheritance shared potentially by one-fifth of the world. It conveys and inculcates in each individual what was once thought of as the given means: the literate inheritance of such traditions as the English Bible, the Book of Common Prayer, the divine genealogies or mythologies, the notation of epic and tragedy, of poetics and the Sublime, the social processions of Festival Calendar, Carnival, Fête, and training in the natural sciences. What Harris discovered is that these institutions are supported by radical strata of alien culture which, once in touch with Europe, 'require windows into reality that are other than the frame of realism'.[1] The whole 'given means' are now seen to include the cross-cultural intrusion as outcrops of arts of the imagination that are perhaps always vanishing. New fictions are written on these outcrops; their role is as new building-blocks of conscious formulation, legacies of Being, not just of Western peoples and languages *but of every people that has sustained contact with the West and its institutions.*

Beside this new annunciation, the contemporary idiom, the social programme, the gender-based writings, the historic revisionism, the realism to which cultures are addicted, seem confined.

By the time the writer comes to think of his origins, the inventory of 'the given means', whether or not there is formal order to it, is already inculcated, and the previous legacy of imaginative writings threatens his own efforts with disappearance. In the bid for literary survival, Harris's fictions and essays engage with and sustain exacting questions. They oppose what has already been consolidated. Harris's hypotheses involving the vanished civilizations of Central and South America also address, by metaphor, the question of literary continuance. How can a body of literature hope to continue when it is pressured toward disappearance by the enormous weight of tradition? In a certain way, by exposing the determinism and partial stance of the conventional narrative; its inherent rigidity; its fixedness in an inadequate conception of the world, Harris has unwittingly undermined a substantial part of the tradition that might have denied him literary survival.

In another way we can say that Harris's dream-book of the culture invests in the creative imagination's inherent capaciousness. There is a refrain in *The Eye of the Scarecrow* (1965) like an epigraph to Idiot Nameless: *My father's house has many mansions.* Idiot Nameless is a christopher or Christ-carrier. *My father's house has many mansions* – the implication being that, if this were not so, how else make room, how else prepare oneself for one's inherent capacity. Thus Harris's readings of disappeared civilizations become, in the parable of Man, an ongoing, unfinished genesis.

1 'Profiles of Myth and the New World' (1966), p.206 in this volume.

APPENDIX

El Dorado and the Grail Legend:
a memorandum with references to
Wilson Harris's fiction

In the ensemble of the novels, which I treat as a single coherent Dreamingbook of the culture, Wilson Harris deploys adversarial twinning as means of transfiguring catastrophic experience into creative potential:

> the historical disasters of the Renaissance reverberate in present-day conflicts ... Monty, for example, imprisoned for a crime he has not committed, is obsessed with the same desire for revenge as Montezuma, the fallen emperor. The mute cry of a child for whose murder Brazilian Leonard feels responsible pursues him in Sorrow Hill. Len takes himself for Leonardo da Vinci and sees the murdered child on da Vinci's *Virgin of the Rocks*. A striking metaphorical web unfolds from the painting, first misused by a fascist league in Brazil as emblem of the ethnically pure virgin state they want to establish, then revealing the possible transubstantiation of the murdered child into the Eucharist.[1]

This skilful précis of the novel *Sorrow Hill* (1993) shows how the possibility of renewal is inherent in the disruptive wounds of history, and it seems to me that the South American legend of El Dorado and the golden city is response to a wound of history and twins with the Grail Quest of Parsifal and the Cry of Merlin in rewritten, reread structures.

Adversarial-twinship[2] in a wholly Western expression is developed by Harris in 'Merlin and Parsifal, Adversarial Twins',[3] whilst the legend of El Dorado,

---

1 Hena Maes-Jelinek, 'Charting the Uncapturable in Wilson Harris's Writing', *Review of Contemporary Fiction*, Summer 1997, p.93.
2 Twinship has been defined in the Preface to Part II (Summary) as the unrealized synchrony between two and more cultures which, at first sight, seem remote in time and circumstance. Adversarial twinship connotes the encounter of two personalities and their world-views that will tend to articulate itself as a dualism.
3 'Merlin and Parsifal, Adversarial Twins', first given at the Temenos Academy, London, April 1997.

although a core-legend for Harris, cannot be assumed to be generally known. Let us look at the two legends in outline; their motifs in the novels and ramification with Harris's vision of a new conceptual language for the arts of the imagination.

Both legends can be understood as epochal responses to loss; the one as persistent oral vestige, the other expressed in epic. The Grail is a work of unstated and hence sustained grief for the death of King Arthur and with the death the closure of mythogenic England–Albion. In a particular way, the Grail legend continues in South America in the legend of El Dorado.

The Grail is the West's most comprehensive legend cycle. El Dorado is barely a fragment. The Grail cycle expresses Christian, Celt and Druid origins. The legend of El Dorado also embodies the encounter of alien civilizations, each one letting slip barely discernible gods that are obscure and unknown even to their own culture. Who might these gods be? Let us consider first the god of the El Dorado legend.

El Dorado is Spanish for 'the gilded one'. From the Carib side, El Dorado is certainly a god, yet he is not associated with the Central and South American flute-bridge. He is not a surviving Mexican, Andean, Arawak or Carib regent. As a divine, the complex royal hierarchy we associate with the Andean civilizations or the ample *periploi* of the ceremonial migrations in the Guiana Highlands are absent from the kingdom of El Dorado. From the Andean or Central American perspective we would expect a royal-divine to have an entourage of 150–200 aristocratic families. Yet this paramount travels out to the far bank of a lake in a single canoe, is bathed in a lake each day by a small number of attendants and his skin renewed in gold. He proceeds *on his own* in a ceremony that seems to point to a daily renewal of time: 'The Maya were torn by the notion of eternity's closure of time and another shape to time, blending pasts and futures to unlock closure or pact or plot' (*Jonestown*, 1996, p.5).

Similarly, the ceremonial bath of El Dorado appears to be a means *to unlock closure or pact or plot* with eternity. If we compare El Dorado with the known ceremonies of prolonging time used elsewhere in Central and South America, no mention is made in his golden city of the central role played by leading families in maintaining the integrity of time. The city-states built on the axis of the so-called 'white-road' of Central America surrounded at their centre a game played with a yellow ball. This game was played in an enclosed court and seems to have been played in perpetuity. It never stopped. The continuing participation of the leading families was required to supply and maintain the game with living human sacrifice and costly gifts. The aristocracy had to live at court because they held indispensable positions in the life-ceremony of perpetuating time.

The just-deciphered hieroglyphs of the Mesoamerican civilization reveal that the city-states at Bonampak, Tikal, Chichén Itzá, Palenque, and the invasions from Teotihuacan in the Mexico valley that brought the 'Bo-Kepie Tree of Life' religion to Central America are endorsed within complex visible human hierarchies.[4] Such visibility is absent in the El Dorado legend. El Dorado's is a prosperous utopia, but the kind of hierarchy implicit, for instance, in the status of the warrior-caste at Chichen Itza does not seem to be implicit in the city of gold. Thus El Dorado is evading structures that are known and recorded at other sites in the founding civilization.

And what of the barely discernible gods on the English side? The legend of El Dorado is reported to Raleigh and his followers in the late 1590s. Seventy years earlier, when the legend is first told to Spain, El Dorado is the head of a tribe who covers himself with gold dust at an annual festival held near Santa Fe de Bogota in present-day Colombia. By the end of the century, when the legend is reported to Raleigh, El Dorado is no longer a tribe's chieftain, but a land of gold called Manoa or Omoa; it is now located some distance inland from the coast on the Orinoco River in the part of the Guianas that is now Venezuela. That is to say, a thousand kilometres east of the Colombian site. To obscure matters further, Martinez, a lieutenant in the Spanish army, claimed to have seen Omoa and to have been entertained by El Dorado himself. 'Elusive El Dorado (City of Gold? City of God?), whose masthead is consumed and refashioned on sacrificial altars in every century around the globe, may have a buried harbour in that compass or "land of waters".'[5]

It is possible that El Dorado – legend of the renewed or returned god – expressed decimation, and that it survives as a vestige of memory, and that such a vestige was still being expressed up to three centuries later.

> The amazing story of the Arekuna Indian Awakaipu is well documented in Georgetown in the 1840s. Arakaipu persuaded representatives from many Indian peoples to offer themselves as a sacrifice at the foot of Mount Roraima in order to recover an 'enchanted kingdom'.[6]

Harris calls such unresolved legend a 'riddle of precipitate breakdown'. The vicious circle of genesis in South America – what Harris calls the flute-bridge – breaks down with the returned god Quetzalcoatl–Hernan Cortez in 1519. Mistaken for the epochal return of Quetzalcoatl, the Spaniard Hernan Cortez causes Montezuma the Aztec king to suspend judgement, and to allow Tenochtitlan (now the site of Mexico City) to fall. Eleven years later, in the Peruvian Andes, Pizarro destroys Atahuallpa, the ninth and last Inca, again in the guise of a returning god, this time Kukulcan. We can say that when conquest came to the Guianas from the early 1540s, Yurokon, the Carib trickster god, who had been borrowing the mask of returned Quetzalcoatl–Kukulcan, was forced by firearms, sexual disease, influenza and famine to strip off. What Yurokon uncovered was

---

4 See Linda Schele (d. 1998), *Maya Cosmos* (1993) with Joy Parker; *A Forest of Kings* (1990); *Blood of Kings: Dynasty and Ritual in Maya* (1986); *Maya Glyphs: The Verbs* (1982).
5 *Jonestown*, 1996, p.5.
6 Ibid.

the hidden mask of alien conquest and the sixteenth-century masque of the Conquistador.

First the Aztec, then the Inca, and finally the Carib mistake a man on horse-back for a half-man/half-animal god. Face to face with the Spanish, the Carib become, as it were, precipitately conscious of the self in others. Their bridge reaching over the abyss of conquest falters in the early 1520s. That recognition is decisive. It ends a predatory span in the indigenous Americas. Seventy years later in the Guianas, Raleigh is as one who arrives in the wake of the obliterated/ obliterating god. Just as the returned god *came home* to Mesoamerica through the person of the Spanish Hernan Cortez in 1519, the obliterated, now-altered king of El Dorado struggles to be found *at home* through Raleigh. Thus, obscurely behind Raleigh, stands a god-king. We do not discern the features clearly; it is an enigma.

Across time, El Dorado stays curiously fixed, rigid in outline. A hard kernel which does not divide and does not increase. In this sense El Dorado is an 'open' myth. It is withholding *closure or pact or plot*. In comparison the Grail legend availed itself of superlative additions, variants and revivals when it entered litera-ture at the turn of the twelfth century. The Grail is recovered. The Arthurian knights Galahad, Gawain and Bors return the sacred Grail chalice – holder of the 'Eucharist' or 'true grace' – to the city of Sarras-Jerusalem. The end of the Grail quest is spiritual accomplishment:

> [Medieval man's] problem was to overcome the purely natural condition in which [the] primitive [in] man is still held captive and to assume a spiritual attitude. For this task the Christian doctrine provided not only the most complete expression but also offered help and guidance.[7]

Next to the Grail, El Dorado has been suspended the past four centuries in *el desdichado*, the disinherited. Loss and disenchantment. Sir Walter Raleigh's failure to find gold in the Orinoco precipitates an epochal parable for the post-Renaissance or modern era. The legend of El Dorado receives and reverses the legend of the Holy Grail, making it possible that, with the modern-era entry of the New World into the consciousness of the West, the legend of El Dorado is a potential summary of our own epoch, and that, like its Grail predecessor, the particular needs of the epoch will enter and breach the rigid monad of legend, so that El Dorado, in its turn, will receive eventual mutations and permutations in the story-line.

If we imagine the problem of the Modern era to be a reversal of the medieval, then, in Sir Walter Raleigh, El Dorado finds a peculiarly English coda, making it an uncanny theme for literatures in English. Looking forward from 1617 and

---

7 Emma Jung and M.-L. von Franz, *The Grail Legend*, trans. A. Dykes, Sigo Press, Boston, 1986, p.377.

Raleigh's return and punishment by beheading, El Dorado sets the problem of the future. Because Raleigh fails to realize the force of will, failure of the 'will-full life' will eventually push modern man back into his hidden nature. Back into the hidden psyche. It is a reversal explored in twentieth-century depth-psychologies. After the long sustained struggle to form the intellect, the West will have begun to move between the twins.

> Until modern psychology [uncovered] the fundamental dual nature of man – the fact that he consists of a conscious and unconscious personal- ity, each of which [completes] the other – [to realise a figure such as the Merlin of the Holy Grail] was practically impossible; it is only with difficulty that the conscious mind was able to free itself from unequivocal single-track formulations.[8]

Language is a threshold or a crosser of rigid boundaries; a thing to mediate rather than to consolidate the imagination. Uniform, mechanistic readings, by their very processes, produce a framed universe of experience. For Harris, a framed universe yields the fiction of absolute knowledge. Paradoxically, language, the maker of such fictions, can also unmake or breach that fiction. 'Language is deeper than "frames", it transgresses against the frames that would make us prisoners of eternity in the name of one creed or dogma or ideology' (*Jonestown*, p.6).

A new conceptual language would seek to breach its own frame. It would be a self-judgement. It would proceed in binary fusion, in figurations that include Parsifal AT THE SAME TIME AS Merlin in the self-confession. It would move backwards and forwards between the twins in a repertory of simultaneous know- ledge. That is to say, the two legends will be found to be quantised or 'entangled' in a 'quantum transference of psyche',[9] the act of reading-measuring the one instantaneously affecting the solid-state of the other.

8 Ibid.
9 *Jonestown*, 1996, p.14.

BIBLIOGRAPHY

Novels

The Guyana Quartet:

Palace of the Peacock (London: Faber and Faber, 1960)

The Far Journey of Oudin (London: Faber and Faber, 1961)

The Whole Armour (London: Faber and Faber, 1962)

The Secret Ladder (London: Faber and Faber, 1963); rpt. in one volume as *The Guyana Quartet* with minor changes and 'A Note on the Genesis of *The Guyana Quartet*' (London: Faber and Faber, 1985)

The Whole Armour and *The Secret Ladder*; rpt. in one volume with an 'Author's Note' (London: Faber and Faber, 1973)

Heartland (London: Faber and Faber, 1964)

The Eye of the Scarecrow (London: Faber and Faber, 1965)

The Waiting Room (London: Faber and Faber, 1967)

Tumatumari (London: Faber and Faber, 1968)

Ascent to Omai (London: Faber and Faber, 1970)

The Sleepers of Roraima, A Carib Trilogy (London: Faber and Faber, 1970)

The Age of the Rainmakers (London: Faber and Faber, 1971)

'Kanaima', in *Black Orpheus Anthology* (Ibadan, 1964); rpt. in Kenneth Ramchand (ed.), *West Indian Narrative* (London: Nelson, 1966), pp.196–205. Also in Anna Rutherford and Donald Hannah (eds), *Commonwealth Short Stories* (London: Edward Arnold, 1971), pp.106–15

Black Marsden (London: Faber and Faber, 1972)

Companions of the Day and Night (London: Faber and Faber, 1975)

Da Silva da Silva's Cultivated Wilderness and *Genesis of the Clowns* (London: Faber and Faber, 1977)

The Tree of the Sun (London: Faber and Faber, 1978)

The Angel at the Gate (London: Faber and Faber, 1982)

Carnival (London: Faber and Faber, 1985)

The Infinite Rehearsal (London: Faber and Faber, 1987)

The Four Banks of the River of Space (London: Faber and Faber, 1990)

Resurrection at Sorrow Hill (London: Faber and Faber, 1993)

Jonestown (London: Faber and Faber, 1996)

Non-fiction

Tradition, the Writer and Society (London: New Beacon Books, 1967); rpt 1973

History, Fable and Myth in the Caribbean and Guianas, The Edgar Mittelholzer Memorial Lectures. Third Series. February 1970. Ministry of Information and Culture, Georgetown, Guyana

History, Fable and Myth in the Caribbean and Guianas. With a new Introduction by Selwyn R. Cudjoe (Wellesley, Mass: Calaloux Publications, 1995)

Enigma of Values, ed. Kirsten Holst Petersen and Anna Rutherford (Aarhus: Dangaroo Press, 1975); contains: introduction by the editors summing up Wilson Harris's ideas; by Wilson Harris, 'Benito Cereno'

Explorations: A Selection of Talks and Articles 1966–1981, ed. Hena Maes-Jelinek (Aarhus: Dangaroo Press, 1981); contains:
'The Place of the Poet in Modern Society'
'Interior of the Novel: Amerindian/European/African Relations'
'History, Fable and Myth in the Caribbean and Guianas', revised version
'The Phenomenal Legacy'
'The Native Phenomenon'
'A Talk on the Subjective Imagination'
'Fossil and Psyche'
'Reflection and Vision'
'The Making of Tradition'
'Some Aspects of Myth and the Intuitive Imagination'
'Scented Gardens for the Blind'
'The Complexity of Freedom'
'Carnival of Psyche: Jean Rhys's *Wide Sargasso Sea*'
'The Frontier on which *Heart of Darkness* Stands'

'Impressions after Seven years', *New World*, 44, 1 (July 1966), pp.17–20

'The Unresolved Constitution', *Caribbean Quarterly*, 14, 1 and 2 (March–June 1968), pp.43–7

'A Comment on *A Passage to India*', *Literary Half-Yearly*, 10 (July 1969), pp.35–40

'Kith and Kin', *Journal of Commonwealth Literature*, 7 (June 1972), pp.1–5

'The Enigma of Values', *New Letters*, 40 (October 1973), pp.141–9

'Journey into the Canje', in Bernth Lindfors and Ulla Schild (eds), *Neo-African Literature and Culture*, Essays in Memory of Janheinz Jahn (Wiesbaden: Heymann, 1976), pp.346–52

'The Imagination on Trial', in Alan Burns and Charles Sugnet (eds), *The Imagination on Trial*, British and American Writers Discuss their Writing Methods (London: Allison and Busby, 1981), pp.51–65

'Metaphor and Myth', in Robert Sellick (ed.), *Myth and Metaphor* (Adelaide: Centre for Research in New Literatures in English, 1982), pp.1–14

The Womb of Space: The Cross-Cultural Imagination (Westport, Conn.: Greenwood Press, 1983)

'Reflections on Faulkner's *Intruder in the Dust* in a Cross-cultural Complex', *World Literature Written in English*, 22, 1 (Spring 1983), pp.98–106

'The Quest for Form', *Kunapipi*, V, 1 (1983), pp.21–7

'Character and Philosophic Myth', in Britta Olinder (ed.), *A Sense of Place*, Essays in Post-Colonial Literatures (Göteborg: The English Department, Gothenburg University, 1984), pp.124–30

'On the Beach', *Landfall* 155, 39, 3 (Sept. 1985), pp.335–41

'A Note on the Genesis of *The Guyana Quartet*', in *The Guyana Quartet* (London: Faber and Faber, 1985), pp.7–14

'Jean Rhys's "Tree of Life"', *Review of Contemporary Fiction*, 5, 2 (Summer 1985), pp.114–17

'Adversarial Contexts and Creativity', *New Left Review*, 154 (Nov.–Dec. 1985), pp.124–8

'Carnival Theatre: A Personal View', in *Masquerading, The Art of the Notting Hill Carnival* (London: The Arts Council of Great Britain, 1986), pp.38–42

'Character and Philosophic Myth' (a different essay from that with same title above), *Hambone*, 6 (Fall 1986), pp.98–107

'Houngan and Shaman', *Hambone*, 6 (Fall 1986), pp.108–28

'Guyanese Folk-Speech', review of *Slave-Song* by David Dabydeen, *The Race Review Today*, 17, 4 (December 1986), pp.24–5

'Guyana Prize Address', *Kyk-Over-Al*, 38 (June 1988), pp.24–7

'Literacy and the Imagination', in Michael Gilkes (ed.), *The Literate Imagination: Essays on the Novels of Wilson Harris* (London: Macmillan, 1989), pp.13–30

'Validation of Fiction: A Personal View of Imaginative Truth', in Maggie Butcher (ed.), *Tibisiri* (Aarhus: Dangaroo Press, 1989), pp.40–51; also in *Kyk-Over-Al*, 38 (June 1988), pp.27–34

'Comedy and Modern Allegory: A Personal View', in Hena Maes-Jelinek, Kirsten Holst Petersen and Anna Rutherford (eds), *Aof Connections, Commonwealth Literature Studies – Then and Now* (Aarhus: Dangaroo Press, 1989), pp.127–40

'A Note on Zulfiker Ghose's "Nature Strategies"', *Review of Contemporary Fiction*, 9, 2 (Summer 1989), pp.172–8

'Oedipus and the Middle Passage', *Landfall* 170, 43, 2 (1989), 198–208; also in Geoffrey V. Davis and Hena Maes-Jelinek, *Crisis and Creativity in the New Literatures in English* (Amsterdam/Atlanta: Rodopi, 1990), pp.9–21

'The Fabric of the Imagination', *Third World Quarterly*, 12, 1, (January 1990), pp.175–86

'An Approach to Couvade', in Michael Gilkes, *Couvade, a Dream-Play of Guyana* (Aarhus: Dangaroo Press, 1990), pp.xi–xiv

'Identities: Whose Europe is it Anyway?', *New Statesman and Society* (22 June 1990), p.3

'In the Name of Liberty', *Third Text*, 11 (Summer 1990), pp.7–15

'Foreword' and 'The Amerindian Legacy', in *Guyana Dreaming, The Art of Aubrey Williams*, compiled by Anne Walmsley (Aarhus: Dangaroo Press, 1990), pp.9, 81

'The Life of Myth and its Possible Bearing on Erna Brodber's Fictions *Jane and Louisa Will Soon Come Home* and *Myal*', *Kunapipi*, XII, 3 (1990), pp.86–92

'The Unfinished Genesis of the Imagination', *Temenos* 13 (1992), pp.69–85; see also *The Journal of Commonwealth Literature*, XXVII, 1 (1992), pp.13–25

'Wilson Harris', an autobiographical essay (Detroit: Gale Research Inc., 1992), pp.121–37

The Radical Imagination, Lectures and Talks (Liège: L³ – Liège Language Literature, Université de Liège, 1992); contains the following essays:

'Judgement and Dream' (University of Cambridge, 1989)

'Wilson Harris interviewed by Alan Riach' (University of Cambridge, 1990), pp.33–65

'The Fabric of the Imagination' (University of Cambridge, 1990), pp.69–79 (a different essay from the one with same title listed above)

'The Absent Presence: The Caribbean, Central and South America (University of Cambridge, 1990), pp.81–92

'Unfinished Genesis: A Personal View of the Cross-cultural Tradition' (University of Cambridge, 1990), pp.93–102 (a different essay from the one listed under the same title in *Tenemos* 13)

'Creative and Re-creative Balance Between Cultures' (University of Cambridge, 1990), pp.103–15

'Originality and Tradition' (Université de Liège, 1991), pp.117–34

'Imagination, Dead, Imagine: Bridging a Chasm', *The Yale Journal of Criticism*, 7, 1 (1994), pp.185–95

'Quetzalcoatl and the Smoking Mirror', *Wasafiri*, 20 (Autumn 1994), pp.38–43; also in *Review: Latin American Literature and Arts*, 50 (Spring 1995), pp.76–83, and in *Review of Contemporary Fiction* (Summer 1997)

'An Open Letter to Janet Frame', in Elizabeth Alley (ed.), *The Inward Sun, Celebrating the Life and Work of Janet Frame* (Wellington: Daphne Brasell Associates Press, 1994), pp.60–6

'Profiles of Myth and the New World', in Wolfgang Zach and Ken L. Goodwin (eds), *Nationalism vs. Internationalism: (Inter)National Dimensions of Literatures in English* (Tübingen: Staufenburg Verlag, 1996), pp.77–86

'Apprenticeship to the Furies', *River City: A Journal of Contemporary Culture*, 16, 2 (Summer 1996), pp.104–15; see also a different essay with the same title, the text of a talk given at the University of Giessen in December 1995

'The Voyaging Imagination. Undreamt-of Resources of Spirit', forthcoming in *How Novelists Work*

'A Note on Alan Burns's Fiction', *Review of Contemporary Fiction*

'The Music of Living Landscapes', radio broadcast, BBC Radio 4, 12 November 1996, and in *Hambone 14*, ed. N. MacKey, Santa Cruz, California, 1998, pp.169–76

Lecture on Aubrey Williams given on 19 January 1996 at the October Gallery, London

Talk given in Milan in May 1996

See also Introduction to the Carnival Trilogy (London: Faber and Faber, 1993), pp.vii–xix

An afterword to *The Four Bank of the River of Space* (unpublished)

Review of Laurence Scott, *Witchbroom*, *Wasafiri*, 16 (Autumn 1992), pp.65–6

Review of Michael Richardson and Krzysztof Fijalkowski, *Refusal of the Shadow: Surrealism and the Caribbean*, *Wasafiri*, 25 (Spring 1997), pp.96–8

'The Open Door', *Journal of Modern Literature*, XX, 1 (Summer 1996), pp.7–12

Essays in this selection: publication and source details

1 'The Music of Living Landscapes', unabridged version of radio broadcast, BBC Radio 4, 12 November 1996, and in *Hambone 14*, ed. N. MacKey, Santa Cruz, California, 1998, pp.169–76

2 'Letter from Francisco Bone to W.H.', in *Jonestown*, (London: Faber and Faber, 1996), pp.3–10

3 'New Preface to *Palace of the Peacock*', in The Faber Caribbean Series, ed. Caryl Phillips (London: Faber and Faber, 1998), pp.2–12

4 'Merlin and Parsifal: Adversarial Twins', address to Temenos Academy, London, 21 April 1997 (London: Temenos Academy, 1997), pp.1–15

5 'Literacy and the Imagination – a Talk', in *The Literate Imagination: Essays on the Novels of Wilson Harris*, ed. Michael Gilkes (London: Macmillan Caribbean, 1989), pp.13–30

6 'Reflections on *Intruder in the Dust* in a Cross-cultural Complex', in *The Womb of Space: The Cross-cultural Imagination* (Westport, CT: Greenwood Press, 1983), pp.3–13

7 'The Schizophrenic Sea', essay on Poe's *Arthur Gordon Pym on Nantucket*, *The Womb of Space*, pp.15–26

8 'Concentric Horizons', essays on Ralph Ellison's *Invisible Man* and Jean Toomer's *Cane*, *The Womb of Space*, pp.27–38

9 'Jean Rhys's "Tree of Life" ', *Review of Contemporary Fiction* (Summer 1985), pp.114–17

10 'Benito Cereno' in *Wilson Harris: Enigma of Values*, ed. Kirsten Holst Petersen and Anna Rutherford (Aarhus: Dangaroo Press, 1975), pp.43–58

11 'Tradition and the West Indian Novel', (West Indian Student's Union: 1964), pp.7–17; also in *Tradition, the Writer and Society* (London and Trinidad: New Beacon Books, 1967, 1973)

12 'History, Fable and Myth in the Caribbean and Guianas', the three-lecture text of the 1970 Edgar Mittelholzer Lectures, including 'The Amerindian Legacy' and 'Continuity and Discontinuity', was first published in 1970 by the National History and Arts Council, Ministry of Information and Culture, Georgetown, Guyana; rev., ed. Selwyn R. Cudjoe (Wellesley, Mass.: Calaloux, 1995), pp.13–50

13 'Quetzelcoatl and the Smoking Mirror: Reflections on Originality and Tradition', address to Temenos Academy, London, 7 February 1994; see also *Review of Contemporary Fiction* (Summer 1997), pp.12–23

14 'Profiles of Myth and the New World', W. Zach and K.L. Goodwin (eds), *Nationalism vs. Internationalism: (Inter)national Dimensions of Literatures in English* (Tübingen: Stauffenburg Verlag, 1996), pp.77–86

15 'In the Name of Liberty', *Third Text*, 'Beyond the Rushdie Affair', special issue (Summer 1990), pp.7–15

16 'Aubrey Williams', *Third Text* (Spring 1996), pp.79–82; and seminar on Aubrey Williams, Institute of International Visual Arts (inIVA), October Gallery, London, 19 January 1996

17 'Apprenticeship to the Furies', River City: *Journal of Contemporary Culture*, University of Memphis, Summer 1996; and keynote address for Festival Week, Cave Hill Campus, University of the West Indies, Barbados, March 1996, pp.104–15

18 'Creoleness, The Crossroads of a Civilization?' in Caribbean Creolization, Reflections on the Cultural Dynamics of Language, Literature and Identity, ed. K.M. Balutansky and M.-A. Sourieau (University Press of Florida, University of the West Indies, 1998), pp.23–35

19 'The Unfinished Genesis of the Imagination', address to Temenos Academy, London, 18 March 1992; and *Temenos Journal*, 13 (1992), pp.69–85

INDEX

Bold numbers represent main entry.

amnesia 51–2, 124–5
analytical psychology: and Harris's work 10
Anancy: imagery in Ellison's *Invisible Man*
  110–11; spider fables 157, 159, 166
ancestors 162, 167, 208
ancient Greece, Greeks 188; epic poetry
  and drama 2; language 1; mythology
  172, 227, 242; Olympian gods 242, 245;
  sculptures 83
ancient Rome 188; tragic drama 2
Andean peoples 264; Inca 22, 266
androgyne: Kukulcan 54
Angel Asturias, Miguel 7, 31n
animals: in *Companions of the Day and Night*
  64; genius of the creature 216, 216–17,
  218, 219; heraldic images 173; kinship
  with human presence 202–4, 205, 209;
  messengers and riddles 189, 191; names
  of Amerindians 52; in pre-Columbian
  art 203–4; in Titian's allegory 209,
  218–19
animism: Amerindian 106, 107
Anthony, Michael: *The Year in San Fernando*
  6n, 181–2
anthropology 5, 10, 17, 22–3, 170, 181
anthropomorphism: in *Intruder in the Dust* 90
Antigone 249, 250
Antoni, Robert 231
apartheid: fixations 158
archetypes 37–9; broken 72, 234; of
  creation myth 120; ground of tradition
  54; Jungian 1, 37n, 169; of phantom limb
  myth 158, 176; of threatened landscape
  229–30; Virgin 51, 234; women and the
  Furies 229
architecture: of consciousness 170, 173,
  174; and the earth 186–7; of
  imagination 62, 169, 183; and literature
  199; and movement in limbo dance 163;
  of space 173, 187, 238, 247; of traditions
  and myths 53, 159
Argentina 30, 31n
Aristotle 249
Armstrong, Louis 110
Arnaldus de Villanova 60
arrival: as a concert 187–8
artifice: of masquerade 56–7
artists: freedom 156; and intuition 177–8;
  status 30
arts: absence of historical correlative in
  Caribbean 161–2, 176, 182; and the
  animal kingdom 203–4, 205; asymmetry

within 11, 71, 72, 101; bearing of limbo
  and vodun 164, 165–6; challenging
  tradition 44, 251; cleavage with history
  in West Indies 165, 167–8, 176, 177;
  depth-resources in 228, 229, 242;
  diversity 61, 62; as escapism or façade
  233; fashions in 238–9; Guyanese 161,
  165–6; of the imagination 31, 62, 71, 72,
  83, 94, 156, 165–6, 169, 177, 183,
  199–200, 231, 262, 264; and intuition
  177–8; and political radicalism 150;
  pre-Columbian 11–12, 33, 53, 76–7, 86,
  203–4, 204; and sciences 210, 238, 243;
  self-confessional and self-judgemental
  61, 63, 64, 117, 208; Toomer's rejection
  of 116–17; West Indian approach 150
Asia: politics and liberty 213
Asian culture: influence on novel 123
Asian literature and writers 220, 231
Asian peoples: migrations into America 41,
  157; in West Indies and the Americas 170
astrology: in India 165
astronomy, astronomers 40, 44, 64, 223
Asturias, Miguel Angel *see* Angel Asturias,
  Miguel
asymmetry 11, 72, 101, 106
Atahuallpa 265
Atlantic Ocean 41
atomic power 244
Australian Aboriginal Dreaming 13n
Australian culture: influence on novel 123
authoritarianism: allegory 250; in *The Far
  Journey of Oudin* 82–3; in Poe's *Arthur
  Gordon Pym* 71; rise in Third World 78; of
  ruling convention 238–9; and the writer
  82–3
Awakaipu: legend of 48, 265

Bachelard, Gaston 10
Bandele, Biyi 6n
Bantu: origin of *loa* 164
Beckett, Samuel: *Imagination Dead Imagine*
  233
Bering Straits 41, 235
Being: bearing of marginality 220–1; and
  creatures 217; *Dasein* 26, 28; geography
  and art of 215, 262; inimitable 214, 216,
  217, 221; and nonbeing 246; parables 3,
  32, 138; partial structures 214, 221
Belize 31n
Benitez Rojo, Antonio: *The Repeating Island*
  191

INDEX

Berkel, Adriaan van: *Travels in South America* 19

Berlin: recent revolution 213

Bible: Gospels 249–50; myth and parable 122, 223; traditions inherited by English language 261

Bim (Barbados literary review) 181–2

black comedy 128–9

black culture: during slavery 122; literature 6n, 53; music 192; nature of blackness 240

Black Widow (film) 229, 230

blindness: classical 249–50; self-confessional 259

body: waking instrument of 259

Bollingen: Tower 59–60

Bonampak 48, 264–5

bone: masks 48

bone-flute/bone-spirit 5, 32, 53–4, 106, 107, 169; bridge 5, 54, 55

Book of Common Prayer: traditions inherited by English language 261

Bosnia: rape and war 229, 230; war of Christians and Muslims 194

boundaries: of persuasion 137–9, 183; of prejudice 164, 176, 177

Brathwaite, Edward 168, 175, 179; *Islands* 157; 'Masks' 178–9; *X/Self* 188

Brazil 17n, 18, 41, 51; culture and language 220; limbo 164; rainforests and jungles 43, 44, 142

breakage/brokenness 38n, 42, 51, 235; of archetype 72, 234; communities 50; and immortal gods 243; in *Palace of the Peacock* 84

bridges: between closed orders 202, 210, 211, 239, 247; between cultures and traditions 70, 110, 112, 210, 238; bone-flute/bone-spirit 5, 54, 55; created by language 202, 242; of love 64; of pre-Columbian myth 54, 96, 104, 105–7

Britain, British: colonial rule of Guyana 41, 50, 51; legacies of empire 120; people in Guyana 25

British Guiana (later Republic of Guyana) 1, 5, 50, 51, 58, 256–7; disappearance of Caribs 48, 54; Harris's childhood and early years in 55, 157, 213, 237–8

Brodber, Erna 231

Brontë, Charlotte: *Jane Eyre* 118, 160

Brotherson, Gordon 192

Brown, C. Barrington 172

Brown, Norman O.: *Love's Body* 87

Brown, Wayne 176

Buber, Martin 10

Bucharest: recent revolution 213

bush-baby: Carib beliefs 25, 33, 137n, 156, 158, 169, 177, 182

Byzantium 183

camera: as weapon or caring eye 257

Cameron, Richard 27

Canada: Harris's research in 5

Canje: interior 18

cannibalism: of Caribs 72, 104, 106, 107, 111–12, 167, 168

capital punishment: in Caribbean and African states 235

Caribbean 22, 105, 106; African myth and legend 156–7; coexistence of cultures 158, 161–2, 180; conquistadors' arrival 39, 188, 266; as context for literature 147, 150; cross-cultural traditions 89, 220, 247; folk-arts as resource for imaginative arts 137n, 164, 176, 179; Froude's reports 154; heritage of slavery 180, 181, 188, 243; historical stasis 152, 161–2, 166, 180; history and imagination 156, 174; lack of status of literary artists 30; literary imagination 33, 123, 182; literary renaissance of 1940s and 1950s 6–7; Middle Passage to 157, 162; native and phenomenal environment 141–2; politics and protest 181; religious ritual of hospitality 170; renascence of sensibility 170–1; status of politicians 30; tradition of melting pot 149; tragedy 222, 223, 224; writers 182, 231, 233; *see also* circum-Caribbean peoples; Haiti; St Lucia; West Indians, West Indies

Caribbean Quarterly 158

Caribbean Sea 240

carnival: of the age 101, 138, 211, 251; block 74, 103, 114; and the classic American novel 12; and conquest 98, 188–9; epic as 38n; etymology 74; in Guyana 25; as imaginative resource 33, 52; and limbo in West Indies 156–7, 167, 170; Lord Death 47, 189; and masks 12, 15, 48, 98, 106, 138, 194, 246, 251; in Toomer's *Cane* 114; tragedy 74, 101, 102; twinships 72, 74, 102–5; women 109–12

276

wars of 229, 230, 235; *see also*
femininity/masculinity
genius: of the creature 216, 216–17, 218,
219; of imagination and creation 236,
245, 250–1; involuntary 246–7
Georgetown 28, 48, 169, 232, 265; Harris's
experiences in 3, 157, 174, 213, 237;
Queen's College 1
German philosophical tradition 4
Gilgamesh 193, 194
gnostic thought 37n, 185, 193
God: City of 55; discarding of term 221;
idea of death of 83, 228, 231
goddess: in *Carnival* 87–8; of death or
killing 227, 228, 229, 230, 235; in
Ellison's *Invisible Man* 110, 111, 113; as
ship 87
gods: African 162; creator 83, 204, 205–6,
208; as densities or veils 184, 193; dying
or death of 109–10, 114, 184; in El
Dorado legend 264–6; evoked in Rhys's
Wide Sargasso Sea 121; and immortality
242–3, 244–5, 245–6; jealous 194, 244;
Olympian 242, 245; phantom limb of
158, 159, 162, 176; *see also* Central and
South American gods; loa
Goethe, Johann Wolfgang von 76, 228, 249
Gogh, Vincent van 168
Goveia, Elsa 160, 160–1, 176; *Slave Society in
the British Leeward Islands* 180–1
Grail *see* Holy Grail
Greaves, Stanley 224, 231
Greece *see* ancient Greece, Greeks
Guatemala 7, 203
Guiana, Guianas 22, 33, 51, 105, 142, 264;
African myth and legend 156–7;
conquests of 177, 265–6; Creoles 238;
cross-cultural traditions 89; etymology
18, 51; exclusion of Amerindians from
population statistics 167; geography and
geology 18; and legend of El Dorado
265; partial recall of the vanishing race
21; pre-Columbian myths 54, 226;
renascence of sensibility 170–1; Timehri
rock markings 222; tribes 22–3
La Guiane Française *see* French Guiana
Guyana, Republic of 22, 51, 170;
anthropological accounts 17, 22–3;
coastlands family in *The Far Journey of
Oudin* 80–1; coexistence of cultures 17,
34, 161–2; colonial rule 41, 50, 51;
demography 19, 22, 25, 41, 50;

divergences from expectations 31;
Essequebo River 44, 45; folk-beliefs and
legends 25, 40, 137n, 256; forfeiture of
Caribbean federation 233; geography
and geology 18–19, 19–20, 41; Harris's
experiences as surveyor 2–3, 5, 18, 20,
40, 41, 46, 55, 58, 77, 207; indigenous
peoples 22, 25, 41, 238; Jonestown 47;
limbo and vodun 25, 137n, 157–8, 164,
165–6, 168; Omai 45; painters 231;
politicians and political office 30;
rainforests 5, 17, 40, 43, 44, 207;
religious denominations 25; religious
ritual of hospitality 170; rise of
imaginative arts 165–6; river in *The Four
Banks of the River of Space* 210; writers 231

Hades: tautology 249, 250
Haiti: and Africa 243; in C.L.R. James's
The Black Jacobins 149; and loa (god)
Legba 242–3, 245, 246, 247; vodun 156,
158, 162, 163–4, 164–5, 168, 182
Hardy, Thomas 228, 230
Harlem: literary renaissance 53, 73, 117
Harris, Wilson: ancestry 1, 220, 237; arrival
and experiences in London 3, 6, 40,
42–3, 45; aspects of his writing 3–6, 10,
37–9, 73–4, 137–9; birth and early life in
Guyana 1, 34, 55, 157, 174, 201, 213,
237–8; broadcasts 40–6; comparative
reading of novels and critical writing
3–4, 8, 13, 17; critical writing 3, 12–13;
and cross-cultural tradition 138, 261–2;
encounters with intuitive clues 240, 261;
essays 1, 8–9, 13, 17, 31–4, 69–74, 261,
262; explorations of vanished
civilizations 262; lectures 1, 31; motifs of
El Dorado and Grail legends 263–7;
novels 1, 5, 9–10, 13, 31, 34, 37–9, 42,
53, 138, 251–60, 262, 263, 264; parallel
texts to his work 10; principal
achievements 261–2; realization of
boundaries of persuasion 137–9; as
surveyor in Guyana 2–3, 5, 18, 20, 40,
41, 46, 55, 58, 77, 207; verse 3; vision
and development of language 261, 264,
267; works: *The Age of the Rainmakers* 15,
19, 20–1; 'The Amerindian Legacy'
167–75; 'Apprenticeship to the Furies'
31, 72n, 199n, **226–36**; 'Aubrey Williams'
33–3, 199n, **222–5**; 'Benito Cereno' 32,
33, 70–1, **123–33**; *Black Marsden* 16;

moral directives: and the writer 147–8
Morrison, Toni: *Song of Solomon* 122
multicultural: distinguished from cross-cultural 38
Murdoch, Iris: *Under the Net* 187
Murray, Patricia 28n
Murray, Stuart 9–10
muses 34, 54, 158, 162; Carib abuse of 54; in Ellison's *Invisible Man* 109, 110, 111, 112; and memory 45; of nature 44, 101; re-assembly of 168, 173
music: black 192; blues in Ellison's *Invisible Man* 110, 114; of bone-flute 169; etymology 14; in Harris's novels 63–4, 65, 186; and language 40–1; and literature 53, 86, 192, 199, 222; of living landscapes 46, 56; as medium of memory 14, 39, 45, 56; orchestration of fiction 42; orchestrations of histories and imageries 185, 190, 209; orchestrations of inner man 43, 45, 124; orchestrations of place 55; orphan song of ancient Mexico 184, 192, 193; in paintings of Aubrey Williams 222, 223; of silence 2, 40–1, 42, 43, 44, 210; as simultaneous text 86; as 'spirit-bone' of the Caribs 53–4; transitive chords 187
Muslims 194
mystery 44, 49, 62; of art and imagination 65, 128, 228; of consciousness 223, 233, 250; of freedom 107
myth: African 156–9, 162; in the age of realism 207; and conscience 96, 208; of creation 120, 122; and creative genesis 11; in dialogue of culture and civilization 151; from N.O. Brown's *Love's Body* 87; and the imaginative tradition 80; and masquerade 105–7; motifs of the womb 172; pre-Columbian bridge of 54, 104, 105–7; re-imagining dream motifs through 4; religious 234; as revealer of inexactitudes 10, 71; shared themes 10; *see also* legend
mythology: traditions inherited by English language 261

Naipaul, V.S. 6n, 137n, 160, 171, 181; *A House for Mr Biswas* 146–7, 181–2
National Assessment of Educational Progress 75
nature: and collective unconscious 201, 204; discarding of 39; humanization of 246; man's exploitation of 208, 228, 235, 244; as muse 44, 101; and Nemesis 43; and ventriloquism of Spirit 207–8; as womb 227, 228, 229
Nazis: ethnic cleansing of Poland 241
Negro, Rio 18
Nelson, Horatio, Admiral 180
nemesis 39, 43, 94, 107, 221, 238, 239
Nettleford, Rex 158
New Amsterdam 1, 28, 47–8, 50
New Beacon Review 161
Newton, Isaac 74n
Nietzschean ideas: death of God 83
Nigeria: capital punishment 235
night-life 96, 99
nihilism 101, 102, 112, 117, 213–14, 216, 221
Nolan, Sidney 168
North America: influence on novel 123; migrations to 157, 235
novel: archetypal 37–9; bearing of limbo and vodun 159, 164; changing shape of narrative 123, 144; classical tradition 148; consolidation of character 140–1, 142, 146; conventional narrative 1, 2, 3, 31, 32, 74, 137n, 140–1, 146, 187, 230, 262; development of 1–2; DreamingBook of 4, 14–15, 17; eighteenth-century 188; English 137n; European 228, 230; literary essay as groundwork 261; nineteenth-century 137n, 140, 150, 188; realism in 9, 141, 146; West Indian 137n 140, 141, 142–3; women portrayed as Furies 227
numinous inexactitudes 71, 194, 204, 205–6, 207

obeah: in Guyana 25
oceans and oceanscapes 41, 58, 62, 229, 246
October Gallery, London 231
Odysseus 111
Oedipus 2, 249
oil fields: burning 229
Olmec: Head from La Venta 203–4, 206
Omai: cyanide overspill 45
Omoa *see* Manoa
O'Neill, Eugene 249
oracle: and West Indian folk consciousness 179
oral traditions 106
Orinoco Basin 18, 266

race: bridges between 238; conflicts of 235; distinctions of 250; obsessions with 218; partial recall of 20, 21

racialism: codes and concepts 11, 201, 202, 204, 206

radicalism 150, 217

Raine, Kathleen 201, 248

rainforests 5, 17, 40, 43, 44, 55, 207, 229, 258

rainmaking: vestiges 33, 137n, 158

Raleigh, Sir Walter 41, 55, 144, 265, 266, 267

Ramchand, Kenneth 53, 159–60, 181–2

rape 229

Reagan, Ronald 78

realism 31, 171, 235; addiction to 204, 206, 262; breaches of by synchronicity 61–2; in C.L.R. James's *The Black Jacobins* 148–50; materialist or conventional 178, 231–2, 238; in the novel 9, 141, 146; as partial model 250; secular 202–3; technocratic and utilitarian 58, 174; technology of 124, 125, 126, 129; *see also* magical realism

reality: different apprehension of 137–8, 183; different language of 137, 139, 142, 183; different reading of texts of 137, 139, 183; Latin American 174–5

re-birth 106, 107, 156, 158; of epic 112, 113, 186, 188, 189–90, 191, 194–5; motifs in Ellison's *Invisible Man* 109, 110, 112; of sensibility 169, 170

refugees: settlements in Guyana 18

rehearsal 7, 50, 81, 85–6, 87, 219; and cross-culturism 28; etymology 137–8; unfinished 28, 137–9

Reid, V.S. 6n; *The Leopard* 151

religions: ancient traditions of Central America 1, 265; Arawaks 167; barriers between 250–1; diversity 194; and the imagination 124; ritual and fanaticism 202–3, 205–6, 208; *see also* sacred, the

resurrection: of Christ 249–50; in Harris's novels 16, 255; parables 45; technology of 39, 46

revealing inexactitudes 10, 71, 92

revenge 227, 229, 230, 235, 256–7, 258

Review of Contemporary Fiction 9, 28n

re-visioning: bridges between cultures and disciplines 238; and the creative artist 33, 43, 45, 51, 86–7, 165, 210; dynamics of 64, 86, 189, 192, 220, 231, 234; histories

and traditions 38, 54, 89, 190, 194, 210, 227

revisitation 16, 37, 45

revolution: in Eastern Europe 212; Russian 212–13, 214

Rhodesia: economic fascism 154

Rhys, Jean 32; *Good Morning, Midnight* 118; *Wide Sargasso Sea* 118–22, 160

Rimbaud, Arthur 96

Ripley, Sir George 72

rivers: abused 44, 45, 58, 229; in *The Four Banks of the River of Space* 210–11; Guyana 18–19, 210–11; and rocks 45–6; and spirit-bone 53

riverscapes 3, 40, 41, 52, 55, 58, 62, 187, 204, 228, 244, 246

rocks: Amerindian legend 41, 45; mythologies 172, 223; and rivers 45–6; Timehri markings in Guianas 222

Rojo, Antonio Benitez *see* Benitez Rojo, Antonio

Romanticism 209

Rome *see* ancient Rome

Roraima, Mount 17n, 18n, 19, 48, 265

Roth, Walter Edmund 5, 17n, 106, 107

Rouse, Dr 167

Royal Astronomical Society 33

Rulfo, Juan 191; *Pedro Paramo* 231

Ruskin, John 150

Russian Revolution 212–13, 214

Rutherford, Ernest 74n

Rwanda: rape and war 229, 230

sacrament 41, 64, 77, 253

sacred, the 203, 206, 208, 209–10, 213–14, 219

sacred sites: in Guyanan interior 20

sacrifice 48, 63, 64, 163

St Lucia: Amerindians as described by Rev. Jesse 167–8

Salkey, Andrew: *West Indian Stories* (ed.) 147

scale: and capacity of imagination 143–5, 150–1, 171

scepticism 213–14

schizophrenia 72–3

Schomburgk, Richard 27; *Travels in British Guiana* 19, 106, 107

Schomburgk, Robert 27

Schopenhauer, Arthur 14n

science, scientists: and the arts 210, 238, 243; consciousness as mystery to 44, 233;

tradition, traditions: abyss or spatiality of 138, 260; archetypal ground of 54; in art 29, 44; Biblical 261; as bridge between past and present 210; classical 1; Commonwealth 30; continuity and divergence 177–8; cross-cultural roots 76, 83, 86, 89, 138, 231; and fiction 145, 201; of the imagination 10, 76, 80, 138, 199; loss of 76, 77, 86; manipulation by post-modernism 243, 251; as mask 137n; partial models 258; philosophical 4; pre-Columbian 33, 119, 120, 168–9, 189, 202–3, 204, 209; and society 150–1; Soul of 192–3, 194–5; visualizations of 53; womb of 49, 177, 194, 261

tragedy 101, 132; and the Caribbean 222, 223, 224; carnival 74, 101, 102, 106; classical 2, 222, 223–4, 249; in C.L.R. James's *The Black Jacobins* 150; in dialogue of culture and civilization 151; idea of the death of 101; as partial model 250; suffering and symmetry 71; traditions inherited by English language 261; tragic premises in Lamming's *Of Age and Innocence* 145–6; and the writer 147

transparencies: and densities in language 239, 242; mirror in Rhys's *Wide Sargasso Sea* 119–20

tree of life: and Amerindian foodbearing tree 119, 120; Bo-Kepie 265; and Lazarus 39; in Rhys's *Wide Sargasso Sea* 119–21, 122

trees: Arawak legend 222; felling of 44, 44–5; Merlin legend 59, 60–1; walking 46

trickster 166, 171, 172, 179, 240, 266

Trinidad 160

Trotsky, Leon 213

Turner, J.M.W. 168

Turner, Nat 102

Tutuola, Amos 6n 144, 176

twinship: adversarial 56, 59, 263–4, 267; between cultures 73–4, 74; carnival 72, 74, 99–105; in Ellison's *Invisible Man* 102–5, 107, 109, 110; and gods 105–6; in *Intruder in the Dust* 97, 97–8; Maya 49; in *Palace of the Peacock* 54, 55–6; structures 32

tyranny: breaking 86; in Melville's 'Benito Cereno' 126; in Poe's *Arthur Gordon Pym* 71,

100; and survival of the fittest 245; tautology 255–6

Ulysses 256, 257

unconscious: collective 201, 233; and creativity 249; discarding of by post-modernists 86; and language 242; medieval 60; need to investigate 170; presence of myth and tradition 87, 210, 215, 217, 246; and revenge 229; symbolic 124

uniform text 77, 82, 86, 138, 267

United States of America (USA): decorative motifs 12; erosion of soils 43; Harris's research in 5; illiteracy 75; McCarthyism 213; nineteenth-century slave-masters 99; *see also* American literature; Americans

Urdu 25

Van Gogh, Vincent *see* Gogh, Vincent van

Venezuela 17n, 18, 41, 44, 51, 220, 265

ventriloquism of Spirit 199, 207–8

Verger, Pierre 162–3, 164

Villanova, Arnaldus de *see* Arnaldus de Villanova

Virgil: in Dante's *Divine Comedy* 192, 250

Virgin: archetype 51, 234

visualization 33, 34, 43, 53, 59, 87, 164, 219

vodun/voodoo 33; African 158, 162–3, 164–5; Guyana 25, 137n; Haitian 156, 158, 162, 163–4, 164–5, 168, 182; in *Intruder in the Dust* 69–70, 94, 95–6; and void 166; and West Indian psyche 173

void 42, 50–1, 166, 223, 225

Volpe, Edmond L.: study of Faulkner 91, 97

Waithe, Keith 40

Walcott, Derek 30, 173–4

war: effects on nature 59, 228; epics of 129–30; fostering of by democracies 256; Melville's writings on 129; and rape 229

Warsaw: recent revolution 213

Warton, Charles: *Wanderings in South America* 19

Waugh, Evelyn: *Ninety-Two Days* 17n

weather: changing patterns 43, 235

Weld, Theodore: *The Bible Against Slavery* 102

West Indian literature 143, 174; New Wave 6–7; novel 33, 137n, 140, 141, 142, 145–8, 150, 151

West Indian writers 145–50, 151, 160–2
West Indians, West Indies: Amerindian
gateways between cultures 159; Anglo-
West Indian society 154; bearing of
African myth 156, 179; cleavage
between history and art 156, 165, 176;
conquest by pre-Columbian Caribs 177;
conventional concepts of 140, 160;
cultural environment 150, 170;
deprivations 223; documentary and
protest literature 159; forfeiture of
Caribbean federation 233; historical
convention and the inbuilt censor 160,
164, 166, 176; historical stasis 152, 156,
168, 176; isolated status as minority
140, 142; limbo 156–7, 164, 165–6,
168; and movements of peoples 171;
native and phenomenal environment
141–2; philistinism of middle and upper
classes 151; politics and intellectualism
181–2; presence in tree of life 120,
121–2; rise of imaginative arts 164,
165–6; self-contempt 160; theatre 157;
University 174; writers on 160–1; *see also*
Caribbean
Western civilization and traditions 1, 10,
220
White, Patrick 6n, 144
Whitman, Walt 213
Williams, Aubrey 33–4, 168, 179, 222,
223–5, 231
Williams, Denis 161–2, 176
Williams, Eric: *Capitalism and Slavery* 148,
160–1; *A History of the People of Trinidad and
Tobago* 161
Williams, Tennessee 249
wings: African dream of 122; in
Amerindian legend 54, 120; images
in Rhys's *Wide Sargasso Sea* 119, 120,
121–2

womb: in *Carnival* 88; of culture and
tradition 49, 177, 194, 227, 261; of
dream 226, 227, 232, 233, 260; in
Ellison's *Invisible Man* 109–10; Kukulcan
54; of nature and civilization 227–8,
229; numinous body of 256; of the sea
103, 107; in shamanic lore 172, 226–7;
of song 45; of space 3, 11, 28–9, 92, 94,
100, 102, 105, 107, 110, 111, 112, 113,
138, 163, 230, 232–3, 234, 236, 239;
surrogates as 71–2; of time 49, 56, 109,
124, 187, 230, 232, 234, 236; of
tradition 49, 177, 194, 261
women: carnival 109–12; priests 254, 256;
rape of 229; *see also* Furies; goddess;
muses; Sirens
the Word/word 55, 62, 86, 187; alchemy of
96, 100; of creation 207; extrahuman
faculties within 246; hollowness of
217–18; and living language 218
writers: authoritarianism 82–3; in
Caribbean and Guyana 182, 231, 233;
conferences of 179–80; connections
between 129; and moral directives
147–8; and the primordial dancer 164;
and re-birth of original epic 191–2; and
their origins 219–20, 262; tragic and
comic 147
writers on Guyana 5, 17n, 19

Yates, Frances 82, 209; *The Art of Memory*
33, 76, 201, 218–19
Yeats, W.B. 178, 183
Yugoslavia, former: rape and war 229,
230

zemi (idols): Arawak 156, 167, 173, 182
Zephaniah, Benjamin 6n
Zimbabwe: decorative motifs 12
Zindika 6n